HAYATE THE COMBAT BUTLER

[ALL-CHARACTER APPEARANCE EVENT, IN ORDER OF POPULARITY (2)]

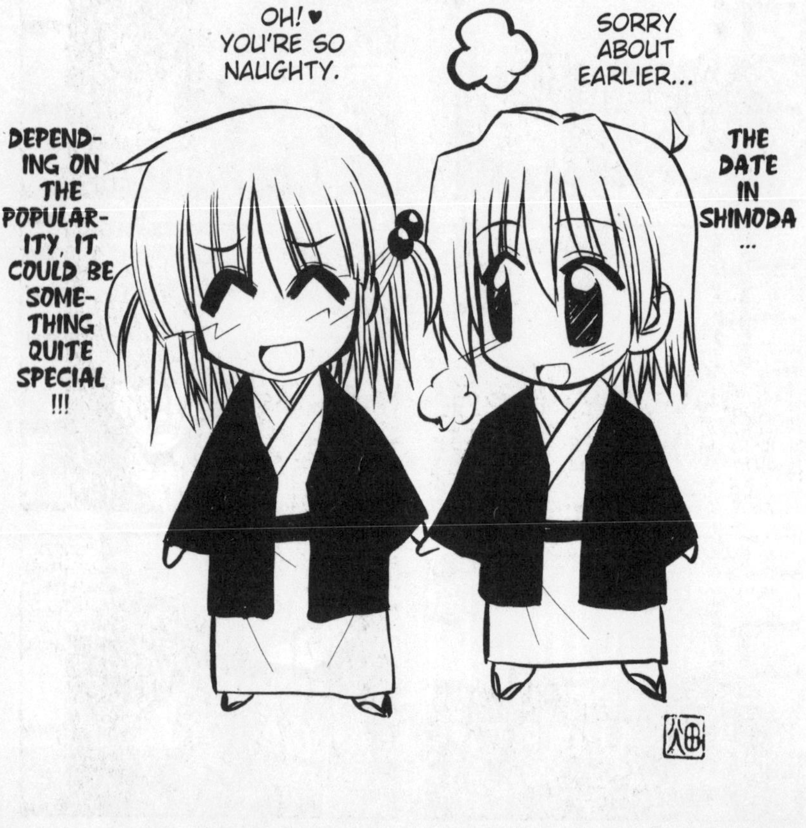
SORRY ABOUT EARLIER...
THE DATE IN SHIMODA ...
OH! ♥ YOU'RE SO NAUGHTY.
DEPENDING ON THE POPULARITY, IT COULD BE SOMETHING QUITE SPECIAL !!!

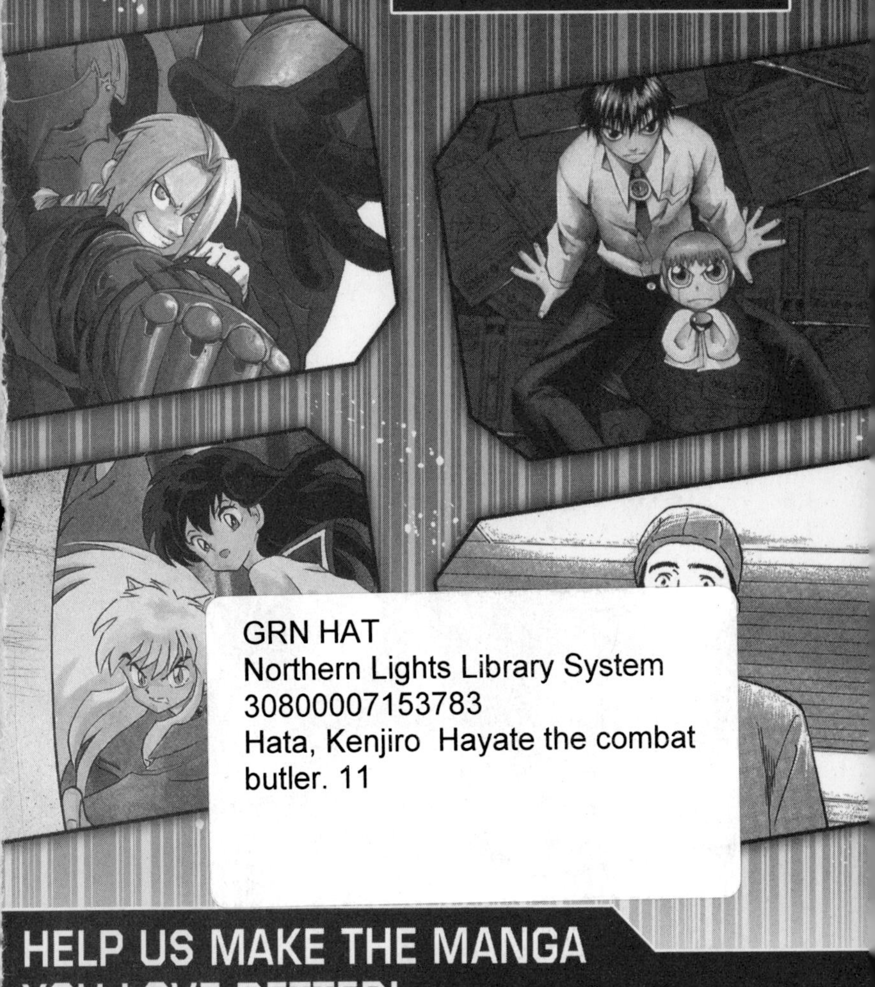

Hayate
the Combat Butler

11

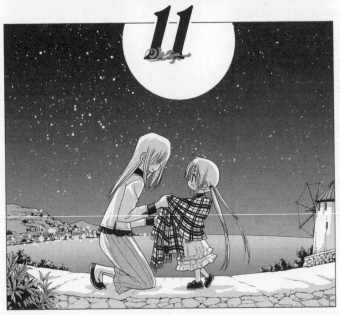

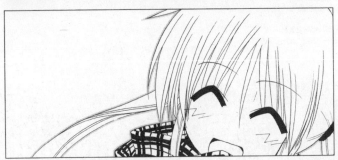

KENJIRO HATA

CONTENTS

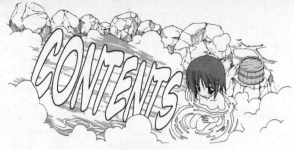

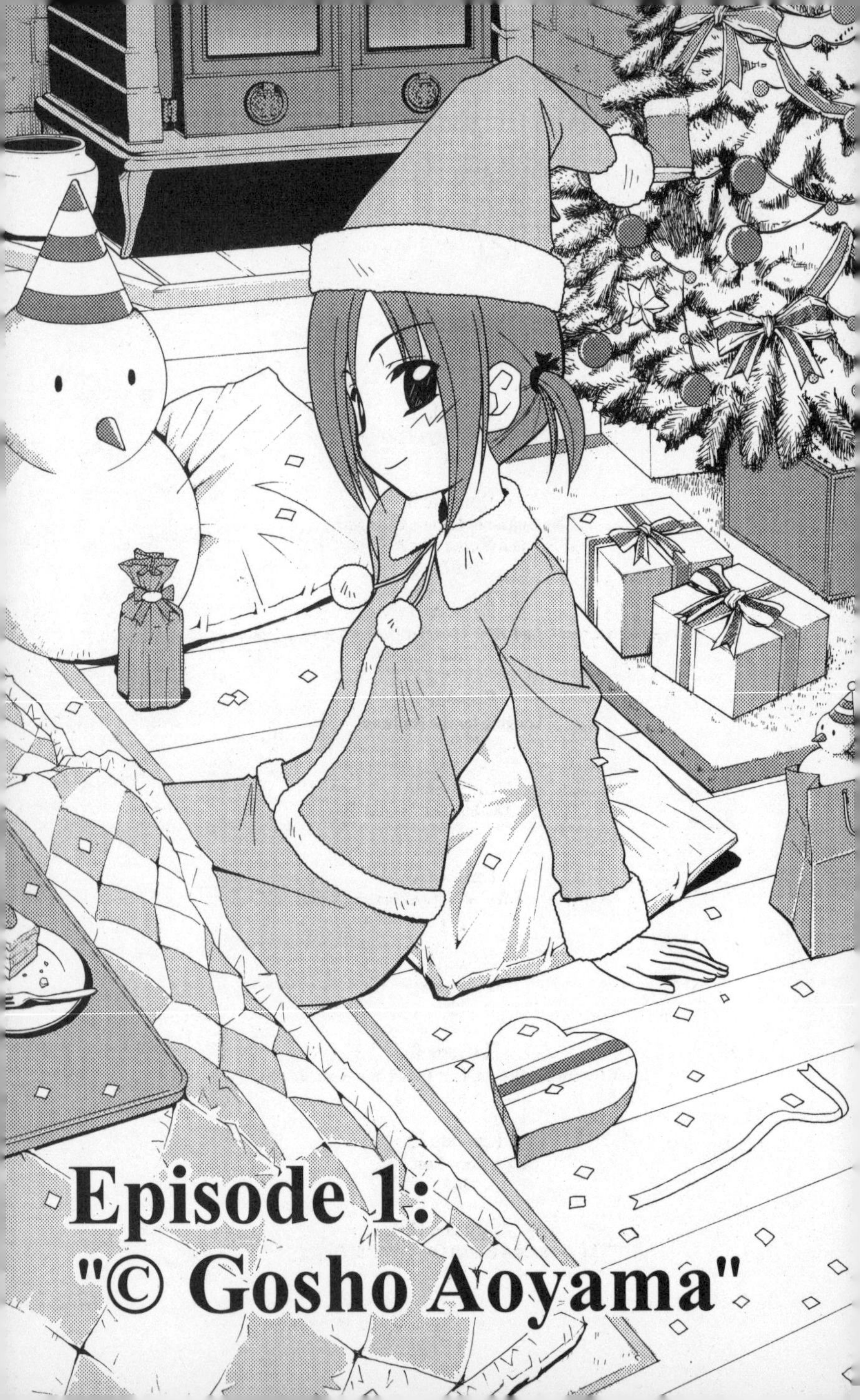
Episode 1:
"© Gosho Aoyama"

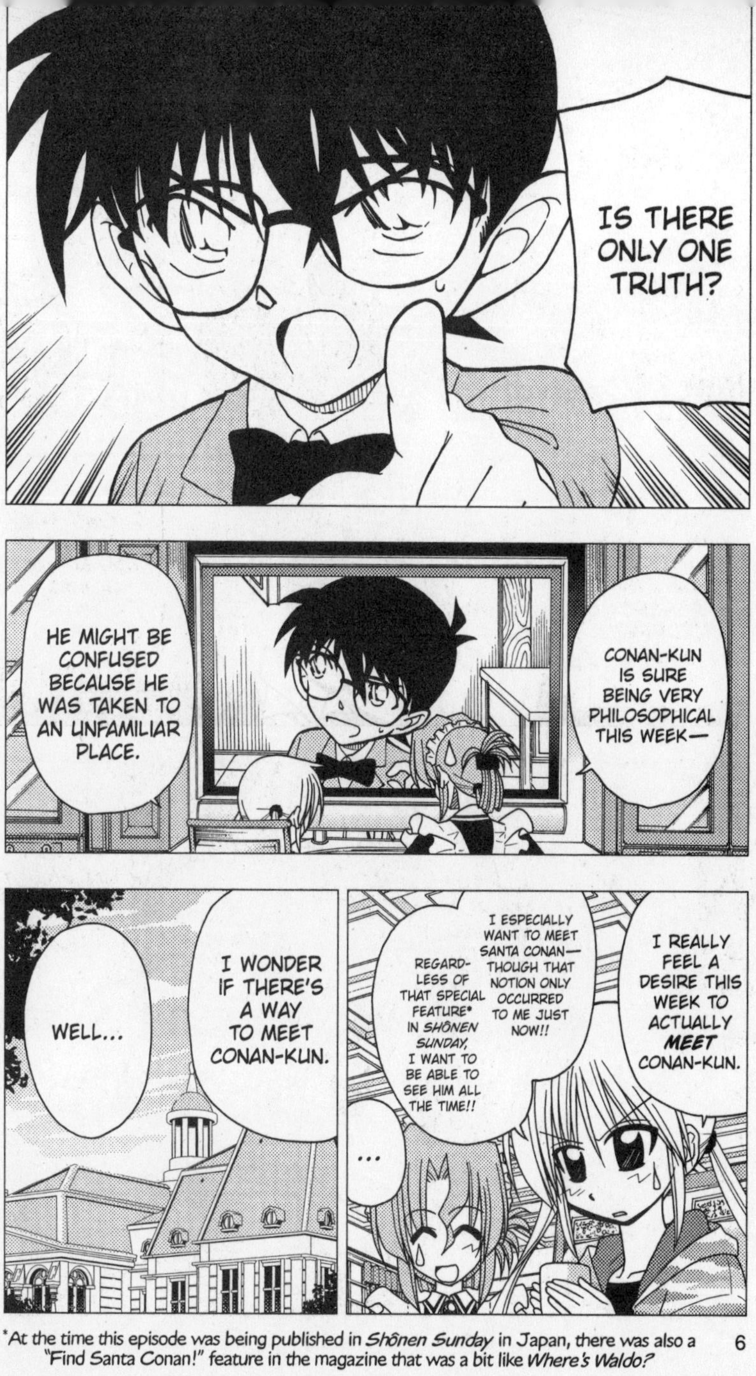
IS THERE ONLY ONE TRUTH?
CONAN-KUN IS SURE BEING VERY PHILOSOPHICAL THIS WEEK—
HE MIGHT BE CONFUSED BECAUSE HE WAS TAKEN TO AN UNFAMILIAR PLACE.
I REALLY FEEL A DESIRE THIS WEEK TO ACTUALLY MEET CONAN-KUN.
I ESPECIALLY WANT TO MEET SANTA CONAN—THOUGH THAT NOTION ONLY OCCURRED TO ME JUST NOW!!
REGARDLESS OF THAT SPECIAL FEATURE* IN SHÔNEN SUNDAY, I WANT TO BE ABLE TO SEE HIM ALL THE TIME!!
...
I WONDER IF THERE'S A WAY TO MEET CONAN-KUN.
WELL...

*At the time this episode was being published in *Shônen Sunday* in Japan, there was also a "Find Santa Conan!" feature in the magazine that was a bit like *Where's Waldo?*

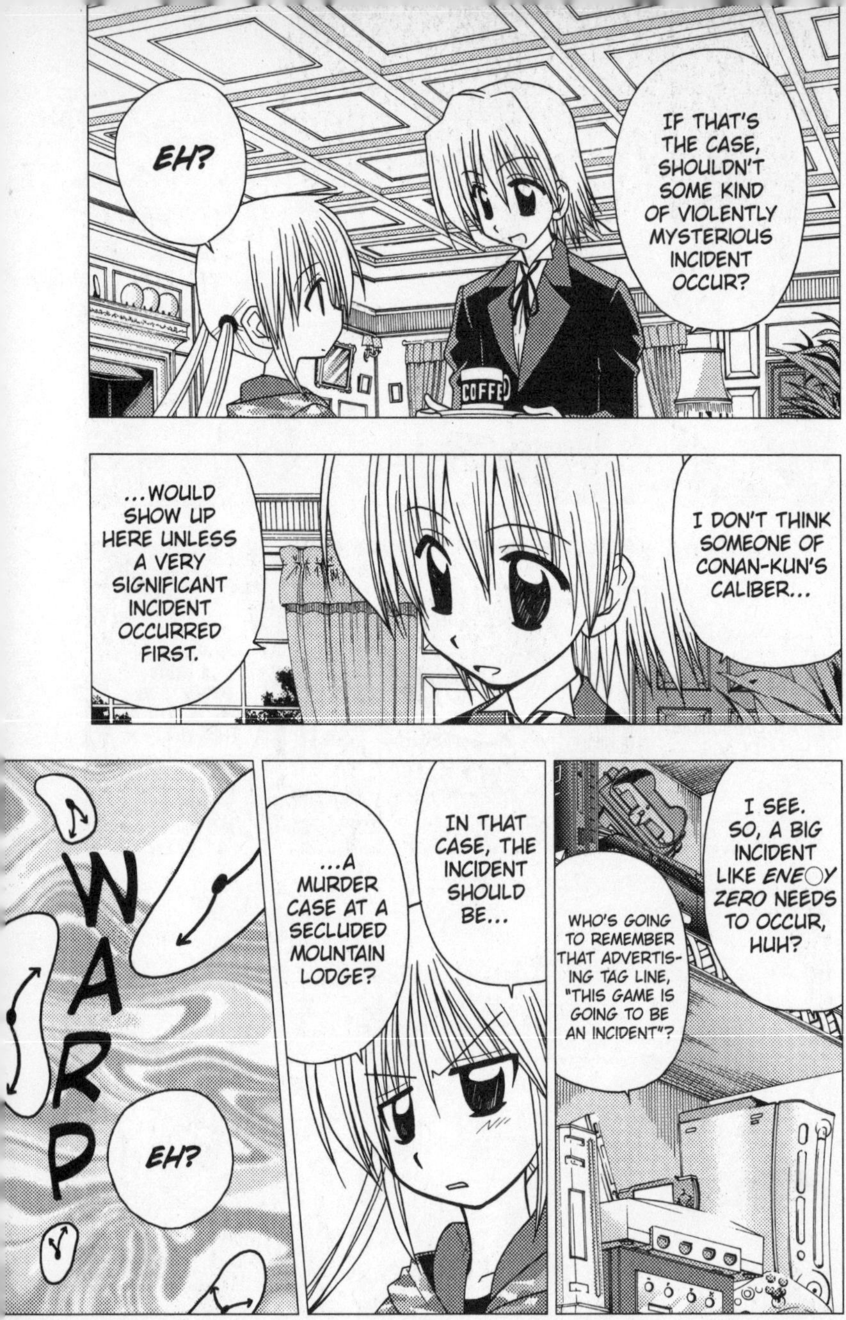
IF THAT'S THE CASE, SHOULDN'T SOME KIND OF VIOLENTLY MYSTERIOUS INCIDENT OCCUR?
EH?
I DON'T THINK SOMEONE OF CONAN-KUN'S CALIBER...
...WOULD SHOW UP HERE UNLESS A VERY SIGNIFICANT INCIDENT OCCURRED FIRST.
I SEE. SO, A BIG INCIDENT LIKE ENE◯Y ZERO NEEDS TO OCCUR, HUH?
WHO'S GOING TO REMEMBER THAT ADVERTISING TAG LINE, "THIS GAME IS GOING TO BE AN INCIDENT"?
IN THAT CASE, THE INCIDENT SHOULD BE...
...A MURDER CASE AT A SECLUDED MOUNTAIN LODGE?
WARP
EH?

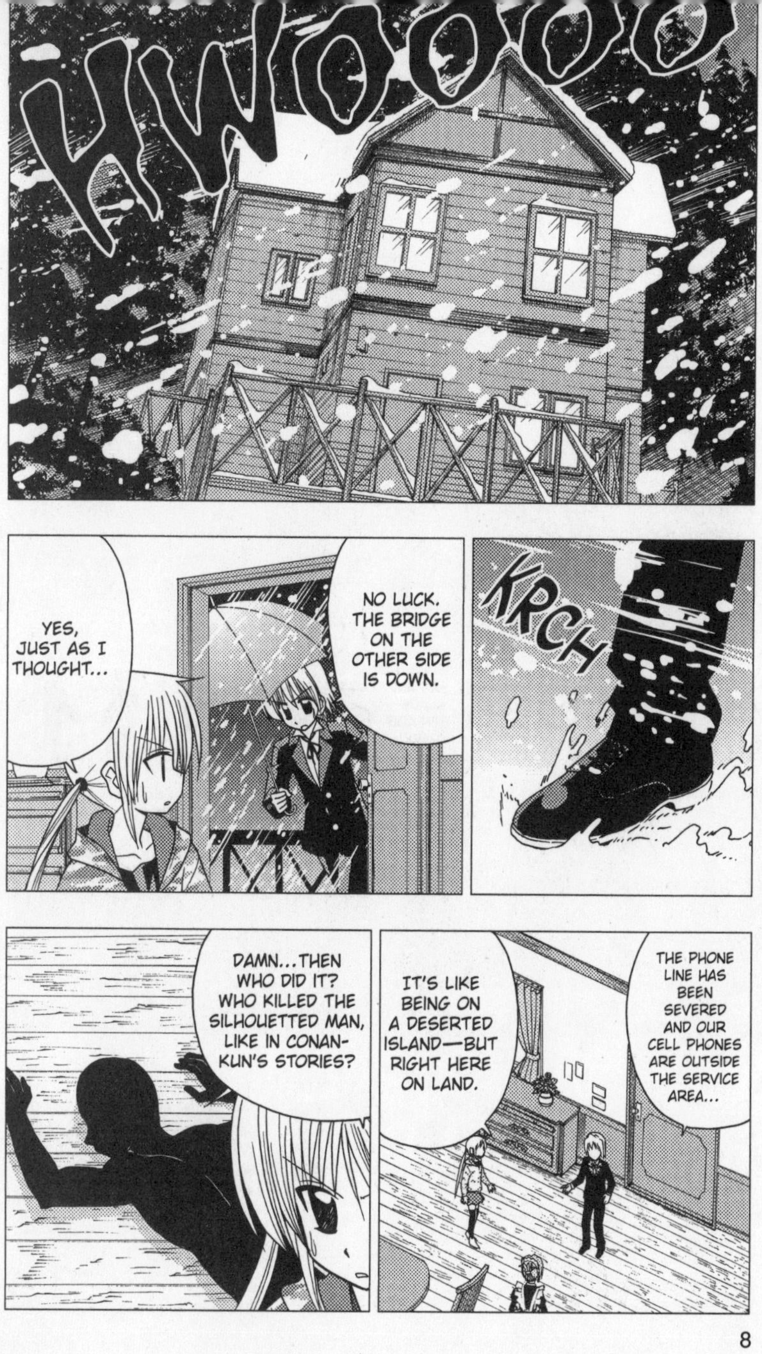
HWOOOOO
KRCH
NO LUCK. THE BRIDGE ON THE OTHER SIDE IS DOWN.
YES, JUST AS I THOUGHT...
THE PHONE LINE HAS BEEN SEVERED AND OUR CELL PHONES ARE OUTSIDE THE SERVICE AREA...
IT'S LIKE BEING ON A DESERTED ISLAND—BUT RIGHT HERE ON LAND.
DAMN...THEN WHO DID IT? WHO KILLED THE SILHOUETTED MAN, LIKE IN CONAN-KUN'S STORIES?

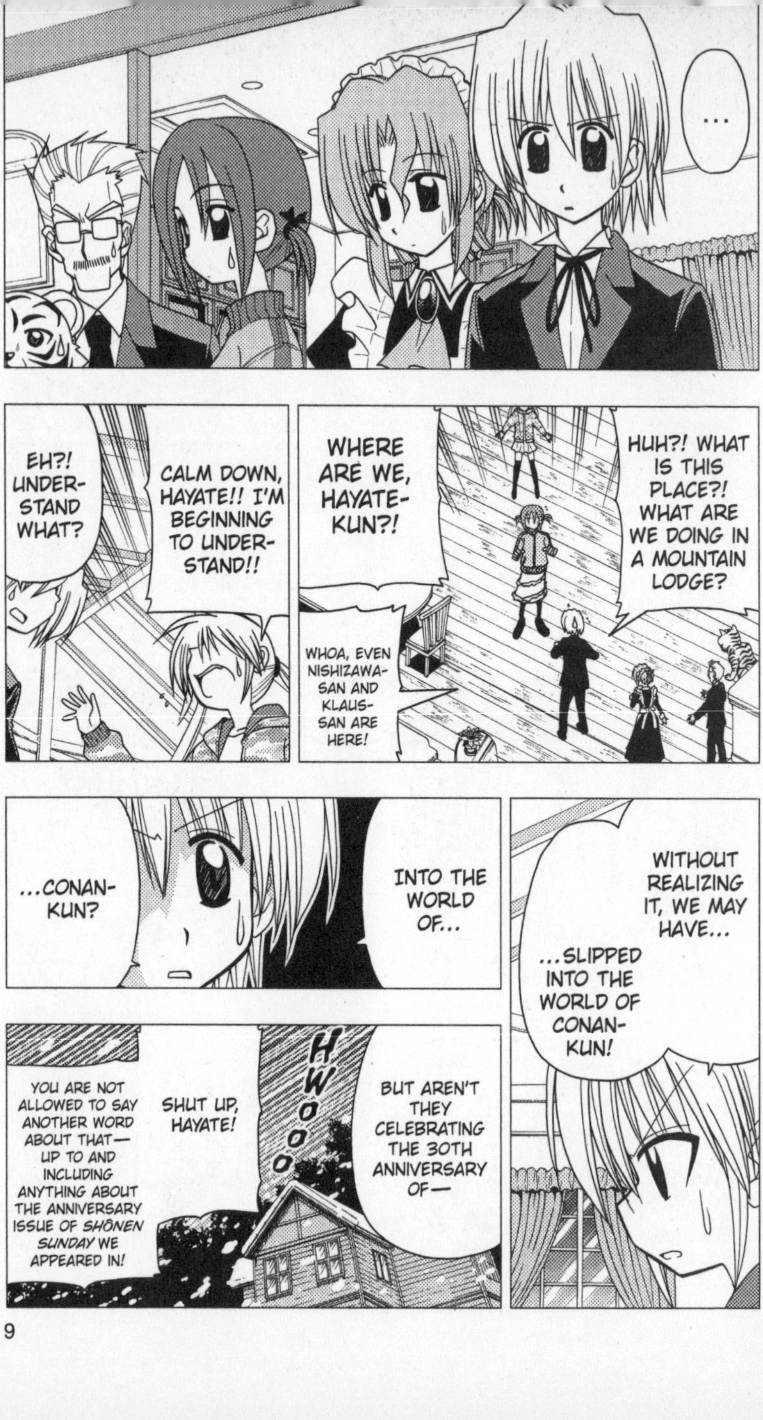
...
HUH?! WHAT IS THIS PLACE?! WHAT ARE WE DOING IN A MOUNTAIN LODGE?
WHERE ARE WE, HAYATE-KUN?!
WHOA, EVEN NISHIZAWA-SAN AND KLAUS-SAN ARE HERE!
CALM DOWN, HAYATE!! I'M BEGINNING TO UNDERSTAND!!
EH?! UNDERSTAND WHAT?
WITHOUT REALIZING IT, WE MAY HAVE...
...SLIPPED INTO THE WORLD OF CONAN-KUN!
INTO THE WORLD OF...
...CONAN-KUN?
BUT AREN'T THEY CELEBRATING THE 30TH ANNIVERSARY OF—
HWOOOO
SHUT UP, HAYATE!
YOU ARE NOT ALLOWED TO SAY ANOTHER WORD ABOUT THAT—UP TO AND INCLUDING ANYTHING ABOUT THE ANNIVERSARY ISSUE OF *SHÔNEN SUNDAY* WE APPEARED IN!

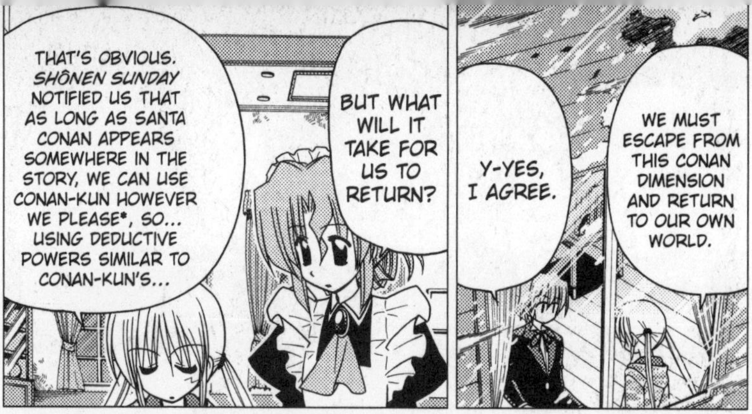
WE MUST ESCAPE FROM THIS CONAN DIMENSION AND RETURN TO OUR OWN WORLD.
Y-YES, I AGREE.
BUT WHAT WILL IT TAKE FOR US TO RETURN?
THAT'S OBVIOUS. *SHÔNEN SUNDAY* NOTIFIED US THAT AS LONG AS SANTA CONAN APPEARS SOMEWHERE IN THE STORY, WE CAN USE CONAN-KUN HOWEVER WE PLEASE*, SO... USING DEDUCTIVE POWERS SIMILAR TO CONAN-KUN'S...

* *SHÔNEN SUNDAY* EDITOR'S NOTE: THAT ISN'T QUITE THE NOTIFICATION WE GAVE...

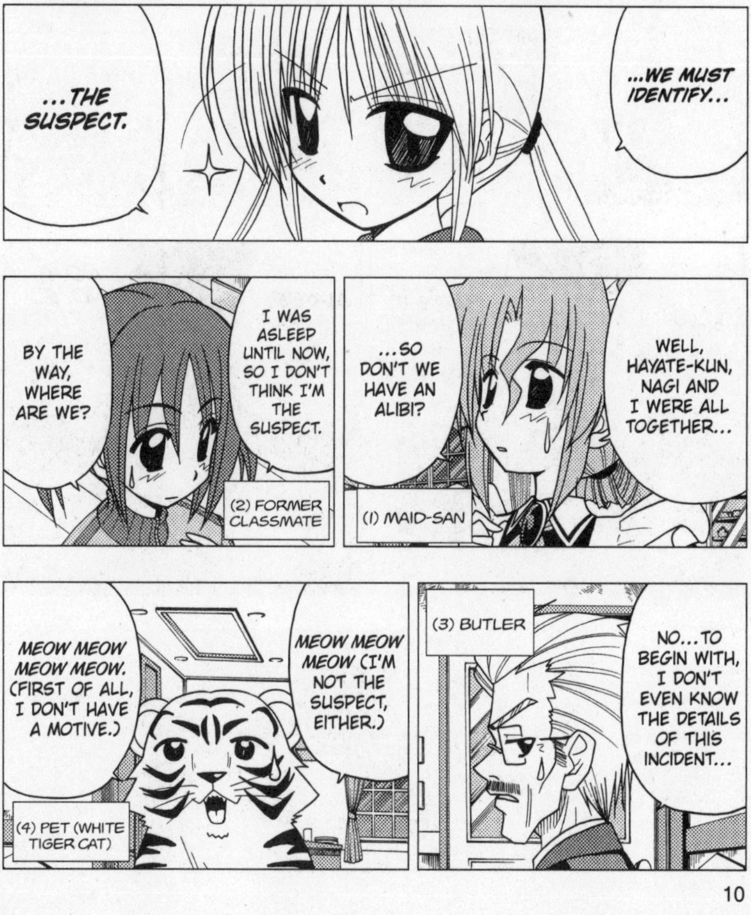
...WE MUST IDENTIFY...
...THE SUSPECT.
WELL, HAYATE-KUN, NAGI AND I WERE ALL TOGETHER...
...SO DON'T WE HAVE AN ALIBI?
(1) MAID-SAN
I WAS ASLEEP UNTIL NOW, SO I DON'T THINK I'M THE SUSPECT.
BY THE WAY, WHERE ARE WE?
(2) FORMER CLASSMATE
(3) BUTLER
NO...TO BEGIN WITH, I DON'T EVEN KNOW THE DETAILS OF THIS INCIDENT...
MEOW MEOW MEOW (I'M NOT THE SUSPECT, EITHER.)
MEOW MEOW MEOW MEOW. (FIRST OF ALL, I DON'T HAVE A MOTIVE.)
(4) PET (WHITE TIGER CAT)

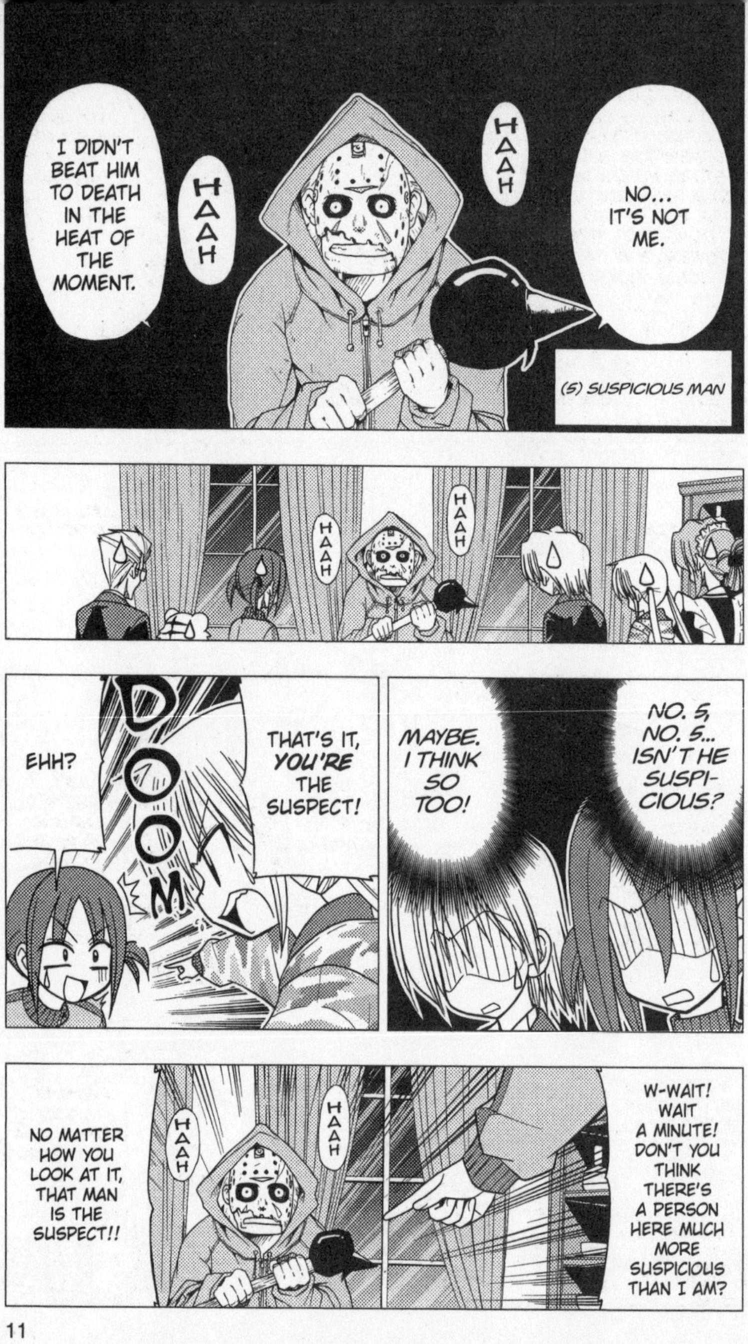
NO... IT'S NOT ME.
HAAH
HAAH
I DIDN'T BEAT HIM TO DEATH IN THE HEAT OF THE MOMENT.
(5) SUSPICIOUS MAN
HAAH
HAAH
NO. 5, NO. 5... ISN'T HE SUSPICIOUS?
MAYBE. I THINK SO TOO!
THAT'S IT, YOU'RE THE SUSPECT!
DOOOM
EHH?
W-WAIT! WAIT A MINUTE! DON'T YOU THINK THERE'S A PERSON HERE MUCH MORE SUSPICIOUS THAN I AM?
HAAH
HAAH
NO MATTER HOW YOU LOOK AT IT, THAT MAN IS THE SUSPECT!!

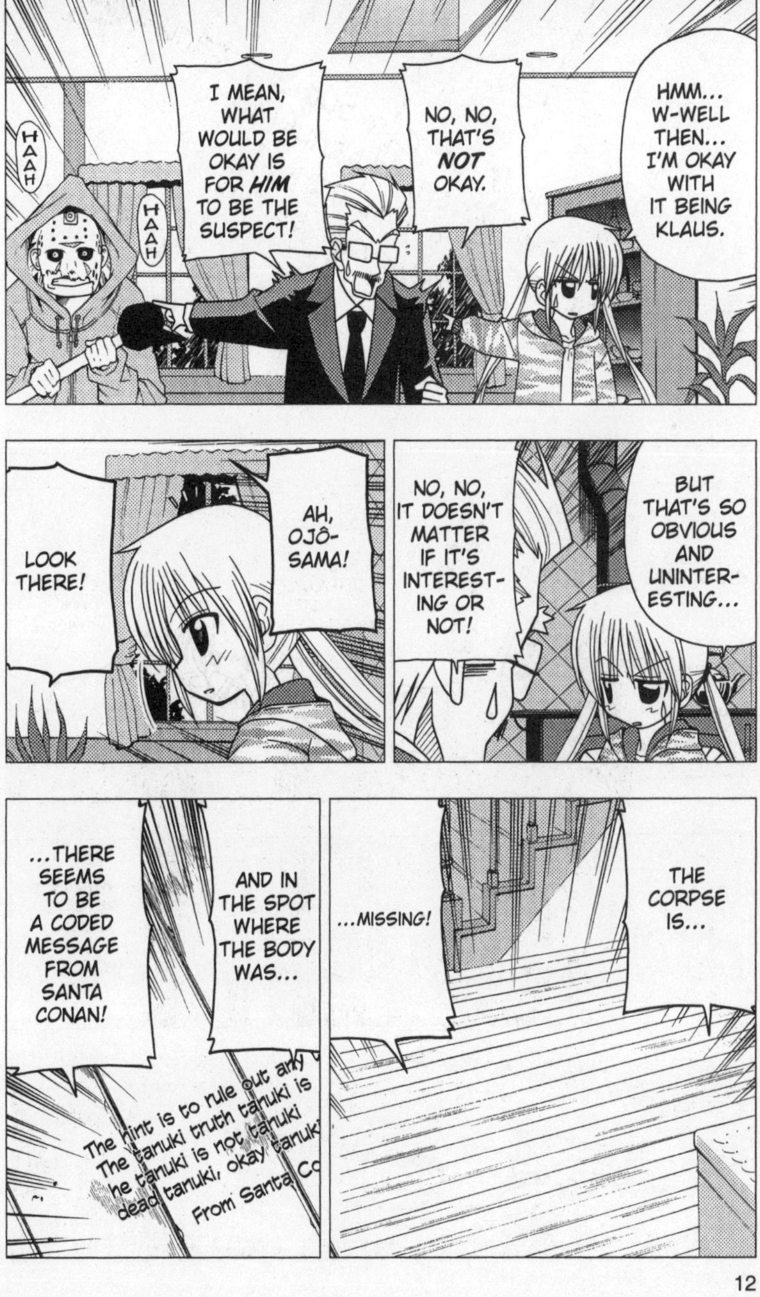
HMM... W-WELL THEN... I'M OKAY WITH IT BEING KLAUS.
NO, NO, THAT'S NOT OKAY.
I MEAN, WHAT WOULD BE OKAY IS FOR HIM TO BE THE SUSPECT!
HAAH
HAAH
BUT THAT'S SO OBVIOUS AND UNINTERESTING...
NO, NO, IT DOESN'T MATTER IF IT'S INTERESTING OR NOT!
AH, OJÔ-SAMA!
LOOK THERE!
THE CORPSE IS...
...MISSING!
AND IN THE SPOT WHERE THE BODY WAS...
...THERE SEEMS TO BE A CODED MESSAGE FROM SANTA CONAN!
The hint is to rule out any
The tanuki truth tanuki is
he tanuki is not tanuki
dead tanuki, okay tanuki
From Santa Co

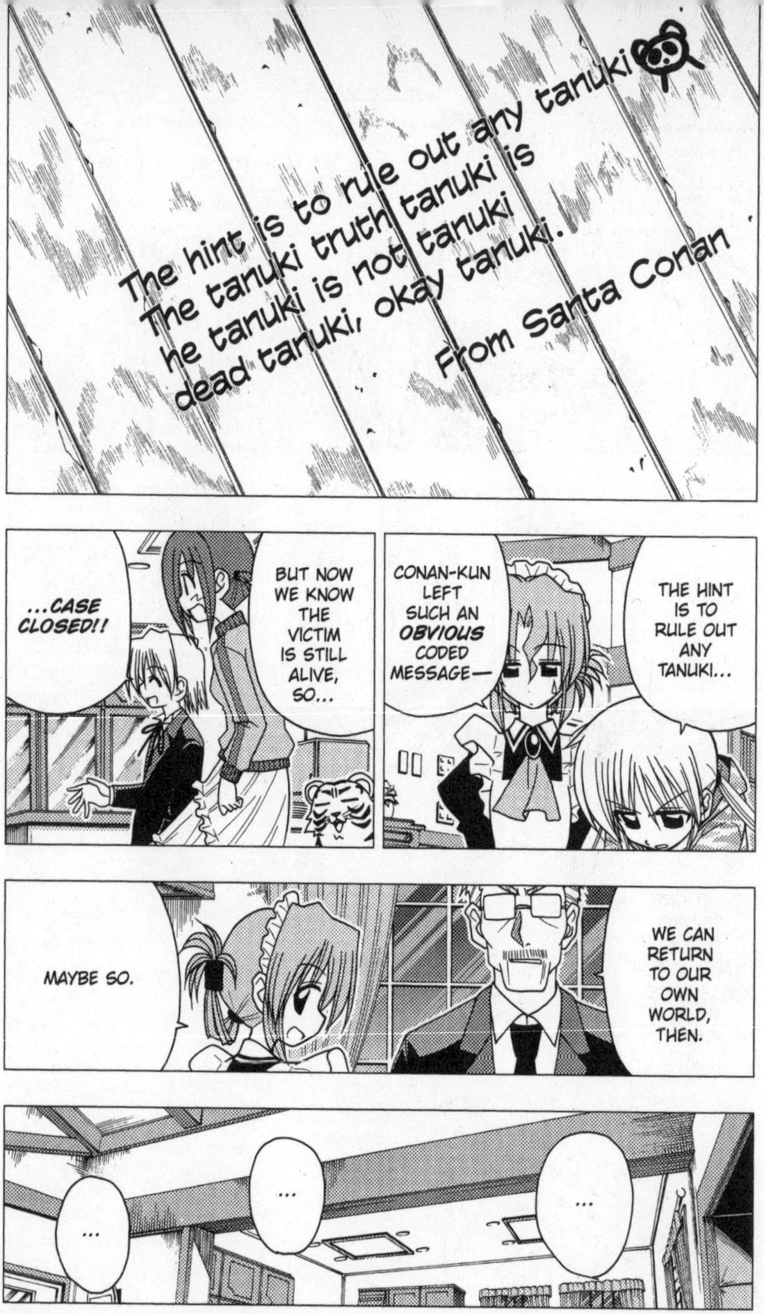

The hint is to rule out any tanuki
The tanuki truth tanuki is
he tanuki is not tanuki
dead tanuki, okay tanuki.
From Santa Conan
THE HINT IS TO RULE OUT ANY TANUKI...
CONAN-KUN LEFT SUCH AN OBVIOUS CODED MESSAGE—
BUT NOW WE KNOW THE VICTIM IS STILL ALIVE, SO...
...CASE CLOSED!!
WE CAN RETURN TO OUR OWN WORLD, THEN.
MAYBE SO.
...
...
...

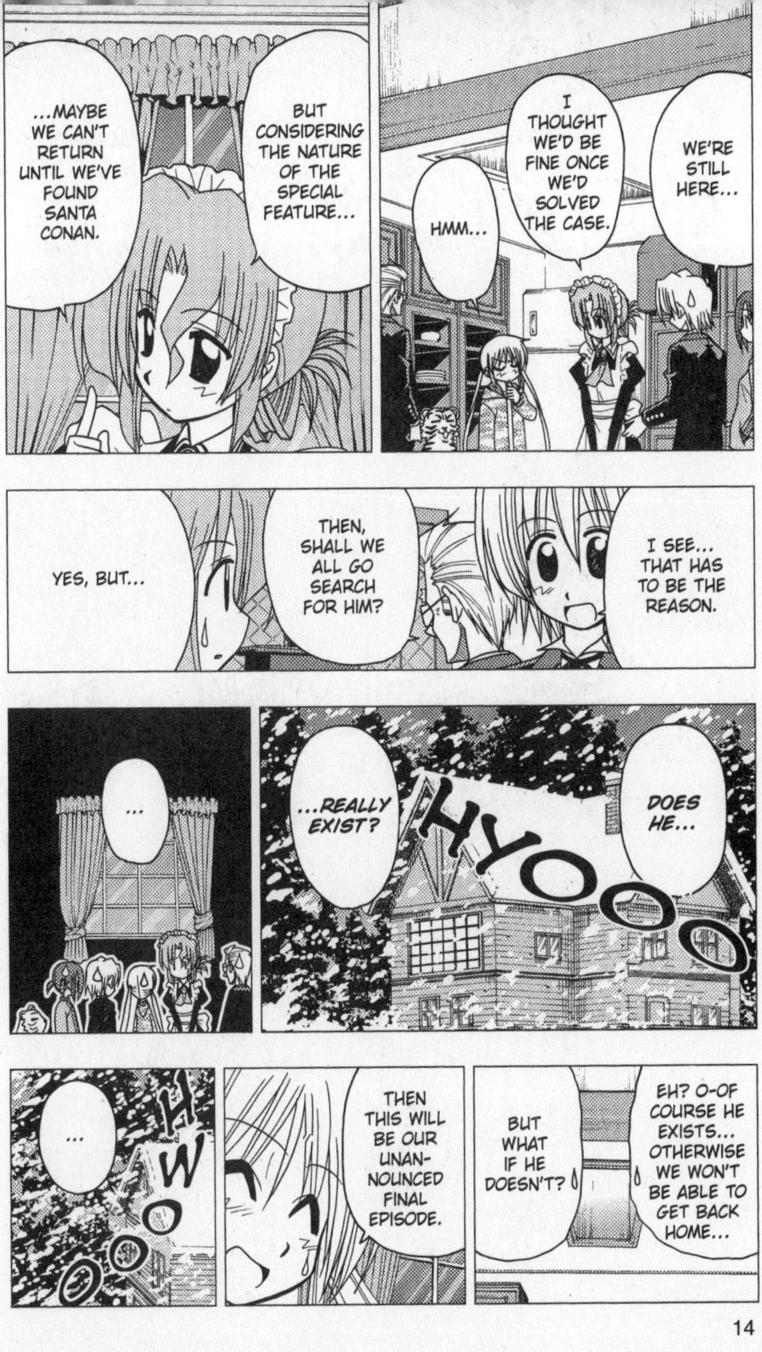
WE'RE STILL HERE...
I THOUGHT WE'D BE FINE ONCE WE'D SOLVED THE CASE.
HMM...
BUT CONSIDERING THE NATURE OF THE SPECIAL FEATURE...
...MAYBE WE CAN'T RETURN UNTIL WE'VE FOUND SANTA CONAN.
I SEE... THAT HAS TO BE THE REASON.
THEN, SHALL WE ALL GO SEARCH FOR HIM?
YES, BUT...
DOES HE...
HYOOOO
...REALLY EXIST?
...
EH? O-OF COURSE HE EXISTS... OTHERWISE WE WON'T BE ABLE TO GET BACK HOME...
BUT WHAT IF HE DOESN'T?
THEN THIS WILL BE OUR UNANNOUNCED FINAL EPISODE.
HWOOOO
...

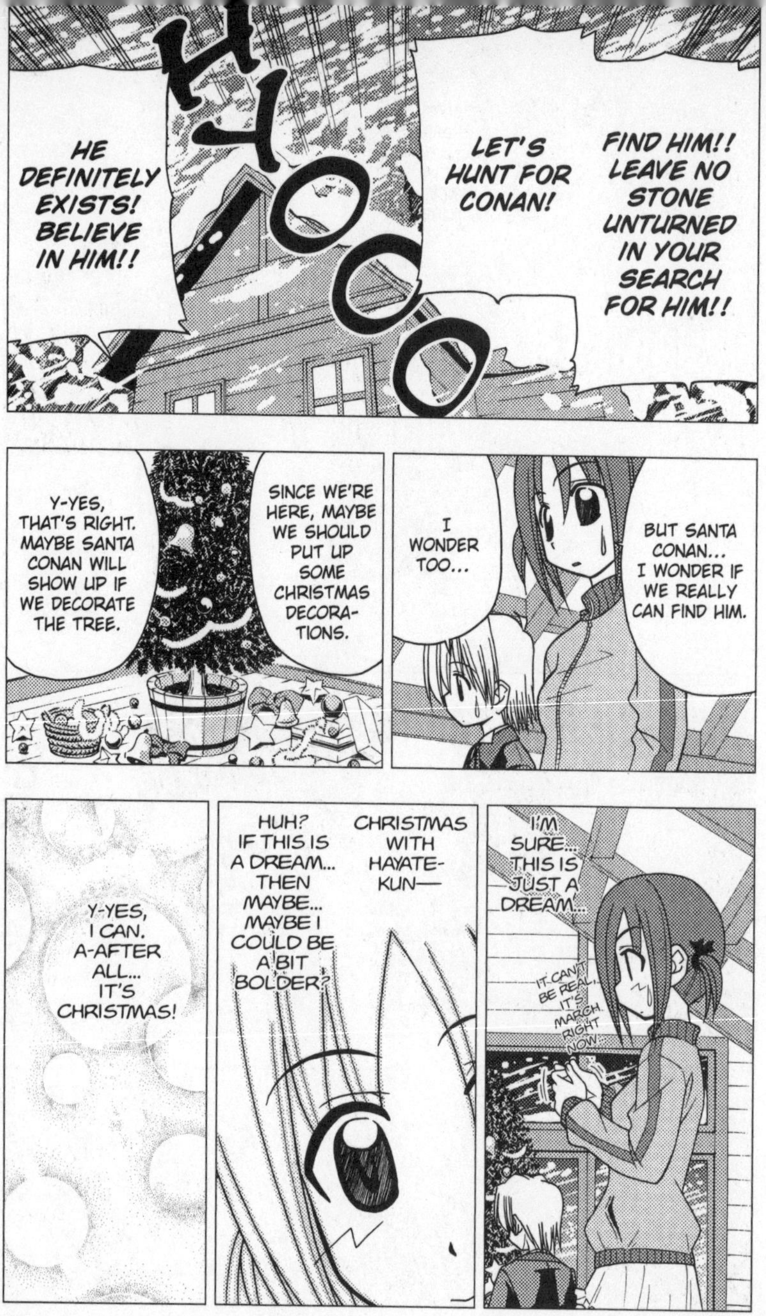
FIND HIM!! LEAVE NO STONE UNTURNED IN YOUR SEARCH FOR HIM!!
LET'S HUNT FOR CONAN!
HYOOOO
HE DEFINITELY EXISTS! BELIEVE IN HIM!!
BUT SANTA CONAN... I WONDER IF WE REALLY CAN FIND HIM.
I WONDER TOO...
SINCE WE'RE HERE, MAYBE WE SHOULD PUT UP SOME CHRISTMAS DECORA-TIONS.
Y-YES, THAT'S RIGHT. MAYBE SANTA CONAN WILL SHOW UP IF WE DECORATE THE TREE.
I'M SURE... THIS IS JUST A DREAM...
IT CAN'T BE REAL. IT'S MARCH RIGHT NOW...
CHRISTMAS WITH HAYATE-KUN—
HUH? IF THIS IS A DREAM... THEN MAYBE... MAYBE I COULD BE A BIT BOLDER?
Y-YES, I CAN. A-AFTER ALL... IT'S CHRISTMAS!

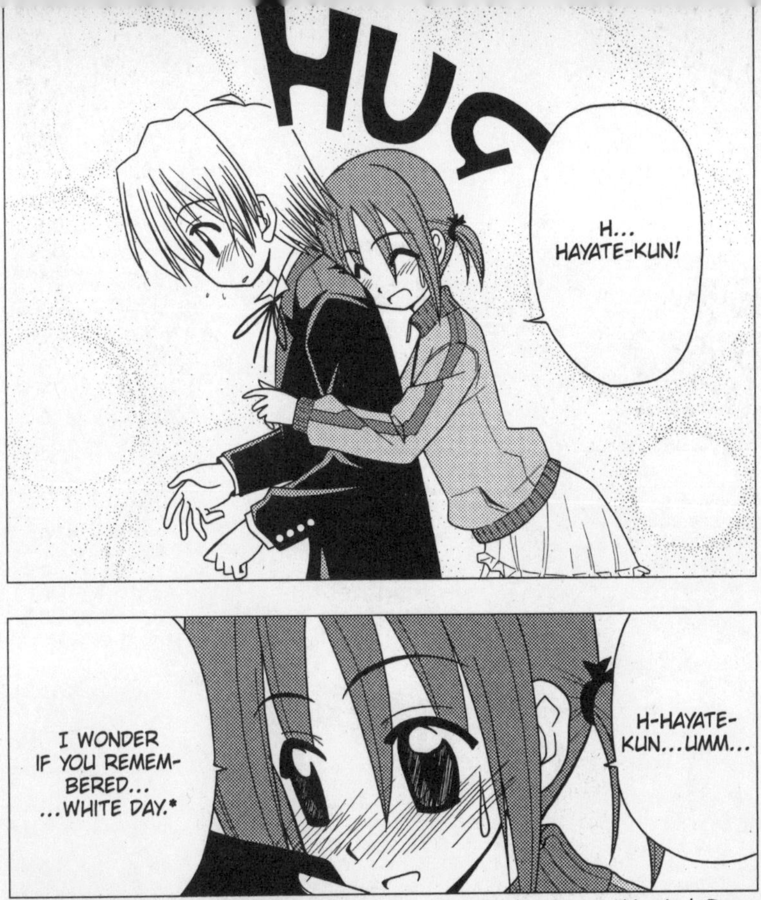
HUG
H... HAYATE-KUN!
H-HAYATE-KUN...UMM...
I WONDER IF YOU REMEMBERED... ...WHITE DAY.*

*A day where men buy gifts for the women who gave them chocolate on Valentine's Day.

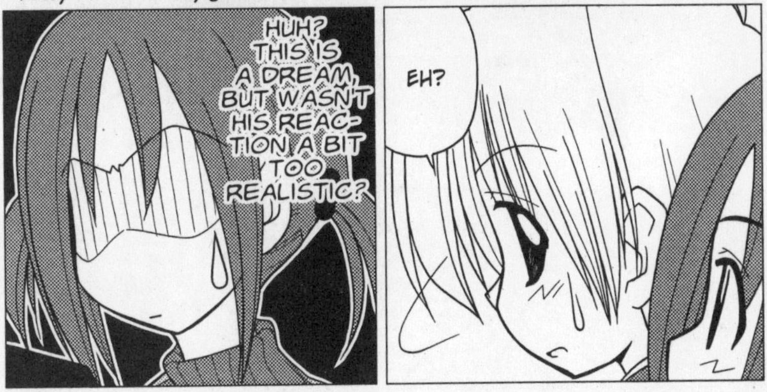
EH?
HUH? THIS IS A DREAM, BUT WASN'T HIS REACTION A BIT TOO REALISTIC?

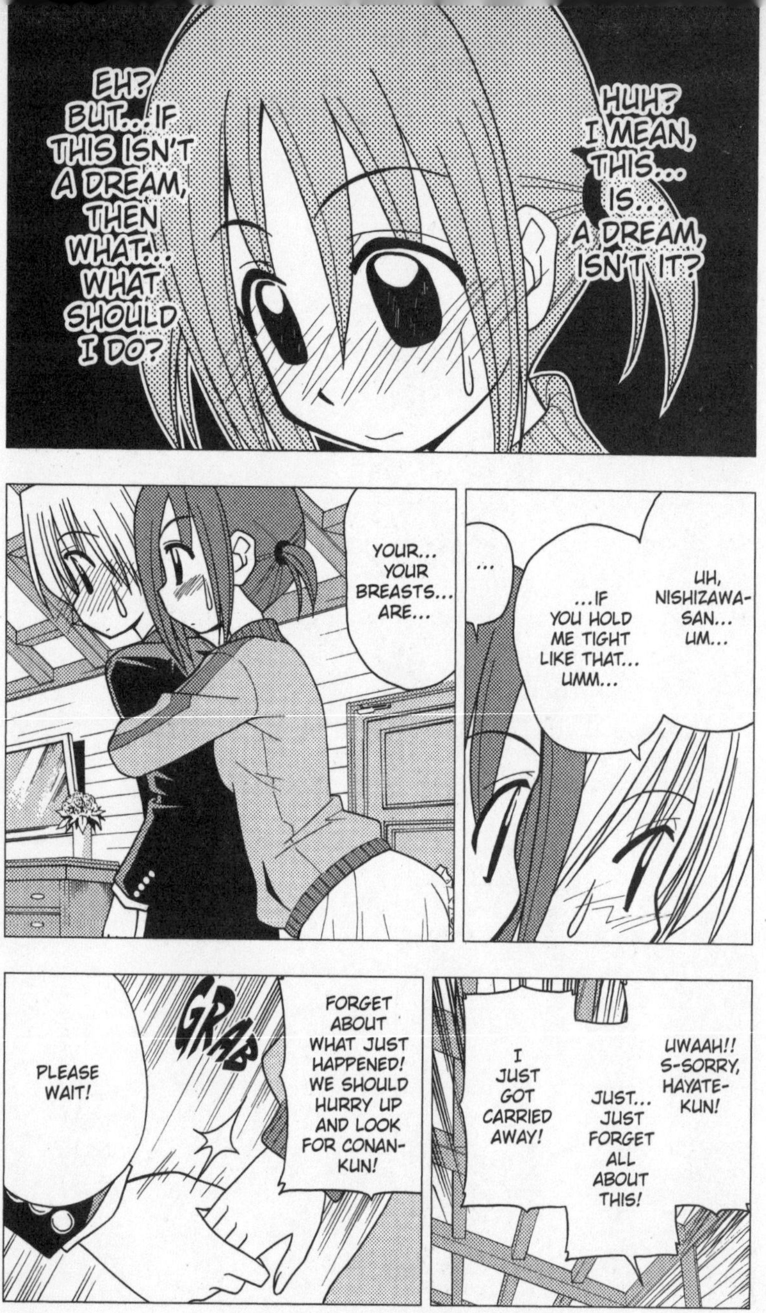
HUH? I MEAN, THIS... IS... A DREAM, ISN'T IT?
EH? BUT... IF THIS ISN'T A DREAM, THEN WHAT... WHAT SHOULD I DO?
UH, NISHIZAWA-SAN... UM...
...IF YOU HOLD ME TIGHT LIKE THAT... UMM...
...
YOUR... YOUR BREASTS... ARE...
UWAAH!! S-SORRY, HAYATE-KUN!
JUST... JUST FORGET ALL ABOUT THIS!
I JUST GOT CARRIED AWAY!
FORGET ABOUT WHAT JUST HAPPENED! WE SHOULD HURRY UP AND LOOK FOR CONAN-KUN!
GRAB
PLEASE WAIT!

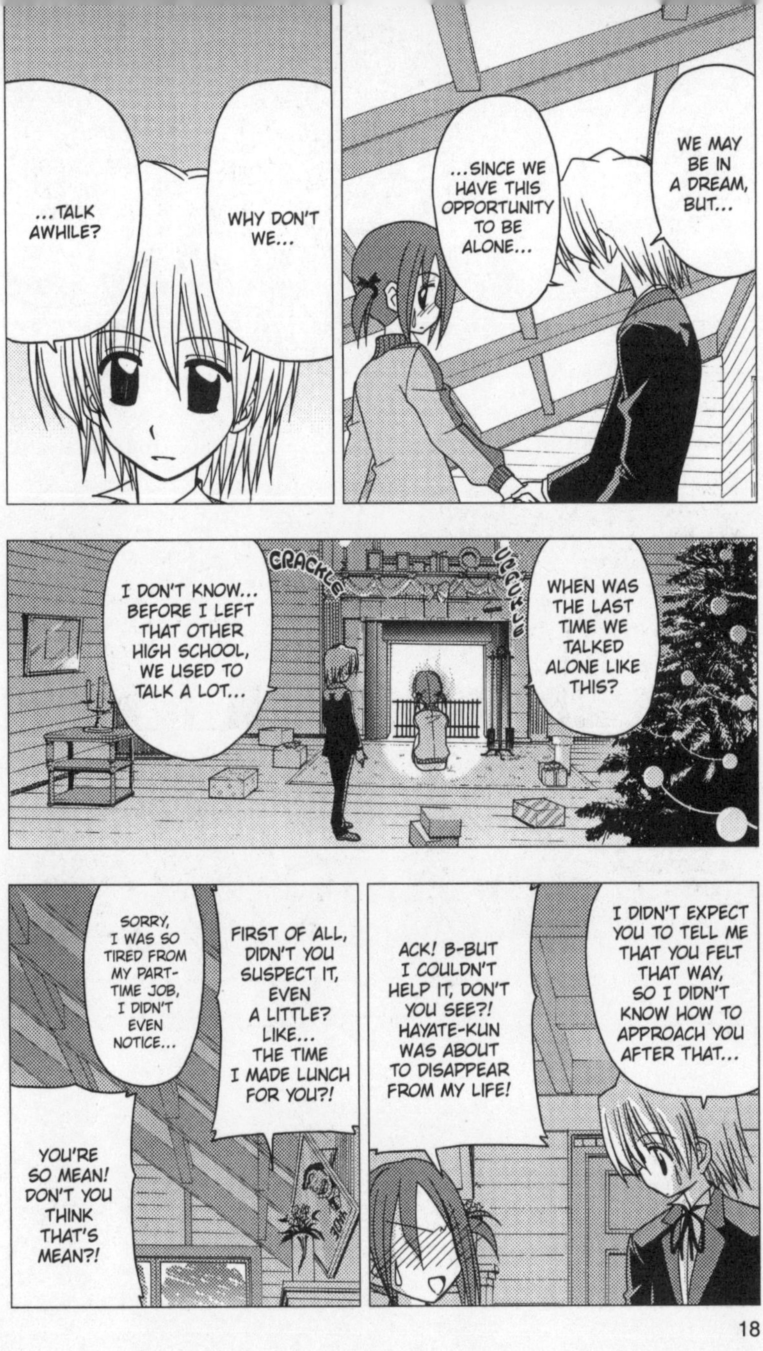
WE MAY BE IN A DREAM, BUT...
...SINCE WE HAVE THIS OPPORTUNITY TO BE ALONE...
WHY DON'T WE...
...TALK AWHILE?
CRACKLE
WHEN WAS THE LAST TIME WE TALKED ALONE LIKE THIS?
CRACKLE
I DON'T KNOW... BEFORE I LEFT THAT OTHER HIGH SCHOOL, WE USED TO TALK A LOT...
I DIDN'T EXPECT YOU TO TELL ME THAT YOU FELT THAT WAY, SO I DIDN'T KNOW HOW TO APPROACH YOU AFTER THAT...
ACK! B-BUT I COULDN'T HELP IT, DON'T YOU SEE?! HAYATE-KUN WAS ABOUT TO DISAPPEAR FROM MY LIFE!
FIRST OF ALL, DIDN'T YOU SUSPECT IT, EVEN A LITTLE? LIKE... THE TIME I MADE LUNCH FOR YOU?!
SORRY, I WAS SO TIRED FROM MY PART-TIME JOB, I DIDN'T EVEN NOTICE...
YOU'RE SO MEAN! DON'T YOU THINK THAT'S MEAN?!

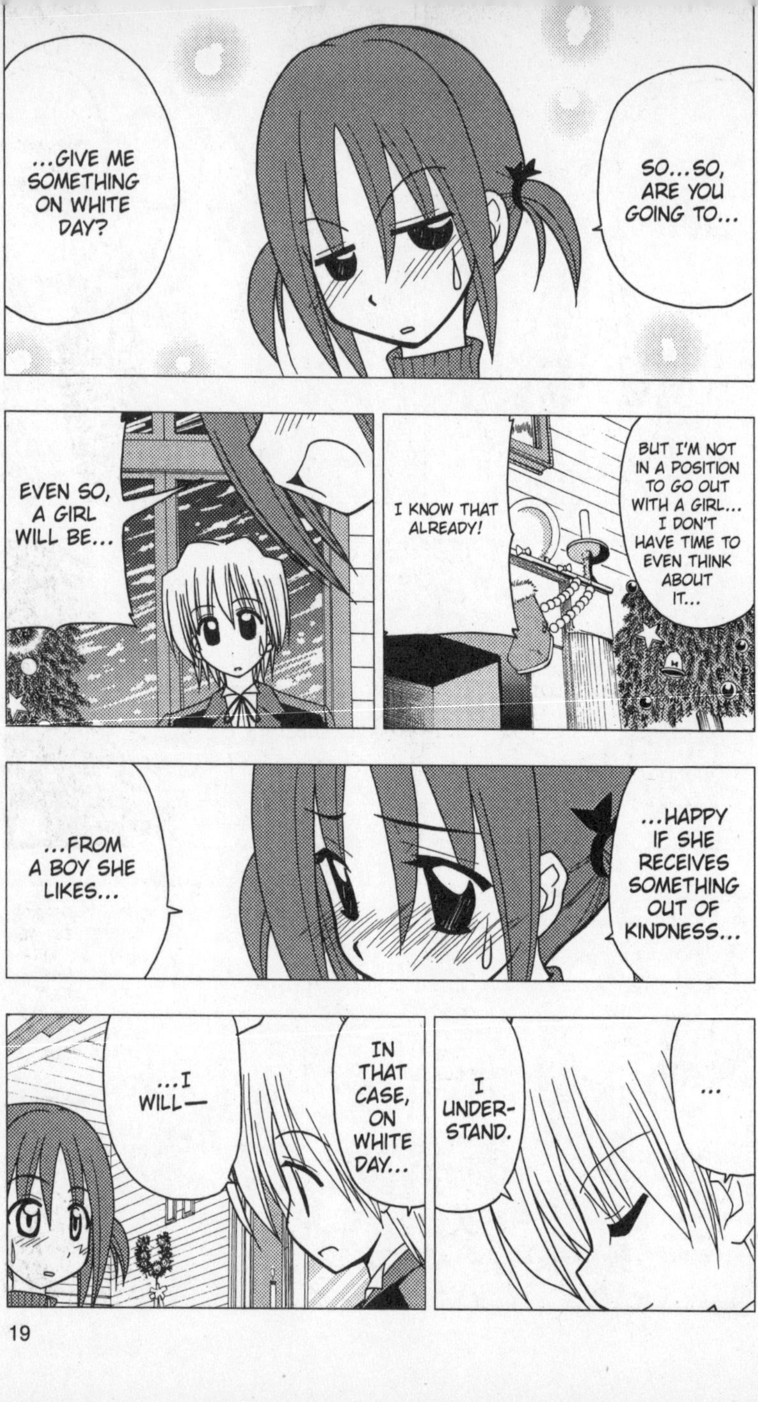
SO...SO, ARE YOU GOING TO...
...GIVE ME SOMETHING ON WHITE DAY?
BUT I'M NOT IN A POSITION TO GO OUT WITH A GIRL... I DON'T HAVE TIME TO EVEN THINK ABOUT IT...
I KNOW THAT ALREADY!
EVEN SO, A GIRL WILL BE...
...HAPPY IF SHE RECEIVES SOMETHING OUT OF KINDNESS...
...FROM A BOY SHE LIKES...
...
I UNDER-STAND.
IN THAT CASE, ON WHITE DAY...
...I WILL—

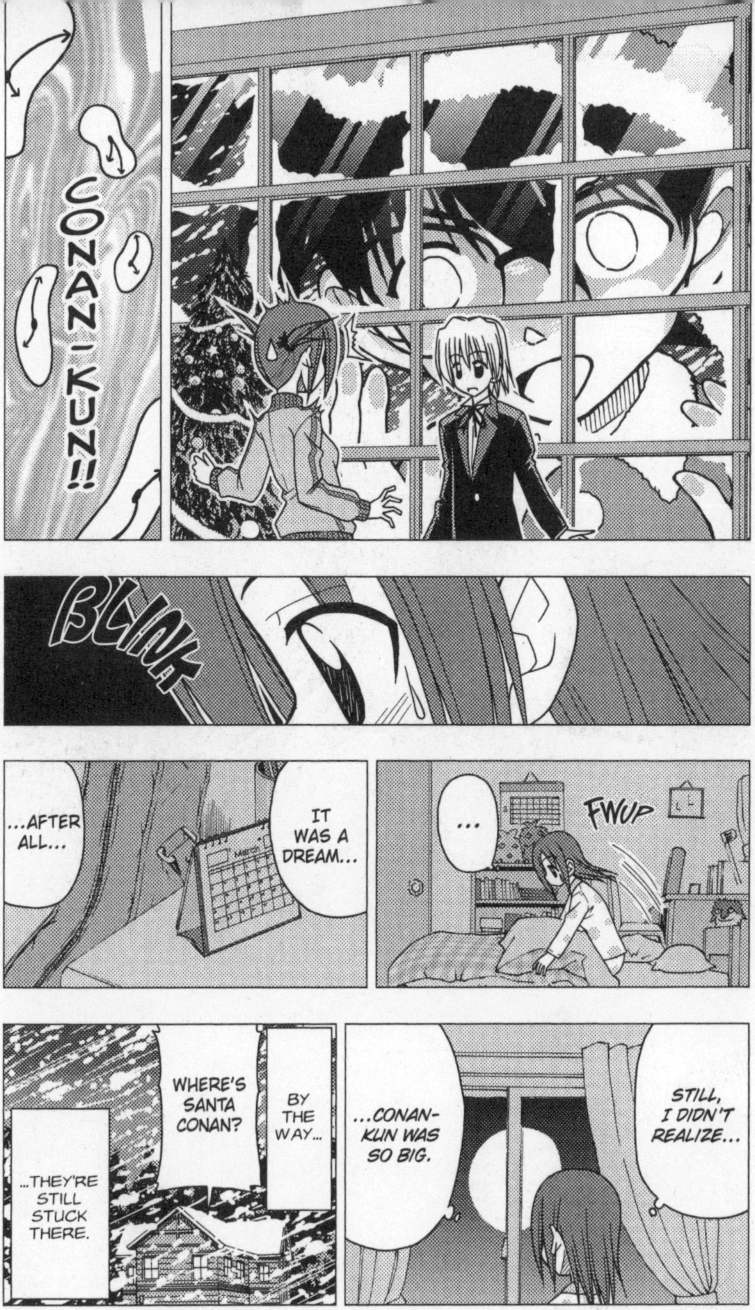
CONAN-KUN!!
BLINK
...
FWUP
IT WAS A DREAM...
...AFTER ALL...
STILL, I DIDN'T REALIZE...
...CONAN-KUN WAS SO BIG.
BY THE WAY...
WHERE'S SANTA CONAN?
...THEY'RE STILL STUCK THERE.

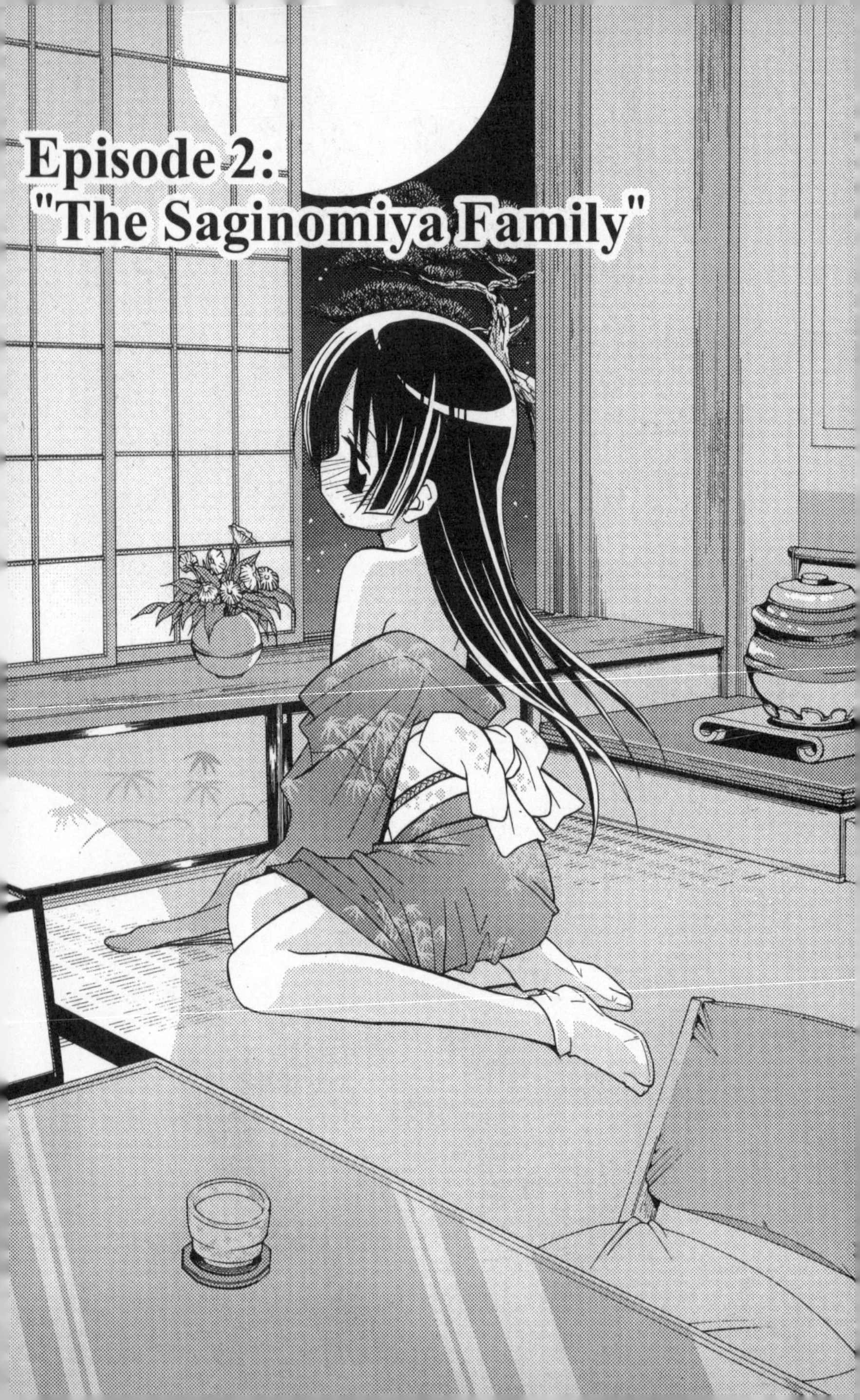
Episode 2:
"The Saginomiya Family"

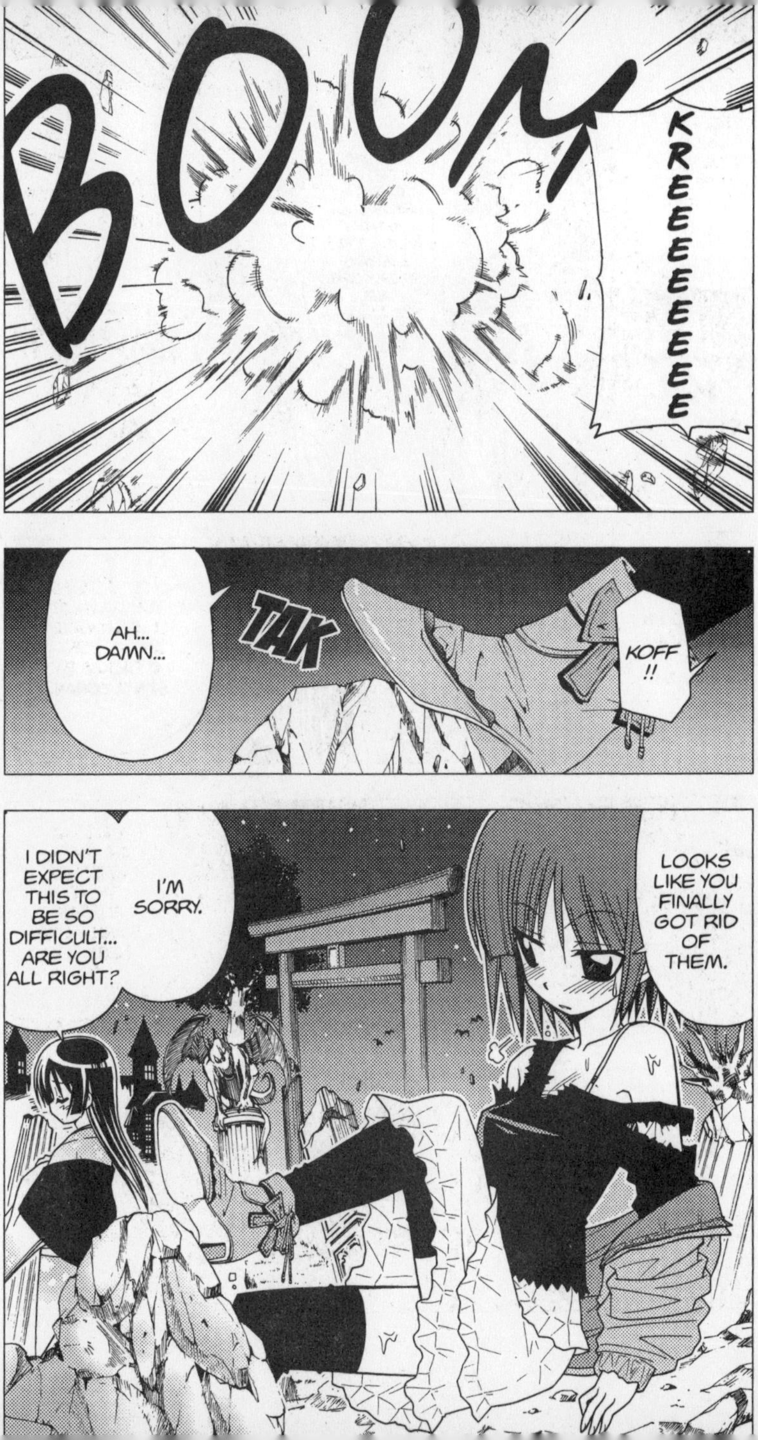
BOOM
KREEEEEEEEE
KOFF !!
TAK
AH... DAMN...
LOOKS LIKE YOU FINALLY GOT RID OF THEM.
I'M SORRY.
I DIDN'T EXPECT THIS TO BE SO DIFFICULT... ARE YOU ALL RIGHT?

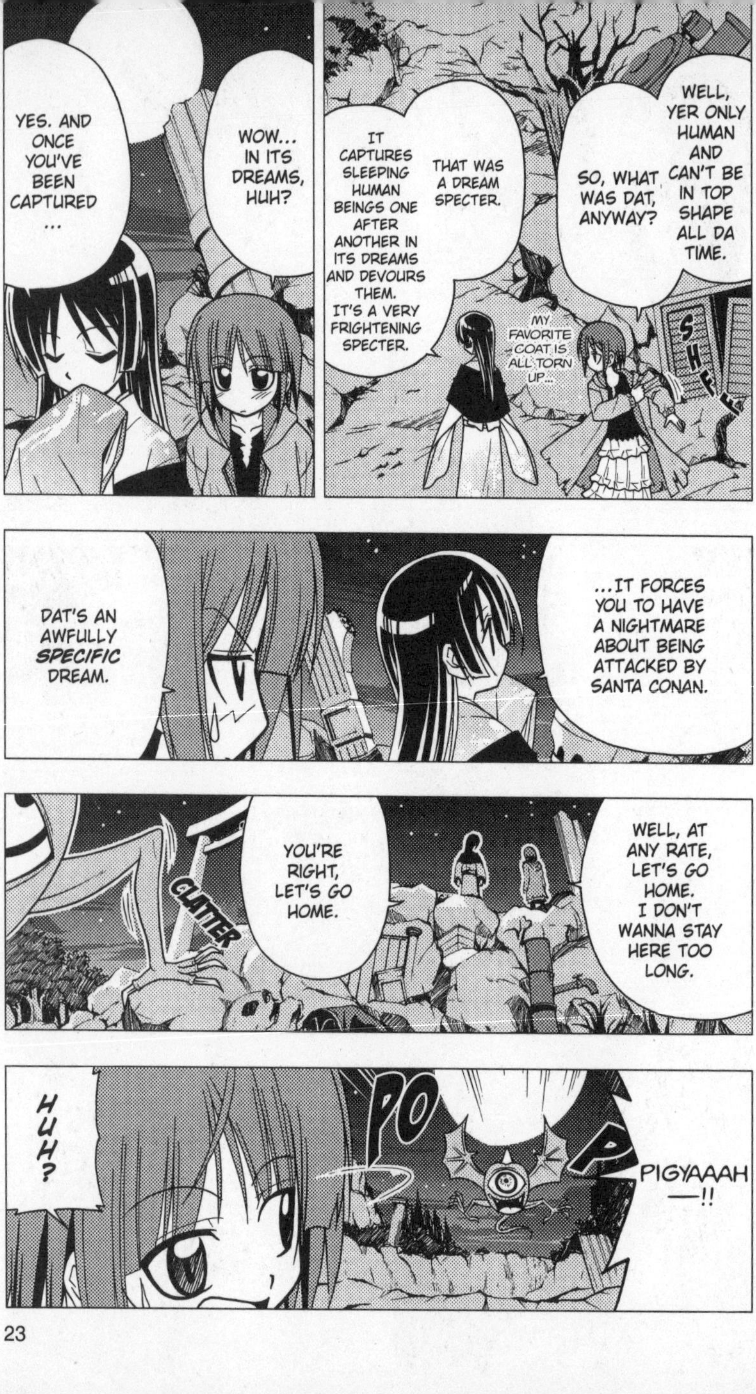

WELL, YER ONLY HUMAN AND CAN'T BE IN TOP SHAPE ALL DA TIME.
SO, WHAT WAS DAT, ANYWAY?
MY FAVORITE COAT IS ALL TORN UP...
THAT WAS A DREAM SPECTER.
IT CAPTURES SLEEPING HUMAN BEINGS ONE AFTER ANOTHER IN ITS DREAMS AND DEVOURS THEM. IT'S A VERY FRIGHTENING SPECTER.
WOW... IN ITS DREAMS, HUH?
YES. AND ONCE YOU'VE BEEN CAPTURED ...
...IT FORCES YOU TO HAVE A NIGHTMARE ABOUT BEING ATTACKED BY SANTA CONAN.
DAT'S AN AWFULLY *SPECIFIC* DREAM.
WELL, AT ANY RATE, LET'S GO HOME. I DON'T WANNA STAY HERE TOO LONG.
YOU'RE RIGHT, LET'S GO HOME.
CLATTER
PIGYAAAH—!!
POP
HUH?

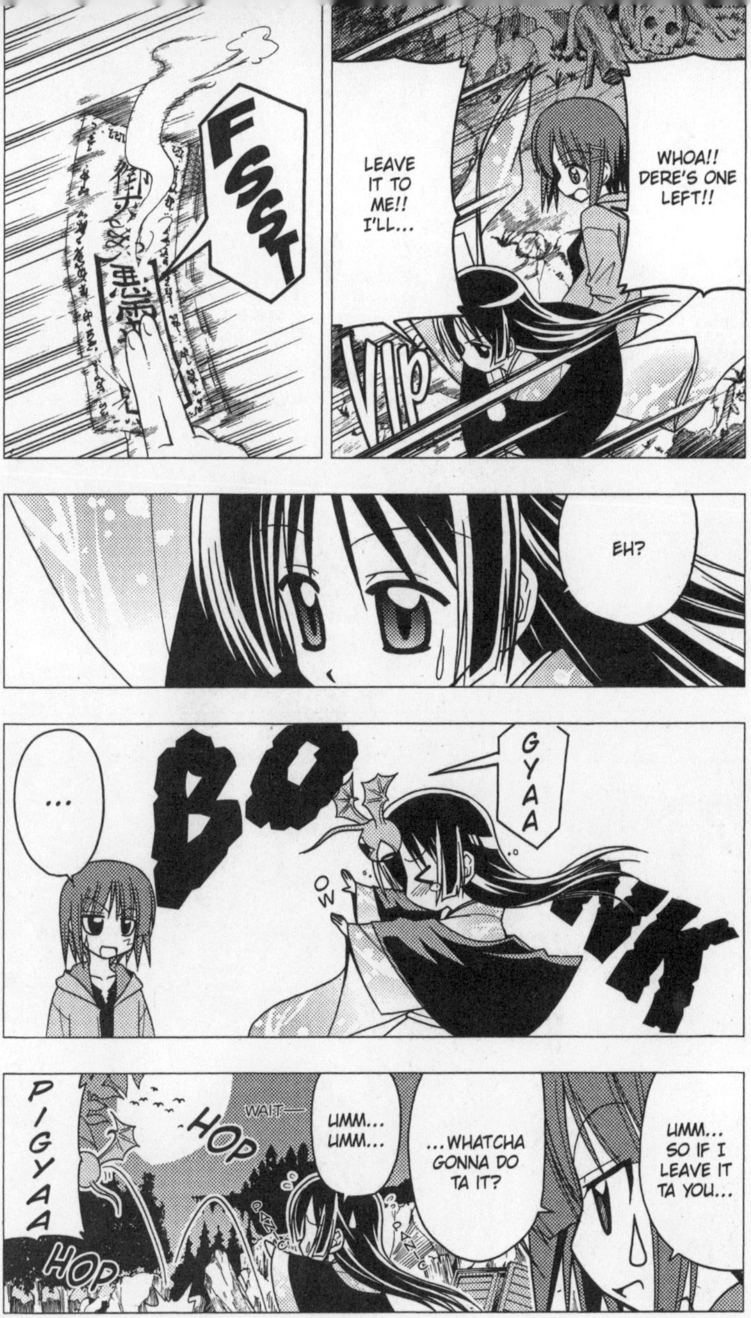

WHOA!! DERE'S ONE LEFT!!
LEAVE IT TO ME!! I'LL...
VIP
FSSST
EH?
GYAA
BONK
OW
...
UMM... SO IF I LEAVE IT TA YOU...
...WHATCHA GONNA DO TA IT?
UMM... UMM...
WAIT—
PANIC
PANIC
HOP
PIGYAA
HOP

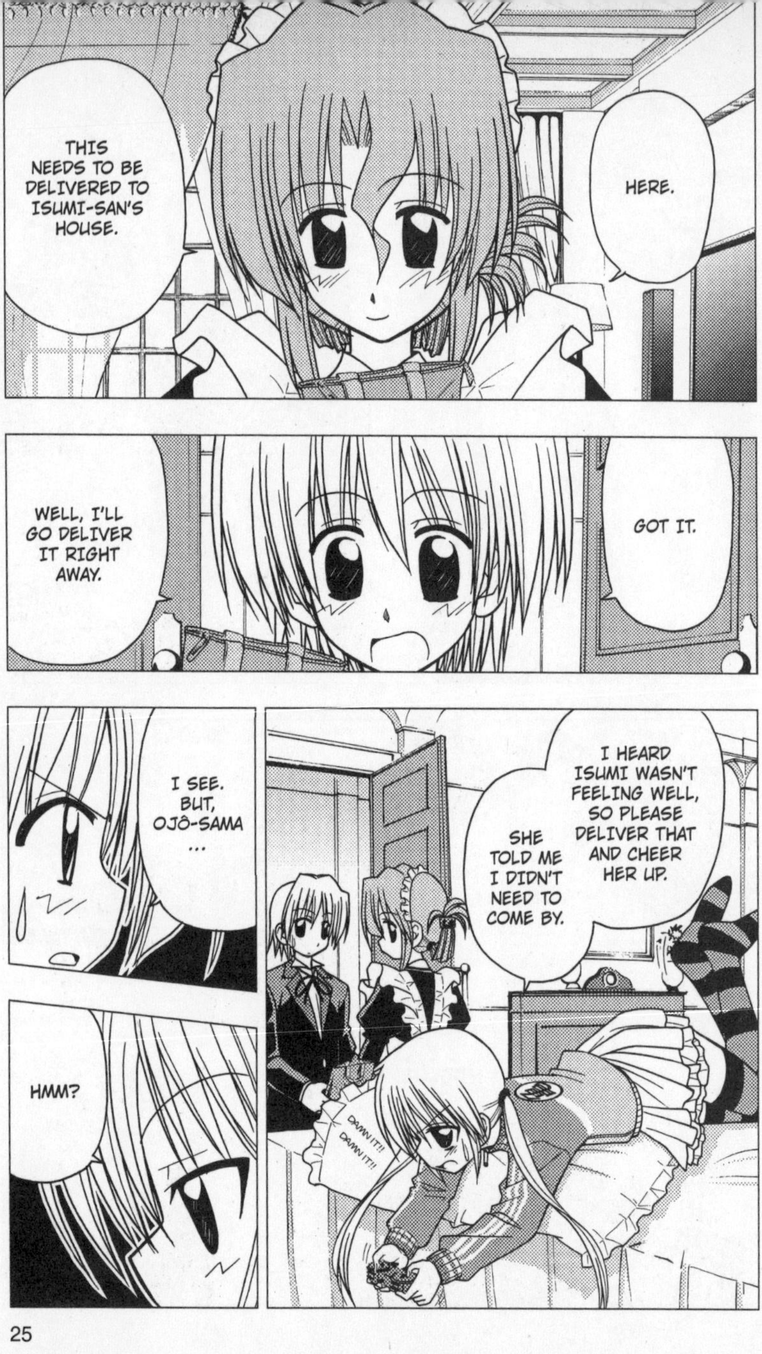
HERE.
THIS NEEDS TO BE DELIVERED TO ISUMI-SAN'S HOUSE.
GOT IT.
WELL, I'LL GO DELIVER IT RIGHT AWAY.
I HEARD ISUMI WASN'T FEELING WELL, SO PLEASE DELIVER THAT AND CHEER HER UP.
SHE TOLD ME I DIDN'T NEED TO COME BY.
DAMN IT!! DAMN IT!!
I SEE. BUT, OJÔ-SAMA ...
HMM?

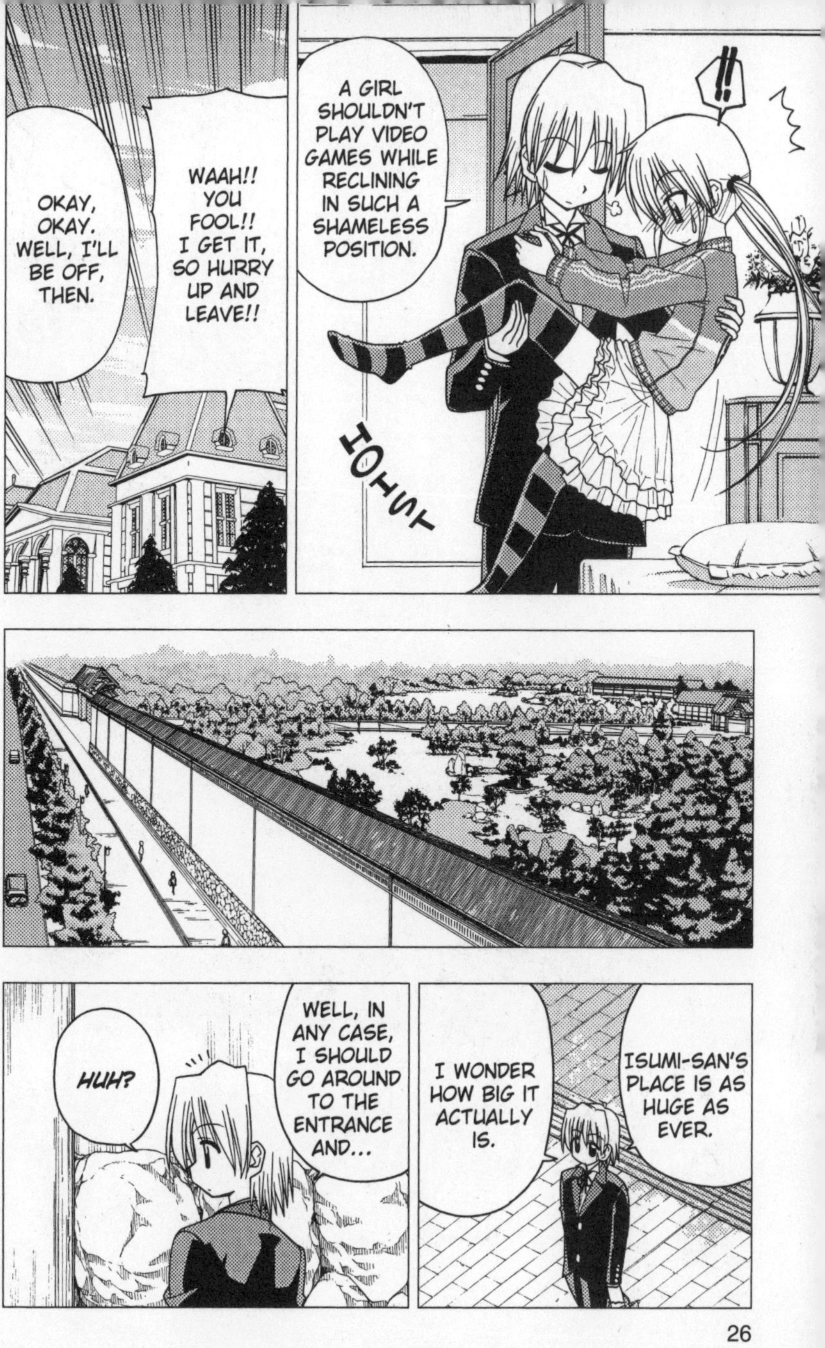
!!
A GIRL SHOULDN'T PLAY VIDEO GAMES WHILE RECLINING IN SUCH A SHAMELESS POSITION.
HOIST
WAAH!! YOU FOOL!! I GET IT, SO HURRY UP AND LEAVE!!
OKAY, OKAY. WELL, I'LL BE OFF, THEN.
ISUMI-SAN'S PLACE IS AS HUGE AS EVER.
I WONDER HOW BIG IT ACTUALLY IS.
WELL, IN ANY CASE, I SHOULD GO AROUND TO THE ENTRANCE AND...
HUH?

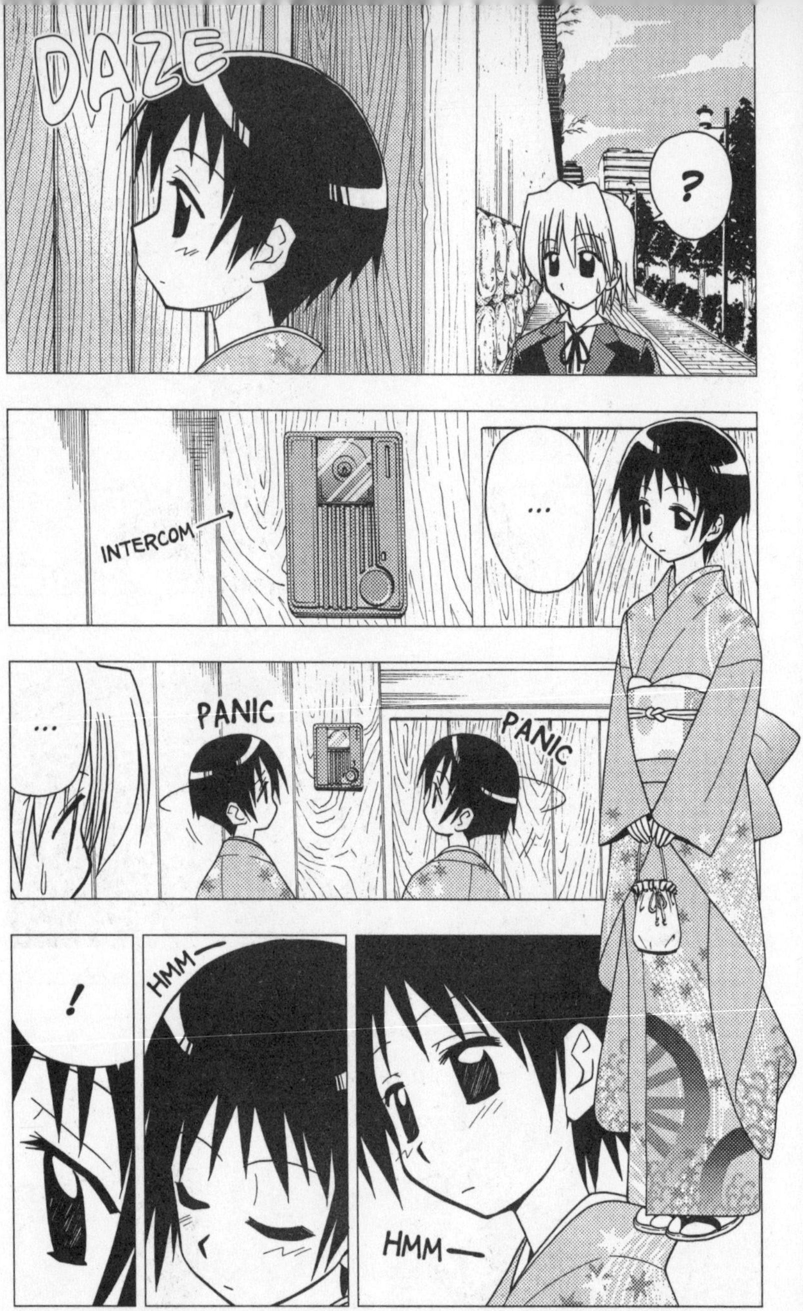
?
DAZE
...
INTERCOM
PANIC
PANIC
...
HMM—
HMM—
!

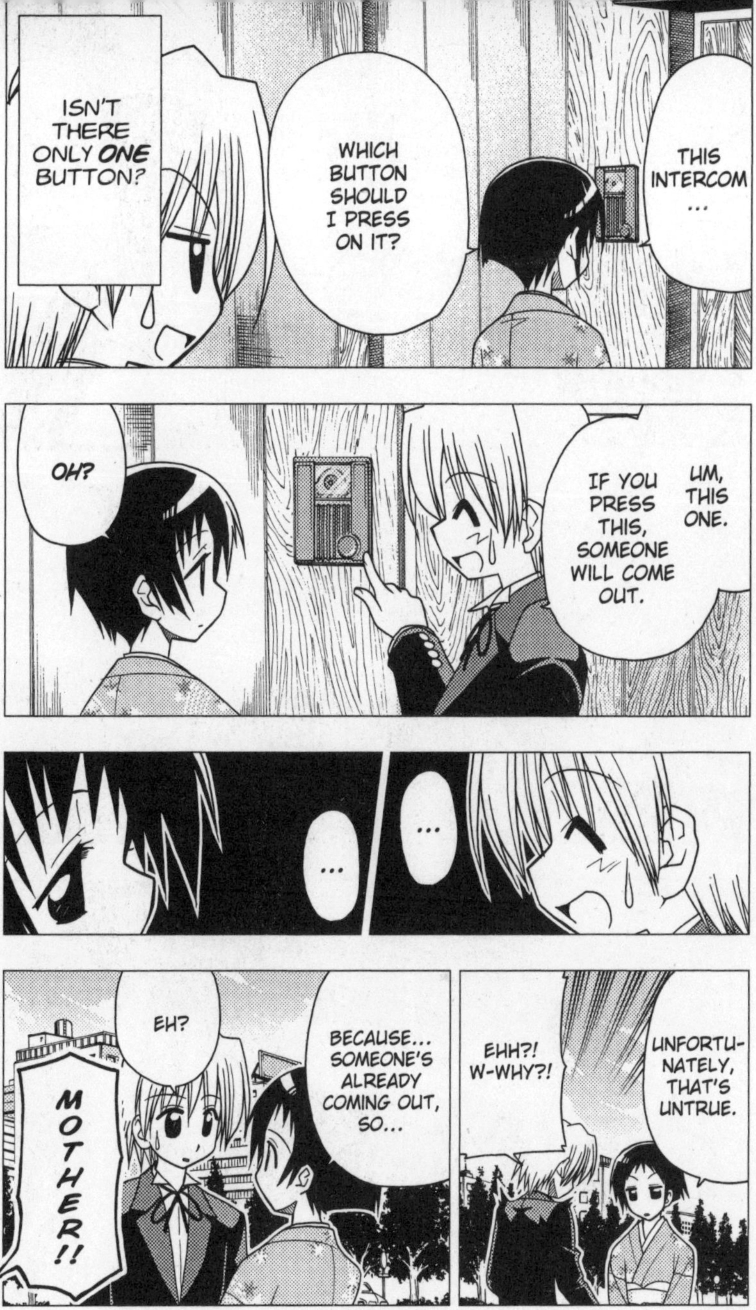
THIS INTERCOM...
WHICH BUTTON SHOULD I PRESS ON IT?
ISN'T THERE ONLY ONE BUTTON?
UM, THIS ONE.
IF YOU PRESS THIS, SOMEONE WILL COME OUT.
OH?
...
...
UNFORTUNATELY, THAT'S UNTRUE.
EHH?! W-WHY?!
BECAUSE... SOMEONE'S ALREADY COMING OUT, SO...
EH?
MOTHER!!

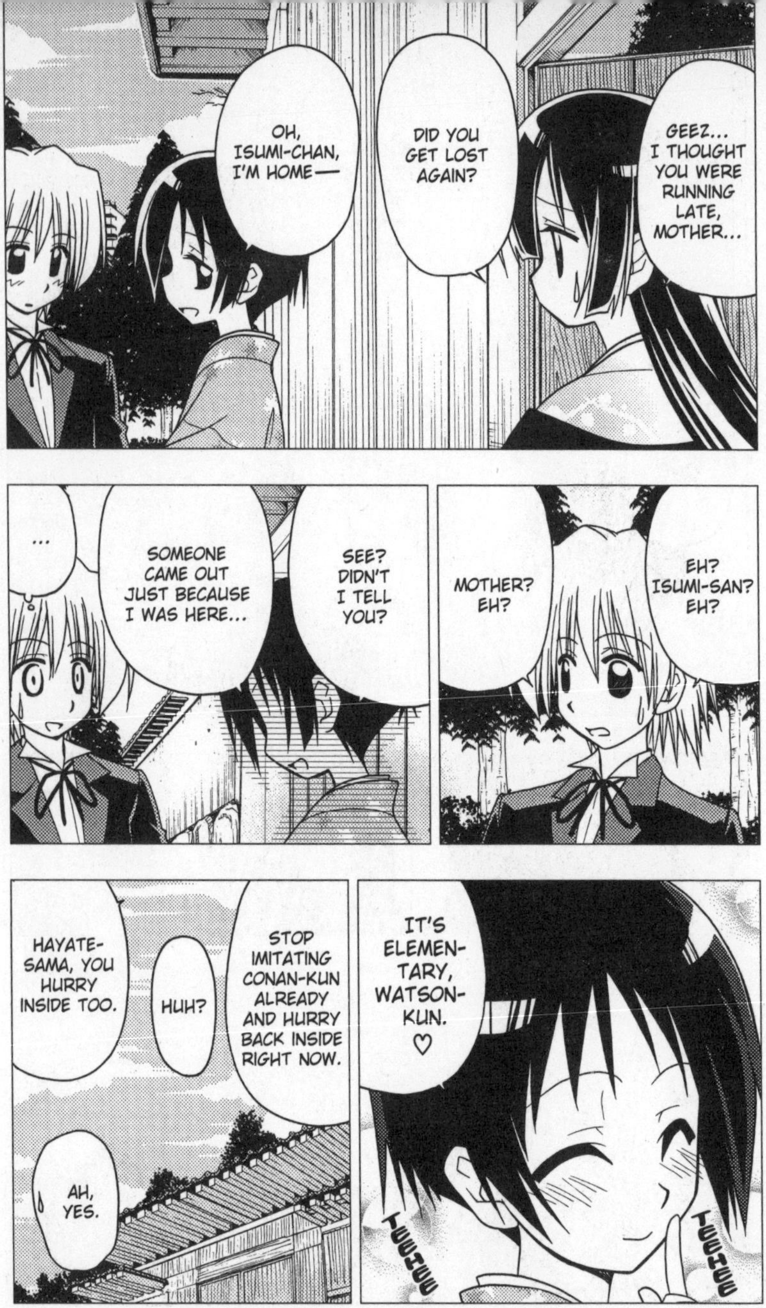
GEEZ... I THOUGHT YOU WERE RUNNING LATE, MOTHER...
DID YOU GET LOST AGAIN?
OH, ISUMI-CHAN, I'M HOME—
EH? ISUMI-SAN? EH?
MOTHER? EH?
SEE? DIDN'T I TELL YOU?
SOMEONE CAME OUT JUST BECAUSE I WAS HERE...
...
IT'S ELEMENTARY, WATSON-KUN. ♡
TEEHEE
TEEHEE
STOP IMITATING CONAN-KUN ALREADY AND HURRY BACK INSIDE RIGHT NOW.
HUH?
HAYATE-SAMA, YOU HURRY INSIDE TOO.
AH, YES.

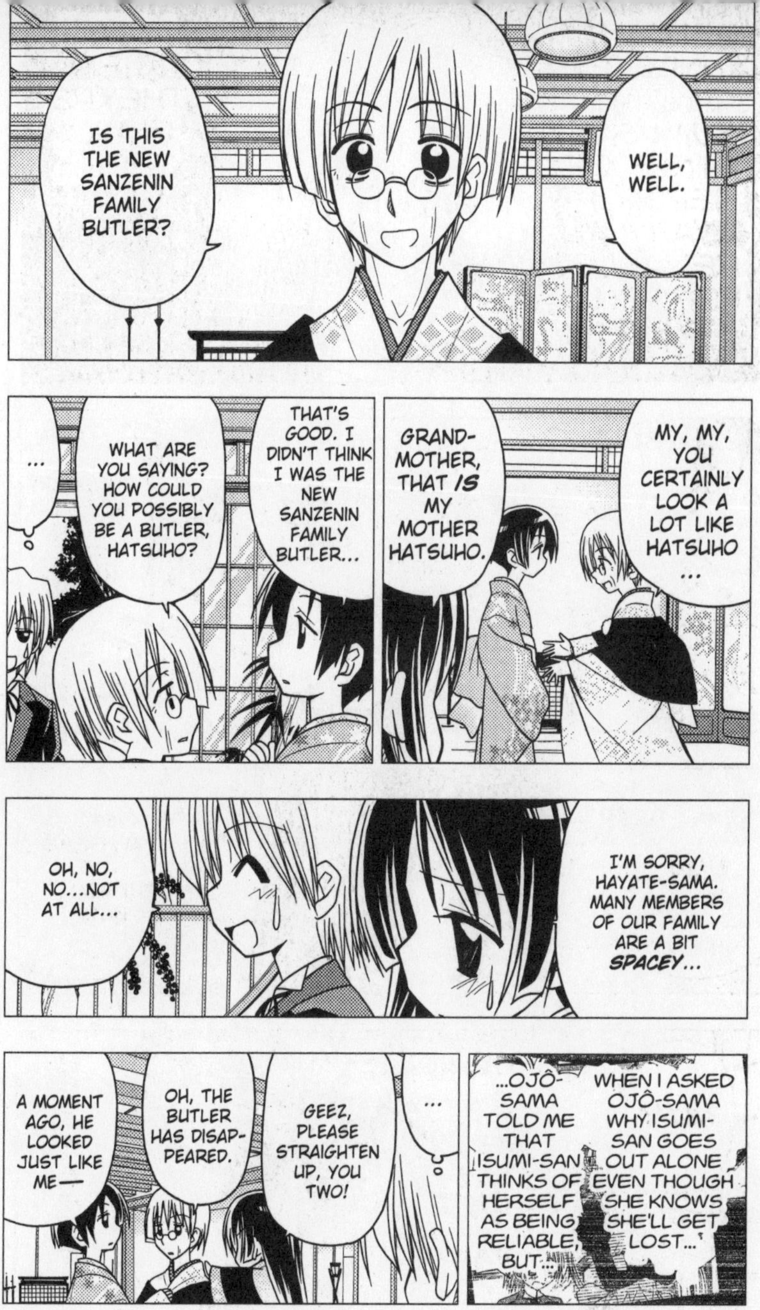
WELL, WELL.
IS THIS THE NEW SANZENIN FAMILY BUTLER?
MY, MY, YOU CERTAINLY LOOK A LOT LIKE HATSUHO ...
GRANDMOTHER, THAT *IS* MY MOTHER HATSUHO.
THAT'S GOOD. I DIDN'T THINK I WAS THE NEW SANZENIN FAMILY BUTLER...
WHAT ARE YOU SAYING? HOW COULD YOU POSSIBLY BE A BUTLER, HATSUHO?
...
I'M SORRY, HAYATE-SAMA. MANY MEMBERS OF OUR FAMILY ARE A BIT **SPACEY**...
OH, NO, NO...NOT AT ALL...
WHEN I ASKED OJÔ-SAMA WHY ISUMI-SAN GOES OUT ALONE EVEN THOUGH SHE KNOWS SHE'LL GET LOST...
...OJÔ-SAMA TOLD ME THAT ISUMI-SAN THINKS OF HERSELF AS BEING RELIABLE, BUT...
...
GEEZ, PLEASE STRAIGHTEN UP, YOU TWO!
OH, THE BUTLER HAS DISAPPEARED.
A MOMENT AGO, HE LOOKED JUST LIKE ME—

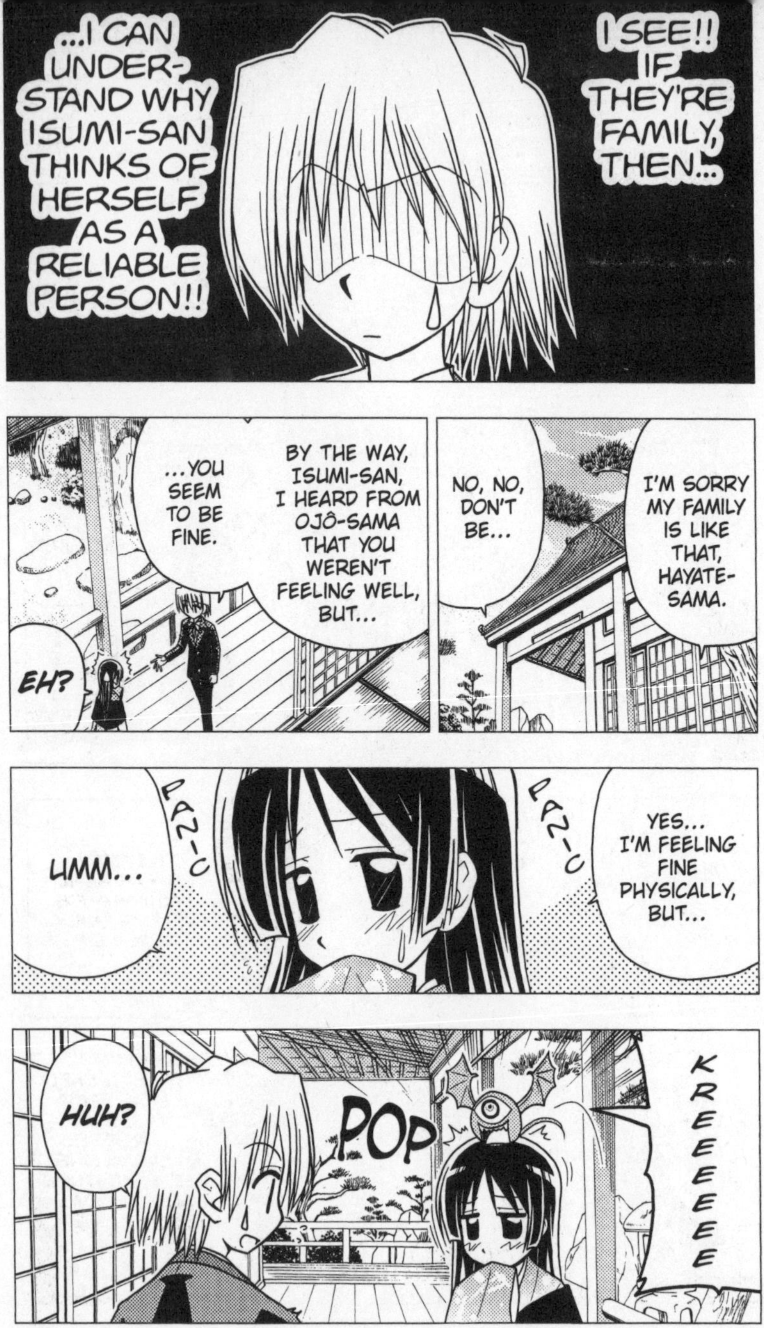
I SEE!! IF THEY'RE FAMILY, THEN...
...I CAN UNDER-STAND WHY ISUMI-SAN THINKS OF HERSELF AS A RELIABLE PERSON!!
I'M SORRY MY FAMILY IS LIKE THAT, HAYATE-SAMA.
NO, NO, DON'T BE...
BY THE WAY, ISUMI-SAN, I HEARD FROM OJÔ-SAMA THAT YOU WEREN'T FEELING WELL, BUT...
...YOU SEEM TO BE FINE.
EH?
YES... I'M FEELING FINE PHYSICALLY, BUT...
PANIC
PANIC
UMM...
KREEEEEEE
POP
HUH?

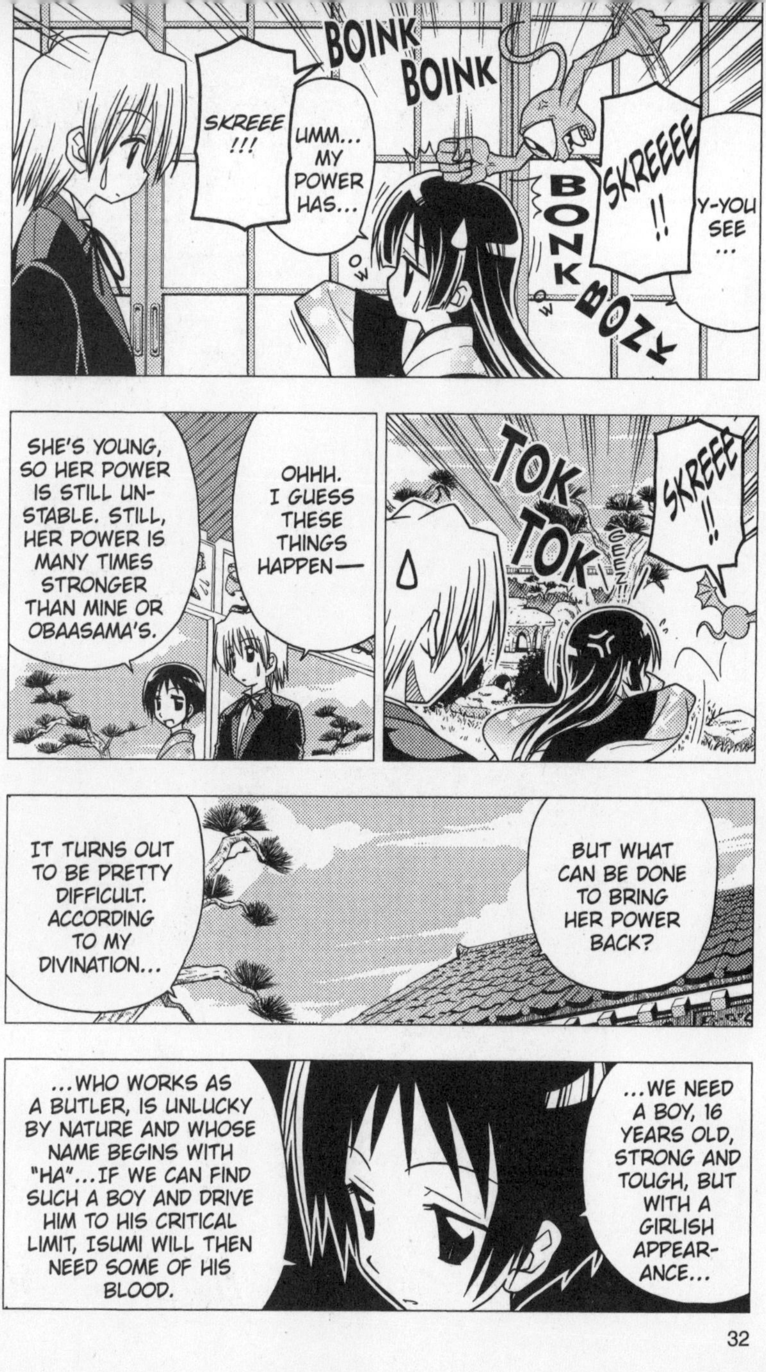
Y-YOU SEE ...
SKREEEE !!
BONK
BONK
BOZK
BOINK
BOINK
UMM... MY POWER HAS...
SKREEE !!!
OW
OW
SKREEE !!
TOK
TOK
GEEZ!!
OHHH. I GUESS THESE THINGS HAPPEN—
SHE'S YOUNG, SO HER POWER IS STILL UN-STABLE. STILL, HER POWER IS MANY TIMES STRONGER THAN MINE OR OBAASAMA'S.
BUT WHAT CAN BE DONE TO BRING HER POWER BACK?
IT TURNS OUT TO BE PRETTY DIFFICULT. ACCORDING TO MY DIVINATION...
...WE NEED A BOY, 16 YEARS OLD, STRONG AND TOUGH, BUT WITH A GIRLISH APPEAR-ANCE...
...WHO WORKS AS A BUTLER, IS UNLUCKY BY NATURE AND WHOSE NAME BEGINS WITH "HA"...IF WE CAN FIND SUCH A BOY AND DRIVE HIM TO HIS CRITICAL LIMIT, ISUMI WILL THEN NEED SOME OF HIS BLOOD.

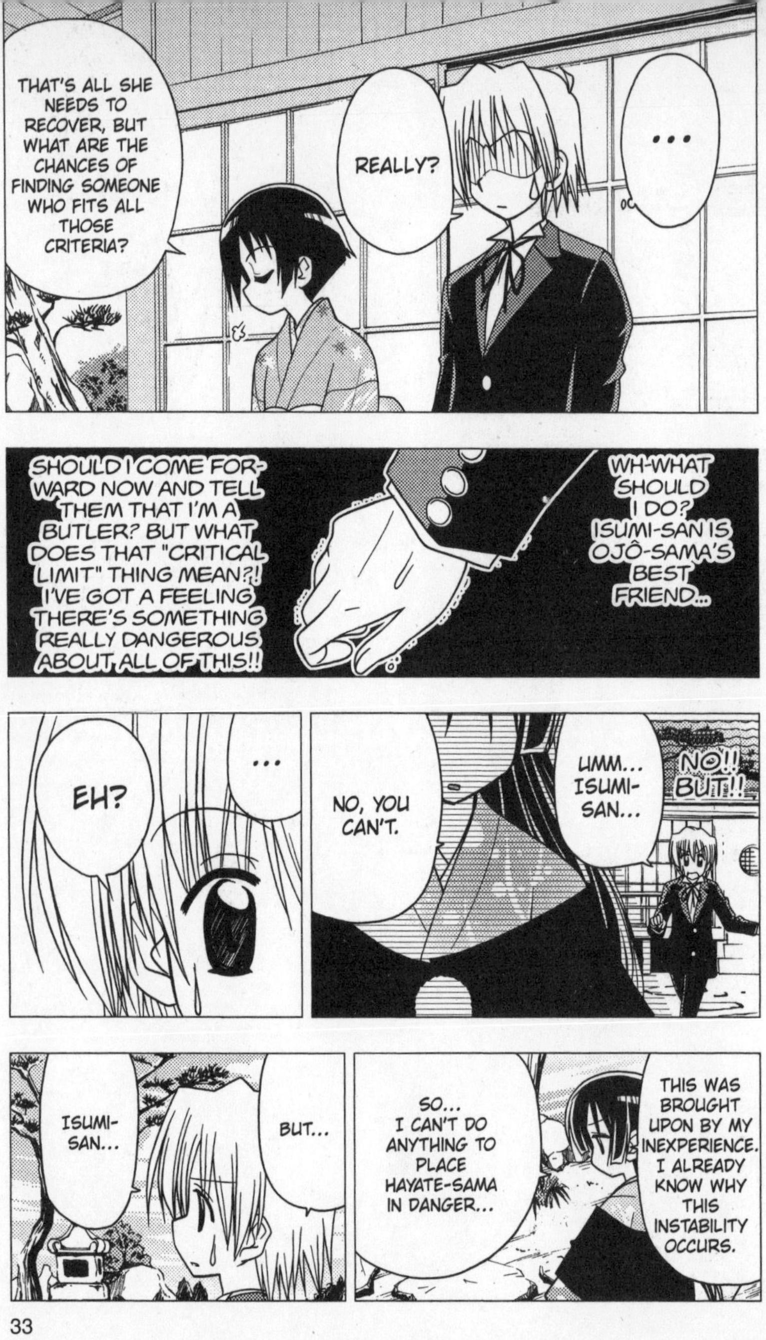
...
REALLY?
THAT'S ALL SHE NEEDS TO RECOVER, BUT WHAT ARE THE CHANCES OF FINDING SOMEONE WHO FITS ALL THOSE CRITERIA?
WH-WHAT SHOULD I DO? ISUMI-SAN IS OJÔ-SAMA'S BEST FRIEND...
SHOULD I COME FORWARD NOW AND TELL THEM THAT I'M A BUTLER? BUT WHAT DOES THAT "CRITICAL LIMIT" THING MEAN?! I'VE GOT A FEELING THERE'S SOMETHING REALLY DANGEROUS ABOUT ALL OF THIS!!
NO!! BUT!!
UMM... ISUMI-SAN...
NO, YOU CAN'T.
...
EH?
THIS WAS BROUGHT UPON BY MY INEXPERIENCE. I ALREADY KNOW WHY THIS INSTABILITY OCCURS.
SO... I CAN'T DO ANYTHING TO PLACE HAYATE-SAMA IN DANGER...
BUT...
ISUMI-SAN...

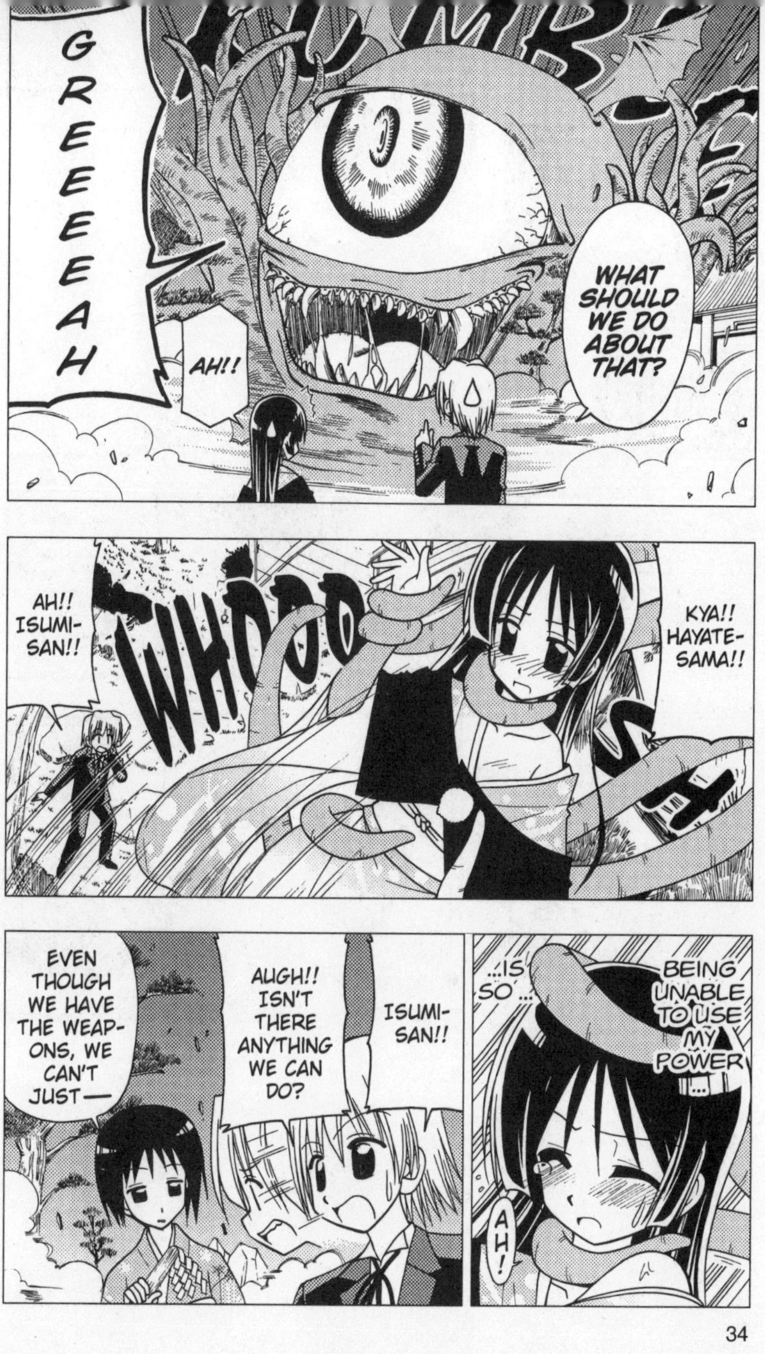
WHAT SHOULD WE DO ABOUT THAT?
AH!!
GREEEEEAH
KYA!! HAYATE-SAMA!!
WHOOSH
AH!! ISUMI-SAN!!
BEING UNABLE TO USE MY POWER...
...IS SO...
AH!
ISUMI-SAN!!
AUGH!! ISN'T THERE ANYTHING WE CAN DO?
EVEN THOUGH WE HAVE THE WEAP-ONS, WE CAN'T JUST—

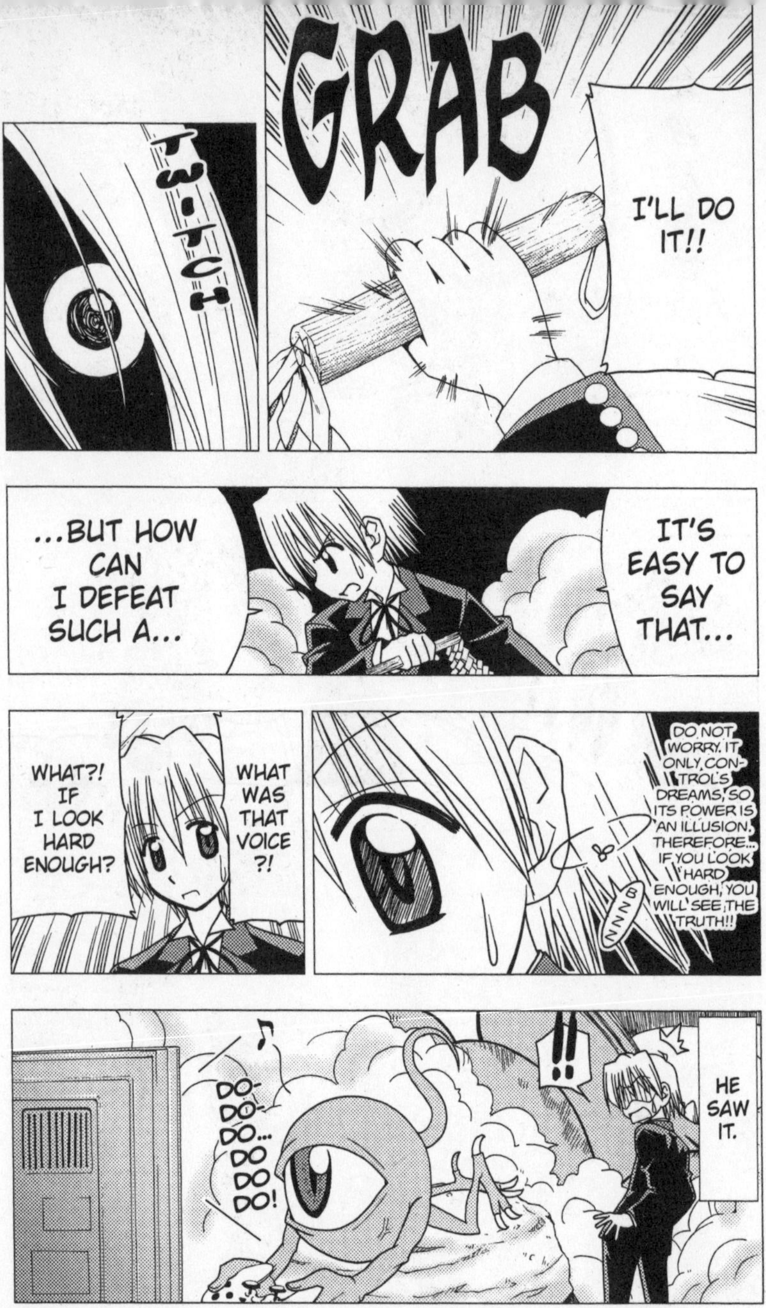
GRAB
I'LL DO IT!!
TWITCH
IT'S EASY TO SAY THAT...
...BUT HOW CAN I DEFEAT SUCH A...
DO NOT WORRY. IT ONLY CONTROLS DREAMS, SO ITS POWER IS AN ILLUSION. THEREFORE... IF YOU LOOK HARD ENOUGH, YOU WILL SEE THE TRUTH!!
BNNN
WHAT WAS THAT VOICE?!
WHAT?! IF I LOOK HARD ENOUGH?
HE SAW IT.
!!
DO-DO-DO... DO DO DO!

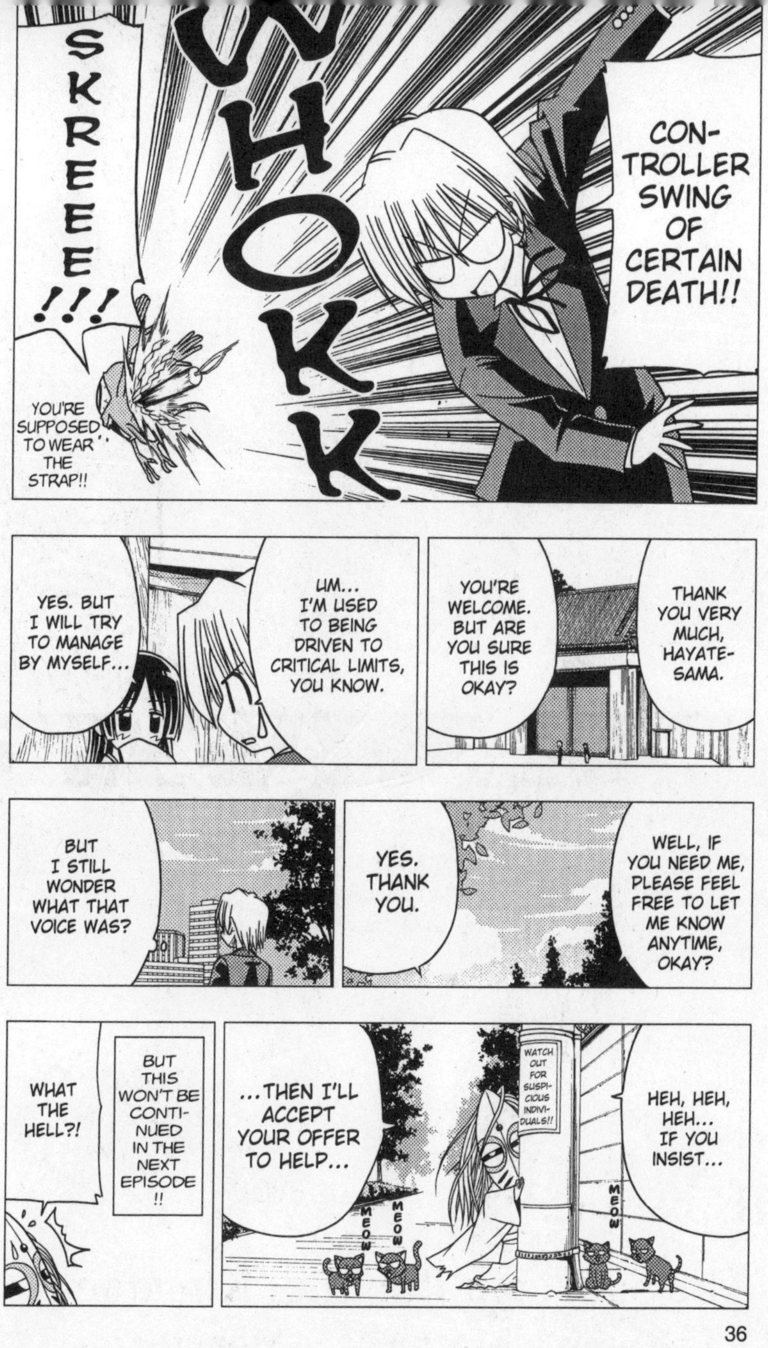
CON-TROLLER SWING OF CERTAIN DEATH!!
SHOKK
SKREEE!!!
YOU'RE SUPPOSED TO WEAR THE STRAP!!
THANK YOU VERY MUCH, HAYATE-SAMA.
YOU'RE WELCOME. BUT ARE YOU SURE THIS IS OKAY?
UM... I'M USED TO BEING DRIVEN TO CRITICAL LIMITS, YOU KNOW.
YES. BUT I WILL TRY TO MANAGE BY MYSELF...
WELL, IF YOU NEED ME, PLEASE FEEL FREE TO LET ME KNOW ANYTIME, OKAY?
YES. THANK YOU.
BUT I STILL WONDER WHAT THAT VOICE WAS?
HEH, HEH, HEH... IF YOU INSIST...
WATCH OUT FOR SUSPICIOUS INDIVIDUALS!!
MEOW
...THEN I'LL ACCEPT YOUR OFFER TO HELP...
MEOW
MEOW
BUT THIS WON'T BE CONTINUED IN THE NEXT EPISODE!!
WHAT THE HELL?!

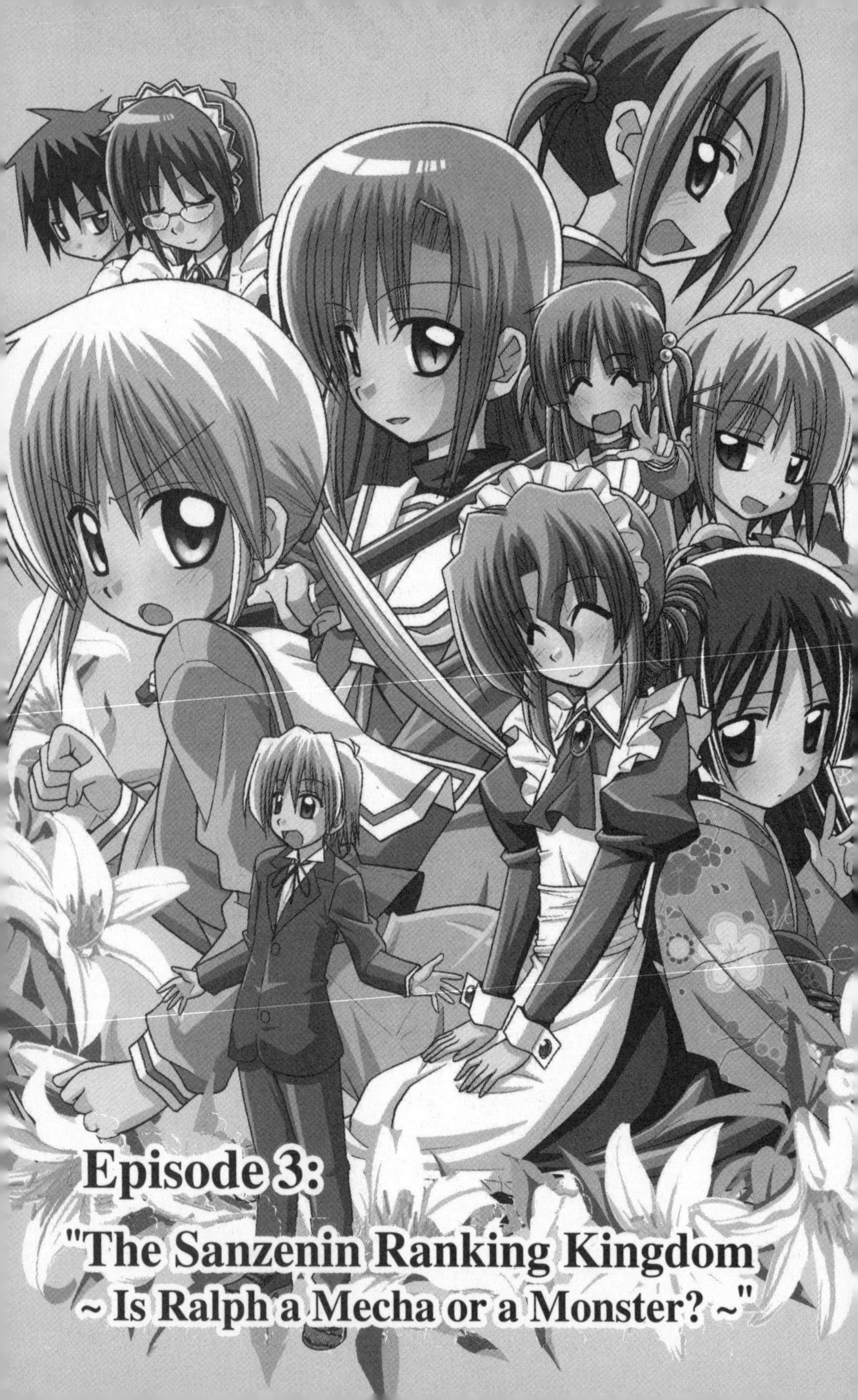

Episode 3:

"The Sanzenin Ranking Kingdom ~ Is Ralph a Mecha or a Monster? ~"

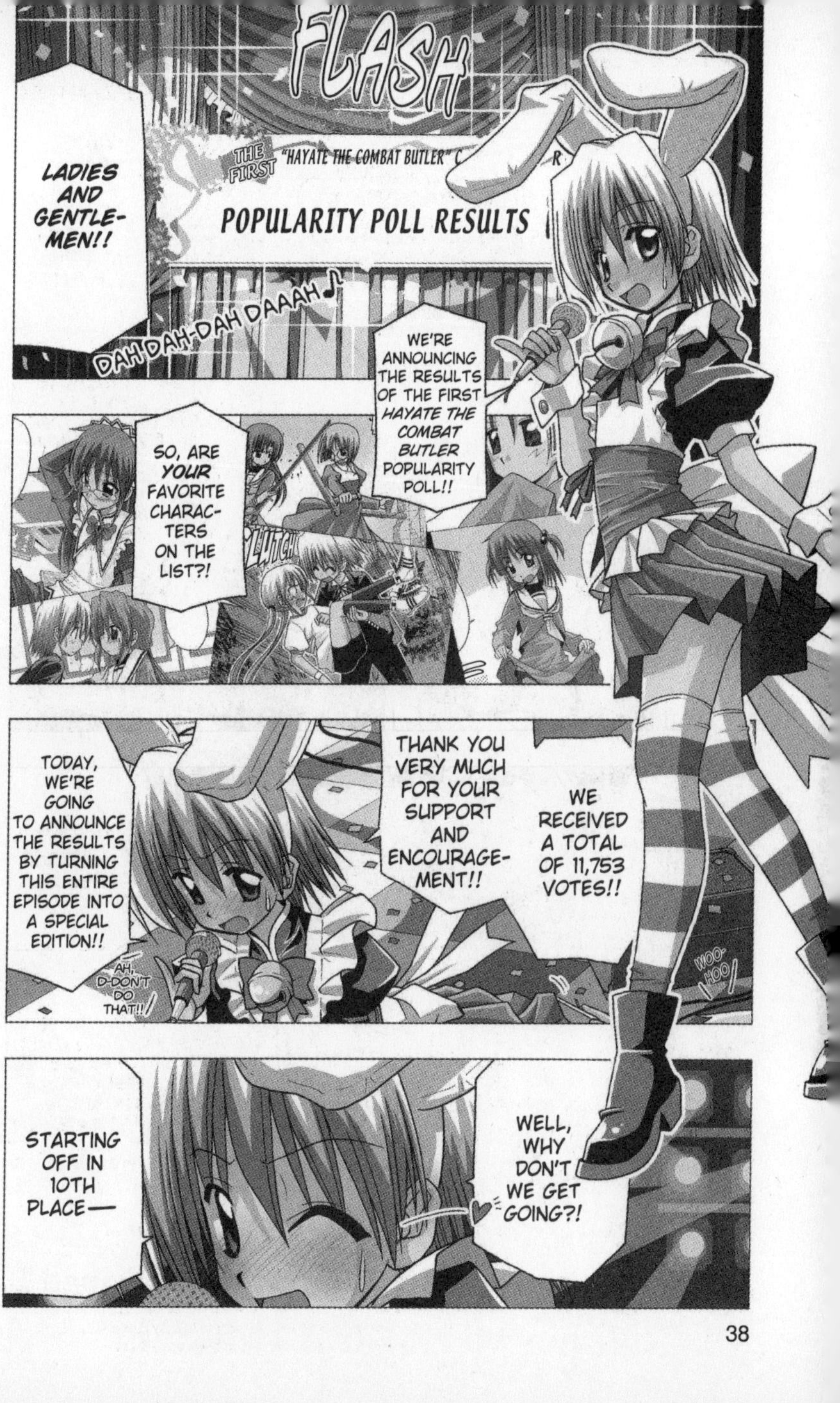
FLASH
THE FIRST "HAYATE THE COMBAT BUTLER"
POPULARITY POLL RESULTS
WE'RE ANNOUNCING THE RESULTS OF THE FIRST HAYATE THE COMBAT BUTLER POPULARITY POLL!!
DAH DAH-DAH DAAAH♪
LADIES AND GENTLE-MEN!!
SO, ARE YOUR FAVORITE CHARAC-TERS ON THE LIST?!
WE RECEIVED A TOTAL OF 11,753 VOTES!!
WOO-HOO
THANK YOU VERY MUCH FOR YOUR SUPPORT AND ENCOURAGE-MENT!!
TODAY, WE'RE GOING TO ANNOUNCE THE RESULTS BY TURNING THIS ENTIRE EPISODE INTO A SPECIAL EDITION!!
AH, D-DON'T DO THAT!!
WELL, WHY DON'T WE GET GOING?!
STARTING OFF IN 10TH PLACE—

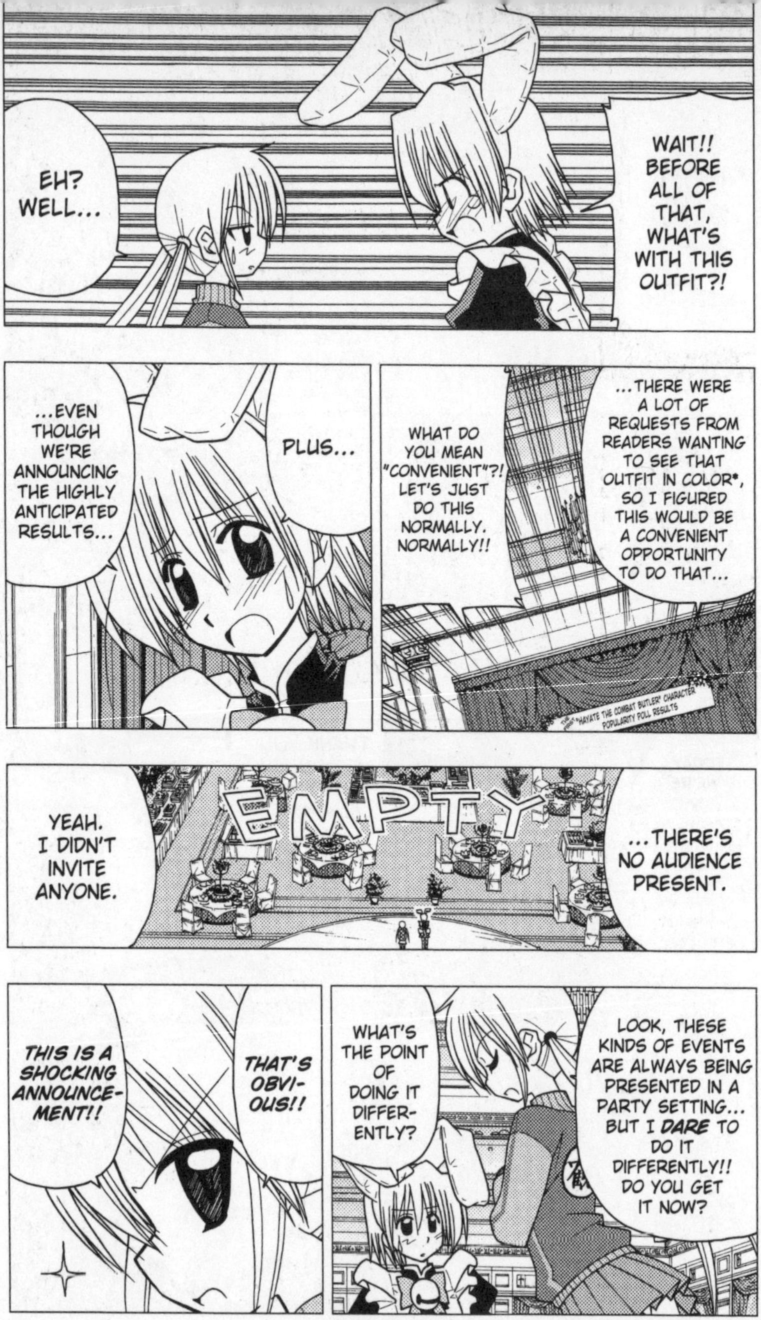
WAIT!! BEFORE ALL OF THAT, WHAT'S WITH THIS OUTFIT?!
EH? WELL...
...THERE WERE A LOT OF REQUESTS FROM READERS WANTING TO SEE THAT OUTFIT IN COLOR*, SO I FIGURED THIS WOULD BE A CONVENIENT OPPORTUNITY TO DO THAT...
WHAT DO YOU MEAN "CONVENIENT"?! LET'S JUST DO THIS NORMALLY. NORMALLY!!
"HAYATE THE COMBAT BUTLER" CHARACTER POPULARITY POLL RESULTS
PLUS...
...EVEN THOUGH WE'RE ANNOUNCING THE HIGHLY ANTICIPATED RESULTS...
...THERE'S NO AUDIENCE PRESENT.
EMPTY
YEAH. I DIDN'T INVITE ANYONE.
LOOK, THESE KINDS OF EVENTS ARE ALWAYS BEING PRESENTED IN A PARTY SETTING... BUT I *DARE* TO DO IT DIFFERENTLY!! DO YOU GET IT NOW?
WHAT'S THE POINT OF DOING IT DIFFER-ENTLY?
THAT'S OBVI-OUS!!
THIS IS A SHOCKING ANNOUNCE-MENT!!

*Some pages of this episode were originally published in color. Regretfully, they appear here in black and white.

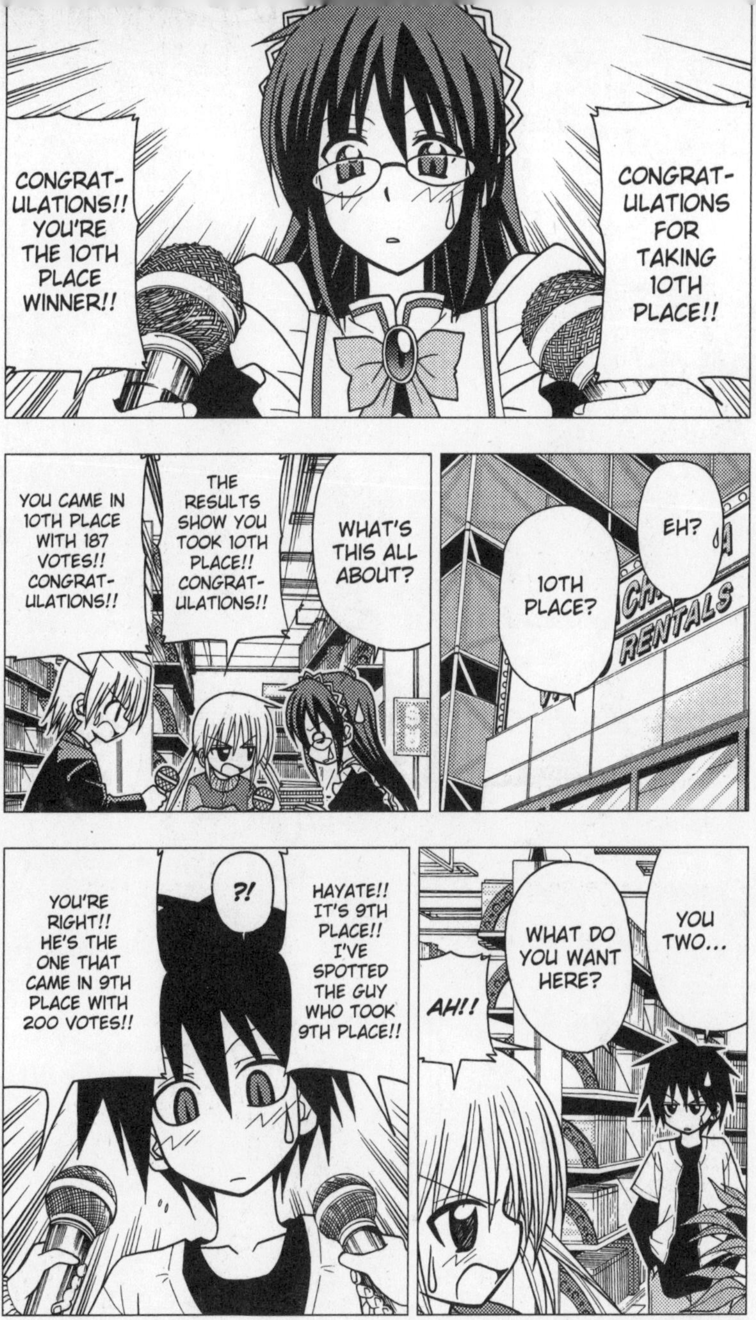
CONGRAT-ULATIONS FOR TAKING 10TH PLACE!!
CONGRAT-ULATIONS!! YOU'RE THE 10TH PLACE WINNER!!
EH?
10TH PLACE?
RENTALS
WHAT'S THIS ALL ABOUT?
THE RESULTS SHOW YOU TOOK 10TH PLACE!! CONGRAT-ULATIONS!!
YOU CAME IN 10TH PLACE WITH 187 VOTES!! CONGRAT-ULATIONS!!
YOU TWO...
WHAT DO YOU WANT HERE?
AH!!
HAYATE!! IT'S 9TH PLACE!! I'VE SPOTTED THE GUY WHO TOOK 9TH PLACE!!
?!
YOU'RE RIGHT!! HE'S THE ONE THAT CAME IN 9TH PLACE WITH 200 VOTES!!

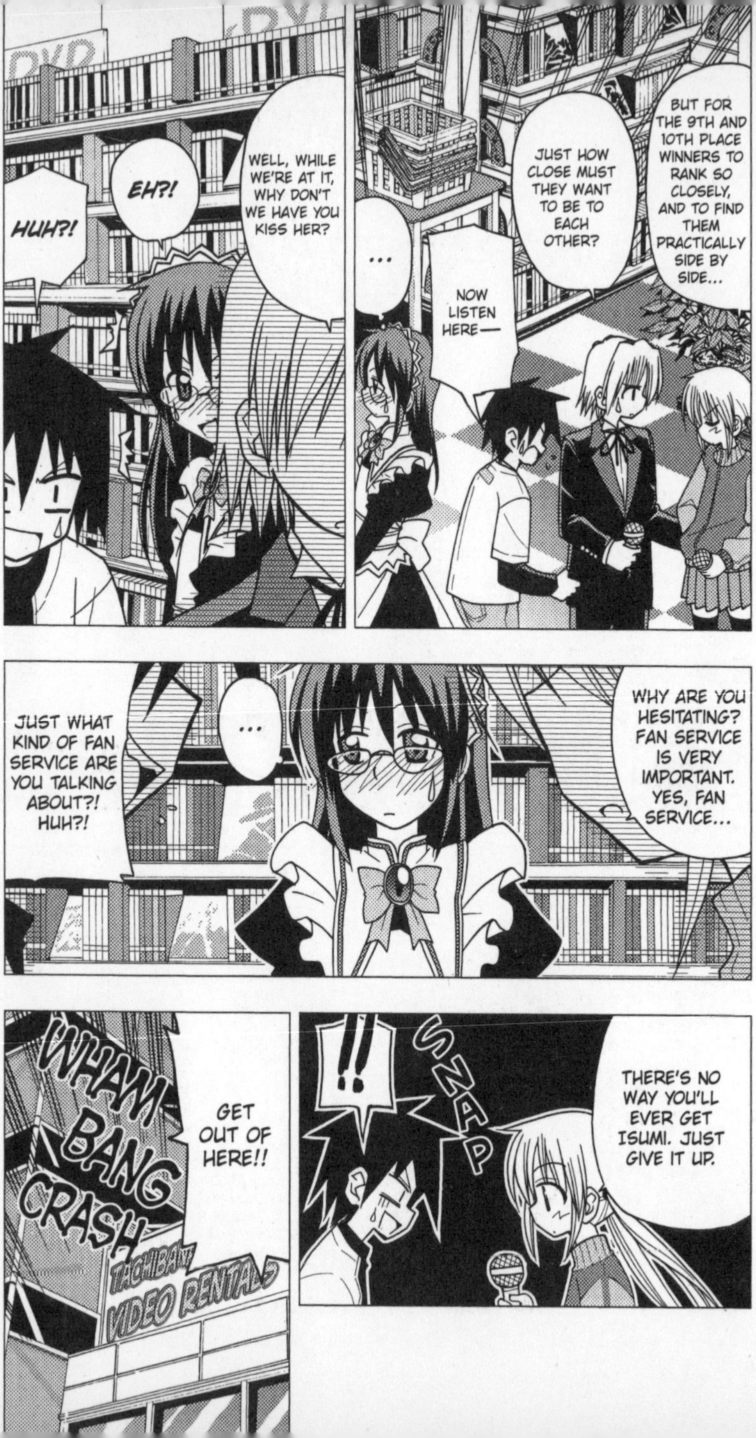
BUT FOR THE 9TH AND 10TH PLACE WINNERS TO RANK SO CLOSELY, AND TO FIND THEM PRACTICALLY SIDE BY SIDE...
JUST HOW CLOSE MUST THEY WANT TO BE TO EACH OTHER?
NOW LISTEN HERE—
...
WELL, WHILE WE'RE AT IT, WHY DON'T WE HAVE YOU KISS HER?
EH?!
HUH?!
WHY ARE YOU HESITATING? FAN SERVICE IS VERY IMPORTANT. YES, FAN SERVICE...
...
JUST WHAT KIND OF FAN SERVICE ARE YOU TALKING ABOUT?! HUH?!
THERE'S NO WAY YOU'LL EVER GET ISUMI. JUST GIVE IT UP.
SNAP
!!
GET OUT OF HERE!!
WHAM
BANG
CRASH
TACHIBANA
VIDEO RENTAL

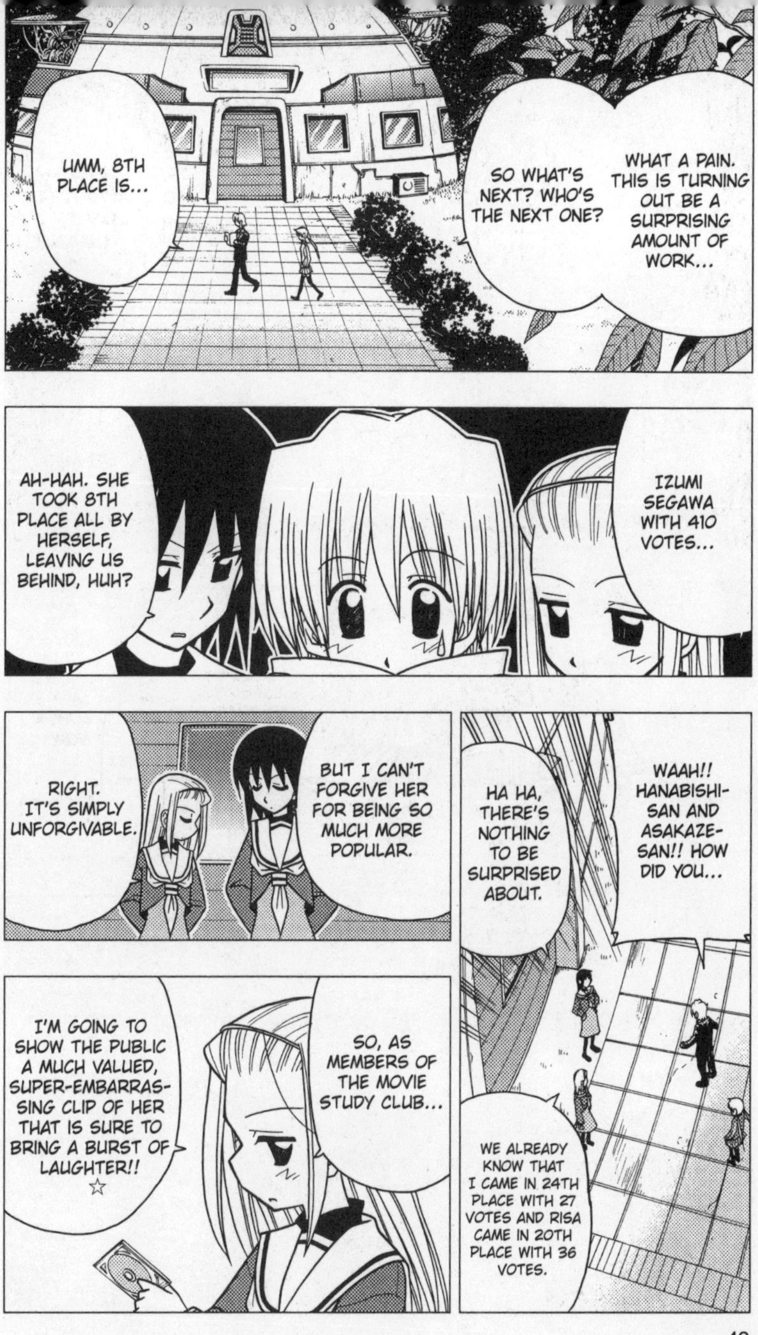
WHAT A PAIN. THIS IS TURNING OUT BE A SURPRISING AMOUNT OF WORK...
SO WHAT'S NEXT? WHO'S THE NEXT ONE?
UMM, 8TH PLACE IS...
IZUMI SEGAWA WITH 410 VOTES...
AH-HAH. SHE TOOK 8TH PLACE ALL BY HERSELF, LEAVING US BEHIND, HUH?
WAAH!! HANABISHI-SAN AND ASAKAZE-SAN!! HOW DID YOU...
HA HA, THERE'S NOTHING TO BE SURPRISED ABOUT.
WE ALREADY KNOW THAT I CAME IN 24TH PLACE WITH 27 VOTES AND RISA CAME IN 20TH PLACE WITH 36 VOTES.
BUT I CAN'T FORGIVE HER FOR BEING SO MUCH MORE POPULAR.
RIGHT. IT'S SIMPLY UNFORGIVABLE.
SO, AS MEMBERS OF THE MOVIE STUDY CLUB...
I'M GOING TO SHOW THE PUBLIC A MUCH VALUED, SUPER-EMBARRASSING CLIP OF HER THAT IS SURE TO BRING A BURST OF LAUGHTER!! ☆

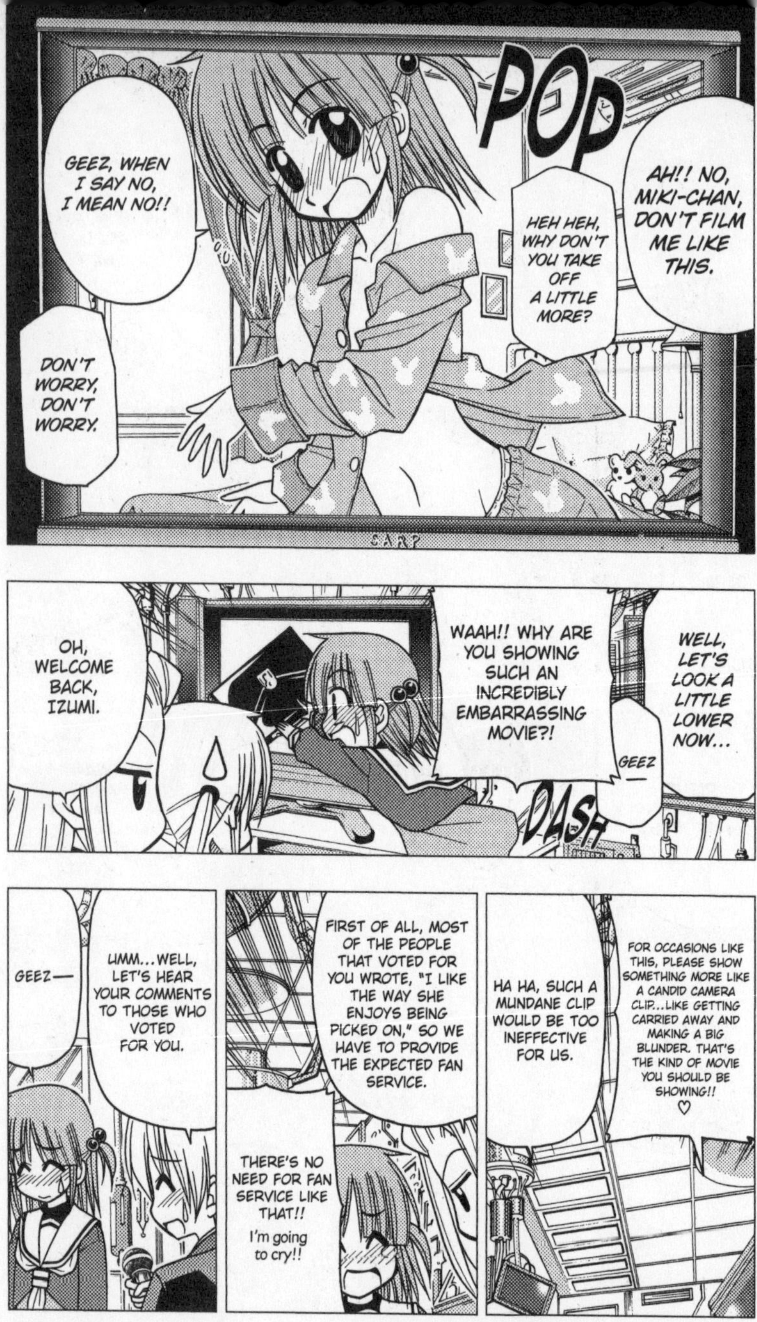
AH!! NO, MIKI-CHAN, DON'T FILM ME LIKE THIS.
HEH HEH, WHY DON'T YOU TAKE OFF A LITTLE MORE?
POP
GEEZ, WHEN I SAY NO, I MEAN NO!!
DON'T WORRY, DON'T WORRY.
WELL, LET'S LOOK A LITTLE LOWER NOW...
GEEZ—
WAAH!! WHY ARE YOU SHOWING SUCH AN INCREDIBLY EMBARRASSING MOVIE?!
DASH
OH, WELCOME BACK, IZUMI.
FOR OCCASIONS LIKE THIS, PLEASE SHOW SOMETHING MORE LIKE A CANDID CAMERA CLIP...LIKE GETTING CARRIED AWAY AND MAKING A BIG BLUNDER. THAT'S THE KIND OF MOVIE YOU SHOULD BE SHOWING!! ♡
HA HA, SUCH A MUNDANE CLIP WOULD BE TOO INEFFECTIVE FOR US.
FIRST OF ALL, MOST OF THE PEOPLE THAT VOTED FOR YOU WROTE, "I LIKE THE WAY SHE ENJOYS BEING PICKED ON," SO WE HAVE TO PROVIDE THE EXPECTED FAN SERVICE.
THERE'S NO NEED FOR FAN SERVICE LIKE THAT!!
I'm going to cry!!
UMM...WELL, LET'S HEAR YOUR COMMENTS TO THOSE WHO VOTED FOR YOU.
GEEZ—

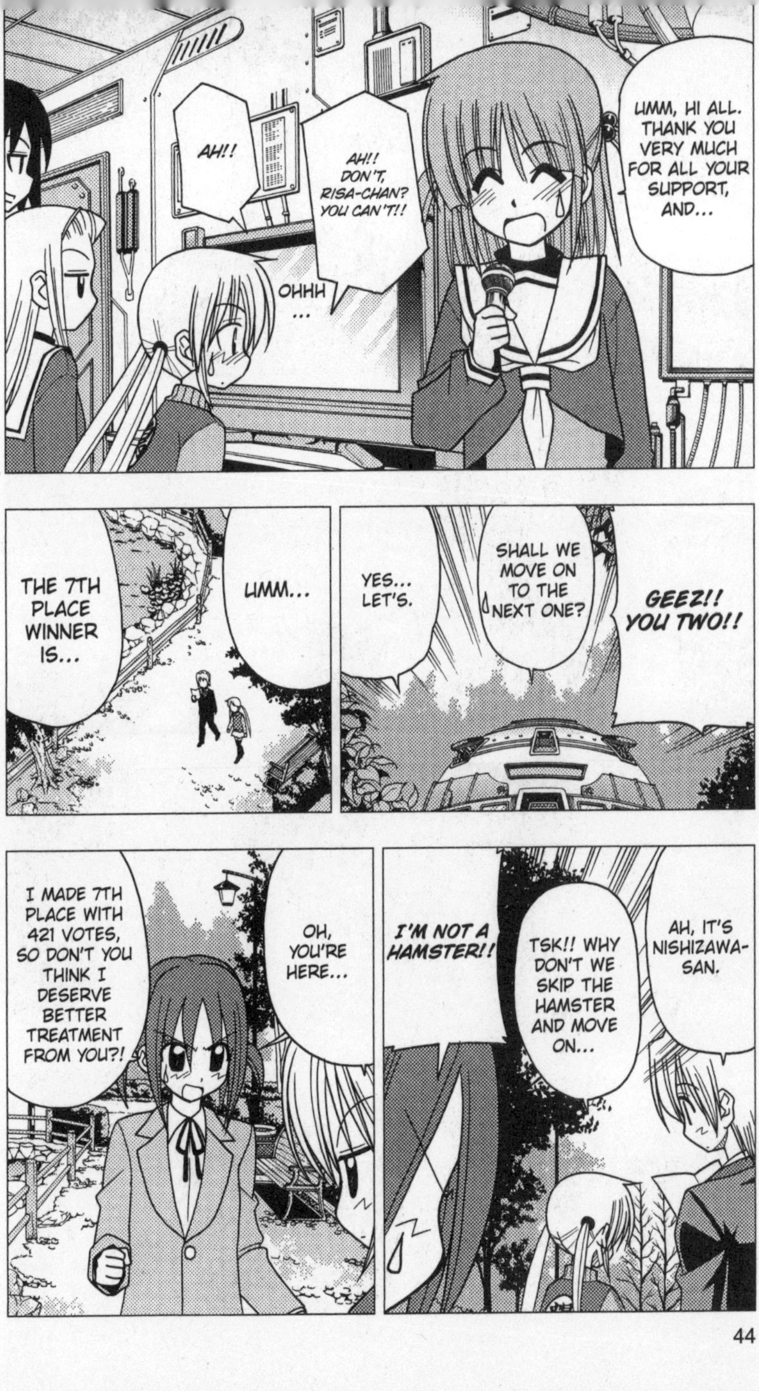
UMM, HI ALL. THANK YOU VERY MUCH FOR ALL YOUR SUPPORT, AND...
AH!! DON'T, RISA-CHAN? YOU CAN'T!!
AH!!
OHHH ...
GEEZ!! YOU TWO!!
SHALL WE MOVE ON TO THE NEXT ONE?
YES... LET'S.
UMM...
THE 7TH PLACE WINNER IS...
AH, IT'S NISHIZAWA-SAN.
TSK!! WHY DON'T WE SKIP THE HAMSTER AND MOVE ON...
I'M NOT A HAMSTER!!
OH, YOU'RE HERE...
I MADE 7TH PLACE WITH 421 VOTES, SO DON'T YOU THINK I DESERVE BETTER TREATMENT FROM YOU?!

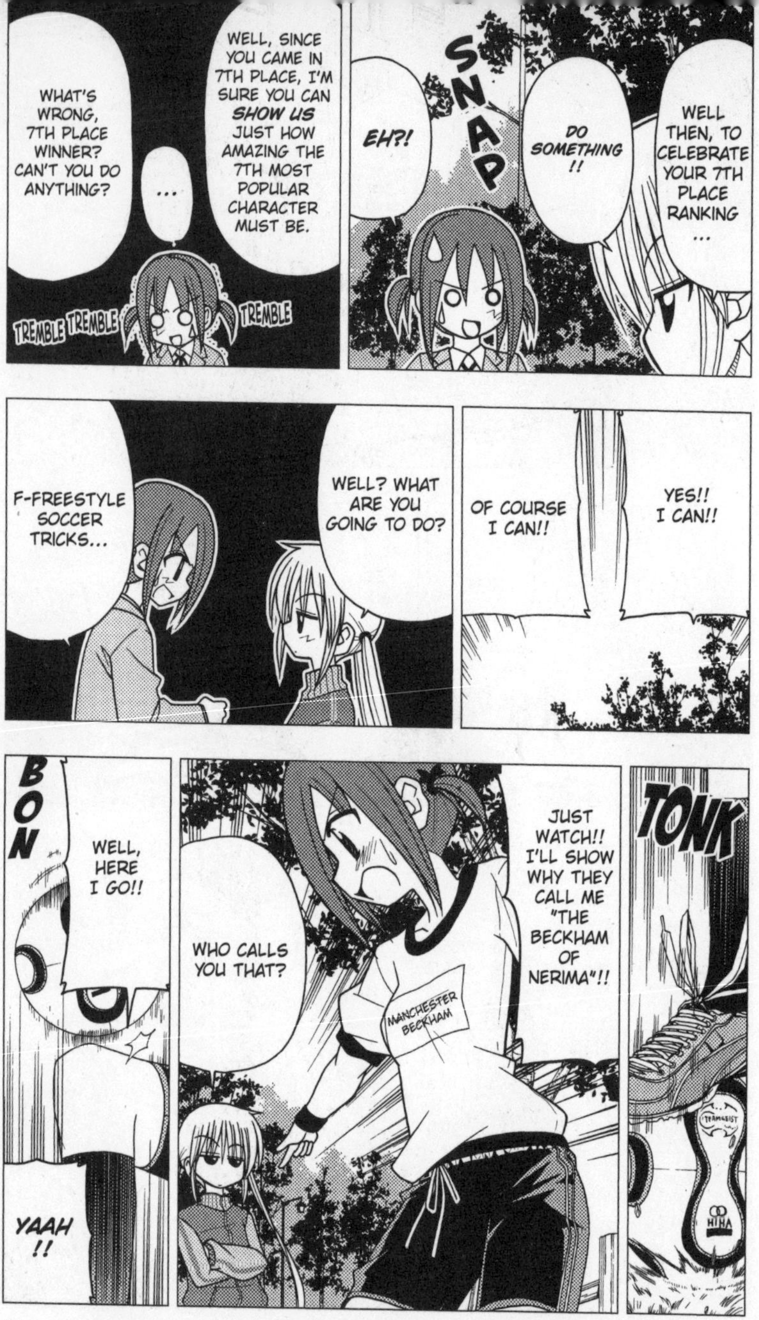
WELL THEN, TO CELEBRATE YOUR 7TH PLACE RANKING ...
DO SOMETHING !!
SNAP
EH?!
WELL, SINCE YOU CAME IN 7TH PLACE, I'M SURE YOU CAN SHOW US JUST HOW AMAZING THE 7TH MOST POPULAR CHARACTER MUST BE.
...
WHAT'S WRONG, 7TH PLACE WINNER? CAN'T YOU DO ANYTHING?
TREMBLE TREMBLE TREMBLE
YES!! I CAN!!
OF COURSE I CAN!!
WELL? WHAT ARE YOU GOING TO DO?
F-FREESTYLE SOCCER TRICKS...
TONK
JUST WATCH!! I'LL SHOW WHY THEY CALL ME "THE BECKHAM OF NERIMA"!!
WHO CALLS YOU THAT?
MANCHESTER BECKHAM
BON
WELL, HERE I GO!!
YAAH !!

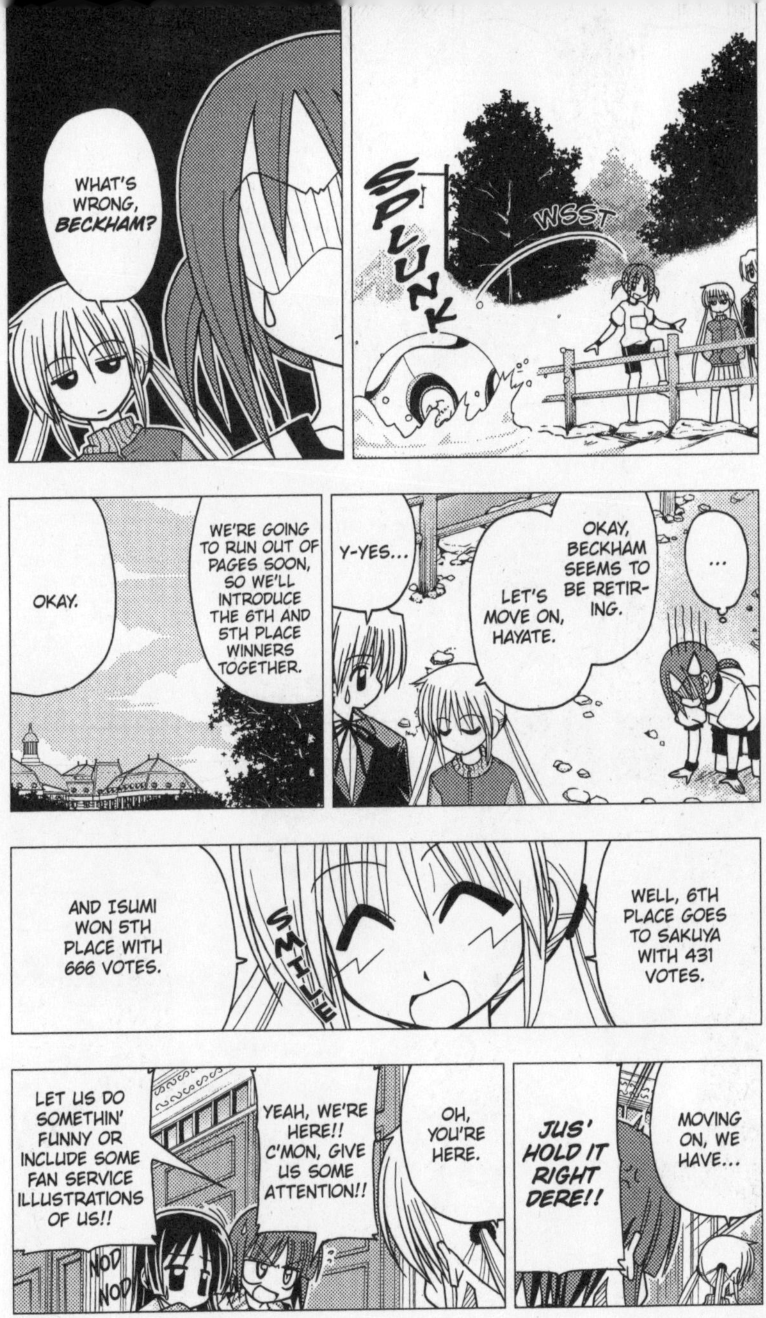
SPLUNK
WSST
WHAT'S WRONG, BECKHAM?
...
OKAY, BECKHAM SEEMS TO BE RETIR-ING.
LET'S MOVE ON, HAYATE.
Y-YES...
WE'RE GOING TO RUN OUT OF PAGES SOON, SO WE'LL INTRODUCE THE 6TH AND 5TH PLACE WINNERS TOGETHER.
OKAY.
WELL, 6TH PLACE GOES TO SAKUYA WITH 431 VOTES.
SMILE
AND ISUMI WON 5TH PLACE WITH 666 VOTES.
MOVING ON, WE HAVE...
JUS' HOLD IT RIGHT DERE!!
OH, YOU'RE HERE.
YEAH, WE'RE HERE!! C'MON, GIVE US SOME ATTENTION!!
LET US DO SOMETHIN' FUNNY OR INCLUDE SOME FAN SERVICE ILLUSTRATIONS OF US!!
NOD NOD

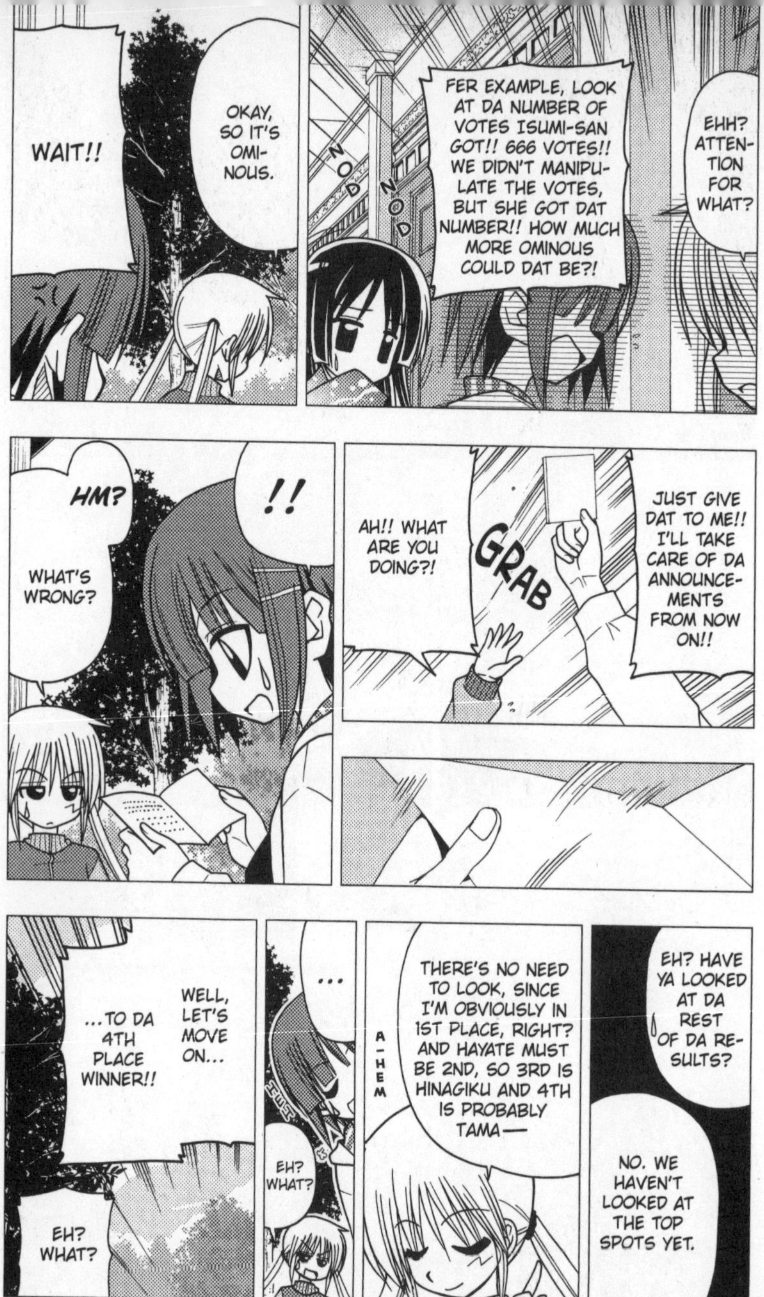
EHH? ATTENTION FOR WHAT?
FER EXAMPLE, LOOK AT DA NUMBER OF VOTES ISUMI-SAN GOT!! 666 VOTES!! WE DIDN'T MANIPULATE THE VOTES, BUT SHE GOT DAT NUMBER!! HOW MUCH MORE OMINOUS COULD DAT BE?!
NOD NOD
OKAY, SO IT'S OMINOUS.
WAIT!!
JUST GIVE DAT TO ME!! I'LL TAKE CARE OF DA ANNOUNCEMENTS FROM NOW ON!!
GRAB
AH!! WHAT ARE YOU DOING?!
!!
HM?
WHAT'S WRONG?
EH? HAVE YA LOOKED AT DA REST OF DA RESULTS?
NO. WE HAVEN'T LOOKED AT THE TOP SPOTS YET.
THERE'S NO NEED TO LOOK, SINCE I'M OBVIOUSLY IN 1ST PLACE, RIGHT? AND HAYATE MUST BE 2ND, SO 3RD IS HINAGIKU AND 4TH IS PROBABLY TAMA—
A-HEM
...
EH? WHAT?
WELL, LET'S MOVE ON...
...TO DA 4TH PLACE WINNER!!
EH? WHAT?

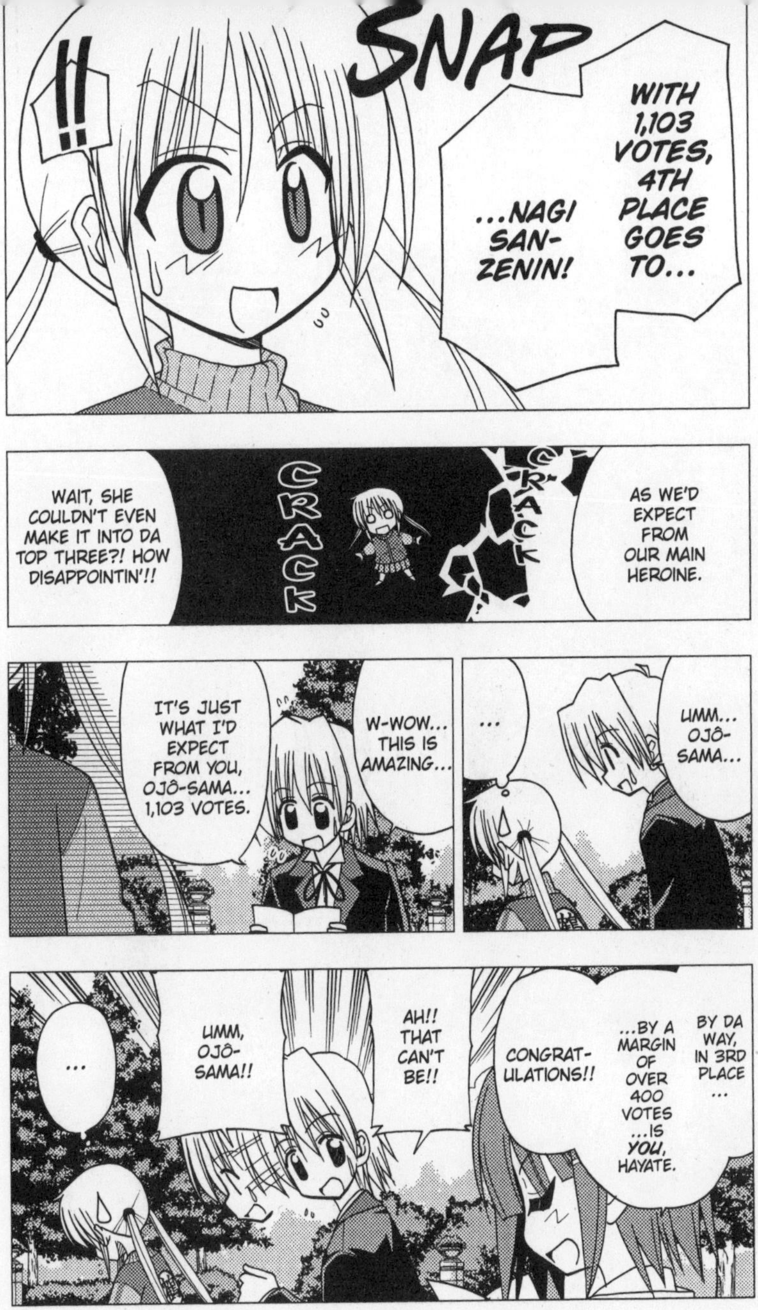
SNAP
WITH 1,103 VOTES, 4TH PLACE GOES TO...
...NAGI SAN-ZENIN!
!!
AS WE'D EXPECT FROM OUR MAIN HEROINE.
CRACK
CRACK
WAIT, SHE COULDN'T EVEN MAKE IT INTO DA TOP THREE?! HOW DISAPPOINTIN'!!
UMM... OJÔ-SAMA...
...
W-WOW... THIS IS AMAZING...
IT'S JUST WHAT I'D EXPECT FROM YOU, OJÔ-SAMA... 1,103 VOTES.
BY DA WAY, IN 3RD PLACE...
...BY A MARGIN OF OVER 400 VOTES ...IS *YOU*, HAYATE.
CONGRAT-ULATIONS!!
AH!! THAT CAN'T BE!!
UMM, OJÔ-SAMA!!
...

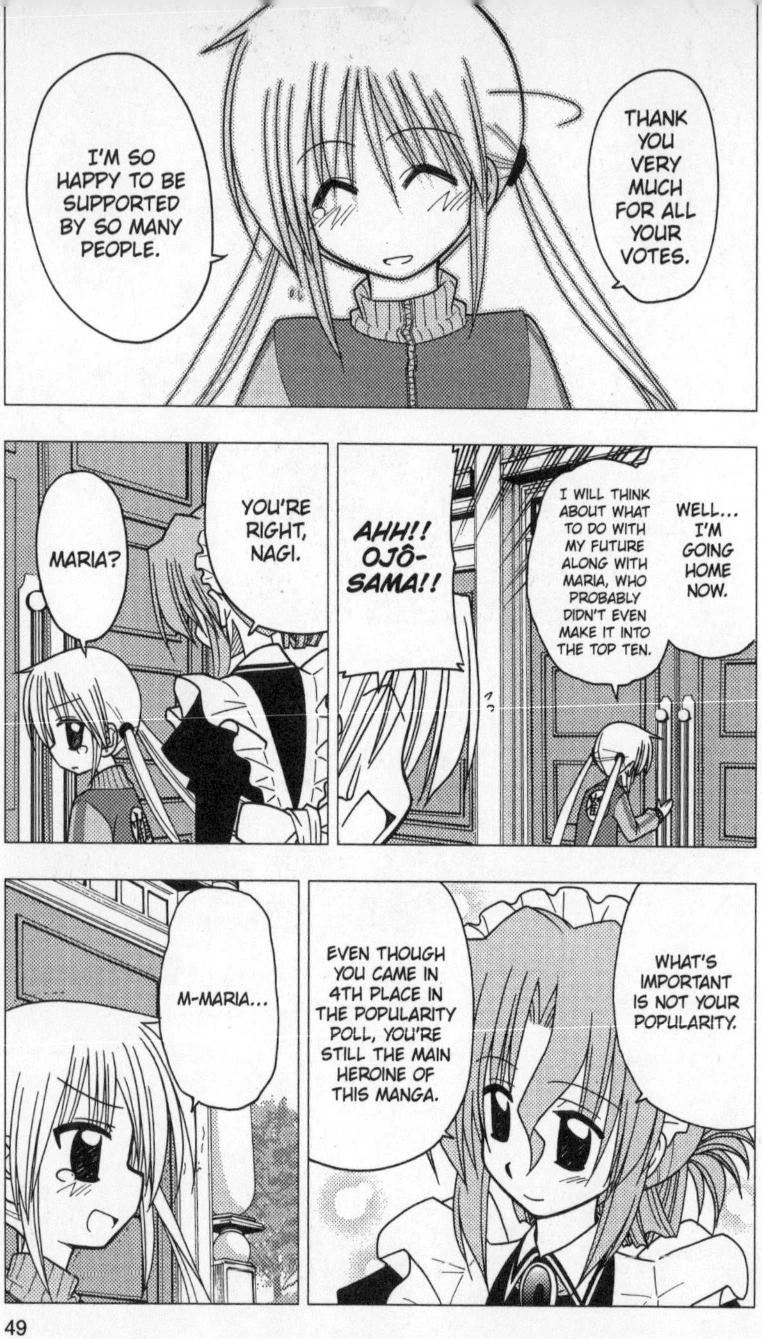
THANK YOU VERY MUCH FOR ALL YOUR VOTES.
I'M SO HAPPY TO BE SUPPORTED BY SO MANY PEOPLE.
WELL... I'M GOING HOME NOW.
I WILL THINK ABOUT WHAT TO DO WITH MY FUTURE ALONG WITH MARIA, WHO PROBABLY DIDN'T EVEN MAKE IT INTO THE TOP TEN.
AHH!! OJÔ-SAMA!!
YOU'RE RIGHT, NAGI.
MARIA?
WHAT'S IMPORTANT IS NOT YOUR POPULARITY.
EVEN THOUGH YOU CAME IN 4TH PLACE IN THE POPULARITY POLL, YOU'RE STILL THE MAIN HEROINE OF THIS MANGA.
M-MARIA...

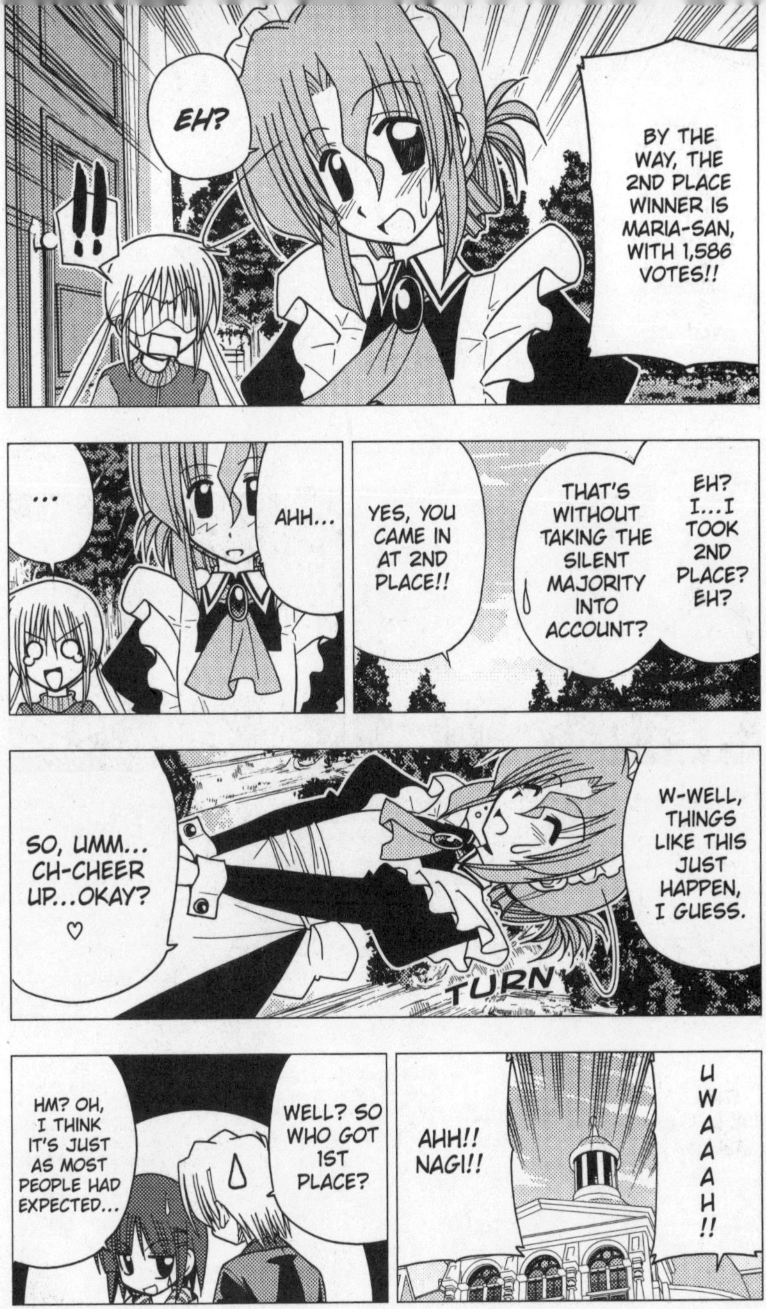
BY THE WAY, THE 2ND PLACE WINNER IS MARIA-SAN, WITH 1,586 VOTES!!
EH?
!!
EH? I...I TOOK 2ND PLACE? EH?
THAT'S WITHOUT TAKING THE SILENT MAJORITY INTO ACCOUNT?
YES, YOU CAME IN AT 2ND PLACE!!
AHH...
...
W-WELL, THINGS LIKE THIS JUST HAPPEN, I GUESS.
TURN
SO, UMM... CH-CHEER UP...OKAY? ♡
UWAAAAH!!
AHH!! NAGI!!
WELL? SO WHO GOT 1ST PLACE?
HM? OH, I THINK IT'S JUST AS MOST PEOPLE HAD EXPECTED...

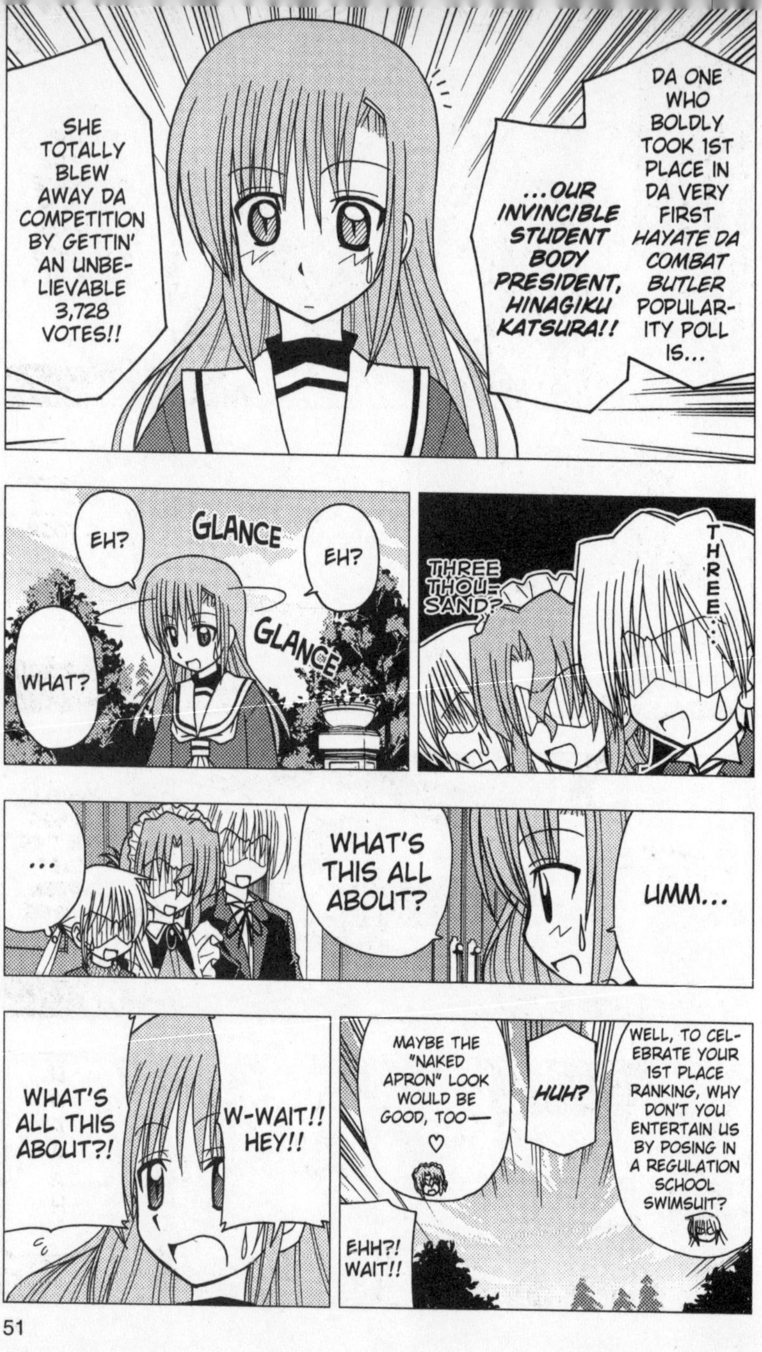
DA ONE WHO BOLDLY TOOK 1ST PLACE IN DA VERY FIRST HAYATE DA COMBAT BUTLER POPULARITY POLL IS...
...OUR INVINCIBLE STUDENT BODY PRESIDENT, HINAGIKU KATSURA!!
SHE TOTALLY BLEW AWAY DA COMPETITION BY GETTIN' AN UNBELIEVABLE 3,728 VOTES!!
THREE...
THREE THOUSAND?
EH?
GLANCE
GLANCE
EH?
WHAT?
UMM...
WHAT'S THIS ALL ABOUT?
...
WELL, TO CELEBRATE YOUR 1ST PLACE RANKING, WHY DON'T YOU ENTERTAIN US BY POSING IN A REGULATION SCHOOL SWIMSUIT?
HUH?
MAYBE THE "NAKED APRON" LOOK WOULD BE GOOD, TOO— ♡
EHH?! WAIT!!
W-WAIT!! HEY!!
WHAT'S ALL THIS ABOUT?!

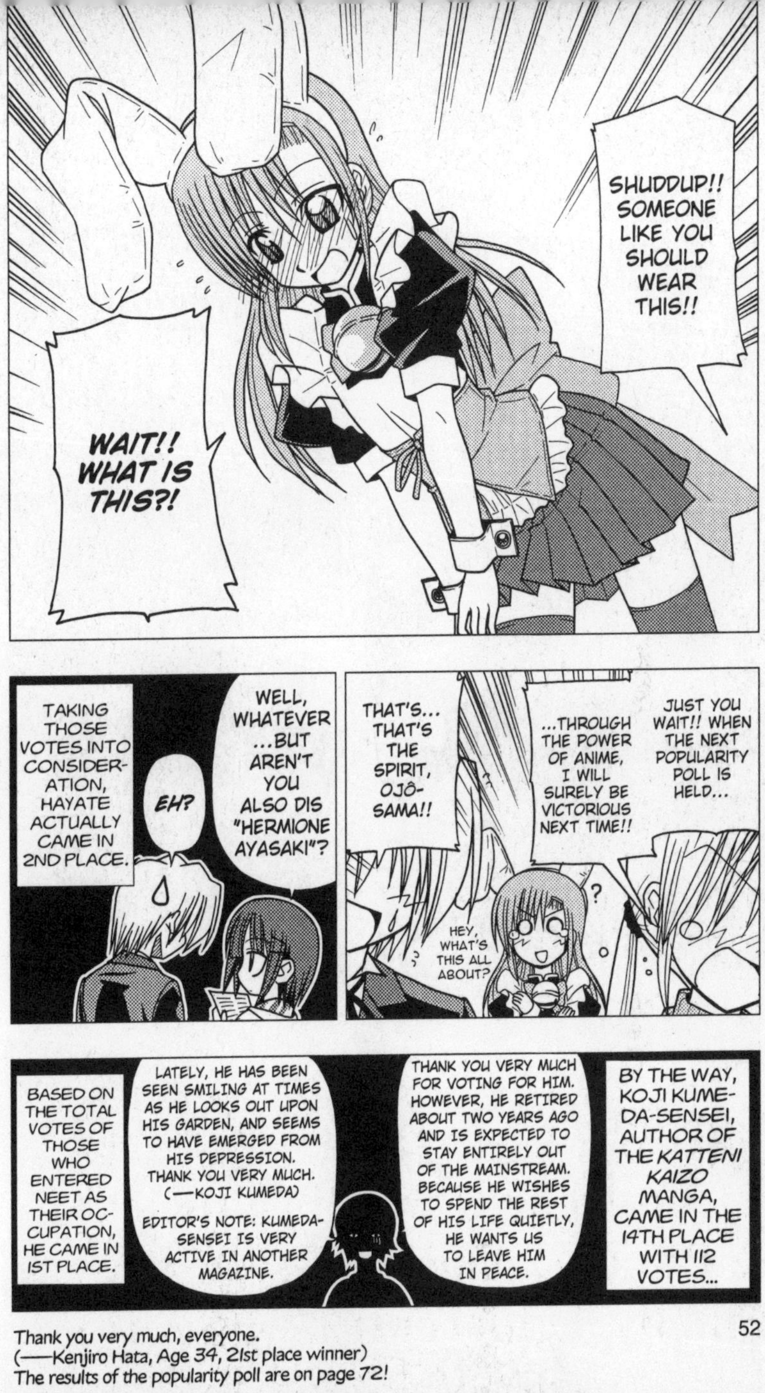
SHUDDUP!! SOMEONE LIKE YOU SHOULD WEAR THIS!!
WAIT!! WHAT IS THIS?!
JUST YOU WAIT!! WHEN THE NEXT POPULARITY POLL IS HELD...
...THROUGH THE POWER OF ANIME, I WILL SURELY BE VICTORIOUS NEXT TIME!!
THAT'S... THAT'S THE SPIRIT, OJÔ-SAMA!!
HEY, WHAT'S THIS ALL ABOUT?
WELL, WHATEVER ...BUT AREN'T YOU ALSO DIS "HERMIONE AYASAKI"?
EH?
TAKING THOSE VOTES INTO CONSIDER-ATION, HAYATE ACTUALLY CAME IN 2ND PLACE.
BY THE WAY, KOJI KUMEDA-SENSEI, AUTHOR OF THE *KATTENI KAIZO* MANGA, CAME IN THE 14TH PLACE WITH 112 VOTES...
THANK YOU VERY MUCH FOR VOTING FOR HIM. HOWEVER, HE RETIRED ABOUT TWO YEARS AGO AND IS EXPECTED TO STAY ENTIRELY OUT OF THE MAINSTREAM. BECAUSE HE WISHES TO SPEND THE REST OF HIS LIFE QUIETLY, HE WANTS US TO LEAVE HIM IN PEACE.
LATELY, HE HAS BEEN SEEN SMILING AT TIMES AS HE LOOKS OUT UPON HIS GARDEN, AND SEEMS TO HAVE EMERGED FROM HIS DEPRESSION. THANK YOU VERY MUCH. (—KOJI KUMEDA)
EDITOR'S NOTE: KUMEDA-SENSEI IS VERY ACTIVE IN ANOTHER MAGAZINE.
BASED ON THE TOTAL VOTES OF THOSE WHO ENTERED NEET AS THEIR OC-CUPATION, HE CAME IN 1ST PLACE.

Thank you very much, everyone.
(—Kenjiro Hata, Age 34, 21st place winner)
The results of the popularity poll are on page 72!

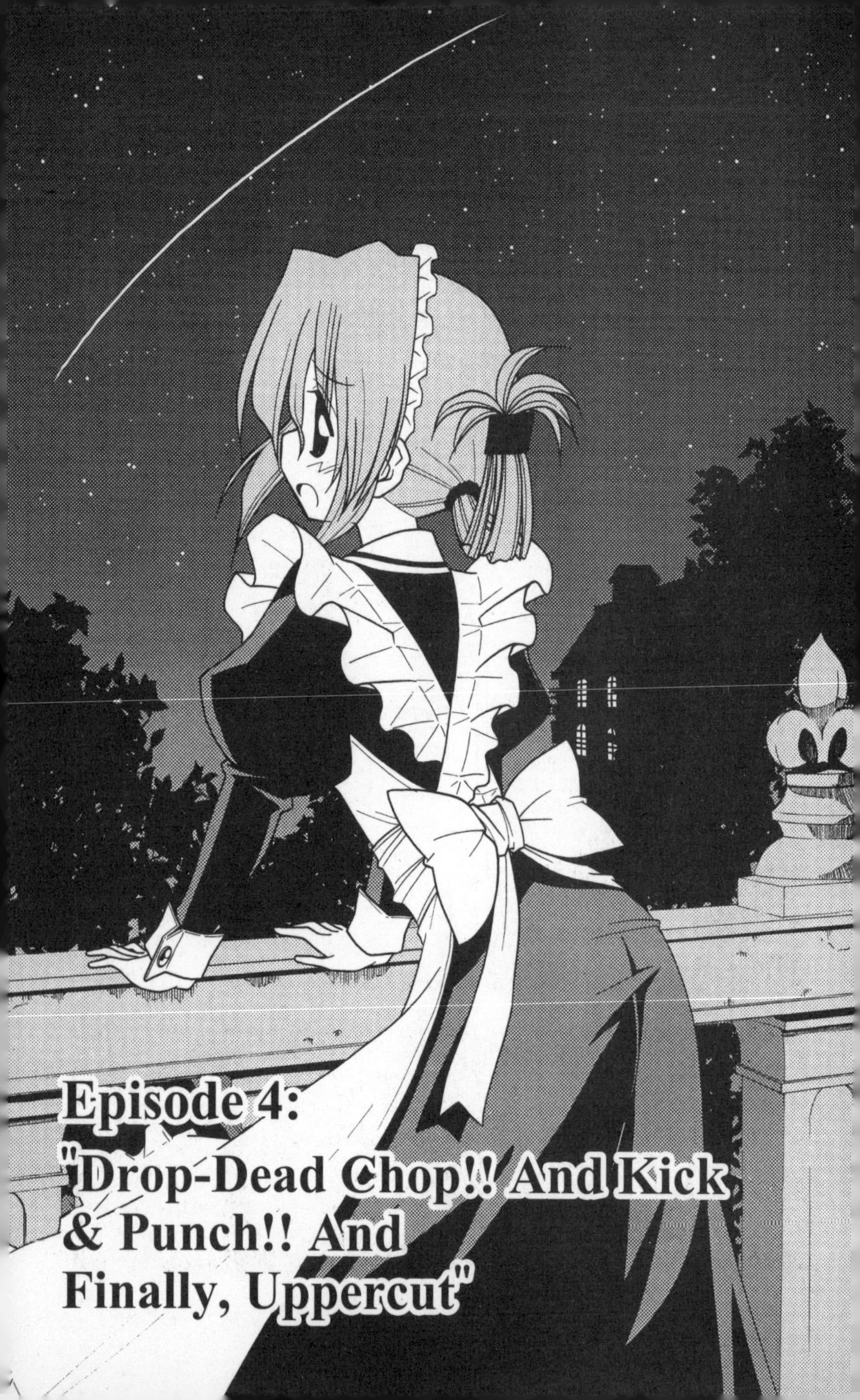
Episode 4:
"Drop-Dead Chop!! And Kick & Punch!! And Finally, Uppercut"

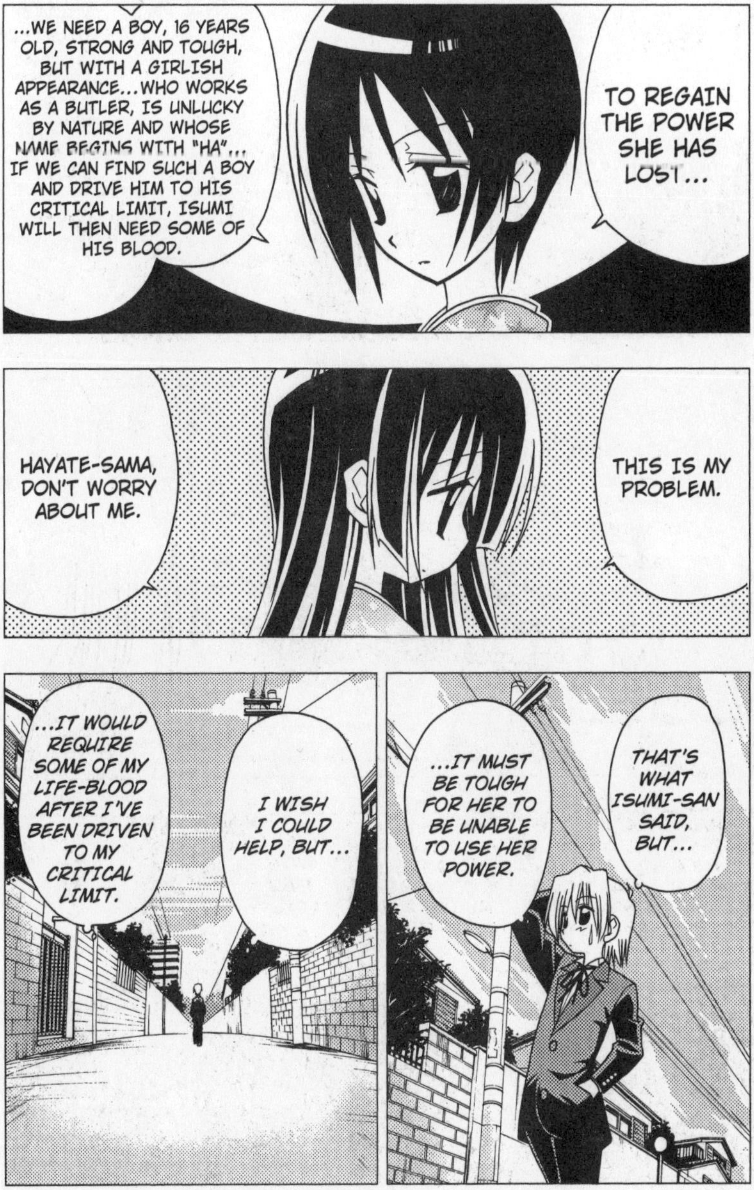
TO REGAIN THE POWER SHE HAS LOST...
...WE NEED A BOY, 16 YEARS OLD, STRONG AND TOUGH, BUT WITH A GIRLISH APPEARANCE...WHO WORKS AS A BUTLER, IS UNLUCKY BY NATURE AND WHOSE NAME BEGINS WITH "HA"... IF WE CAN FIND SUCH A BOY AND DRIVE HIM TO HIS CRITICAL LIMIT, ISUMI WILL THEN NEED SOME OF HIS BLOOD.
THIS IS MY PROBLEM.
HAYATE-SAMA, DON'T WORRY ABOUT ME.
THAT'S WHAT ISUMI-SAN SAID, BUT...
...IT MUST BE TOUGH FOR HER TO BE UNABLE TO USE HER POWER.
I WISH I COULD HELP, BUT...
...IT WOULD REQUIRE SOME OF MY LIFE-BLOOD AFTER I'VE BEEN DRIVEN TO MY CRITICAL LIMIT.

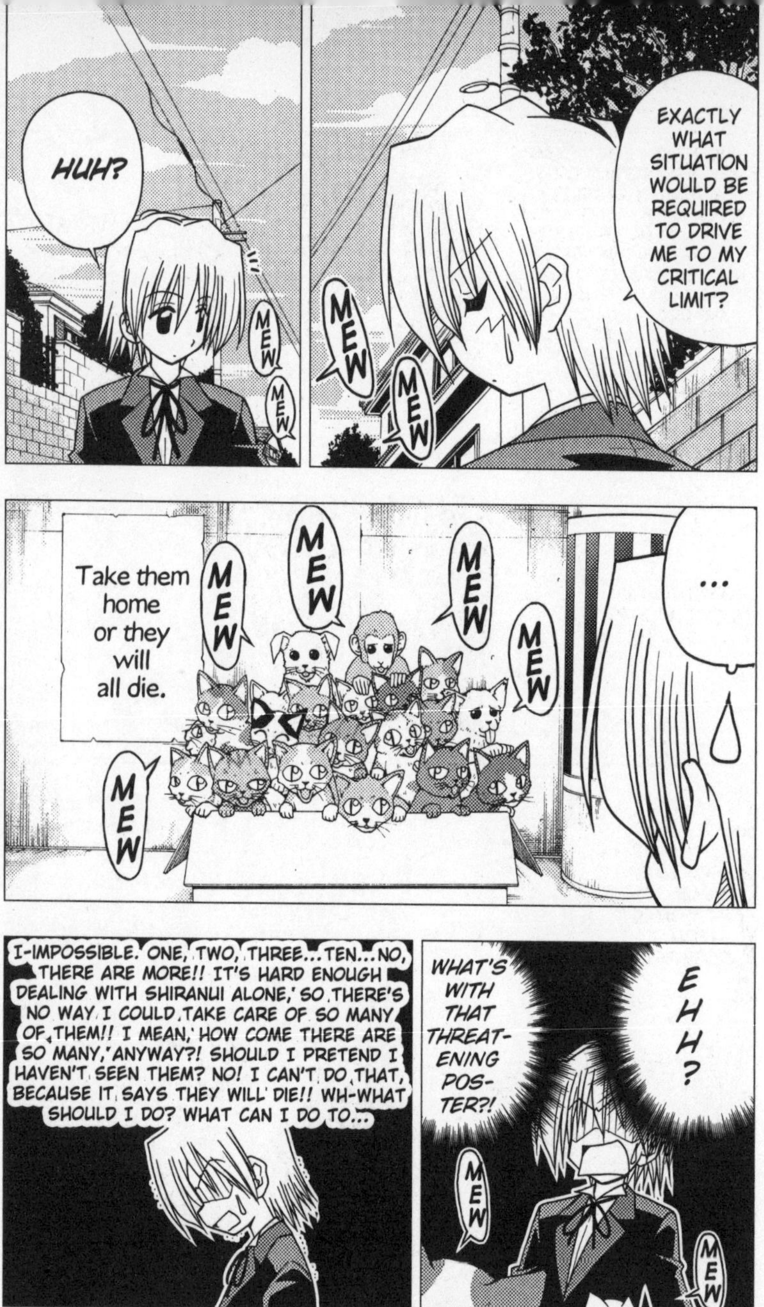
EXACTLY WHAT SITUATION WOULD BE REQUIRED TO DRIVE ME TO MY CRITICAL LIMIT?
MEW
MEW
HUH?
MEW
MEW
...
MEW
MEW
MEW
MEW
Take them home or they will all die.
MEW
EHHH?
WHAT'S WITH THAT THREAT-ENING POS-TER?!
MEW
MEW
I-IMPOSSIBLE. ONE, TWO, THREE... TEN... NO, THERE ARE MORE!! IT'S HARD ENOUGH DEALING WITH SHIRANUI ALONE, SO THERE'S NO WAY I COULD TAKE CARE OF SO MANY OF THEM!! I MEAN, HOW COME THERE ARE SO MANY, ANYWAY?! SHOULD I PRETEND I HAVEN'T SEEN THEM? NO! I CAN'T DO THAT, BECAUSE IT SAYS THEY WILL DIE!! WH-WHAT SHOULD I DO? WHAT CAN I DO TO...

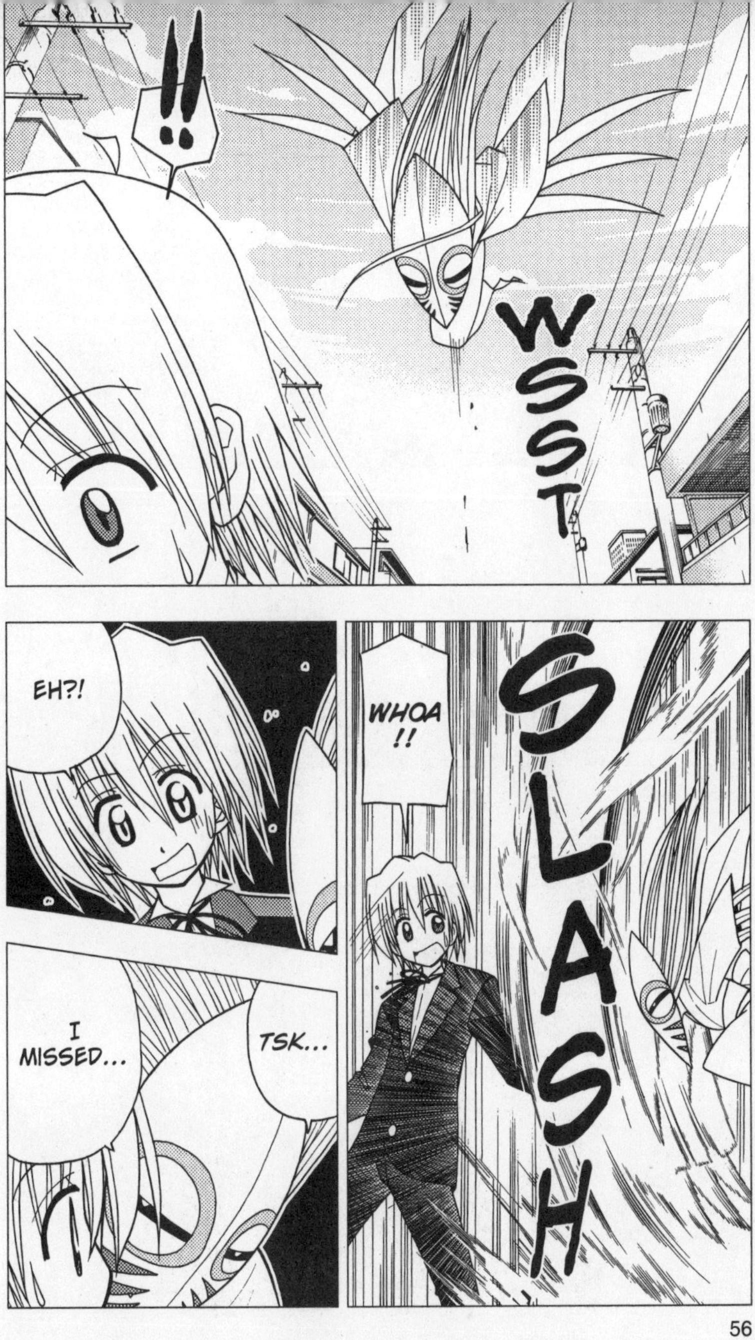
!!
WSST
WHOA!!
SLASH
EH?!
TSK...
I MISSED...

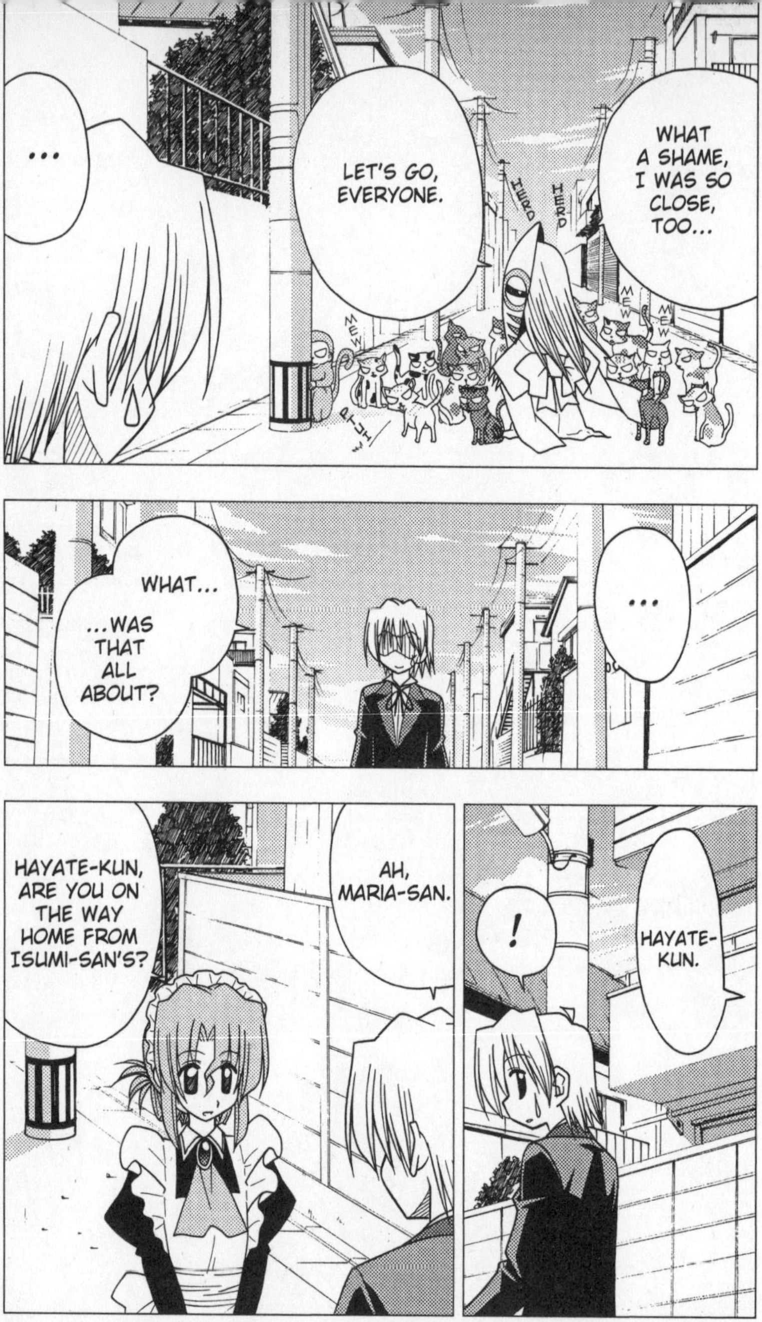
WHAT A SHAME, I WAS SO CLOSE, TOO...
HERD HERD
LET'S GO, EVERYONE.
MEW MEW MEW
...
...
WHAT... ...WAS THAT ALL ABOUT?
HAYATE-KUN.
!
AH, MARIA-SAN.
HAYATE-KUN, ARE YOU ON THE WAY HOME FROM ISUMI-SAN'S?

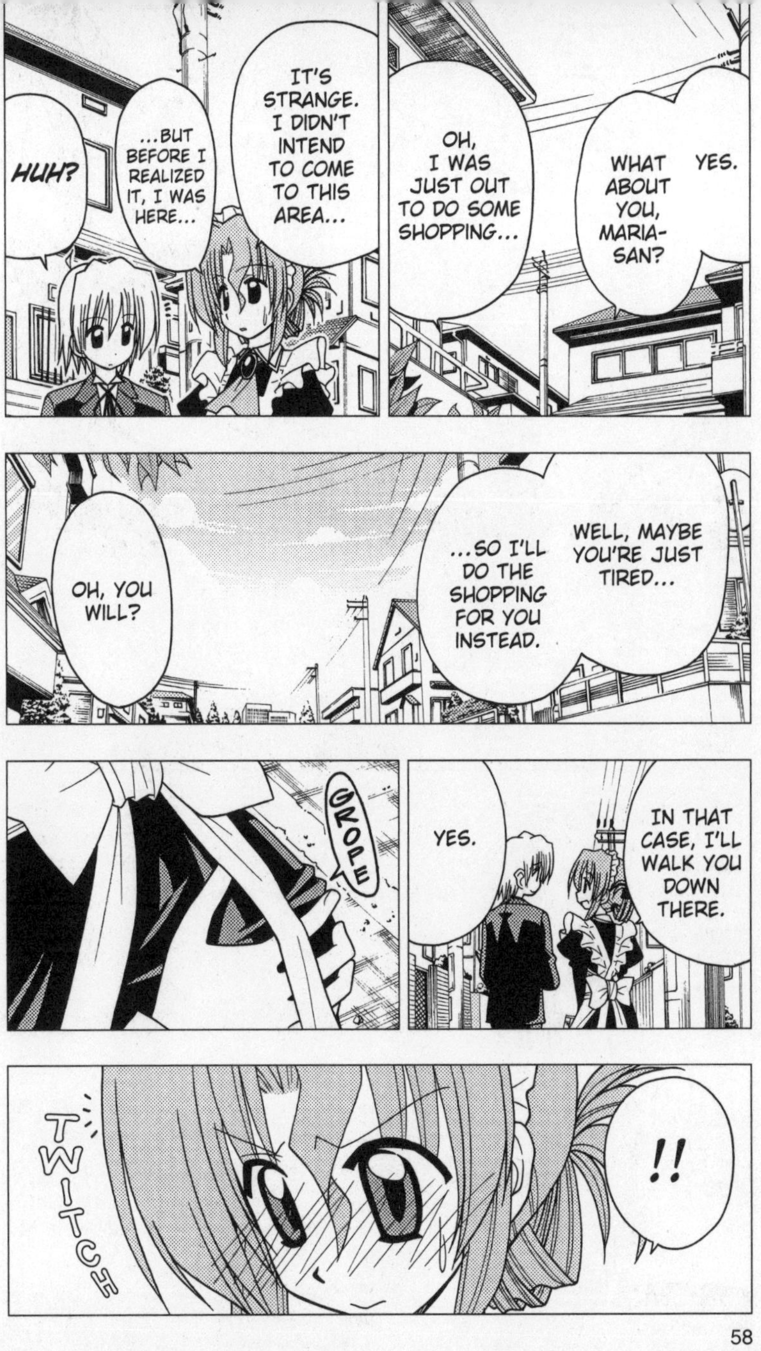
YES.
WHAT ABOUT YOU, MARIA-SAN?
OH, I WAS JUST OUT TO DO SOME SHOPPING...
IT'S STRANGE. I DIDN'T INTEND TO COME TO THIS AREA...
...BUT BEFORE I REALIZED IT, I WAS HERE...
HUH?
WELL, MAYBE YOU'RE JUST TIRED...
...SO I'LL DO THE SHOPPING FOR YOU INSTEAD.
OH, YOU WILL?
IN THAT CASE, I'LL WALK YOU DOWN THERE.
YES.
GROPE
!!
TWITCH

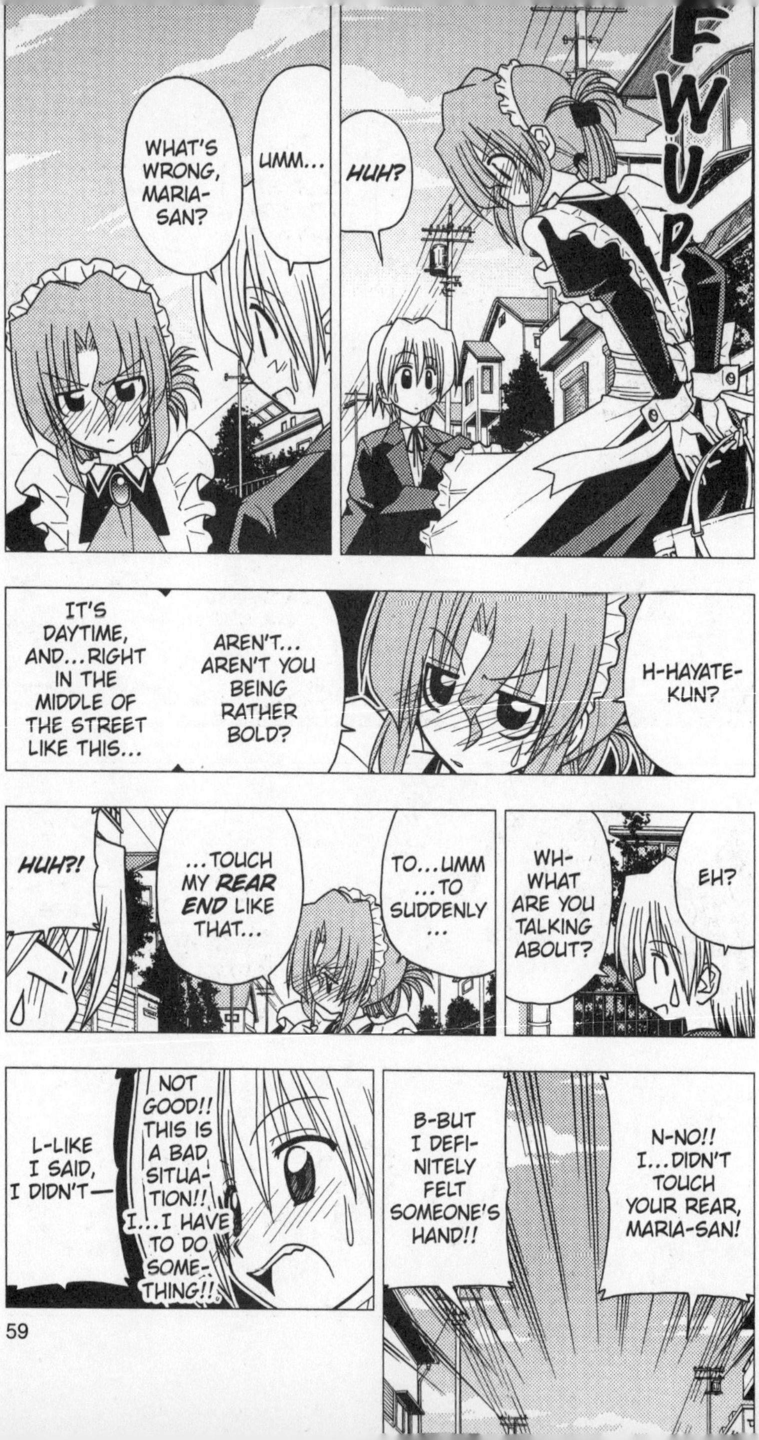
FWUP
HUH?
UMM...
WHAT'S WRONG, MARIA-SAN?
H-HAYATE-KUN?
AREN'T... AREN'T YOU BEING RATHER BOLD?
IT'S DAYTIME, AND...RIGHT IN THE MIDDLE OF THE STREET LIKE THIS...
EH?
WH-WHAT ARE YOU TALKING ABOUT?
TO...UMM ...TO SUDDENLY ...
...TOUCH MY REAR END LIKE THAT...
HUH?!
N-NO!! I...DIDN'T TOUCH YOUR REAR, MARIA-SAN!
B-BUT I DEFINITELY FELT SOMEONE'S HAND!!
NOT GOOD!! THIS IS A BAD SITUATION!! I...I HAVE TO DO SOMETHING!!
L-LIKE I SAID, I DIDN'T—

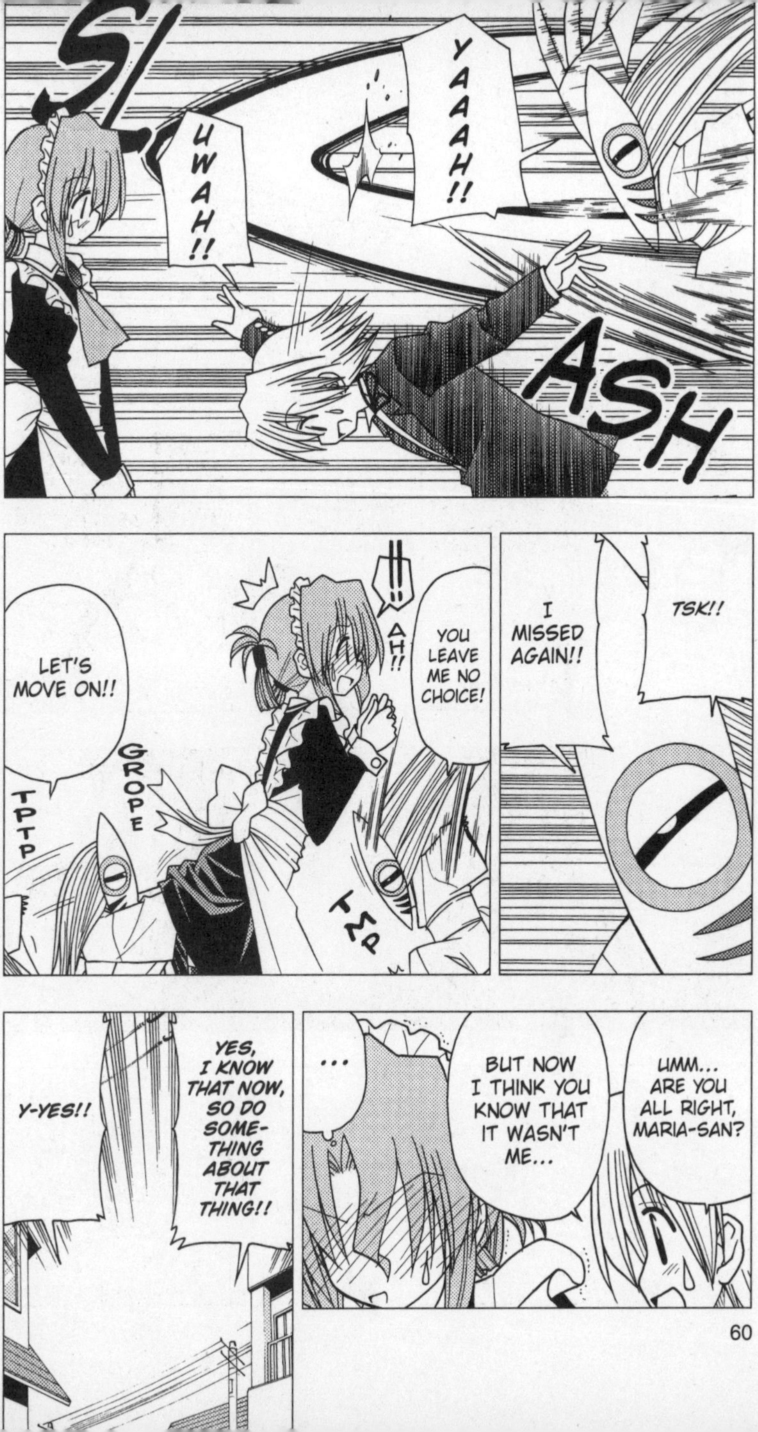
YAAAAH!!
UWAH!!
S/
ASH
TSK!!
I MISSED AGAIN!!
!!
AH!!
YOU LEAVE ME NO CHOICE!
GROPE
TPTP
LET'S MOVE ON!!
UMM... ARE YOU ALL RIGHT, MARIA-SAN?
BUT NOW I THINK YOU KNOW THAT IT WASN'T ME...
...
YES, I KNOW THAT NOW, SO DO SOME-THING ABOUT THAT THING!!
Y-YES!!

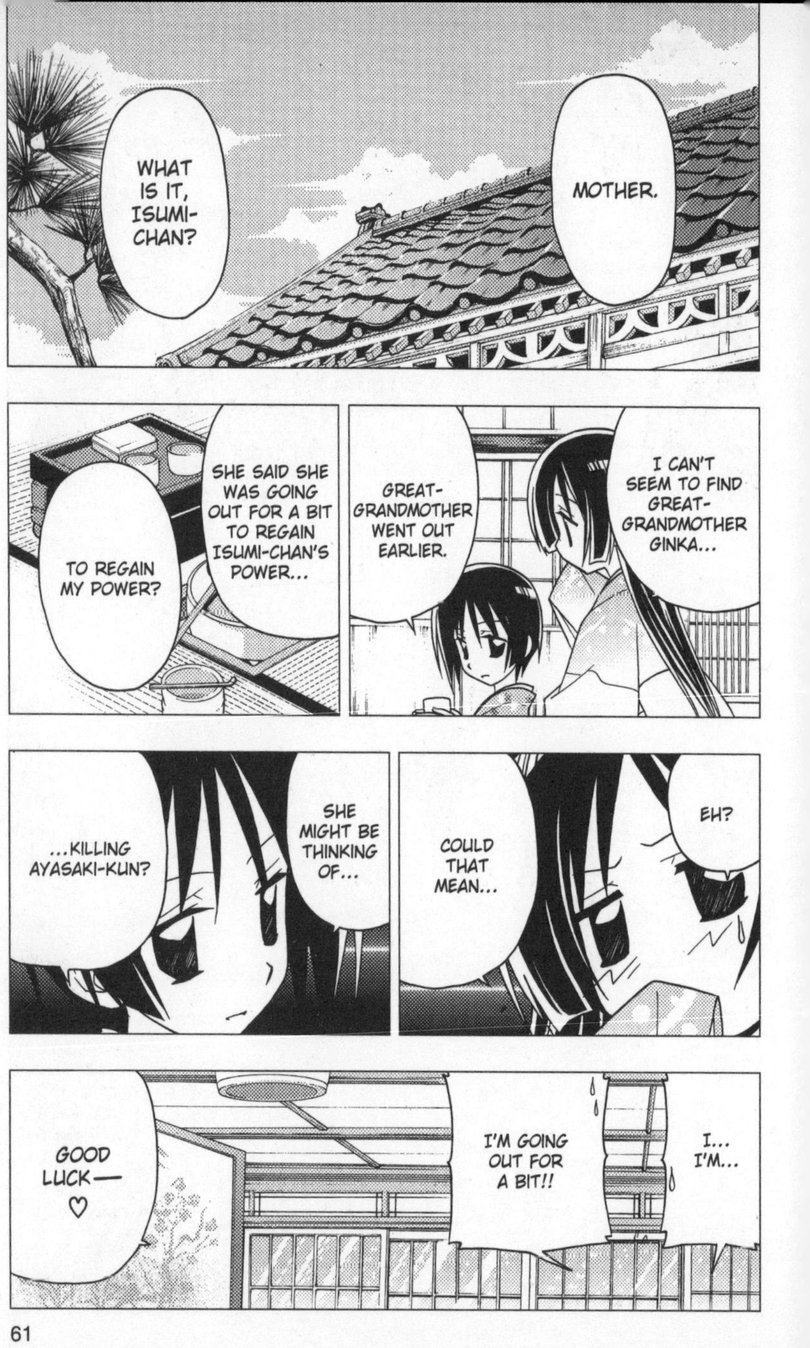
MOTHER.
WHAT IS IT, ISUMI-CHAN?
I CAN'T SEEM TO FIND GREAT-GRANDMOTHER GINKA...
GREAT-GRANDMOTHER WENT OUT EARLIER.
SHE SAID SHE WAS GOING OUT FOR A BIT TO REGAIN ISUMI-CHAN'S POWER...
TO REGAIN MY POWER?
EH?
COULD THAT MEAN...
SHE MIGHT BE THINKING OF...
...KILLING AYASAKI-KUN?
I... I'M...
I'M GOING OUT FOR A BIT!!
GOOD LUCK— ♡

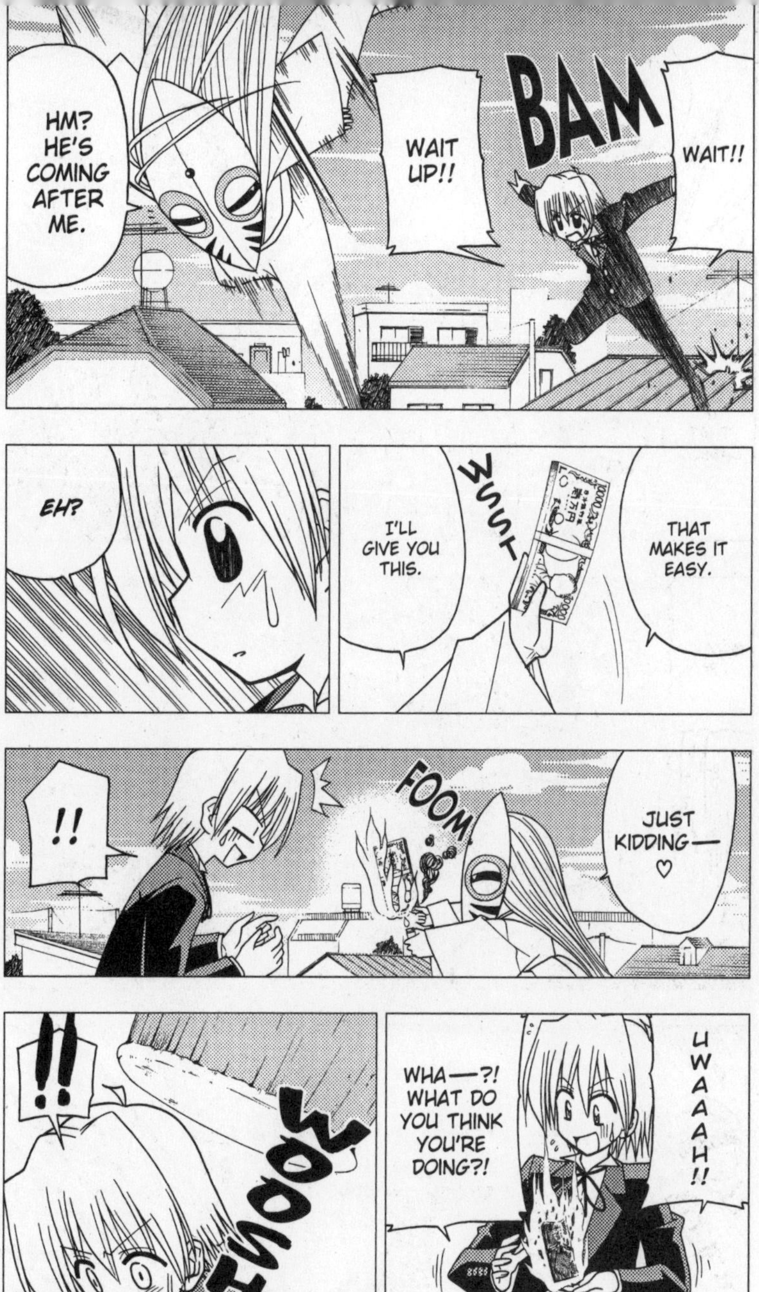

WAIT!!
BAM
WAIT UP!!
HM? HE'S COMING AFTER ME.
THAT MAKES IT EASY.
WSST
I'LL GIVE YOU THIS.
EH?
JUST KIDDING— ♡
FOOM
!!
UWAAAAH!!
WHA—?! WHAT DO YOU THINK YOU'RE DOING?!
WOOSH
!!

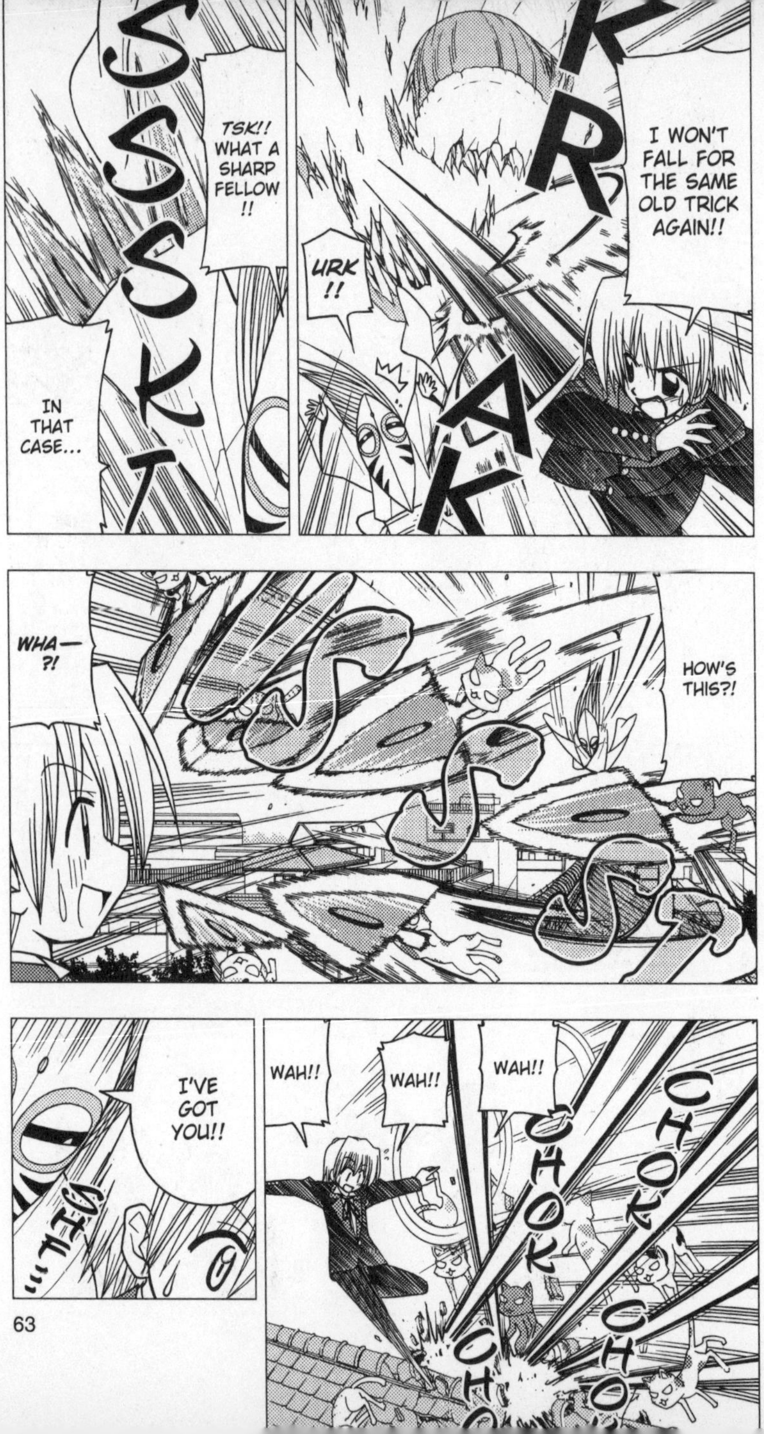
KRAK
I WON'T FALL FOR THE SAME OLD TRICK AGAIN!!
URK!!
TSK!! WHAT A SHARP FELLOW!!
SSKT
IN THAT CASE...
HOW'S THIS?!
WHA—?!
WAH!!
WAH!!
WAH!!
CHOK CHOK
CHOK CHOK
I'VE GOT YOU!!

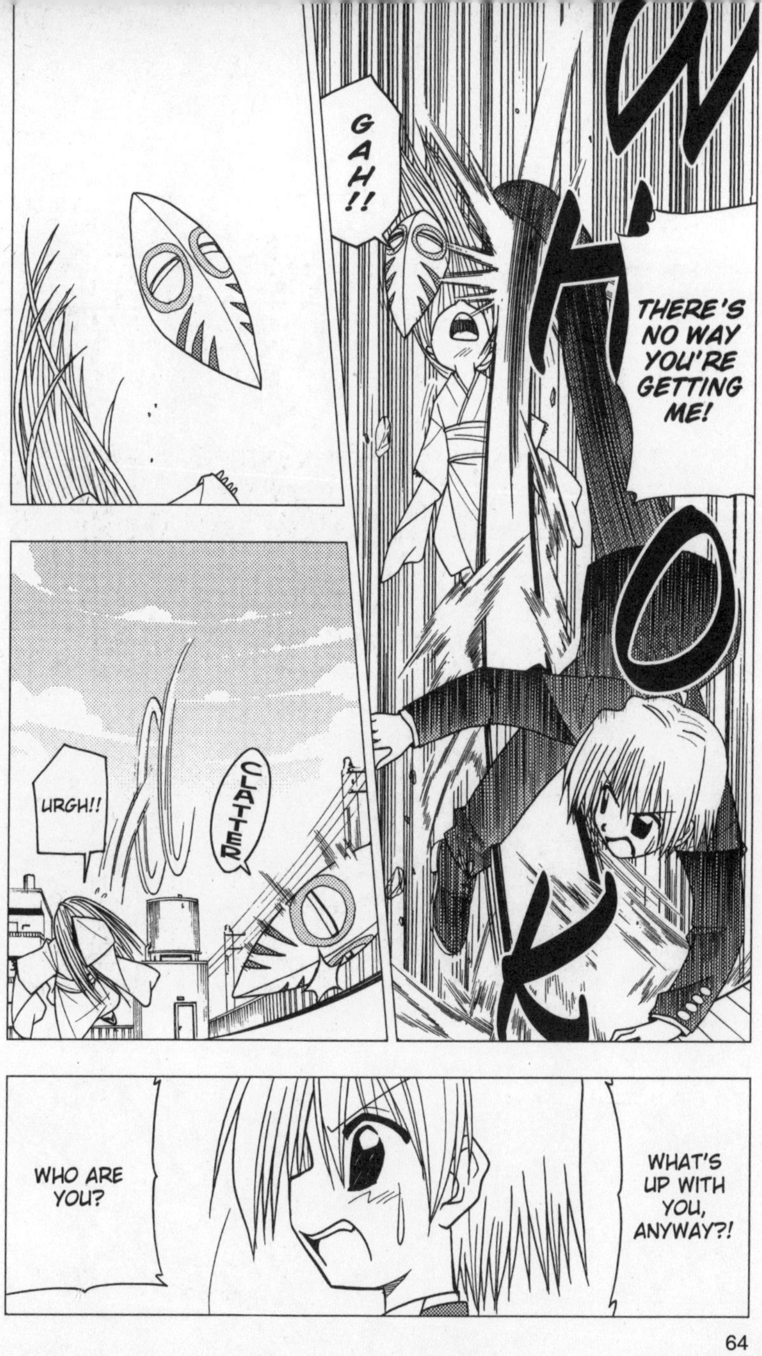
WHOK
GAH!!
THERE'S NO WAY YOU'RE GETTING ME!
CLATTER
URGH!!
WHAT'S UP WITH YOU, ANYWAY?!
WHO ARE YOU?

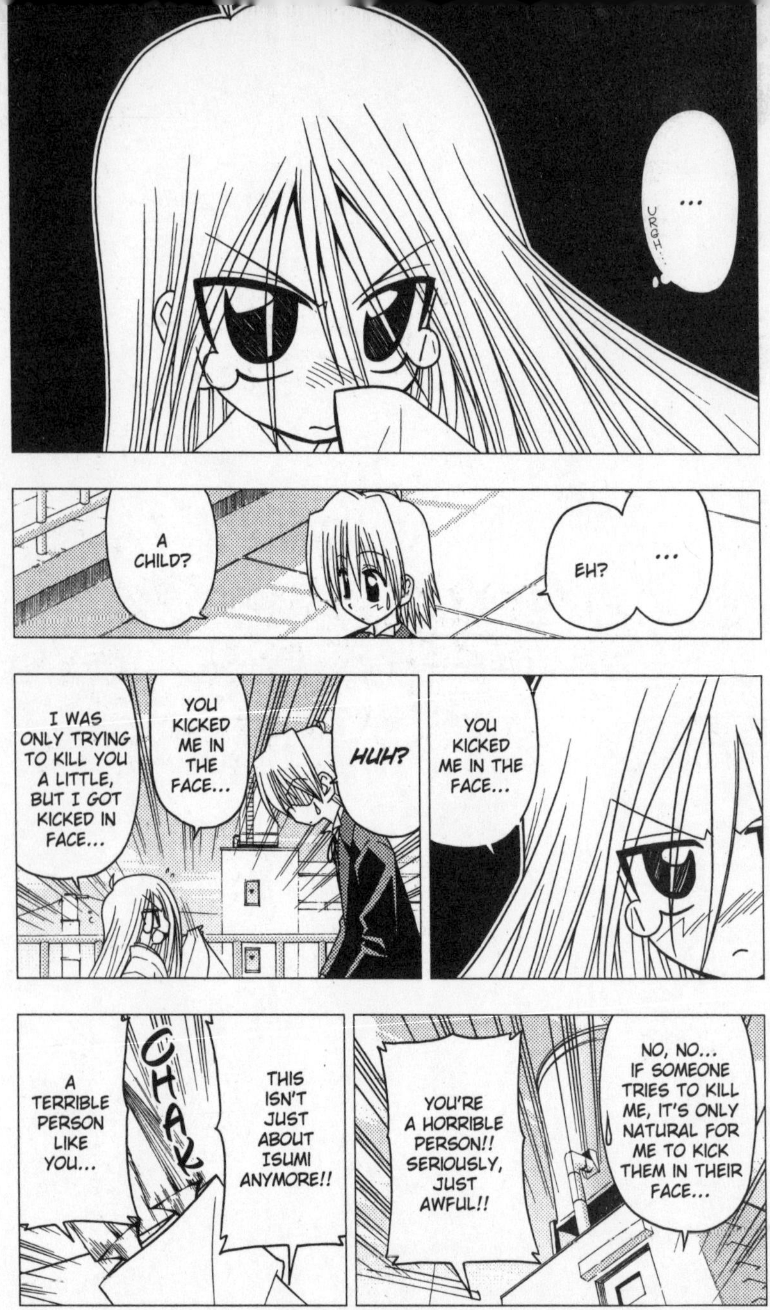
…
URGH…
…
EH?
A CHILD?
YOU KICKED ME IN THE FACE…
HUH?
YOU KICKED ME IN THE FACE…
I WAS ONLY TRYING TO KILL YOU A LITTLE, BUT I GOT KICKED IN FACE…
NO, NO… IF SOMEONE TRIES TO KILL ME, IT'S ONLY NATURAL FOR ME TO KICK THEM IN THEIR FACE…
YOU'RE A HORRIBLE PERSON!! SERIOUSLY, JUST AWFUL!!
THIS ISN'T JUST ABOUT ISUMI ANYMORE!!
CHAK
A TERRIBLE PERSON LIKE YOU…

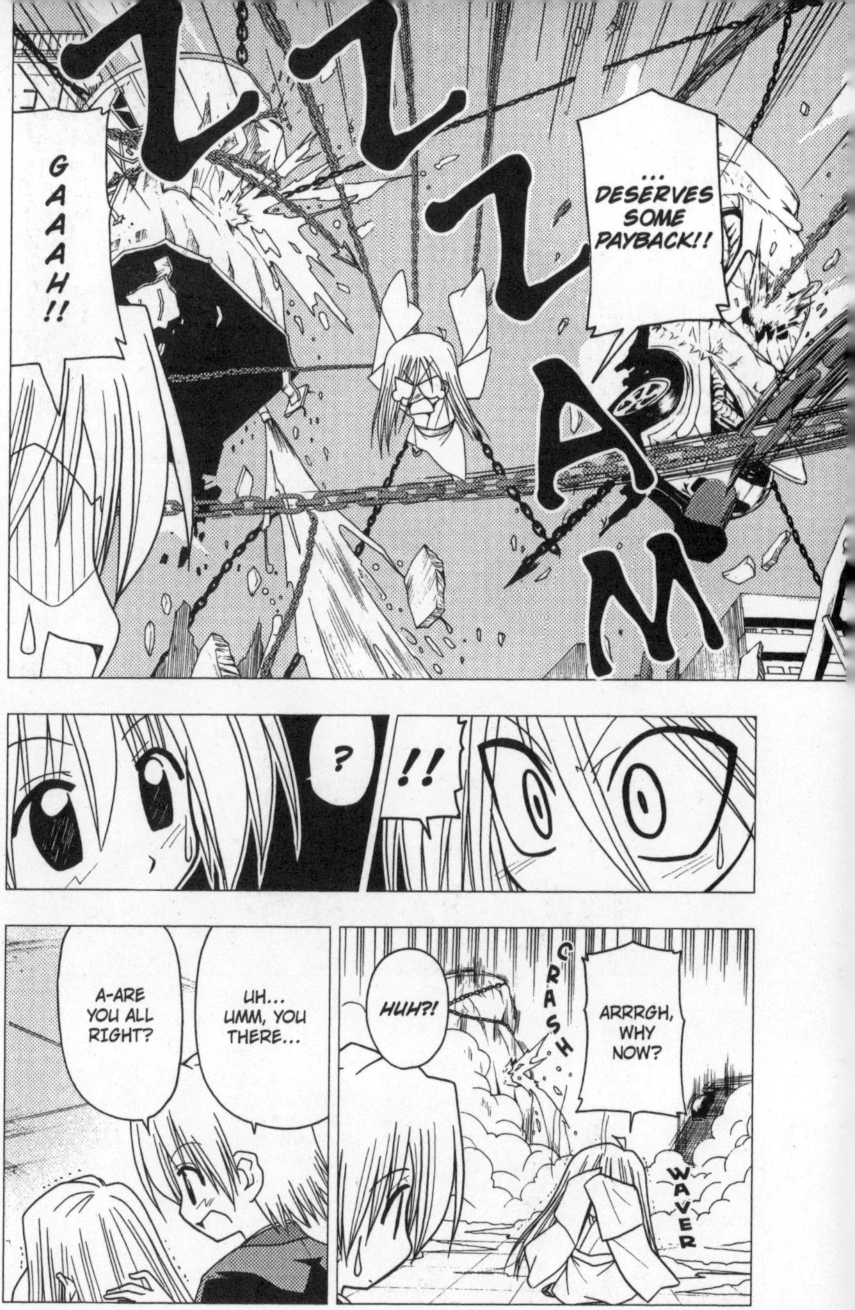
...DESERVES SOME PAYBACK!!
ZZZAM
GAAAAH!!
!!
?
ARRRGH, WHY NOW?
CRASH
HUH?!
WAVER
UH... UMM, YOU THERE...
A-ARE YOU ALL RIGHT?

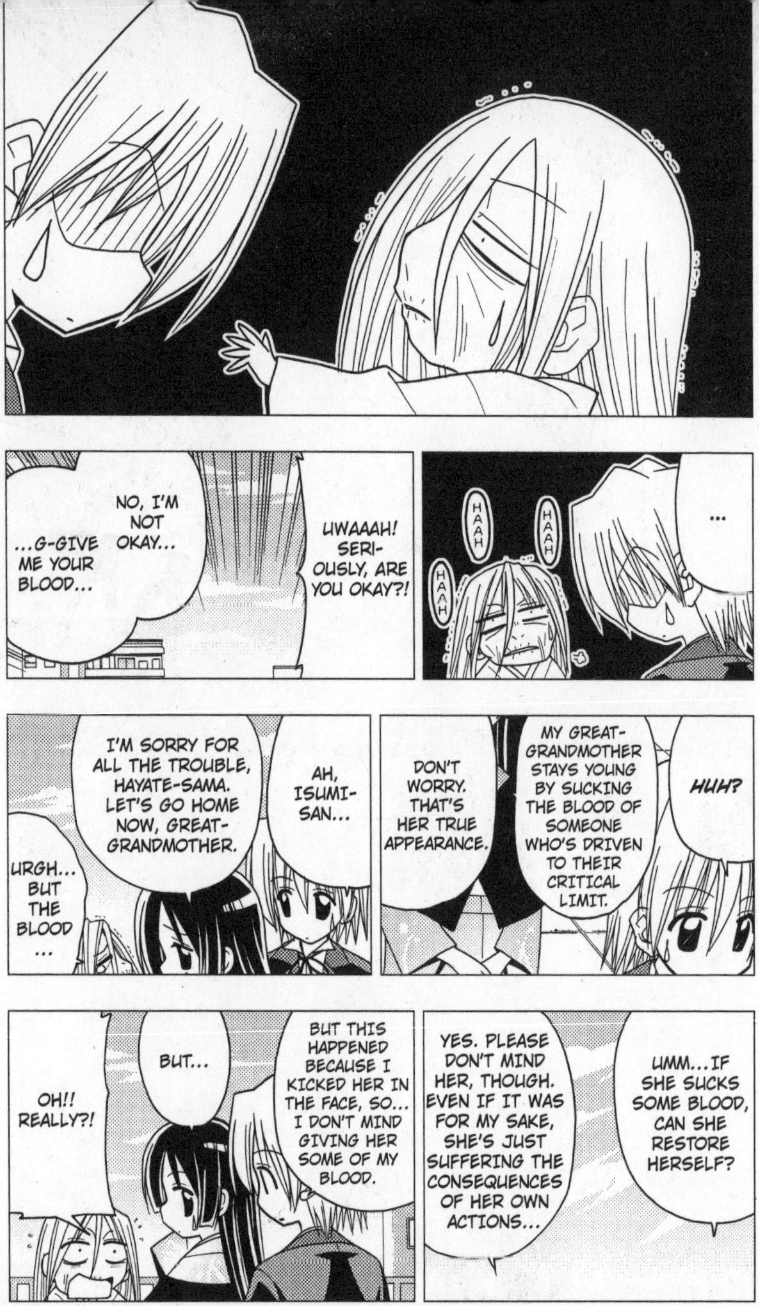
...
HAAH
HAAH
HAAH
UWAAAH! SERIOUSLY, ARE YOU OKAY?!
NO, I'M NOT OKAY...
...G-GIVE ME YOUR BLOOD...
HUH?
MY GREAT-GRANDMOTHER STAYS YOUNG BY SUCKING THE BLOOD OF SOMEONE WHO'S DRIVEN TO THEIR CRITICAL LIMIT.
DON'T WORRY. THAT'S HER TRUE APPEARANCE.
AH, ISUMI-SAN...
I'M SORRY FOR ALL THE TROUBLE, HAYATE-SAMA. LET'S GO HOME NOW, GREAT-GRANDMOTHER.
URGH... BUT THE BLOOD...
UMM...IF SHE SUCKS SOME BLOOD, CAN SHE RESTORE HERSELF?
YES. PLEASE DON'T MIND HER, THOUGH. EVEN IF IT WAS FOR MY SAKE, SHE'S JUST SUFFERING THE CONSEQUENCES OF HER OWN ACTIONS...
BUT THIS HAPPENED BECAUSE I KICKED HER IN THE FACE, SO... I DON'T MIND GIVING HER SOME OF MY BLOOD.
BUT...
OH!! REALLY?!

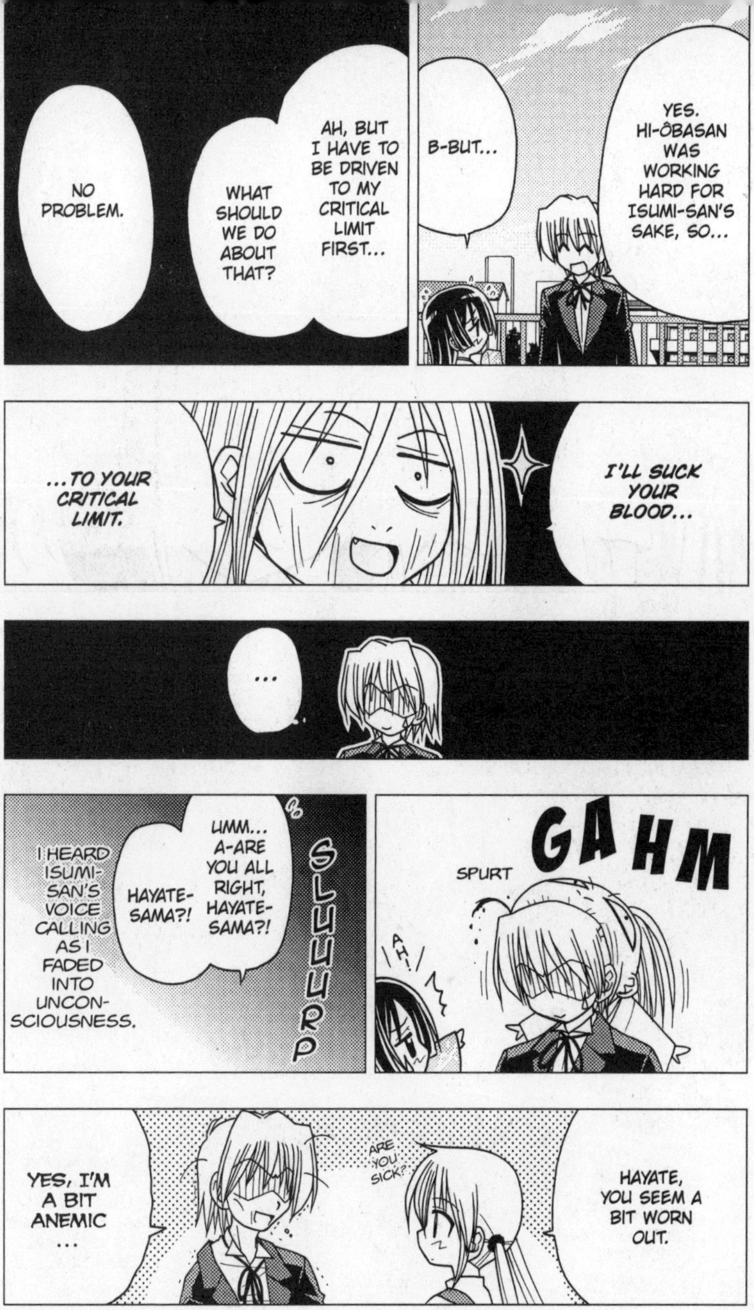
YES. HI-ÔBASAN WAS WORKING HARD FOR ISUMI-SAN'S SAKE, SO...
B-BUT...
AH, BUT I HAVE TO BE DRIVEN TO MY CRITICAL LIMIT FIRST...
WHAT SHOULD WE DO ABOUT THAT?
NO PROBLEM.
I'LL SUCK YOUR BLOOD...
...TO YOUR CRITICAL LIMIT.
...
GAHM
SPURT
AH!
SLUUURP
UMM... A-ARE YOU ALL RIGHT, HAYATE-SAMA?!
HAYATE-SAMA?!
I HEARD ISUMI-SAN'S VOICE CALLING AS I FADED INTO UNCONSCIOUSNESS.
HAYATE, YOU SEEM A BIT WORN OUT.
ARE YOU SICK?
YES, I'M A BIT ANEMIC...

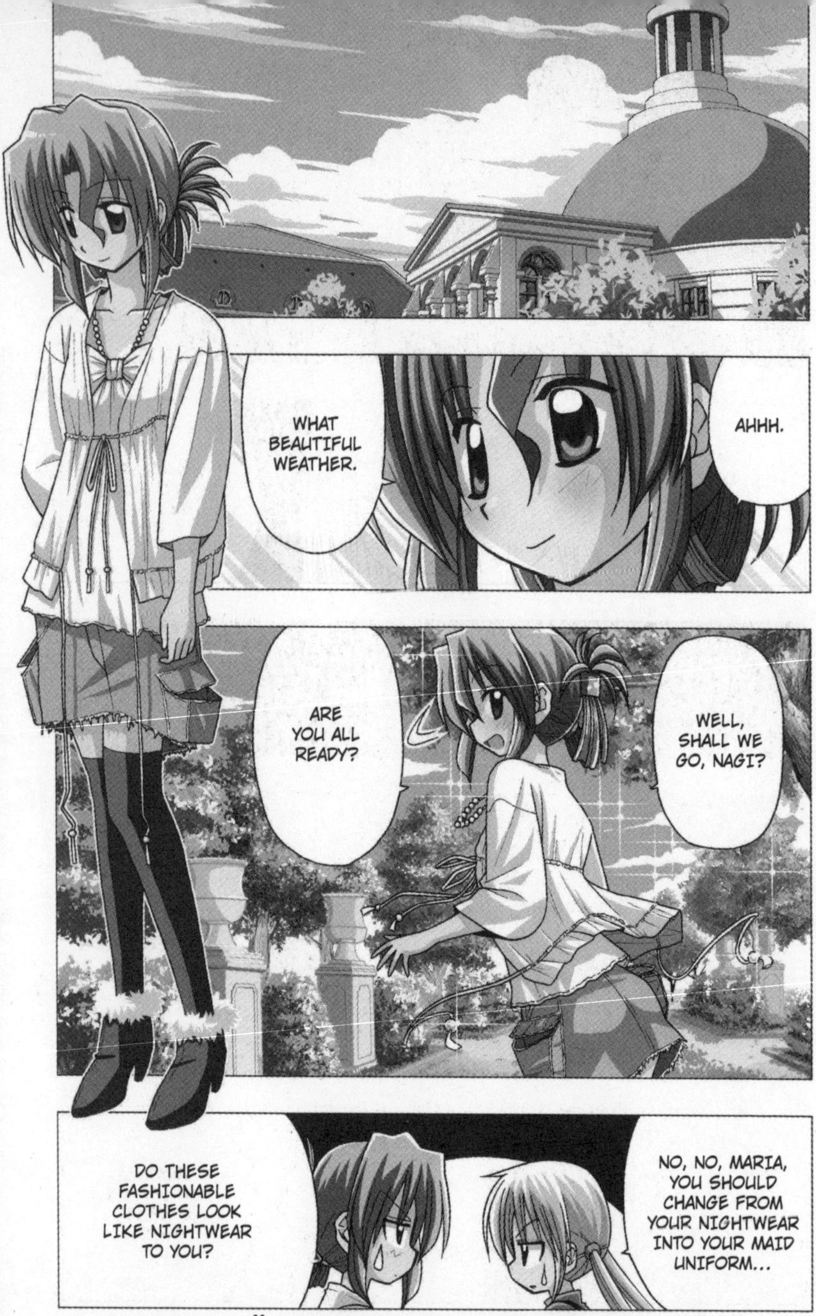
AHHH.
WHAT BEAUTIFUL WEATHER.
WELL, SHALL WE GO, NAGI?
ARE YOU ALL READY?
NO, NO, MARIA, YOU SHOULD CHANGE FROM YOUR NIGHTWEAR INTO YOUR MAID UNIFORM...
DO THESE FASHIONABLE CLOTHES LOOK LIKE NIGHTWEAR TO YOU?

Episode 5: "Longing for the Railway"

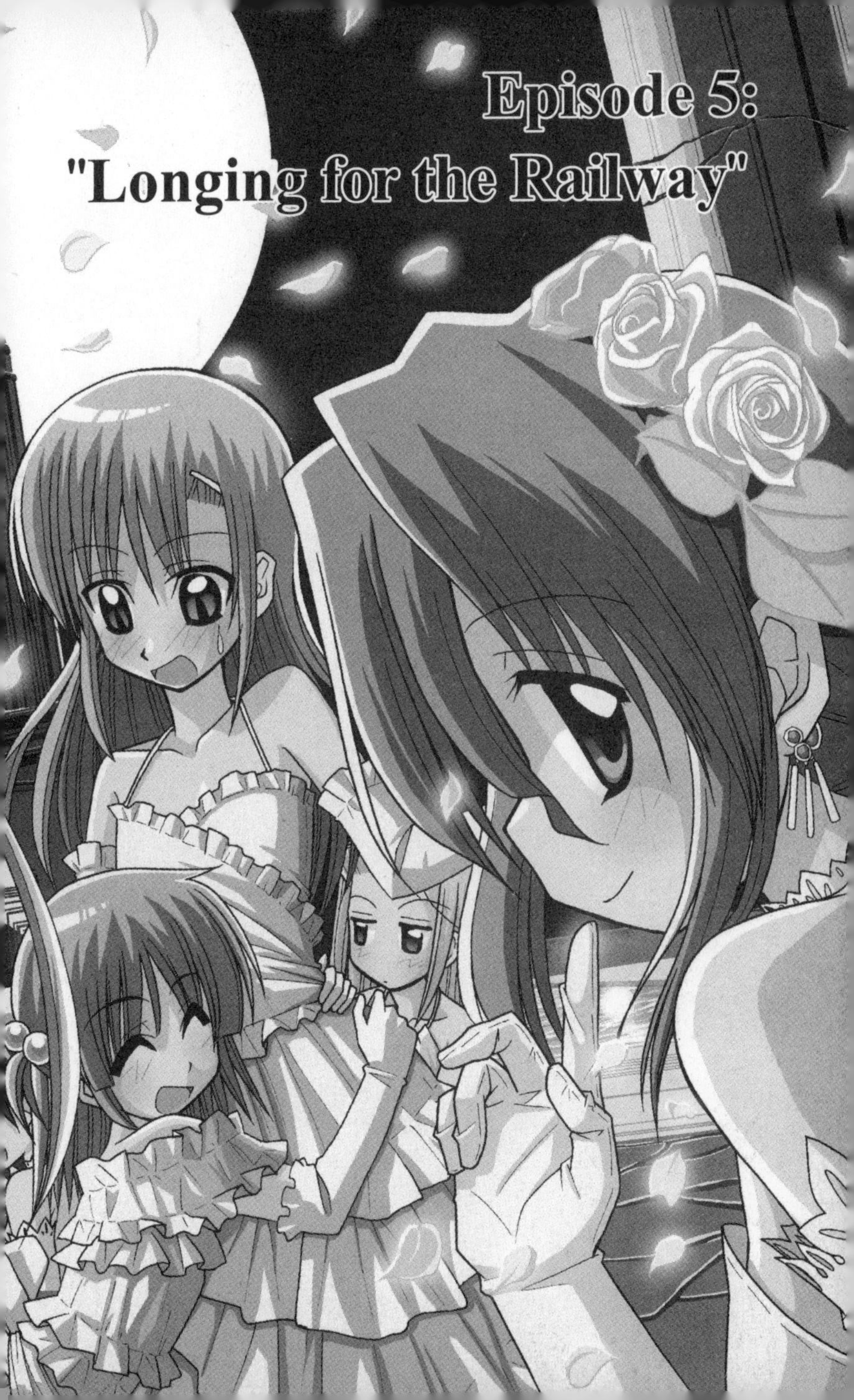
Episode 5:
"Longing for the Railway"

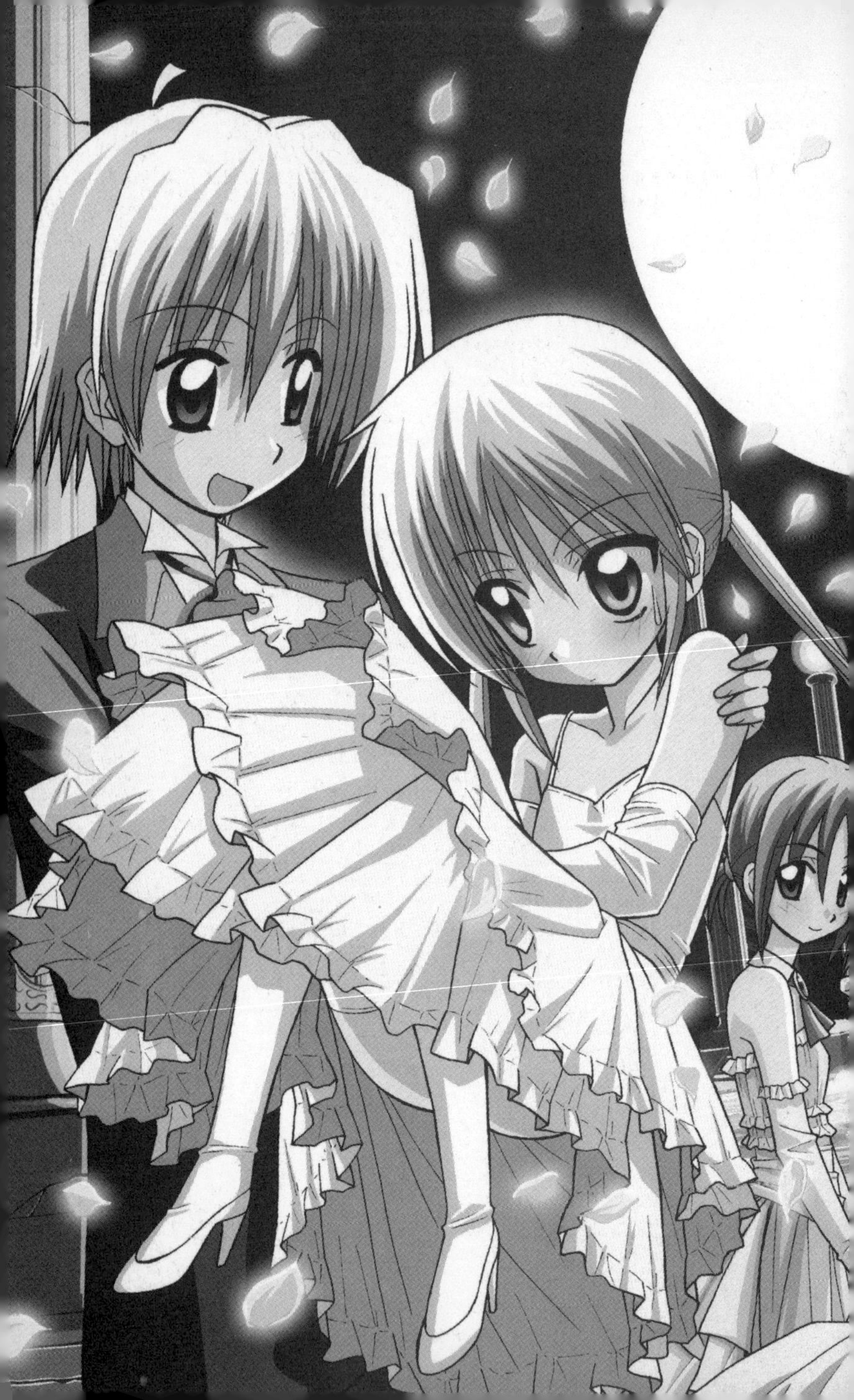

THE FIRST CHARACTER POPULARITY POLL

RESULT SUMMARY!

THERE WERE A TOTAL OF 11,753 VALID VOTES. HERE ARE THE RESULTS OF THE POPULARITY POLL AS REPORTED IN *SHÔNEN SUNDAY* MAGAZINE!

	NO. 1	HINAGIKU KATSURA	3,728 VOTES	I DIDN'T EXPECT HER TO BE SO POPULAR...
LATELY, SHE'S GAINED POPULARITY AMONG LITTLE KIDS, TOO...	NO. 2	MARIA	1,586 VOTES	
	NO. 3	HAYATE AYASAKI	1,543 VOTES	HE CAME IN 3RD PLACE BECAUSE THE VOTES FOR HIM DRESSED IN GIRL'S CLOTHING WERE COUNTED SEPARATELY.
SHE ACTUALLY CAME IN 1ST PLACE AMONG VOTERS UNDER 10 YEARS OLD.	NO. 4	NAGI SANZENIN	1,103 VOTES	
	NO. 5	ISUMI SAGINOMIYA	666 VOTES	FOR SOME REASON, MANY VOTES WERE IN KOREAN...
	NO. 6	SAKUYA AIZAWA	431 VOTES	
THIS IS SO ORDINARY...	NO. 7	AYUMU NISHIZAWA	421 VOTES	
	NO. 8	IZUMI SEGAWA	410 VOTES	I'M SURPRISED SHE'S SO POPULAR.
HE'S A VALUABLE MALE CHARACTER.	NO. 9	WATARU TACHIBANA	220 VOTES	
	NO. 10	SAKI KIJIMA	187 VOTES	BECAUSE SHE'S HAD FEW APPEARANCES LATELY, SHE'S IN THE BONUS PAGES...
KEN NAGAI-SENSEI, THANK YOU VERY MUCH.	NO. 11	FATHER (*SHINSEI MOTEMOTE OUKOKU* BY KEN NAGAI)	176 VOTES	
	NO. 12	TAMA	136 VOTES	
	NO. 13	HERMIONE AYASAKI	125 VOTES	RECEIVED OVERWHELMING SUPPORT FROM MALES IN THEIR 20'S!!
MASTER TEACHER...	NO. 14	KOJI KUMEDA	112 VOTES	
	NO. 15	YUKIJI KATSURA	111 VOTES	
	NO. 16	FATHER (THE DEAD PRIEST)	86 VOTES	I'D LIKE TO HAVE HIM APPEAR MORE OFTEN.
	NO. 17	SHIRANUI	63 VOTES	
	NO. 18	KLAUS	57 VOTES	
RECEIVED OVERWHELMING SUPPORT FROM MALES IN THEIR 20'S!!	NO. 19	HAYATE DRESSED IN GIRL'S CLOTHES	52 VOTES	
	NO. 20	RISA ASAKAZE	36 VOTES	
	NO. 21	KENJIRO HATA	34 VOTES	THANK YOU VERY MUCH.
HAYATE'S VERSION OF BRITNEY WAS ACTUALLY THE MOST POPULAR.	NO. 22	BRITNEY-CHAN	33 VOTES	
	NO. 23	HIMURO SAEKI	30 VOTES	
	NO. 24	MIKI HANABISHI	27 VOTES	
	NO. 25	NADJA ORUMUZUTO (GODDESS)	25 VOTES	I'M HAPPY FOR YOU, GODDESS...
	NO. 26	SISTER	24 VOTES	
	NO. 27	SHIORI MAKIMURA	24 VOTES	
	NO. 28	EIGHT	23 VOTES	
	NO. 29	KAEDE NONOHARA	19 VOTES	
	NO. 30	KYONOSUKE KAORU	16 VOTES	

I THOUGHT THE RANKINGS WOULDN'T BE TAKEN SERIOUSLY, SO I WAS SURPRISED THE OUTCOME WAS SO HEARTFELT.
(—KENJIRO HATA)

THANK YOU VERY MUCH FOR ALL YOUR VOTES!

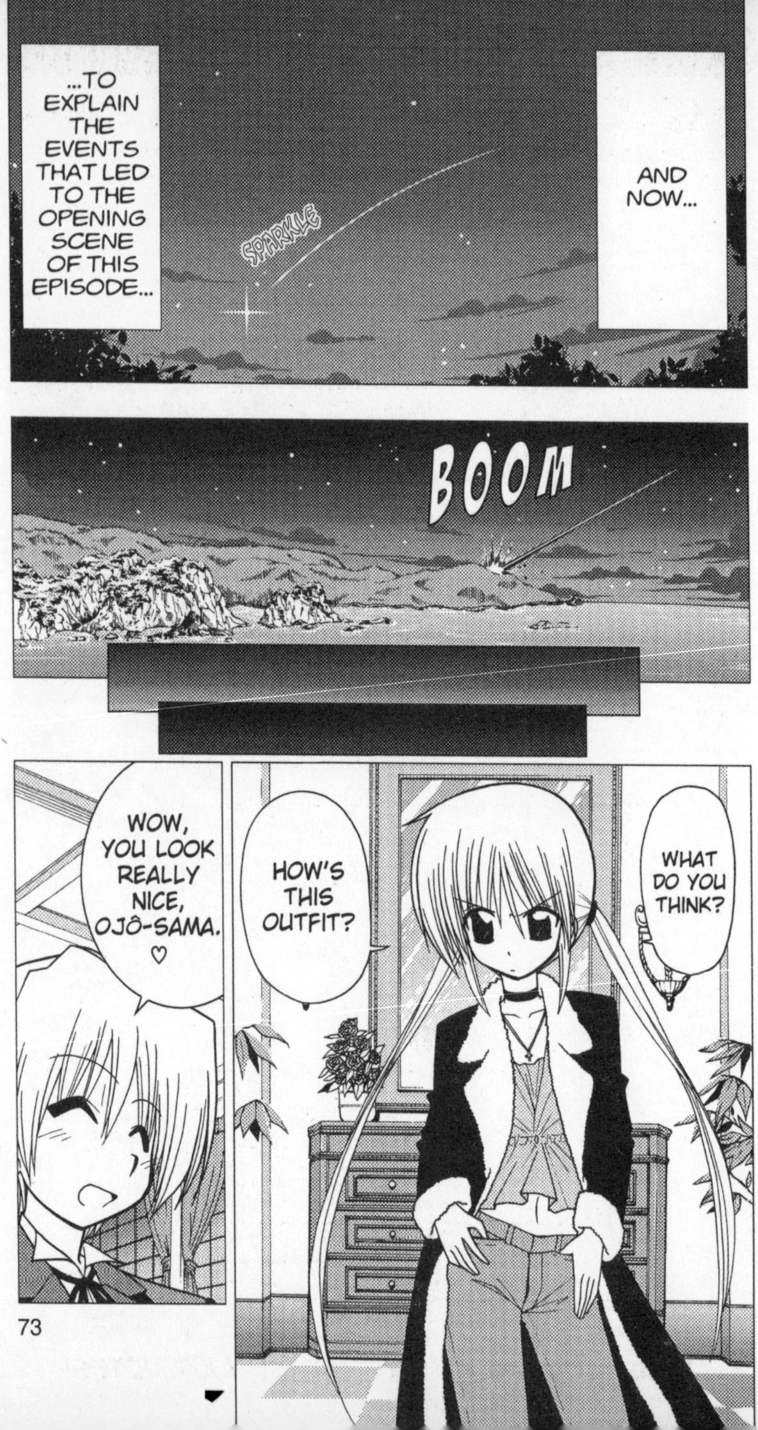
AND NOW...
...TO EXPLAIN THE EVENTS THAT LED TO THE OPENING SCENE OF THIS EPISODE...
SPARKLE
BOOM
WHAT DO YOU THINK?
HOW'S THIS OUTFIT?
WOW, YOU LOOK REALLY NICE, OJÔ-SAMA. ♡

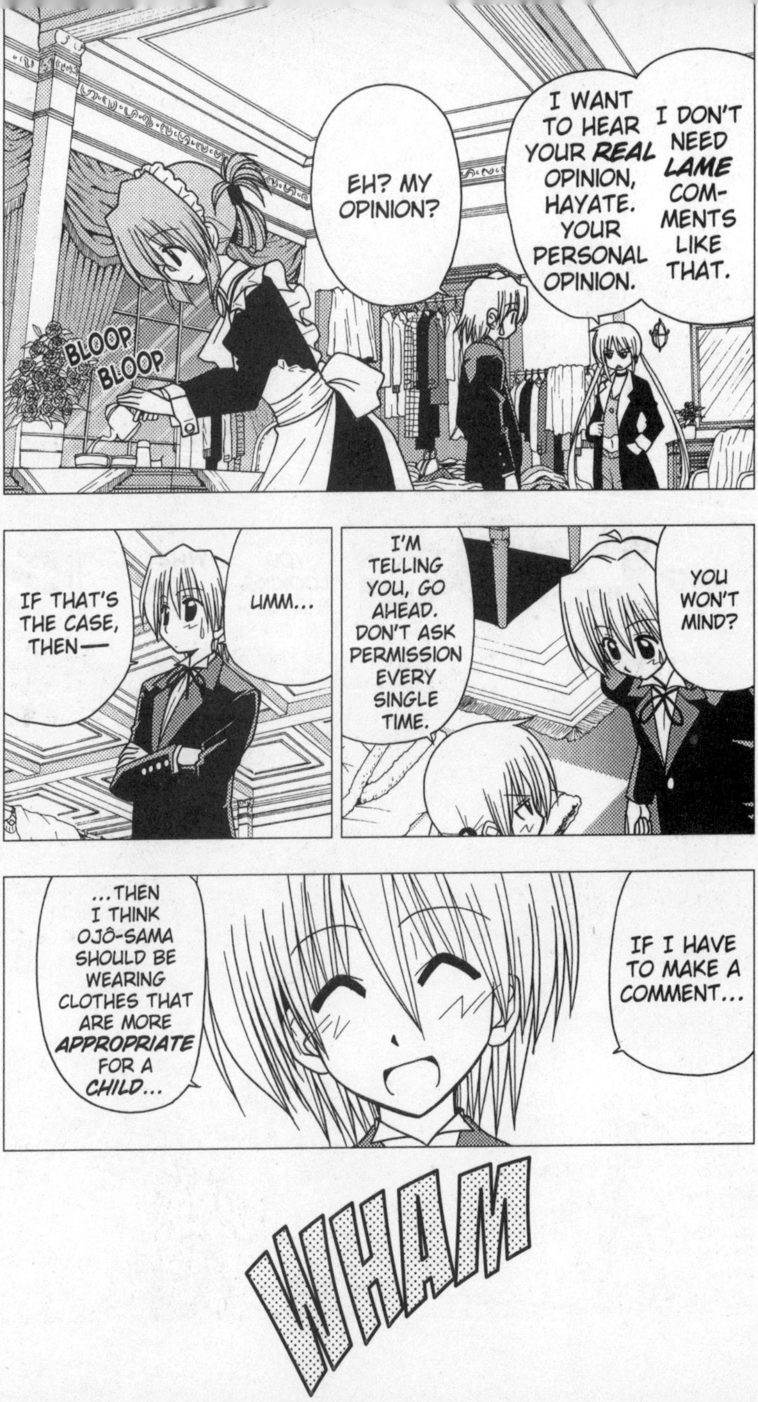
I DON'T NEED LAME COMMENTS LIKE THAT.
I WANT TO HEAR YOUR REAL OPINION, HAYATE. YOUR PERSONAL OPINION.
EH? MY OPINION?
BLOOP BLOOP
YOU WON'T MIND?
I'M TELLING YOU, GO AHEAD. DON'T ASK PERMISSION EVERY SINGLE TIME.
UMM...
IF THAT'S THE CASE, THEN—
IF I HAVE TO MAKE A COMMENT...
...THEN I THINK OJÔ-SAMA SHOULD BE WEARING CLOTHES THAT ARE MORE APPROPRIATE FOR A CHILD...
WHAM

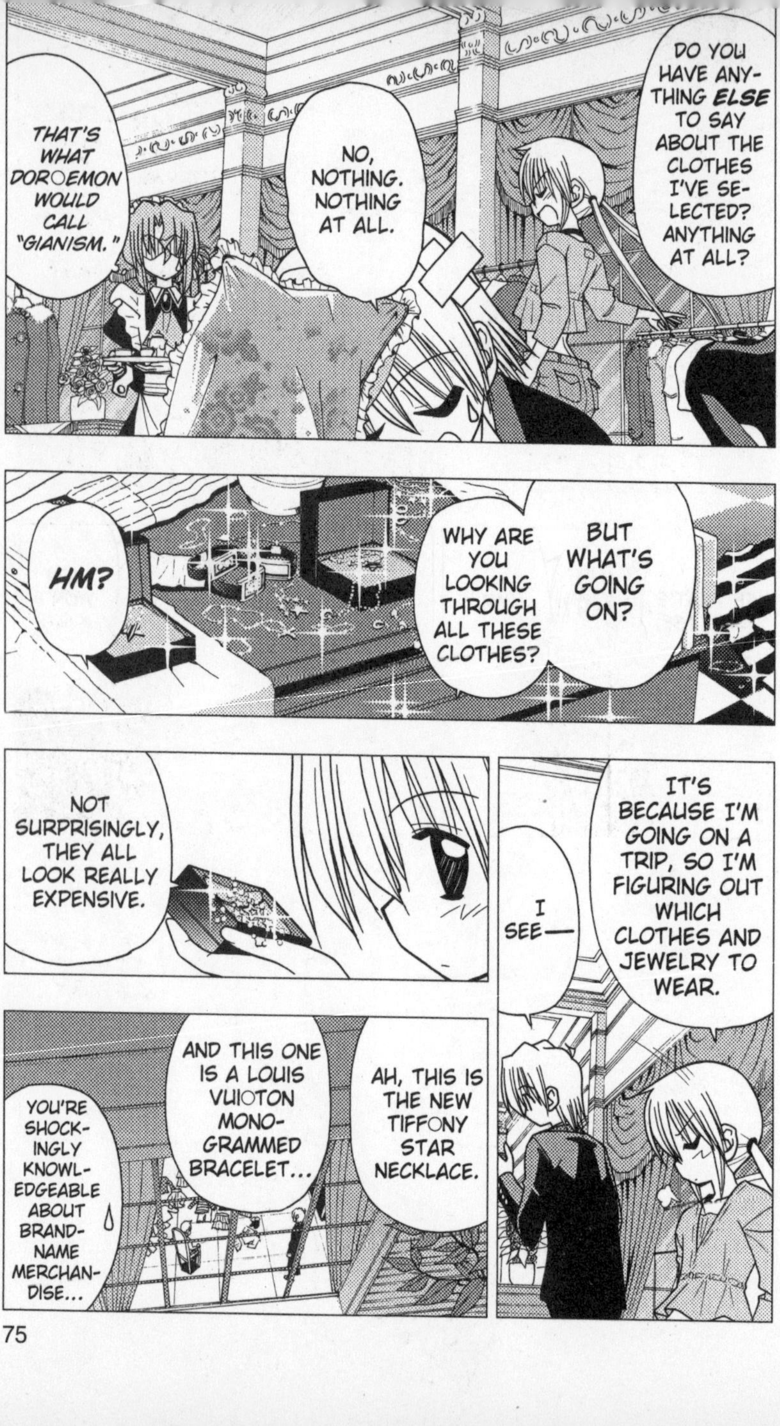
DO YOU HAVE ANYTHING ELSE TO SAY ABOUT THE CLOTHES I'VE SELECTED? ANYTHING AT ALL?
NO, NOTHING. NOTHING AT ALL.
THAT'S WHAT DOR○EMON WOULD CALL "GIANISM."
BUT WHAT'S GOING ON?
WHY ARE YOU LOOKING THROUGH ALL THESE CLOTHES?
HM?
IT'S BECAUSE I'M GOING ON A TRIP, SO I'M FIGURING OUT WHICH CLOTHES AND JEWELRY TO WEAR.
I SEE—
NOT SURPRISINGLY, THEY ALL LOOK REALLY EXPENSIVE.
AH, THIS IS THE NEW TIFF○NY STAR NECKLACE.
AND THIS ONE IS A LOUIS VUI○TON MONOGRAMMED BRACELET...
YOU'RE SHOCKINGLY KNOWLEDGEABLE ABOUT BRAND-NAME MERCHANDISE...

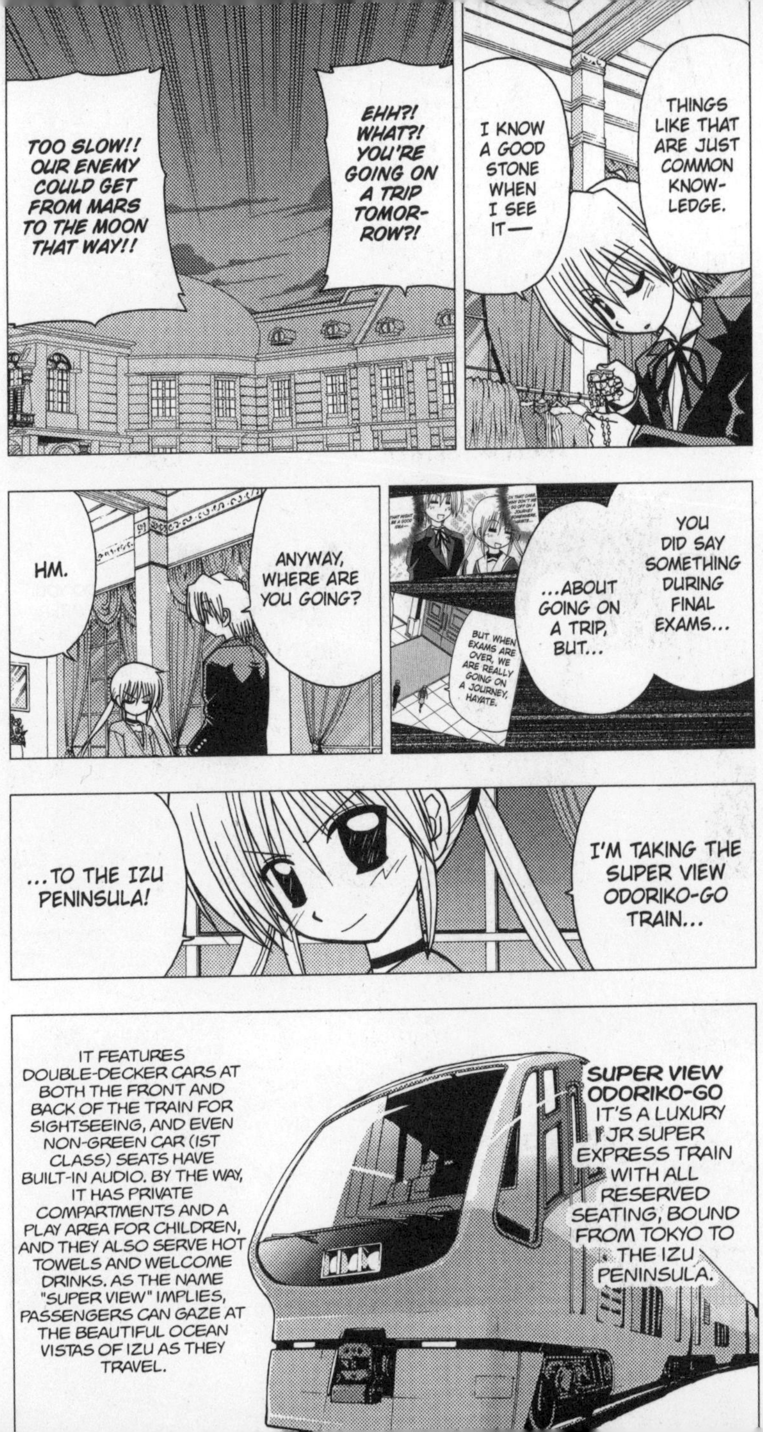
THINGS LIKE THAT ARE JUST COMMON KNOW-LEDGE.
I KNOW A GOOD STONE WHEN I SEE IT—
EHH?! WHAT?! YOU'RE GOING ON A TRIP TOMORROW?!
TOO SLOW!! OUR ENEMY COULD GET FROM MARS TO THE MOON THAT WAY!!
YOU DID SAY SOMETHING DURING FINAL EXAMS...
...ABOUT GOING ON A TRIP, BUT...
IN THAT CASE, WHY DON'T WE GO OFF ON A JOURNEY SOMEWHERE, HAYATE...
THAT MIGHT BE A GOOD IDEA—
BUT WHEN EXAMS ARE OVER, WE ARE REALLY GOING ON A JOURNEY, HAYATE.
ANYWAY, WHERE ARE YOU GOING?
HM.
I'M TAKING THE SUPER VIEW ODORIKO-GO TRAIN...
...TO THE IZU PENINSULA!
SUPER VIEW ODORIKO-GO IT'S A LUXURY JR SUPER EXPRESS TRAIN WITH ALL RESERVED SEATING, BOUND FROM TOKYO TO THE IZU PENINSULA.
IT FEATURES DOUBLE-DECKER CARS AT BOTH THE FRONT AND BACK OF THE TRAIN FOR SIGHTSEEING, AND EVEN NON-GREEN CAR (1ST CLASS) SEATS HAVE BUILT-IN AUDIO. BY THE WAY, IT HAS PRIVATE COMPARTMENTS AND A PLAY AREA FOR CHILDREN, AND THEY ALSO SERVE HOT TOWELS AND WELCOME DRINKS. AS THE NAME "SUPER VIEW" IMPLIES, PASSENGERS CAN GAZE AT THE BEAUTIFUL OCEAN VISTAS OF IZU AS THEY TRAVEL.

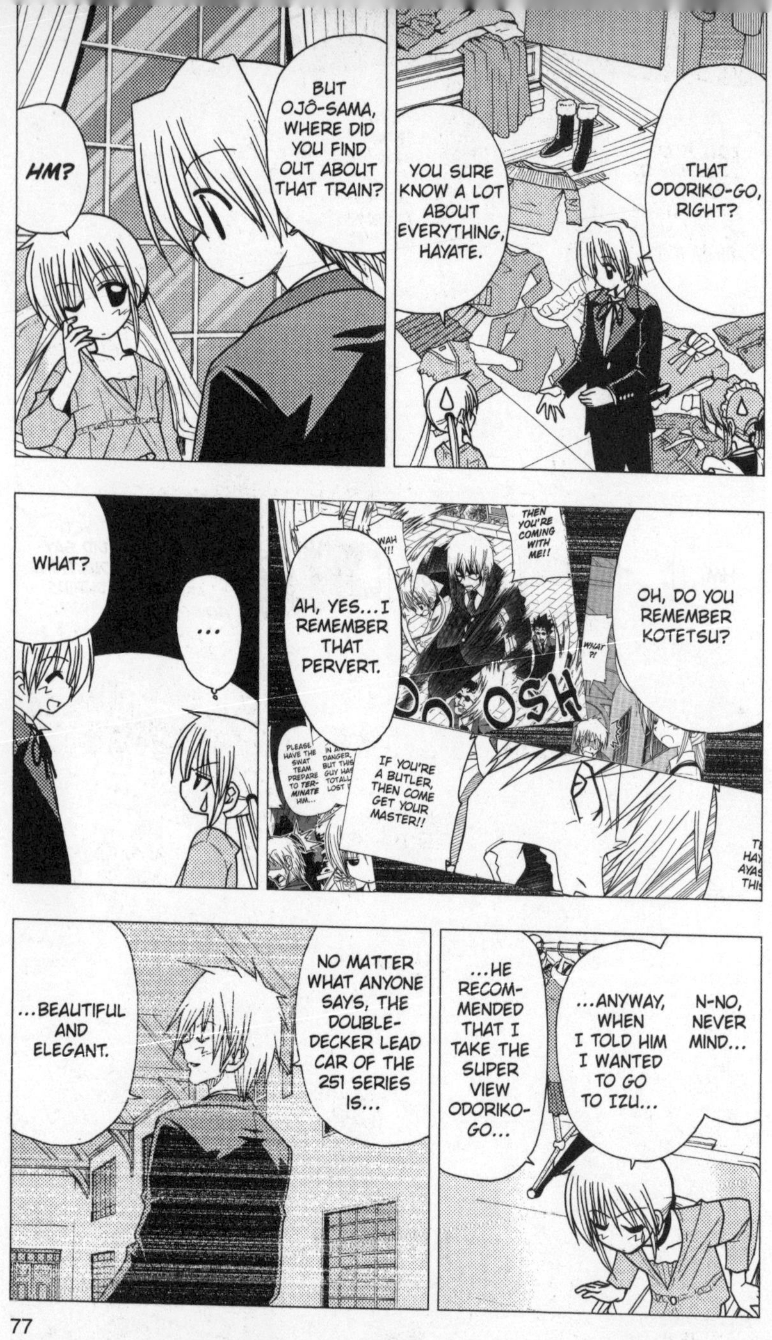
THAT ODORIKO-GO, RIGHT?
YOU SURE KNOW A LOT ABOUT EVERYTHING, HAYATE.
BUT OJÔ-SAMA, WHERE DID YOU FIND OUT ABOUT THAT TRAIN?
HM?
OH, DO YOU REMEMBER KOTETSU?
WHAT ?!
THEN YOU'RE COMING WITH ME!!
IF YOU'RE A BUTLER, THEN COME GET YOUR MASTER!!
PLEASE HAVE THE SWAT TEAM PREPARE TO TERMINATE HIM...
AH, YES...I REMEMBER THAT PERVERT.
...
WHAT?
N-NO, NEVER MIND...
...ANYWAY, WHEN I TOLD HIM I WANTED TO GO TO IZU...
...HE RECOMMENDED THAT I TAKE THE SUPER VIEW ODORIKO-GO...
NO MATTER WHAT ANYONE SAYS, THE DOUBLE-DECKER LEAD CAR OF THE 251 SERIES IS...
...BEAUTIFUL AND ELEGANT.

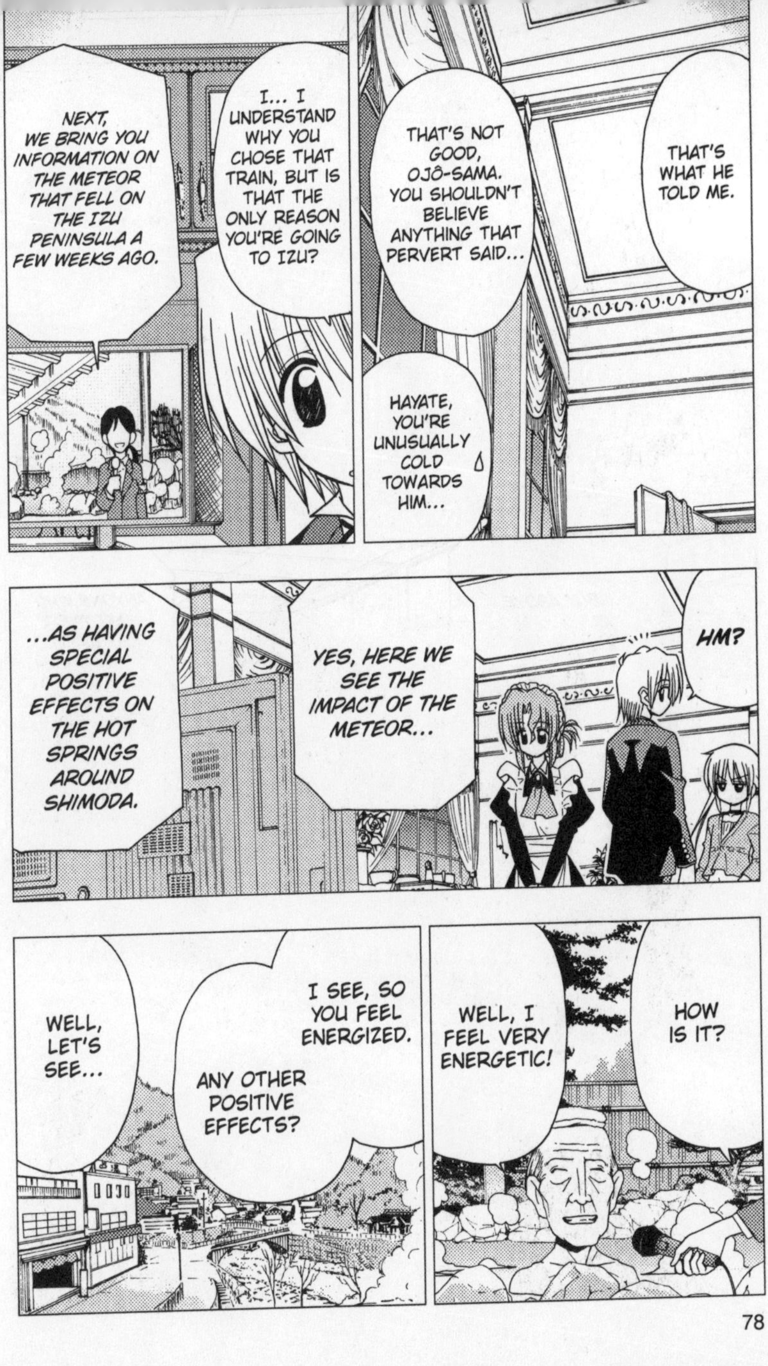
THAT'S WHAT HE TOLD ME.
THAT'S NOT GOOD, OJÔ-SAMA. YOU SHOULDN'T BELIEVE ANYTHING THAT PERVERT SAID...
HAYATE, YOU'RE UNUSUALLY COLD TOWARDS HIM...
I... I UNDERSTAND WHY YOU CHOSE THAT TRAIN, BUT IS THAT THE ONLY REASON YOU'RE GOING TO IZU?
NEXT, WE BRING YOU INFORMATION ON THE METEOR THAT FELL ON THE IZU PENINSULA A FEW WEEKS AGO.
HM?
YES, HERE WE SEE THE IMPACT OF THE METEOR...
...AS HAVING SPECIAL POSITIVE EFFECTS ON THE HOT SPRINGS AROUND SHIMODA.
HOW IS IT?
WELL, I FEEL VERY ENERGETIC!
I SEE, SO YOU FEEL ENERGIZED.
ANY OTHER POSITIVE EFFECTS?
WELL, LET'S SEE...

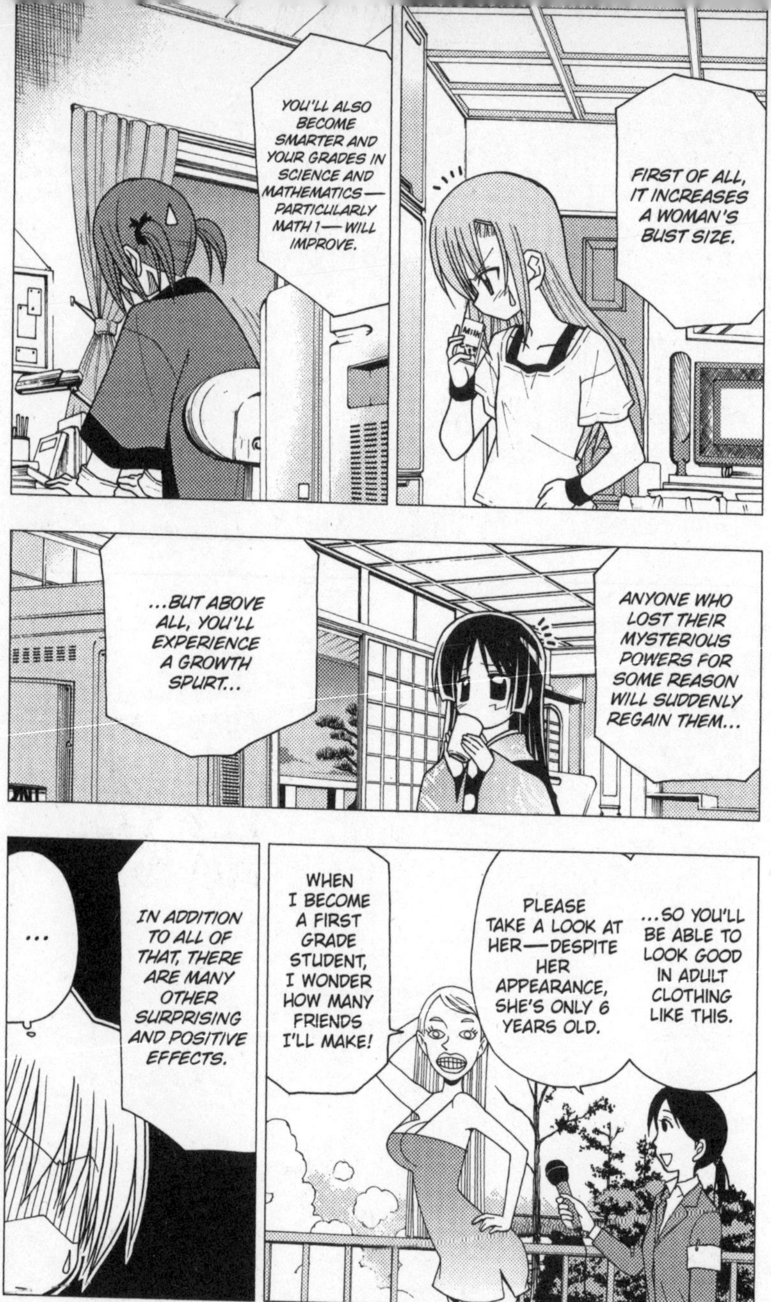
FIRST OF ALL, IT INCREASES A WOMAN'S BUST SIZE.
YOU'LL ALSO BECOME SMARTER AND YOUR GRADES IN SCIENCE AND MATHEMATICS—PARTICULARLY MATH 1—WILL IMPROVE.
ANYONE WHO LOST THEIR MYSTERIOUS POWERS FOR SOME REASON WILL SUDDENLY REGAIN THEM...
...BUT ABOVE ALL, YOU'LL EXPERIENCE A GROWTH SPURT...
...SO YOU'LL BE ABLE TO LOOK GOOD IN ADULT CLOTHING LIKE THIS.
PLEASE TAKE A LOOK AT HER—DESPITE HER APPEARANCE, SHE'S ONLY 6 YEARS OLD.
WHEN I BECOME A FIRST GRADE STUDENT, I WONDER HOW MANY FRIENDS I'LL MAKE!
IN ADDITION TO ALL OF THAT, THERE ARE MANY OTHER SURPRISING AND POSITIVE EFFECTS.
...

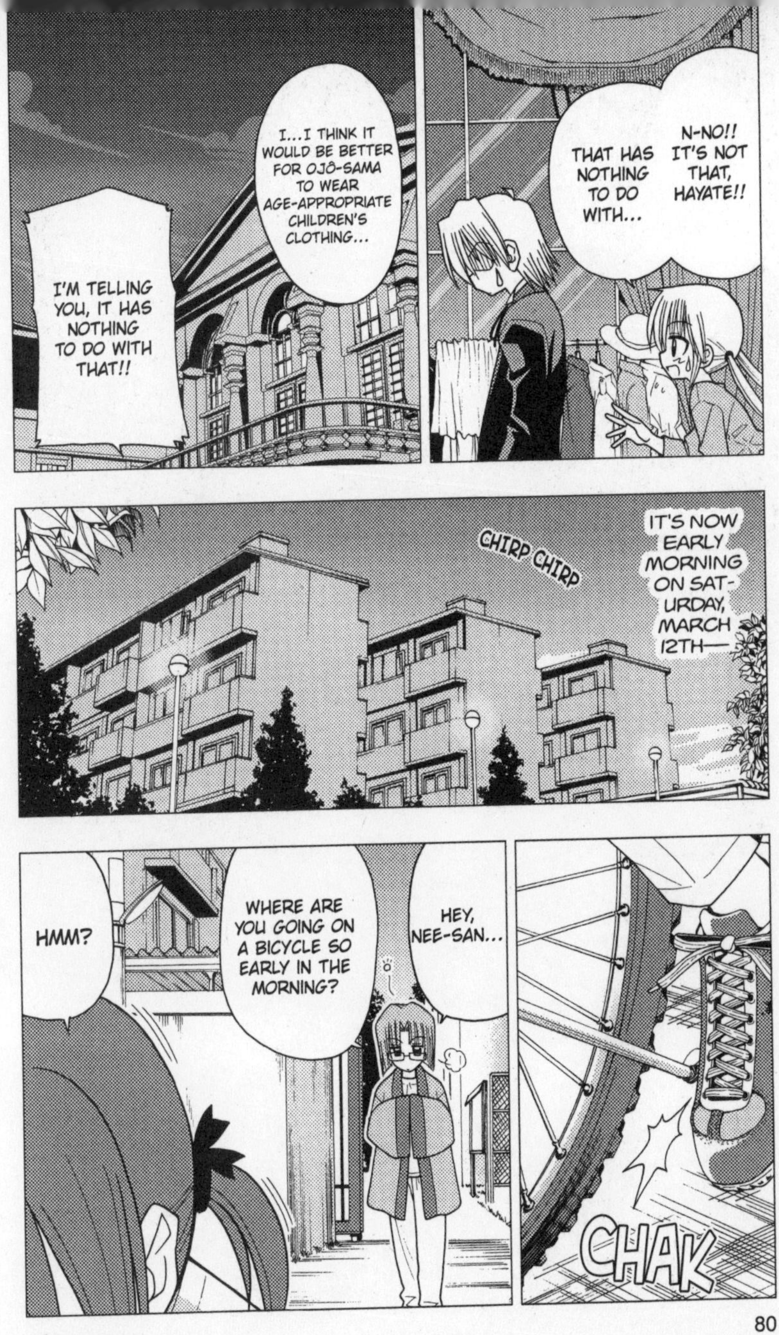
N-NO!! IT'S NOT THAT, HAYATE!!
THAT HAS NOTHING TO DO WITH...
I...I THINK IT WOULD BE BETTER FOR OJŌ-SAMA TO WEAR AGE-APPROPRIATE CHILDREN'S CLOTHING...
I'M TELLING YOU, IT HAS NOTHING TO DO WITH THAT!!
IT'S NOW EARLY MORNING ON SAT-URDAY, MARCH 12TH—
CHIRP CHIRP
CHAK
HEY, NEE-SAN...
WHERE ARE YOU GOING ON A BICYCLE SO EARLY IN THE MORNING?
HMM?

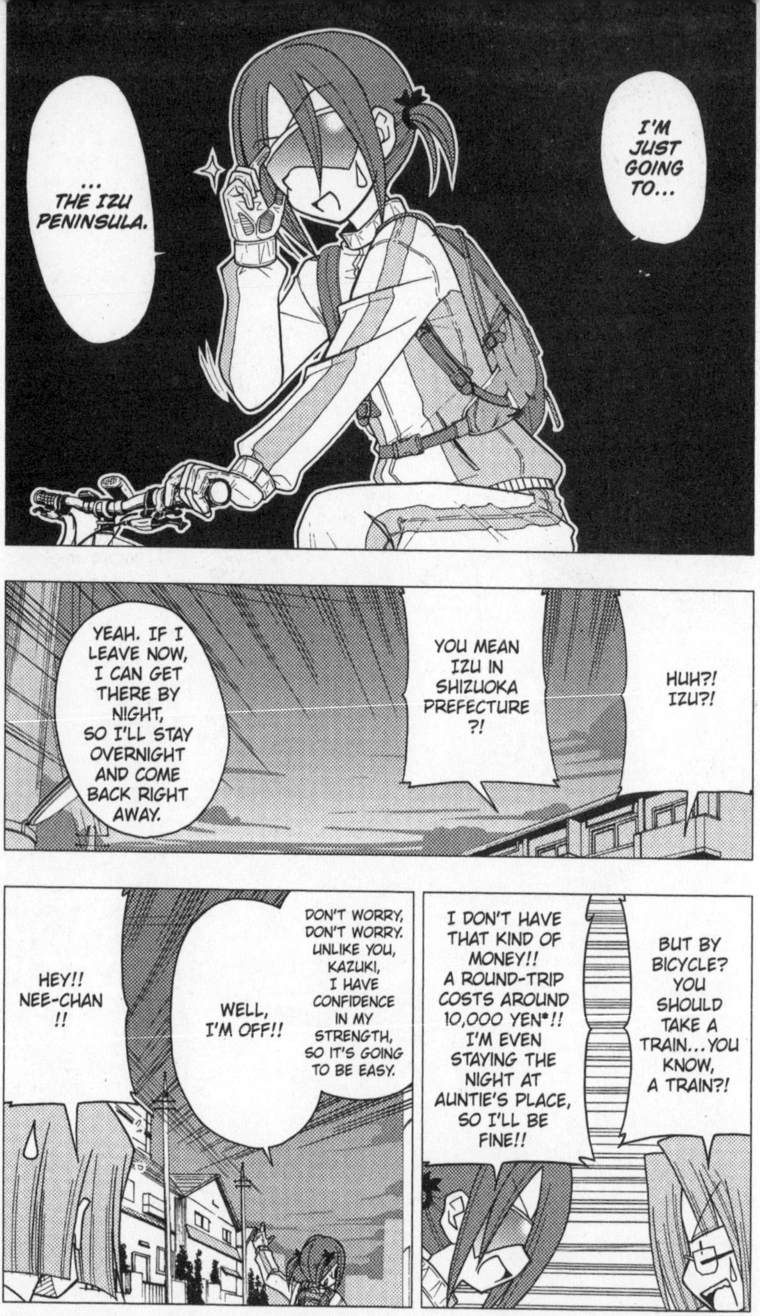
I'M JUST GOING TO...
... THE IZU PENINSULA.
HUH?! IZU?!
YOU MEAN IZU IN SHIZUOKA PREFECTURE ?!
YEAH. IF I LEAVE NOW, I CAN GET THERE BY NIGHT, SO I'LL STAY OVERNIGHT AND COME BACK RIGHT AWAY.
BUT BY BICYCLE? YOU SHOULD TAKE A TRAIN... YOU KNOW, A TRAIN?!
I DON'T HAVE THAT KIND OF MONEY!! A ROUND-TRIP COSTS AROUND 10,000 YEN*!! I'M EVEN STAYING THE NIGHT AT AUNTIE'S PLACE, SO I'LL BE FINE!!
DON'T WORRY, DON'T WORRY. UNLIKE YOU, KAZUKI, I HAVE CONFIDENCE IN MY STRENGTH, SO IT'S GOING TO BE EASY.
WELL, I'M OFF!!
HEY!! NEE-CHAN !!

*About $93

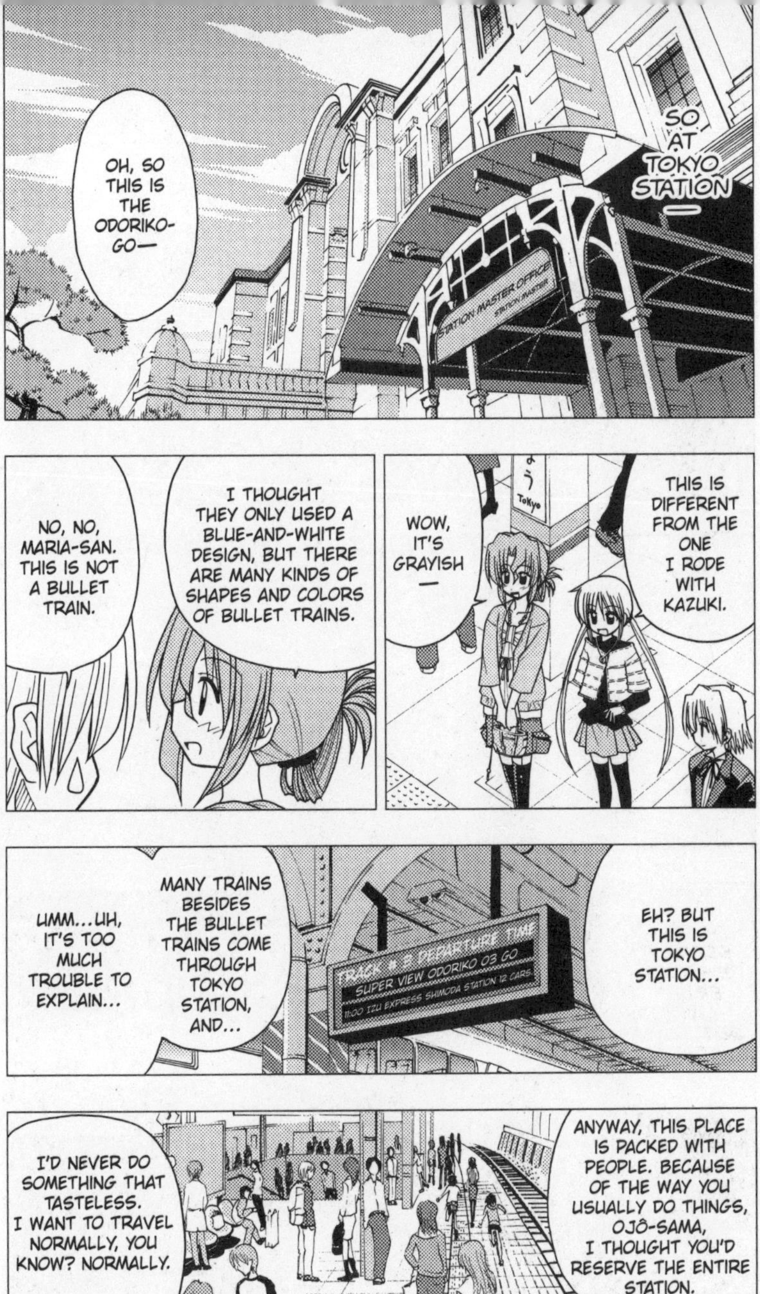
SO AT TOKYO STATION—
STATION MASTER OFFICE
STATION MASTER
OH, SO THIS IS THE ODORIKO-GO—
THIS IS DIFFERENT FROM THE ONE I RODE WITH KAZUKI.
Tokyo
WOW, IT'S GRAYISH—
I THOUGHT THEY ONLY USED A BLUE-AND-WHITE DESIGN, BUT THERE ARE MANY KINDS OF SHAPES AND COLORS OF BULLET TRAINS.
NO, NO, MARIA-SAN. THIS IS NOT A BULLET TRAIN.
EH? BUT THIS IS TOKYO STATION...
TRACK # 3 DEPARTURE TIME
SUPER VIEW ODORIKO 03 GO
11:00 IZU EXPRESS SHIMODA STATION 12 CARS
MANY TRAINS BESIDES THE BULLET TRAINS COME THROUGH TOKYO STATION, AND...
UMM...UH, IT'S TOO MUCH TROUBLE TO EXPLAIN...
ANYWAY, THIS PLACE IS PACKED WITH PEOPLE. BECAUSE OF THE WAY YOU USUALLY DO THINGS, OJÔ-SAMA, I THOUGHT YOU'D RESERVE THE ENTIRE STATION.
I'D NEVER DO SOMETHING THAT TASTELESS. I WANT TO TRAVEL NORMALLY, YOU KNOW? NORMALLY.

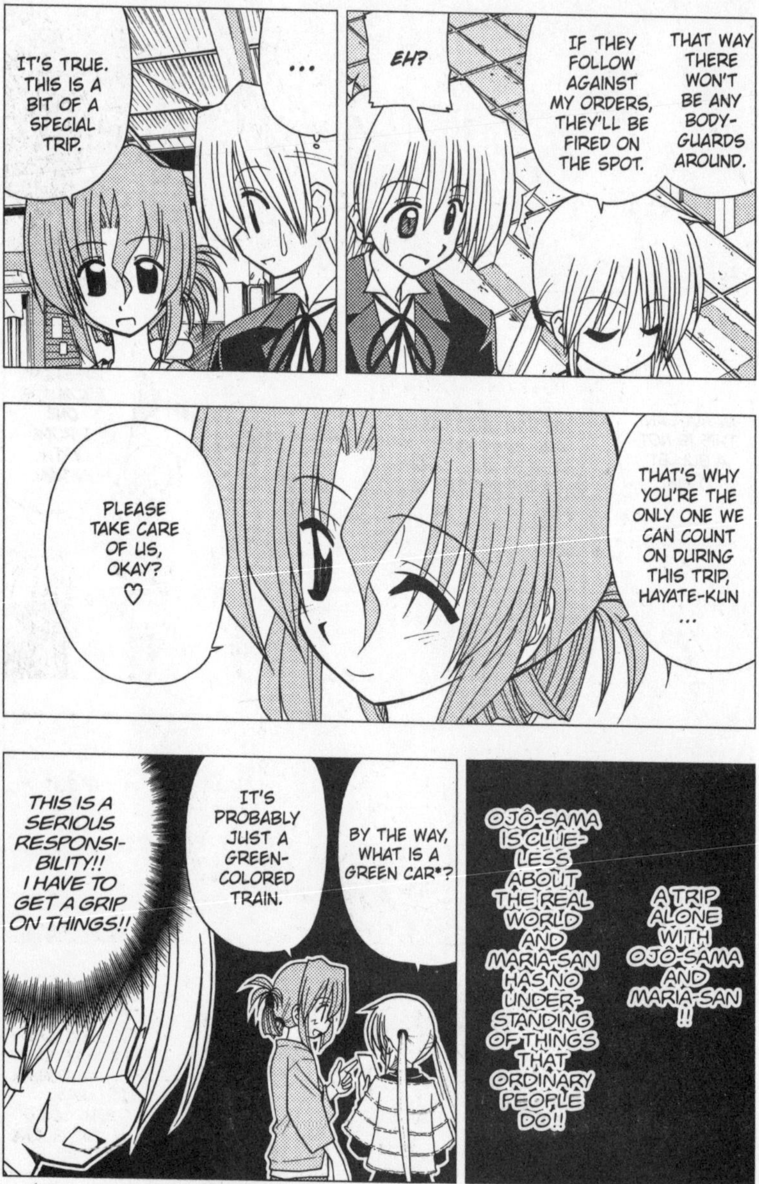
THAT WAY THERE WON'T BE ANY BODY-GUARDS AROUND.
IF THEY FOLLOW AGAINST MY ORDERS, THEY'LL BE FIRED ON THE SPOT.
EH?
...
IT'S TRUE. THIS IS A BIT OF A SPECIAL TRIP.
THAT'S WHY YOU'RE THE ONLY ONE WE CAN COUNT ON DURING THIS TRIP, HAYATE-KUN ...
PLEASE TAKE CARE OF US, OKAY? ♡
A TRIP ALONE WITH OJÔ-SAMA AND MARIA-SAN !!
OJÔ-SAMA IS CLUE-LESS ABOUT THE REAL WORLD AND MARIA-SAN HAS NO UNDER-STANDING OF THINGS THAT ORDINARY PEOPLE DO!!
BY THE WAY, WHAT IS A GREEN CAR*?
IT'S PROBABLY JUST A GREEN-COLORED TRAIN.
THIS IS A SERIOUS RESPONSI-BILITY!! I HAVE TO GET A GRIP ON THINGS!!

* First-Class car marked with a green clover near the door.

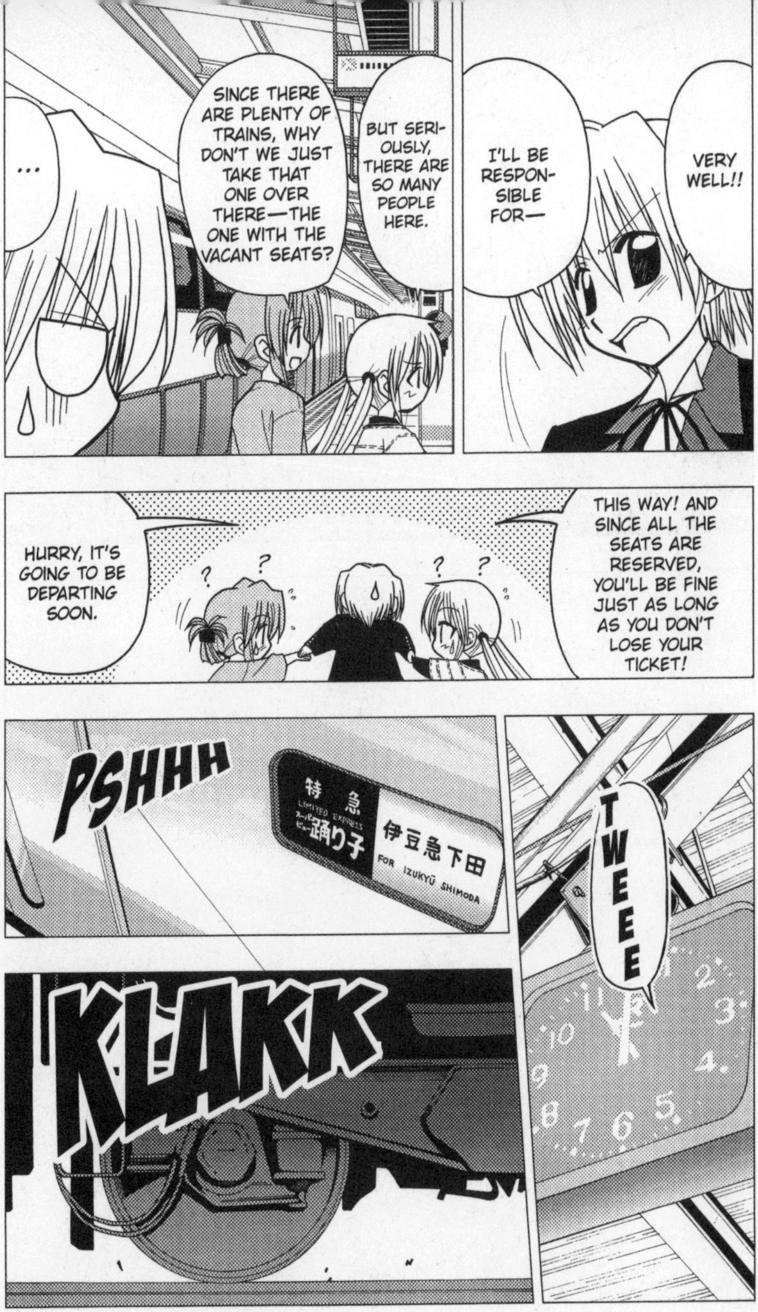
VERY WELL!!
I'LL BE RESPON-SIBLE FOR—
BUT SERI-OUSLY, THERE ARE SO MANY PEOPLE HERE.
SINCE THERE ARE PLENTY OF TRAINS, WHY DON'T WE JUST TAKE THAT ONE OVER THERE—THE ONE WITH THE VACANT SEATS?
...
THIS WAY! AND SINCE ALL THE SEATS ARE RESERVED, YOU'LL BE FINE JUST AS LONG AS YOU DON'T LOSE YOUR TICKET!
HURRY, IT'S GOING TO BE DEPARTING SOON.
? ? ? ?
TWEEE
PSHHH
特急
LIMITED EXPRESS
スーパービュー踊り子
伊豆急下田
FOR IZUKYŪ SHIMODA
KLAKK

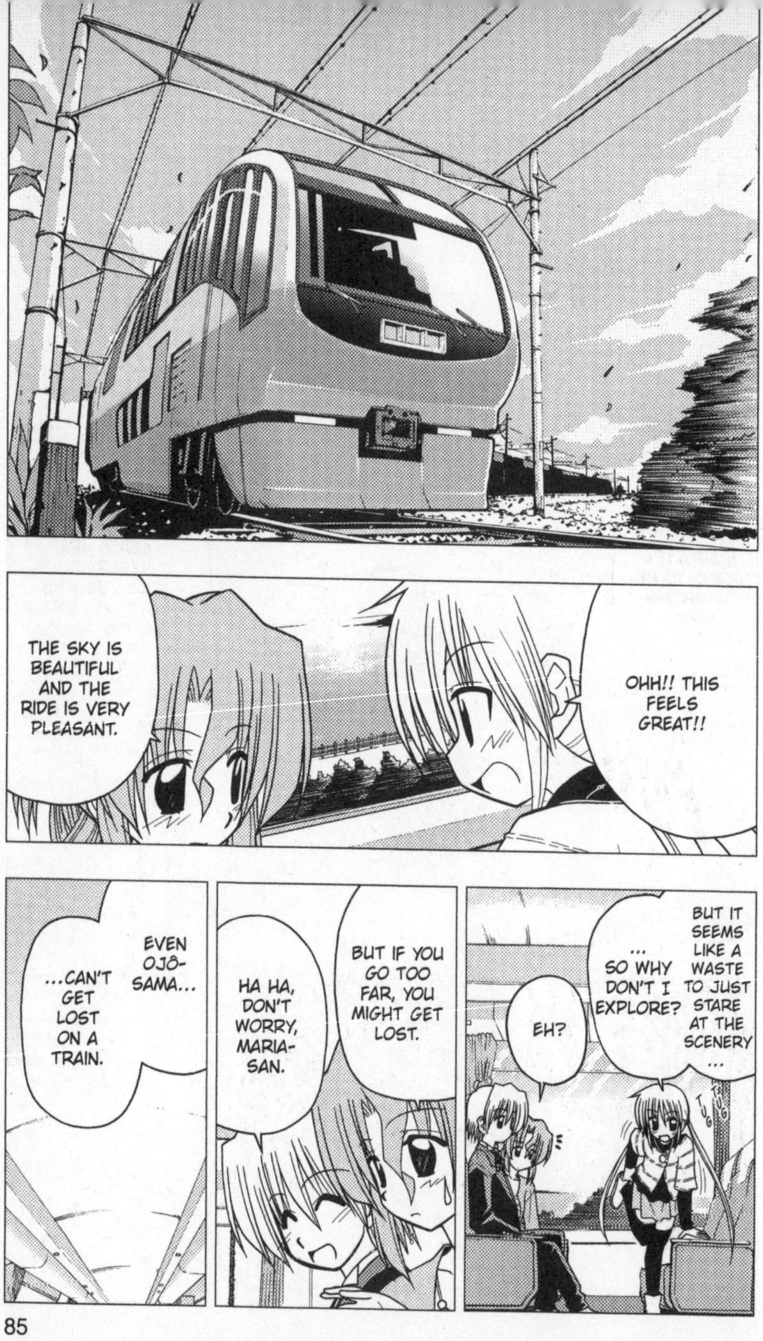
OHH!! THIS FEELS GREAT!!
THE SKY IS BEAUTIFUL AND THE RIDE IS VERY PLEASANT.
BUT IT SEEMS LIKE A WASTE TO JUST STARE AT THE SCENERY...
...SO WHY DON'T I EXPLORE?
EH?
TUG TUG
BUT IF YOU GO TOO FAR, YOU MIGHT GET LOST.
HA HA, DON'T WORRY, MARIA-SAN.
EVEN OJÔ-SAMA...
...CAN'T GET LOST ON A TRAIN.

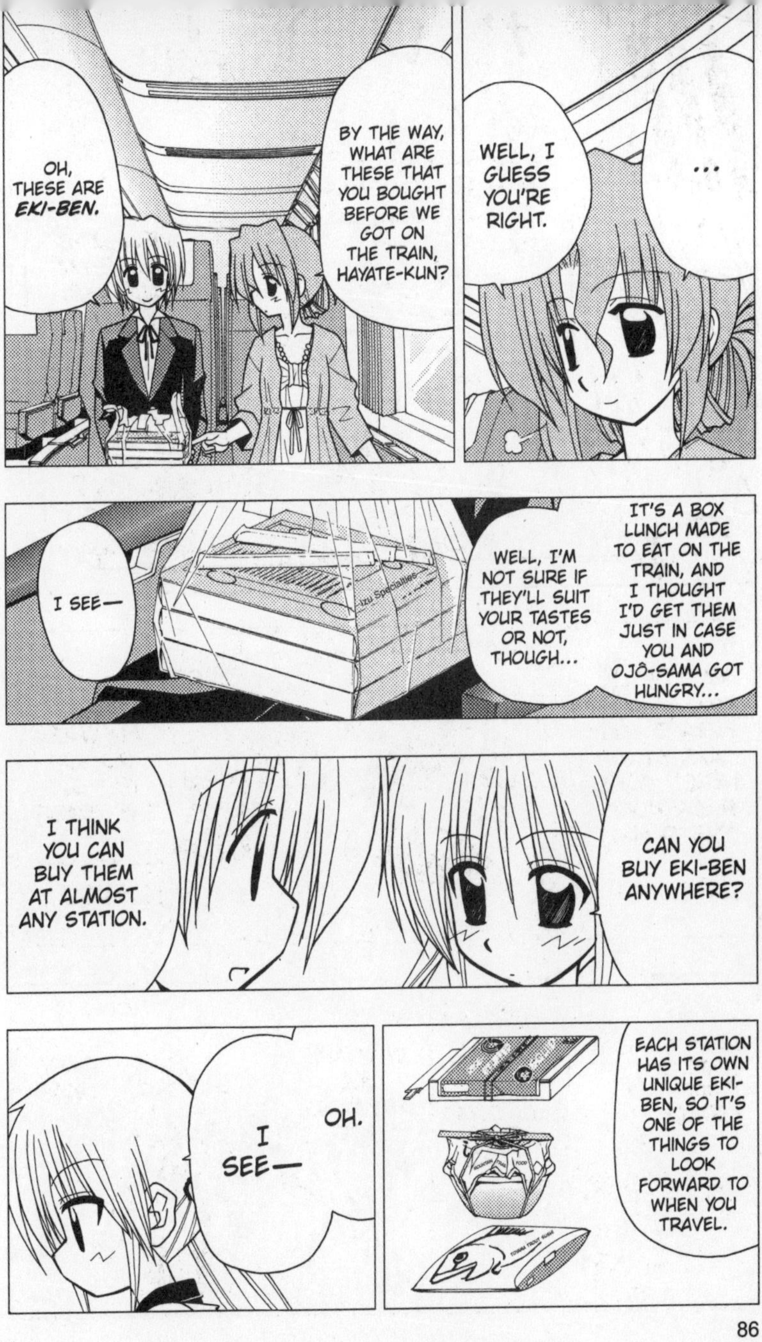
...
WELL, I GUESS YOU'RE RIGHT.
BY THE WAY, WHAT ARE THESE THAT YOU BOUGHT BEFORE WE GOT ON THE TRAIN, HAYATE-KUN?
OH, THESE ARE *EKI-BEN.*
IT'S A BOX LUNCH MADE TO EAT ON THE TRAIN, AND I THOUGHT I'D GET THEM JUST IN CASE YOU AND OJÔ-SAMA GOT HUNGRY...
WELL, I'M NOT SURE IF THEY'LL SUIT YOUR TASTES OR NOT, THOUGH...
Izu Specialties
I SEE—
CAN YOU BUY EKI-BEN ANYWHERE?
I THINK YOU CAN BUY THEM AT ALMOST ANY STATION.
EACH STATION HAS ITS OWN UNIQUE EKI-BEN, SO IT'S ONE OF THE THINGS TO LOOK FORWARD TO WHEN YOU TRAVEL.
OH.
I SEE—

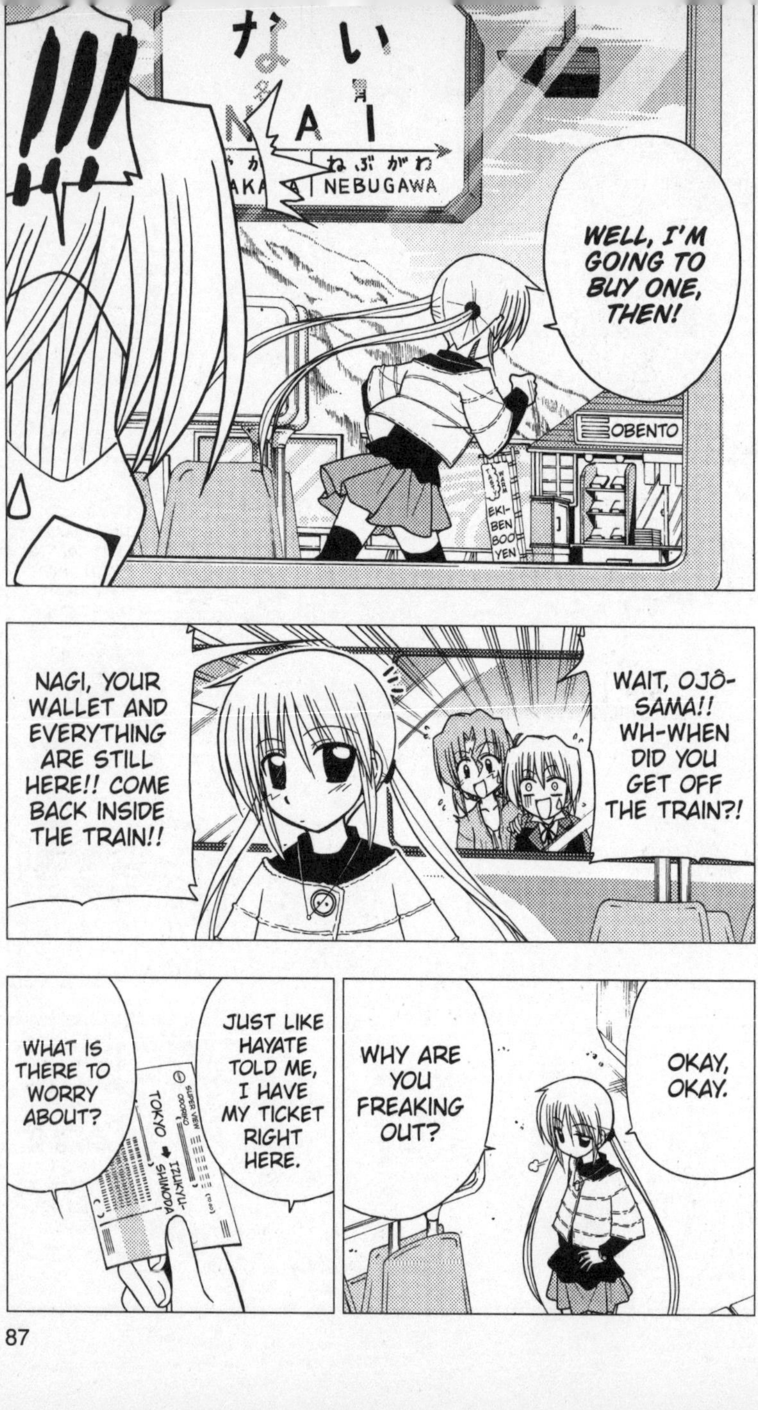

ない
NAI
ねぶがわ
NEBUGAWA
!!!
WELL, I'M GOING TO BUY ONE, THEN!
OBENTO
EKI-BEN 800 YEN
WAIT, OJÔ-SAMA!! WH-WHEN DID YOU GET OFF THE TRAIN?!
NAGI, YOUR WALLET AND EVERYTHING ARE STILL HERE!! COME BACK INSIDE THE TRAIN!!
OKAY, OKAY.
WHY ARE YOU FREAKING OUT?
JUST LIKE HAYATE TOLD ME, I HAVE MY TICKET RIGHT HERE.
WHAT IS THERE TO WORRY ABOUT?
SUPER VIEW ODORIKO
TOKYO ➡ IZUKYU-SHIMODA

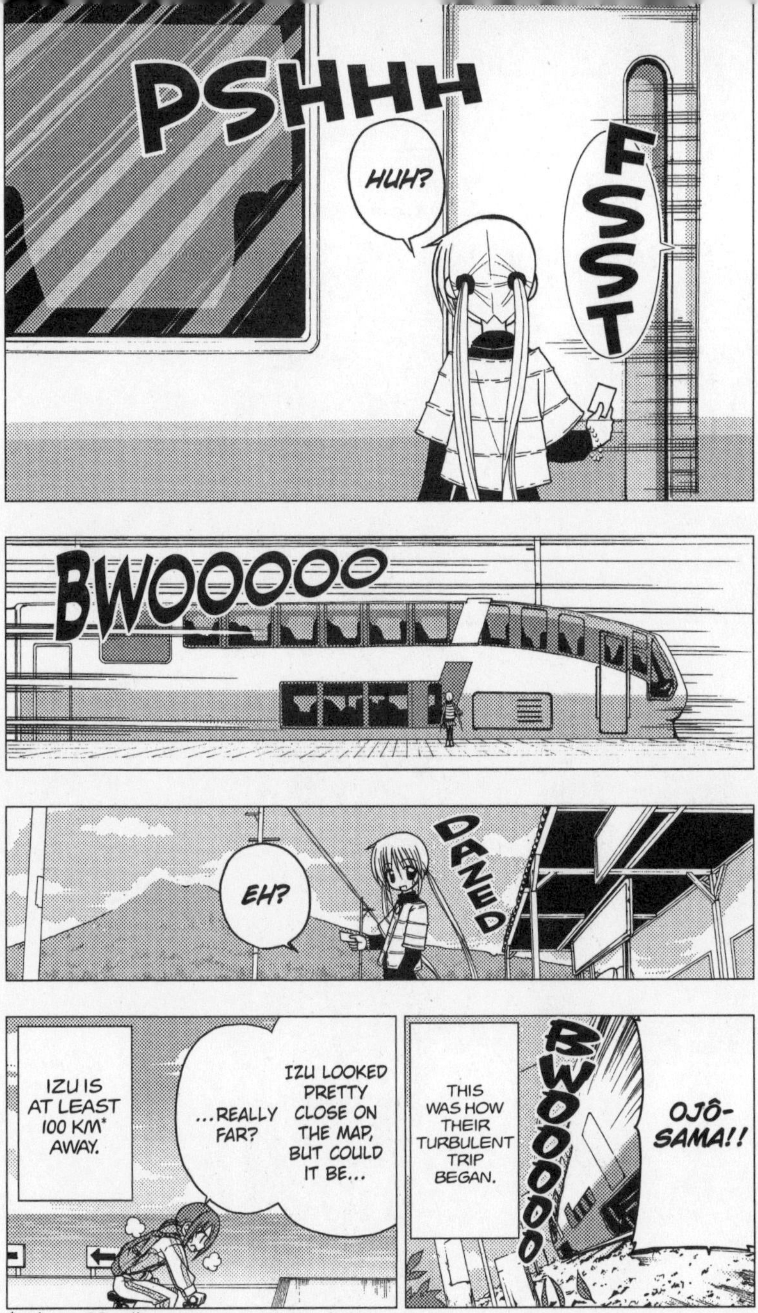
PSHHH
FSST
HUH?
BWOOOOO
DAZED
EH?
OJÔ-SAMA!!
BWOOOOOO
THIS WAS HOW THEIR TURBULENT TRIP BEGAN.
IZU LOOKED PRETTY CLOSE ON THE MAP, BUT COULD IT BE...
...REALLY FAR?
IZU IS AT LEAST 100 KM* AWAY.

* About 62 miles

Episode 6:

"When in Doubt, Just Paint It Red"

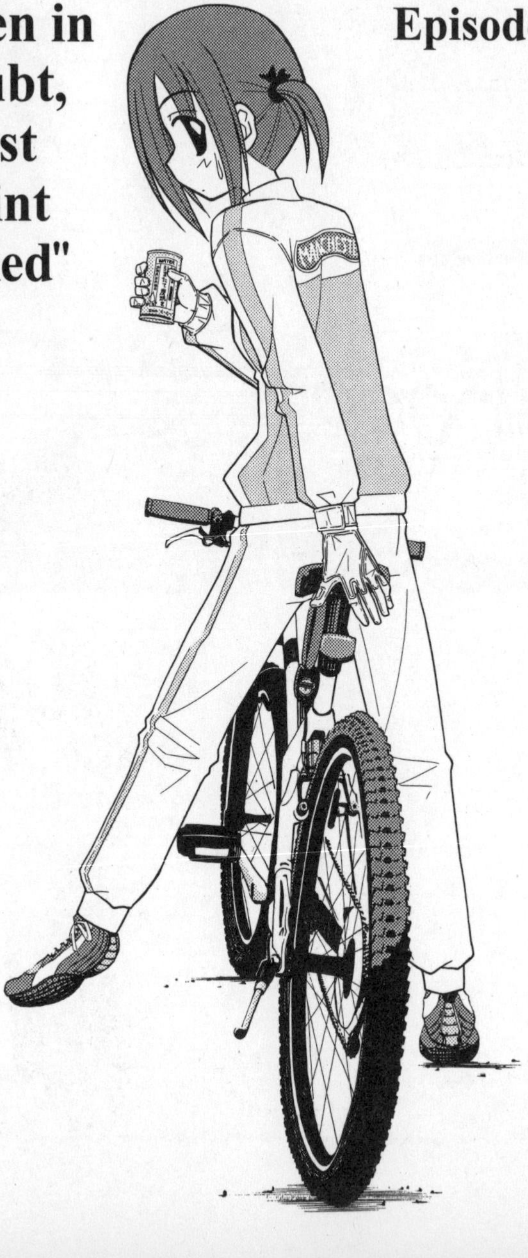

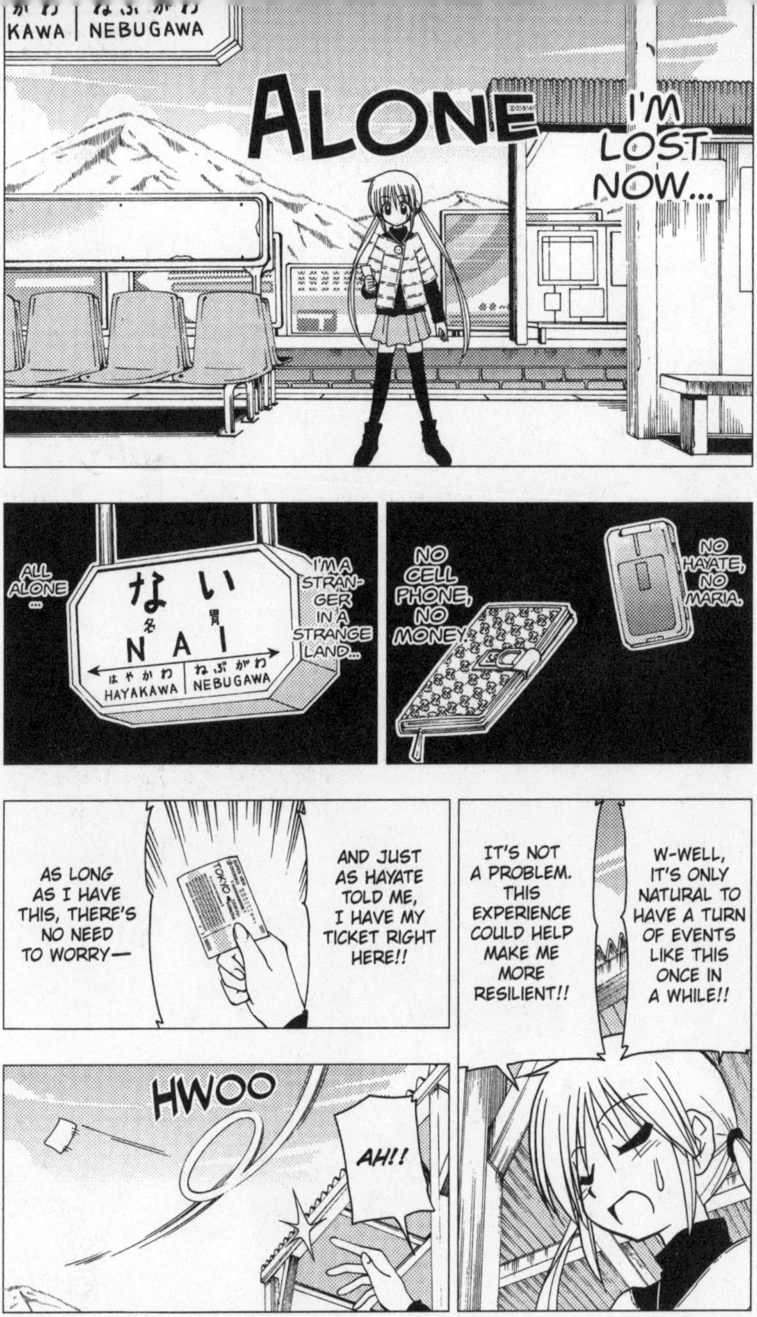

かわ KAWA | ねぶがわ NEBUGAWA
ALONE
I'M LOST NOW...
NO HAYATE, NO MARIA.
NO CELL PHONE, NO MONEY.
I'M A STRANGER IN A STRANGE LAND...
ない
名 胃
NAI
はやかわ HAYAKAWA
ねぶがわ NEBUGAWA
ALL ALONE...
W-WELL, IT'S ONLY NATURAL TO HAVE A TURN OF EVENTS LIKE THIS ONCE IN A WHILE!!
IT'S NOT A PROBLEM. THIS EXPERIENCE COULD HELP MAKE ME MORE RESILIENT!!
AND JUST AS HAYATE TOLD ME, I HAVE MY TICKET RIGHT HERE!!
TOKYO
AS LONG AS I HAVE THIS, THERE'S NO NEED TO WORRY—
AH!!
HWOO

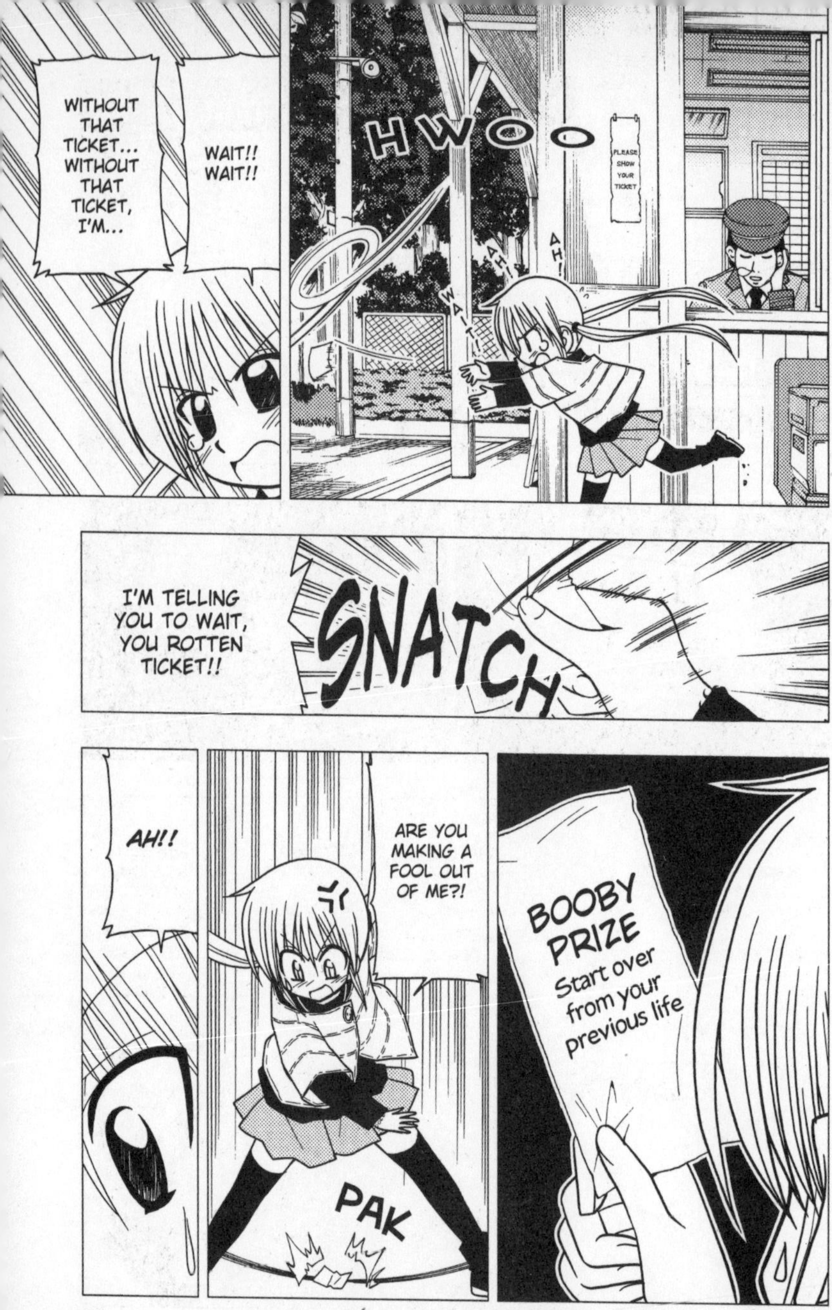
HWOO
PLEASE SHOW YOUR TICKET
AH! AH!
WAIT!!
WAIT!! WAIT!!
WITHOUT THAT TICKET... WITHOUT THAT TICKET, I'M...
I'M TELLING YOU TO WAIT, YOU ROTTEN TICKET!!
SNATCH
BOOBY PRIZE
Start over from your previous life
ARE YOU MAKING A FOOL OUT OF ME?!
PAK
AH!!

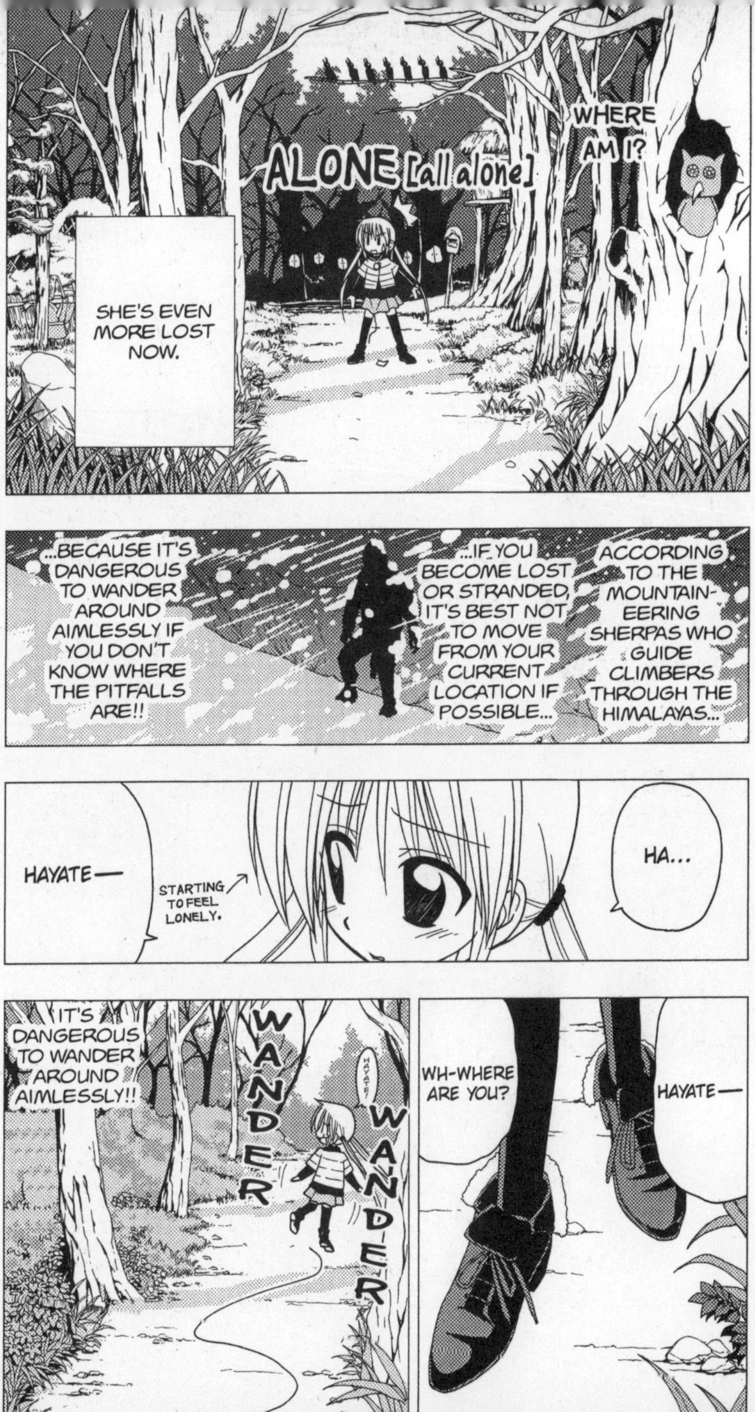
WHERE AM I?
ALONE [all alone]
SHE'S EVEN MORE LOST NOW.
ACCORDING TO THE MOUNTAIN-EERING SHERPAS WHO GUIDE CLIMBERS THROUGH THE HIMALAYAS...
...IF YOU BECOME LOST OR STRANDED, IT'S BEST NOT TO MOVE FROM YOUR CURRENT LOCATION IF POSSIBLE...
...BECAUSE IT'S DANGEROUS TO WANDER AROUND AIMLESSLY IF YOU DON'T KNOW WHERE THE PITFALLS ARE!!
HA...
STARTING TO FEEL LONELY.
HAYATE—
HAYATE—
WH-WHERE ARE YOU?
WANDER
HAYATE!
WANDER
IT'S DANGEROUS TO WANDER AROUND AIMLESSLY!!

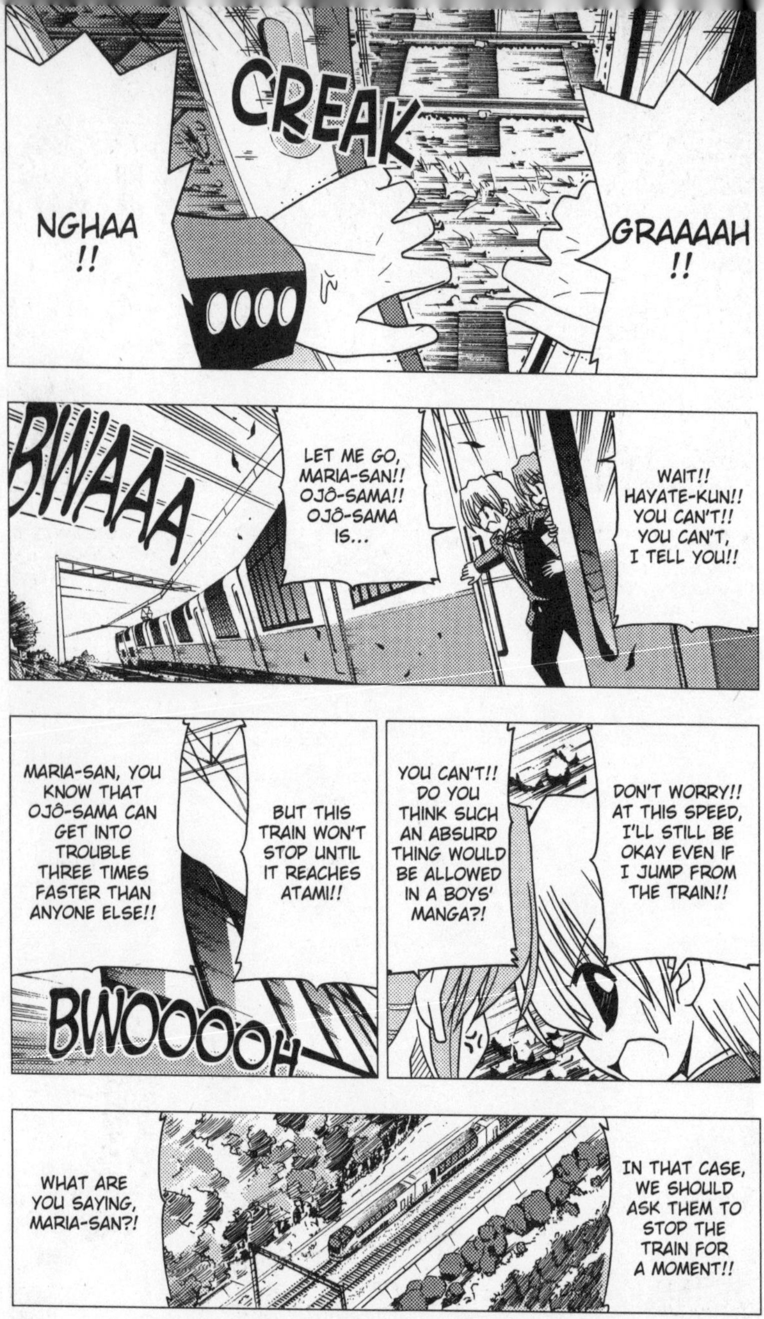
CREAK
GRAAAAH!!
NGHAA!!
WAIT!! HAYATE-KUN!! YOU CAN'T!! YOU CAN'T, I TELL YOU!!
LET ME GO, MARIA-SAN!! OJÔ-SAMA!! OJÔ-SAMA IS...
BWAAAA
DON'T WORRY!! AT THIS SPEED, I'LL STILL BE OKAY EVEN IF I JUMP FROM THE TRAIN!!
YOU CAN'T!! DO YOU THINK SUCH AN ABSURD THING WOULD BE ALLOWED IN A BOYS' MANGA?!
BUT THIS TRAIN WON'T STOP UNTIL IT REACHES ATAMI!!
MARIA-SAN, YOU KNOW THAT OJÔ-SAMA CAN GET INTO TROUBLE THREE TIMES FASTER THAN ANYONE ELSE!!
BWOOOOOH
IN THAT CASE, WE SHOULD ASK THEM TO STOP THE TRAIN FOR A MOMENT!!
WHAT ARE YOU SAYING, MARIA-SAN?!

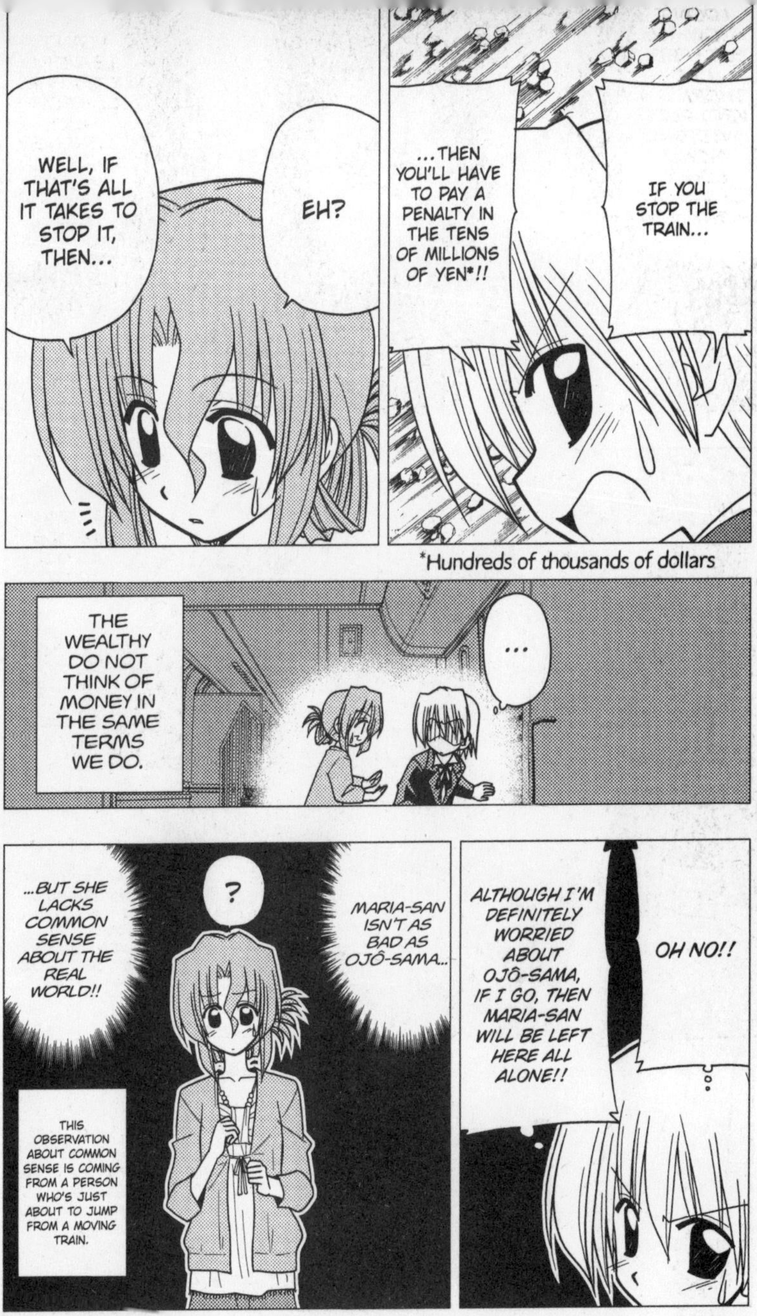
IF YOU STOP THE TRAIN...
...THEN YOU'LL HAVE TO PAY A PENALTY IN THE TENS OF MILLIONS OF YEN*!!
EH?
WELL, IF THAT'S ALL IT TAKES TO STOP IT, THEN...
...
THE WEALTHY DO NOT THINK OF MONEY IN THE SAME TERMS WE DO.
OH NO!!
ALTHOUGH I'M DEFINITELY WORRIED ABOUT OJÔ-SAMA, IF I GO, THEN MARIA-SAN WILL BE LEFT HERE ALL ALONE!!
MARIA-SAN ISN'T AS BAD AS OJÔ-SAMA...
?
...BUT SHE LACKS COMMON SENSE ABOUT THE REAL WORLD!!
THIS OBSERVATION ABOUT COMMON SENSE IS COMING FROM A PERSON WHO'S JUST ABOUT TO JUMP FROM A MOVING TRAIN.
*Hundreds of thousands of dollars

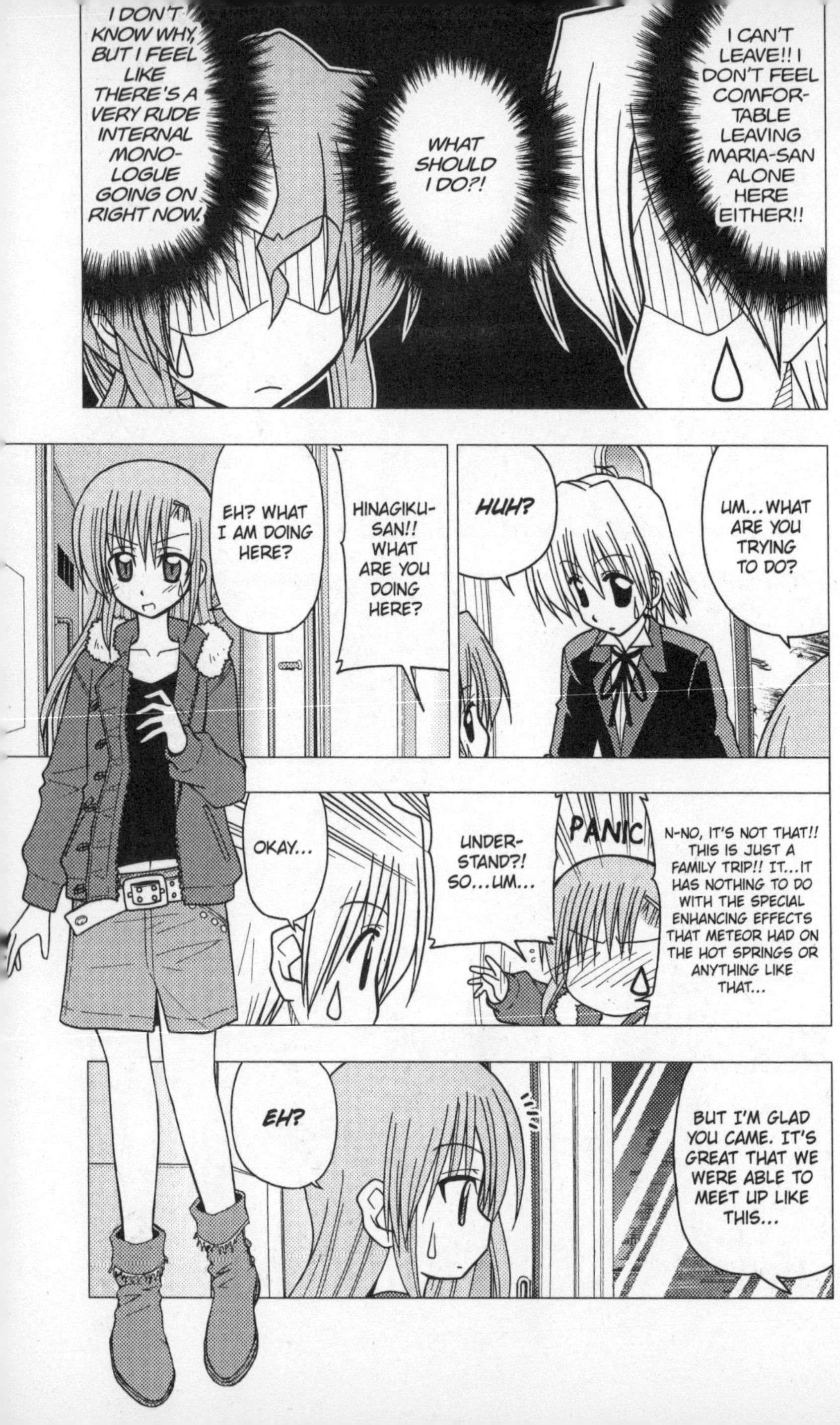
I CAN'T LEAVE!! I DON'T FEEL COMFORTABLE LEAVING MARIA-SAN ALONE HERE EITHER!!
WHAT SHOULD I DO?!
I DON'T KNOW WHY, BUT I FEEL LIKE THERE'S A VERY RUDE INTERNAL MONOLOGUE GOING ON RIGHT NOW.
UM...WHAT ARE YOU TRYING TO DO?
HUH?
HINAGIKU-SAN!! WHAT ARE YOU DOING HERE?
EH? WHAT I AM DOING HERE?
PANIC
N-NO, IT'S NOT THAT!! THIS IS JUST A FAMILY TRIP!! IT...IT HAS NOTHING TO DO WITH THE SPECIAL ENHANCING EFFECTS THAT METEOR HAD ON THE HOT SPRINGS OR ANYTHING LIKE THAT...
UNDERSTAND?! SO...UM...
OKAY...
BUT I'M GLAD YOU CAME. IT'S GREAT THAT WE WERE ABLE TO MEET UP LIKE THIS...
EH?

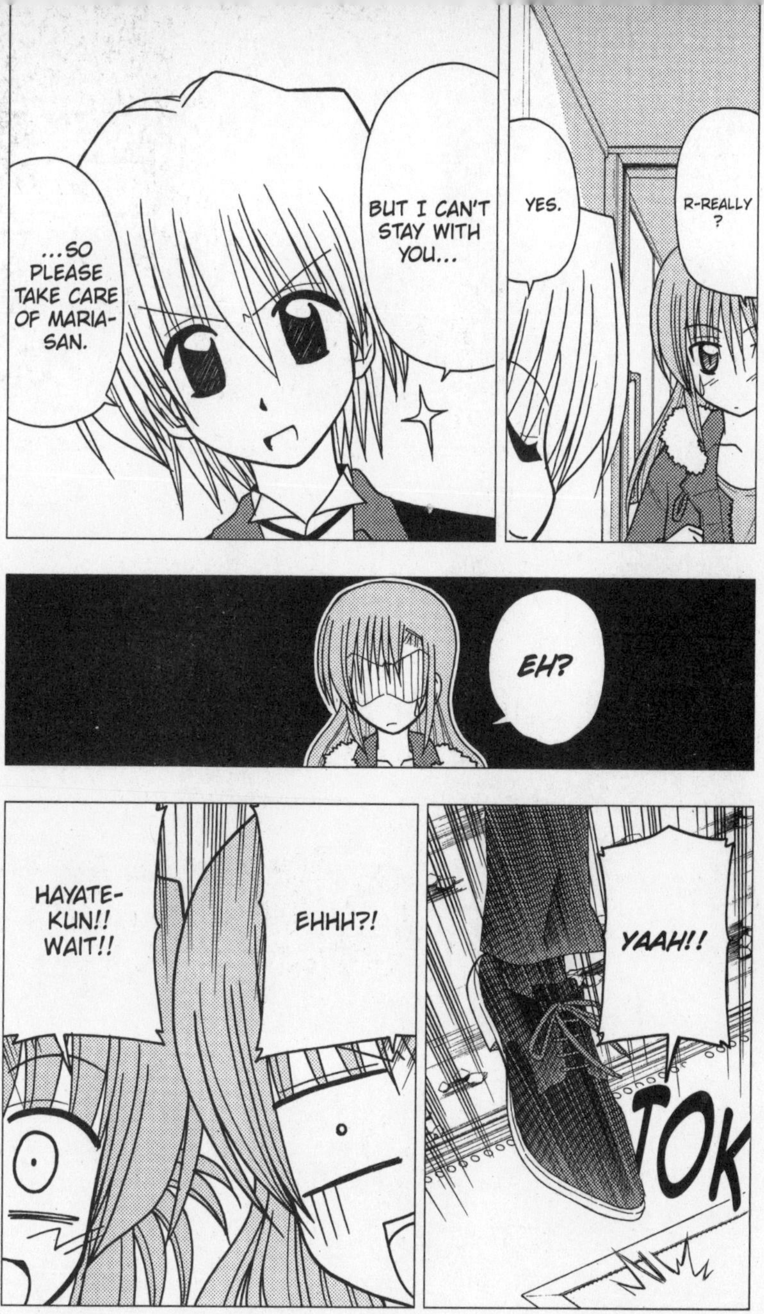
R-REALLY ?
YES.
BUT I CAN'T STAY WITH YOU...
...SO PLEASE TAKE CARE OF MARIA-SAN.
EH?
YAAH!!
TOK
EHHH?!
HAYATE-KUN!! WAIT!!

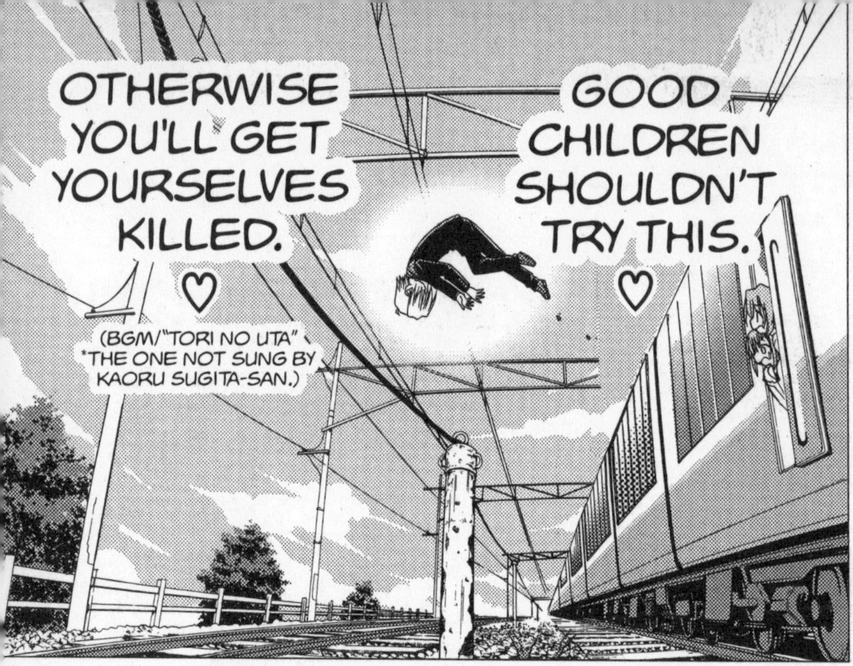
GOOD CHILDREN SHOULDN'T TRY THIS. ♡
OTHERWISE YOU'LL GET YOURSELVES KILLED. ♡
(BGM/"TORI NO UTA" *THE ONE NOT SUNG BY KAORU SUGITA-SAN.)
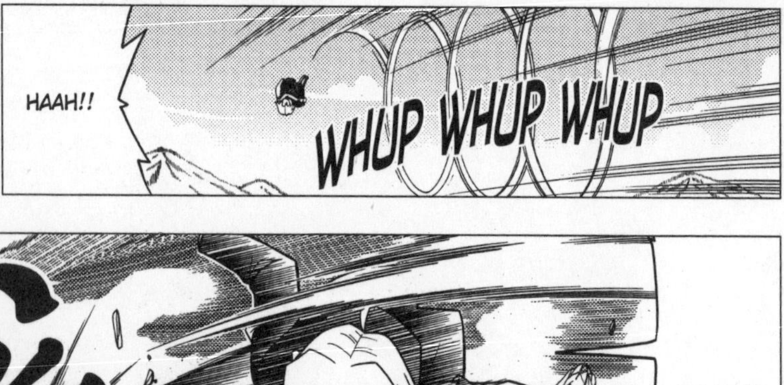
WHUP WHUP WHUP
HAAH!!
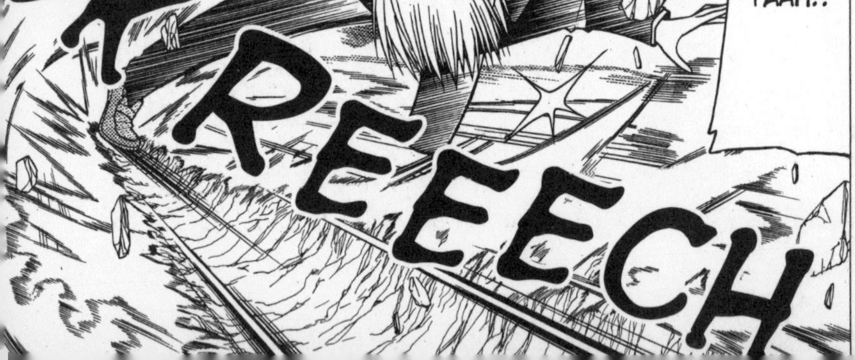
TAAH!!
SKREEECH

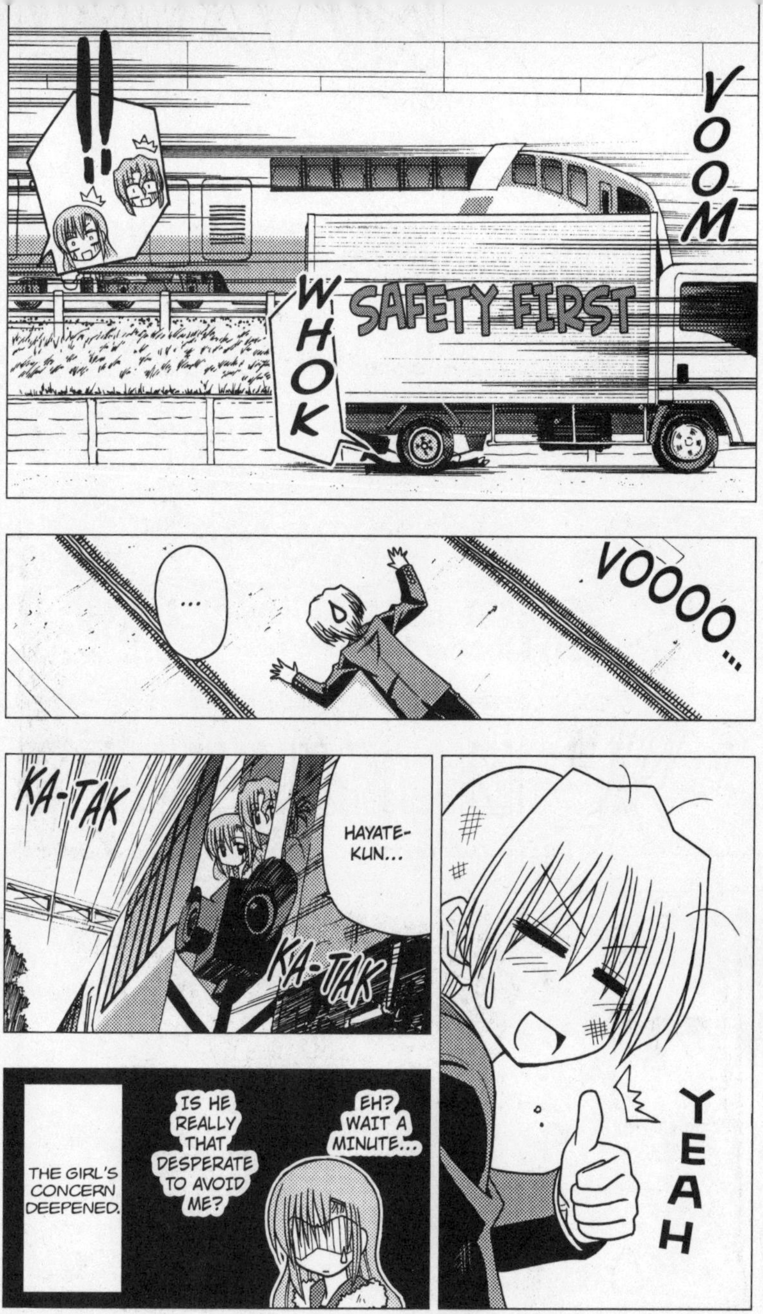
VOOM
!!
SAFETY FIRST
WHOK
VOOOO...
...
YEAH
HAYATE-KUN...
KA-TAK
KA-TAK
EH? WAIT A MINUTE...
IS HE REALLY THAT DESPERATE TO AVOID ME?
THE GIRL'S CONCERN DEEPENED.

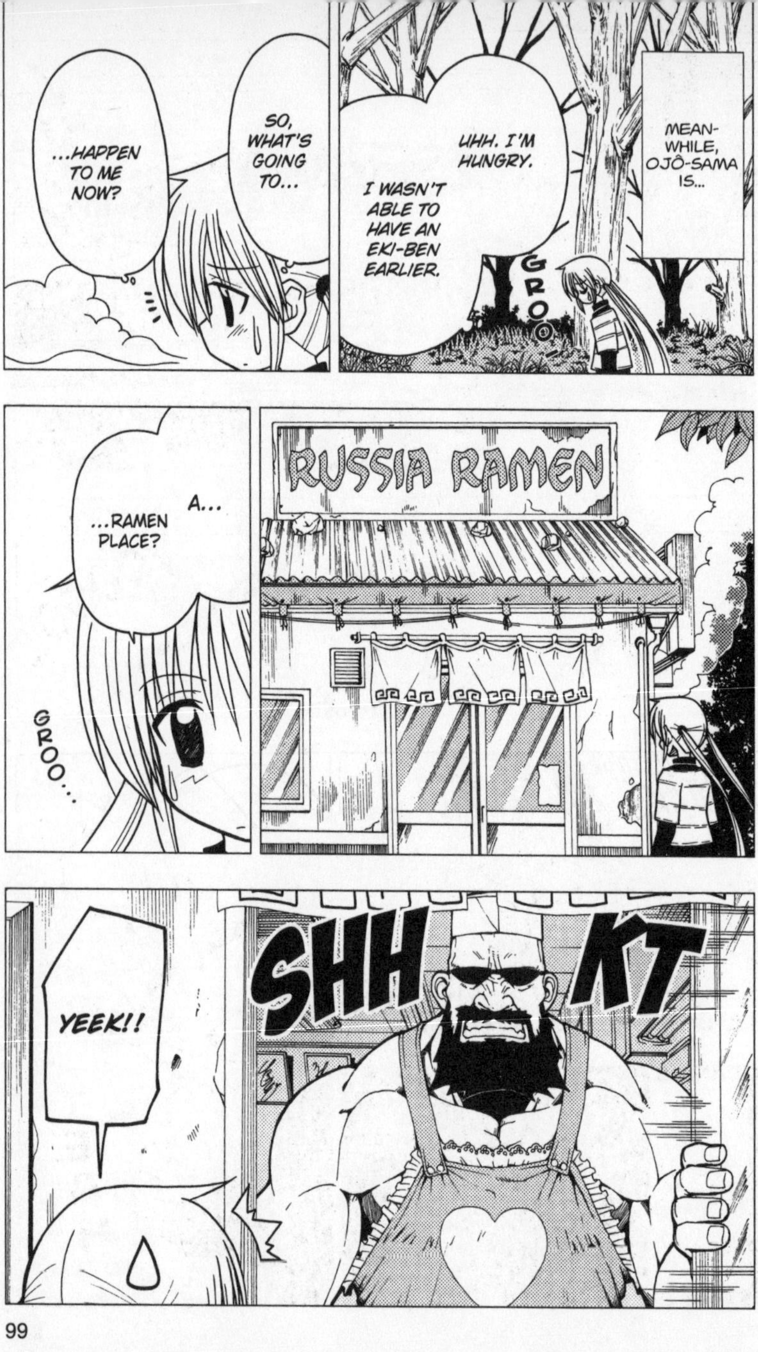
MEAN-WHILE, OJÔ-SAMA IS...
UHH. I'M HUNGRY.
I WASN'T ABLE TO HAVE AN EKI-BEN EARLIER.
GROO...
SO, WHAT'S GOING TO...
...HAPPEN TO ME NOW?
RUSSIA RAMEN
A...
...RAMEN PLACE?
GROO...
SHH KT
YEEK!!

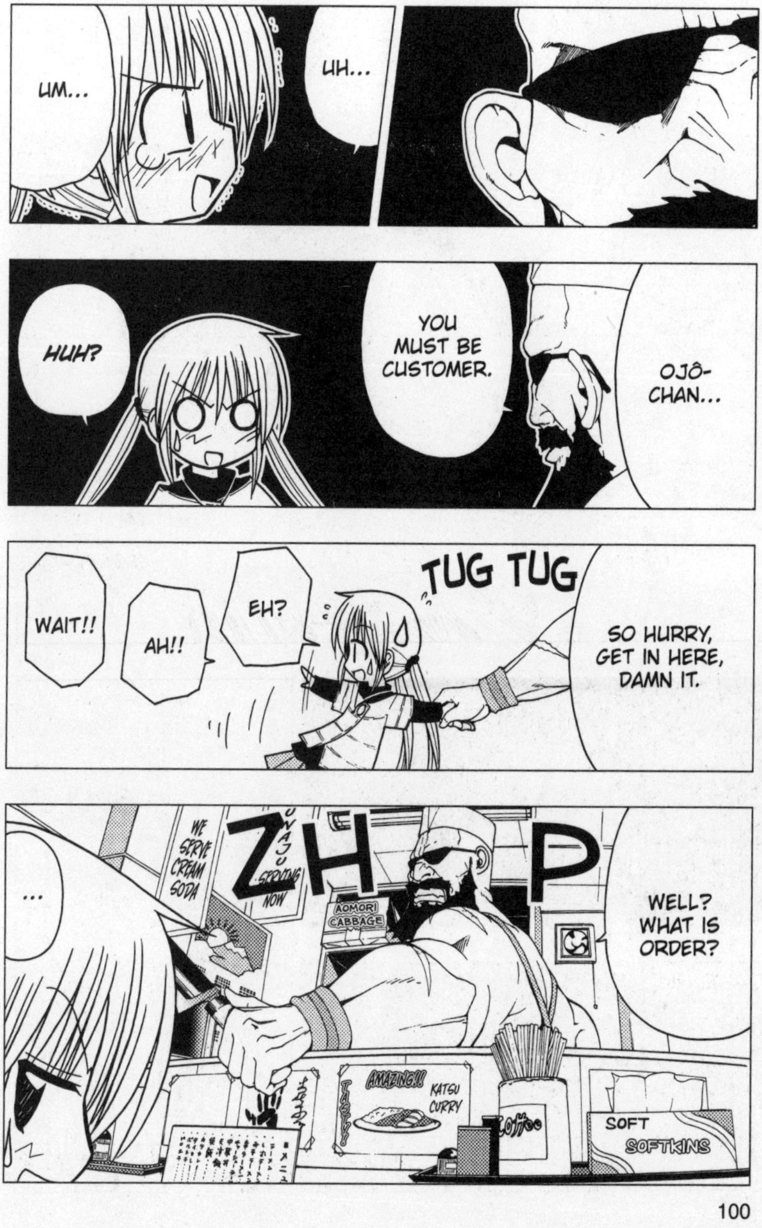
UH...
UM...
OJÔ-CHAN...
YOU MUST BE CUSTOMER.
HUH?
SO HURRY, GET IN HERE, DAMN IT.
TUG TUG
EH?
AH!!
WAIT!!
WELL? WHAT IS ORDER?
ZHP
AOMORI CABBAGE
UNAJU SERVING NOW
WE SERVE CREAM SODA
...
SOFT
SOFTKINS
Coffee
KATSU CURRY
AMAZING!!
TASTY!

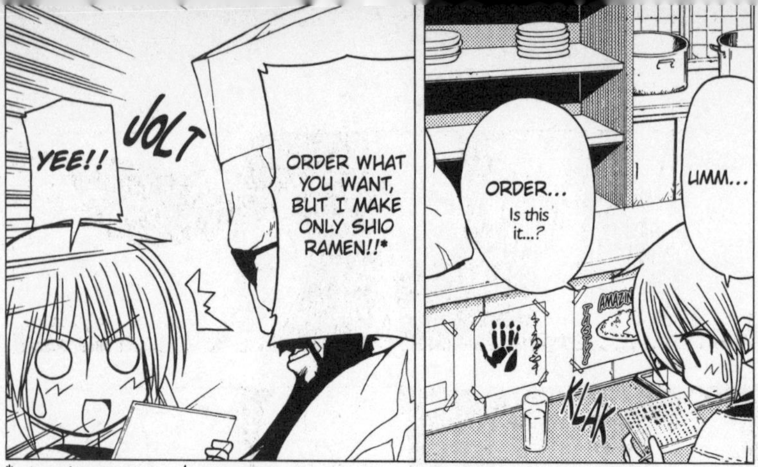
UMM...
ORDER...
Is this it...?
KLAK
ORDER WHAT YOU WANT, BUT I MAKE ONLY SHIO RAMEN!!*
JOLT
YEE!!

* A salt-seasoned ramen

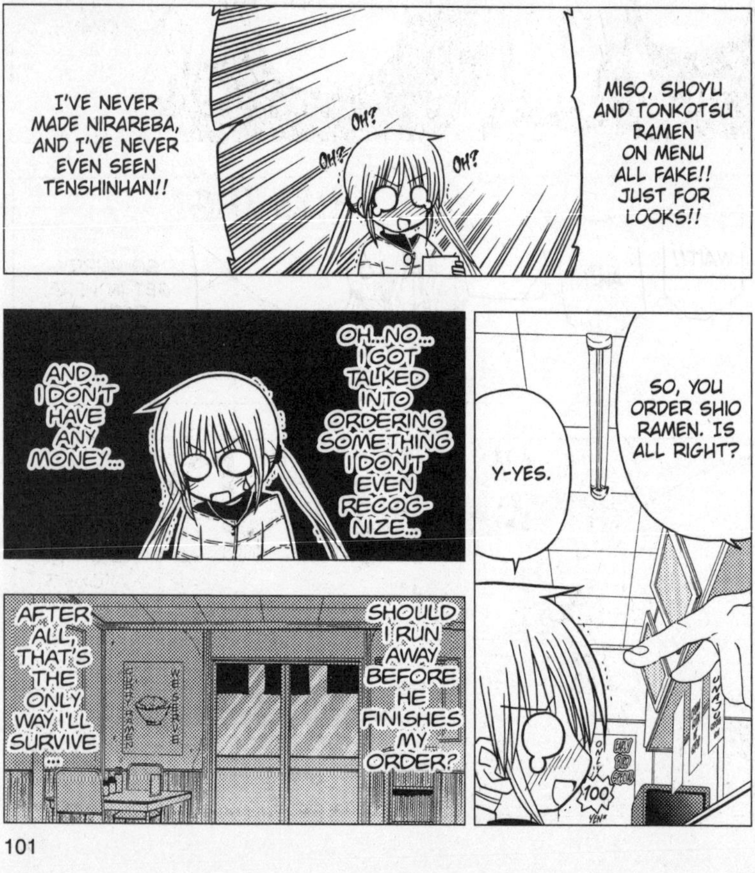
MISO, SHOYU AND TONKOTSU RAMEN ON MENU ALL FAKE!! JUST FOR LOOKS!!
OH?
OH?
OH?
I'VE NEVER MADE NIRAREBA, AND I'VE NEVER EVEN SEEN TENSHINHAN!!
SO, YOU ORDER SHIO RAMEN. IS ALL RIGHT?
Y-YES.
ONLY 100 YEN
OH...NO... I GOT TALKED INTO ORDERING SOMETHING I DON'T EVEN RECOG-NIZE...
AND... I DON'T HAVE ANY MONEY...
SHOULD I RUN AWAY BEFORE HE FINISHES MY ORDER?
AFTER ALL, THAT'S THE ONLY WAY I'LL SURVIVE...

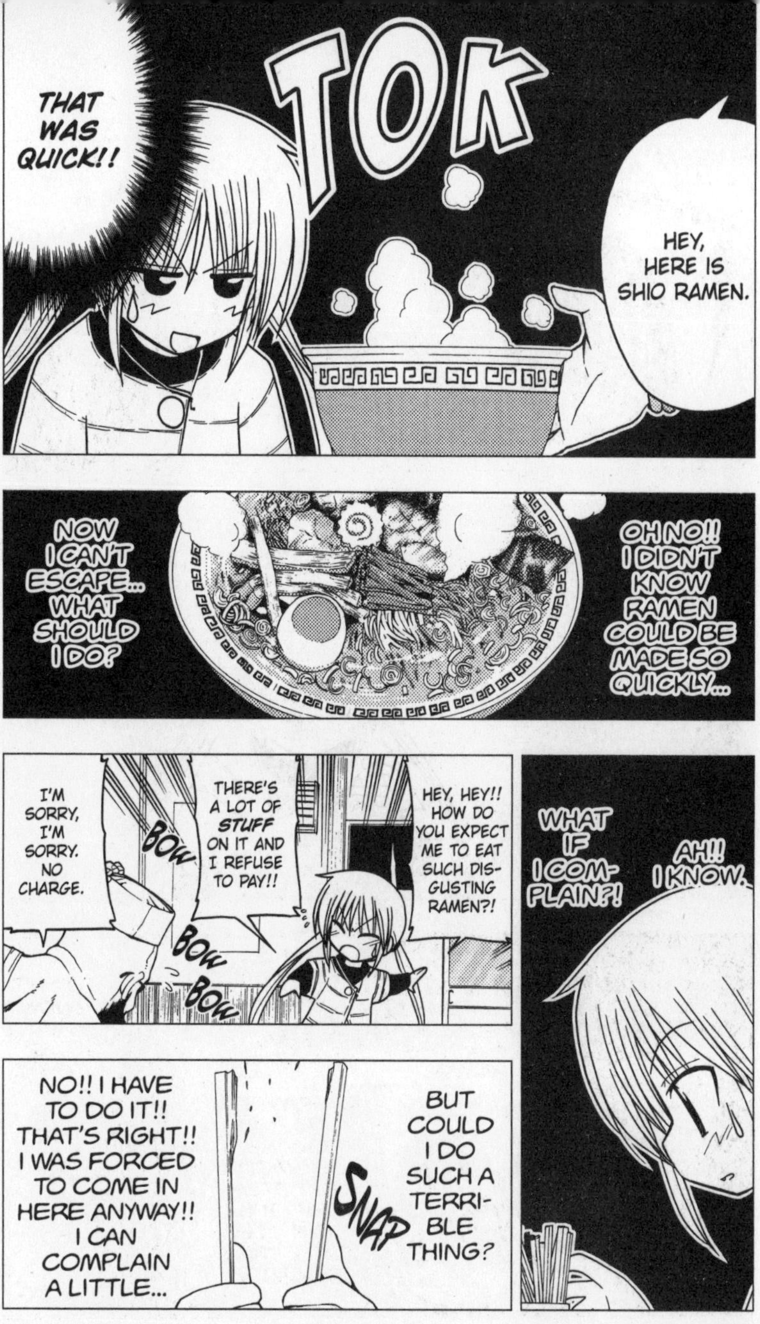
HEY, HERE IS SHIO RAMEN.
TOK
THAT WAS QUICK!!
OH NO!! I DIDN'T KNOW RAMEN COULD BE MADE SO QUICKLY...
NOW I CAN'T ESCAPE... WHAT SHOULD I DO?
AH!! I KNOW.
WHAT IF I COMPLAIN?!
HEY, HEY!! HOW DO YOU EXPECT ME TO EAT SUCH DISGUSTING RAMEN?!
THERE'S A LOT OF STUFF ON IT AND I REFUSE TO PAY!!
I'M SORRY, I'M SORRY. NO CHARGE.
BOW
BOW
BOW
BUT COULD I DO SUCH A TERRIBLE THING?
SNAP
NO!! I HAVE TO DO IT!! THAT'S RIGHT!! I WAS FORCED TO COME IN HERE ANYWAY!! I CAN COMPLAIN A LITTLE...

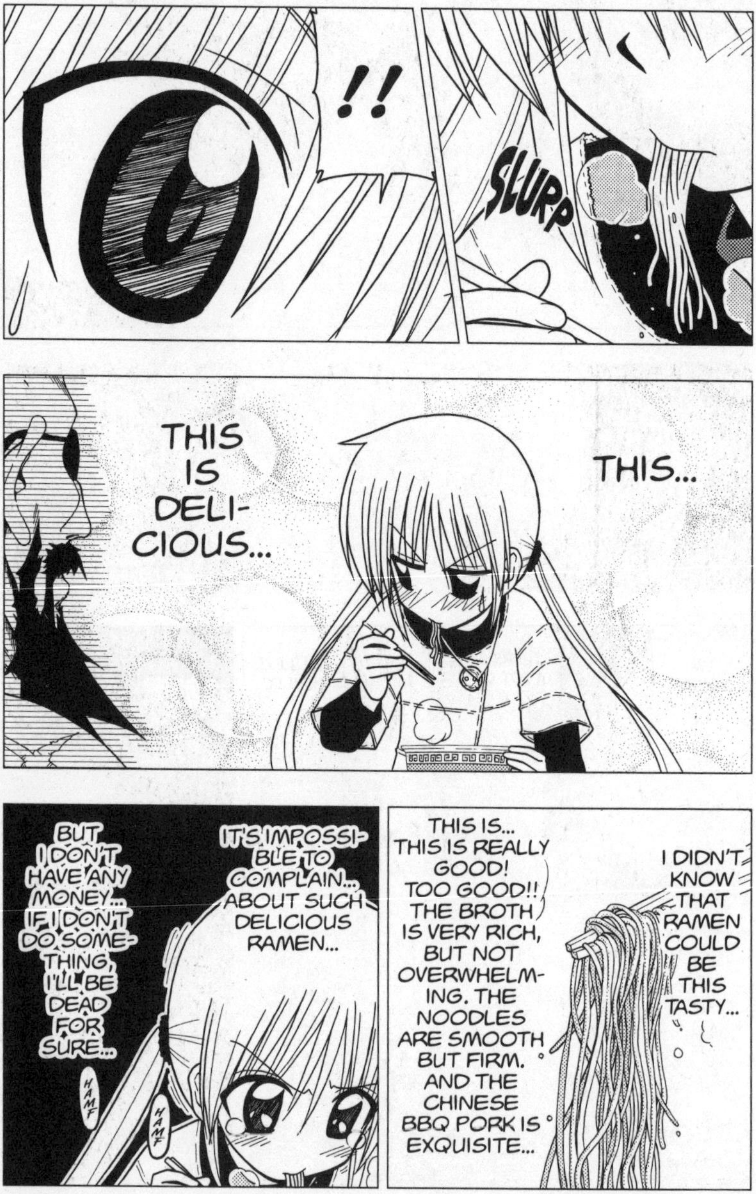
SLURP
!!
THIS...
THIS IS DELICIOUS...
THIS IS... THIS IS REALLY GOOD! TOO GOOD!! THE BROTH IS VERY RICH, BUT NOT OVERWHELMING. THE NOODLES ARE SMOOTH BUT FIRM. AND THE CHINESE BBQ PORK IS EXQUISITE...
I DIDN'T KNOW THAT RAMEN COULD BE THIS TASTY...
IT'S IMPOSSIBLE TO COMPLAIN... ABOUT SUCH DELICIOUS RAMEN...
BUT I DON'T HAVE ANY MONEY... IF I DON'T DO SOMETHING, I'LL BE DEAD FOR SURE...
HAMF
HAMF

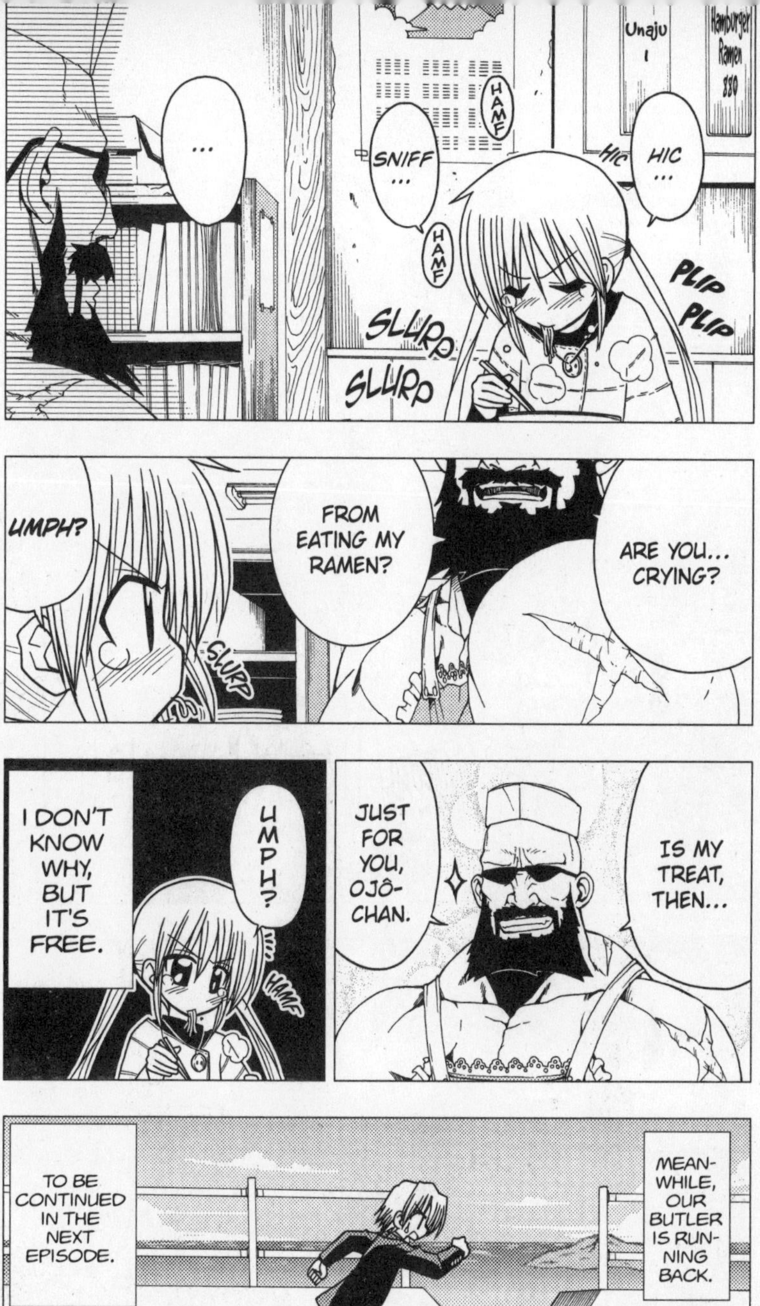
Hamburger Ramen 880
Unaju
HIC HIC...
PLIP PLIP
HAMF
SNIFF...
HAMF
SLURP SLURP
...
ARE YOU... CRYING?
FROM EATING MY RAMEN?
UMPH?
SLURP
IS MY TREAT, THEN...
JUST FOR YOU, OJÔ-CHAN.
UMPH?
HAMF
I DON'T KNOW WHY, BUT IT'S FREE.
MEAN-WHILE, OUR BUTLER IS RUN-NING BACK.
TO BE CONTINUED IN THE NEXT EPISODE.

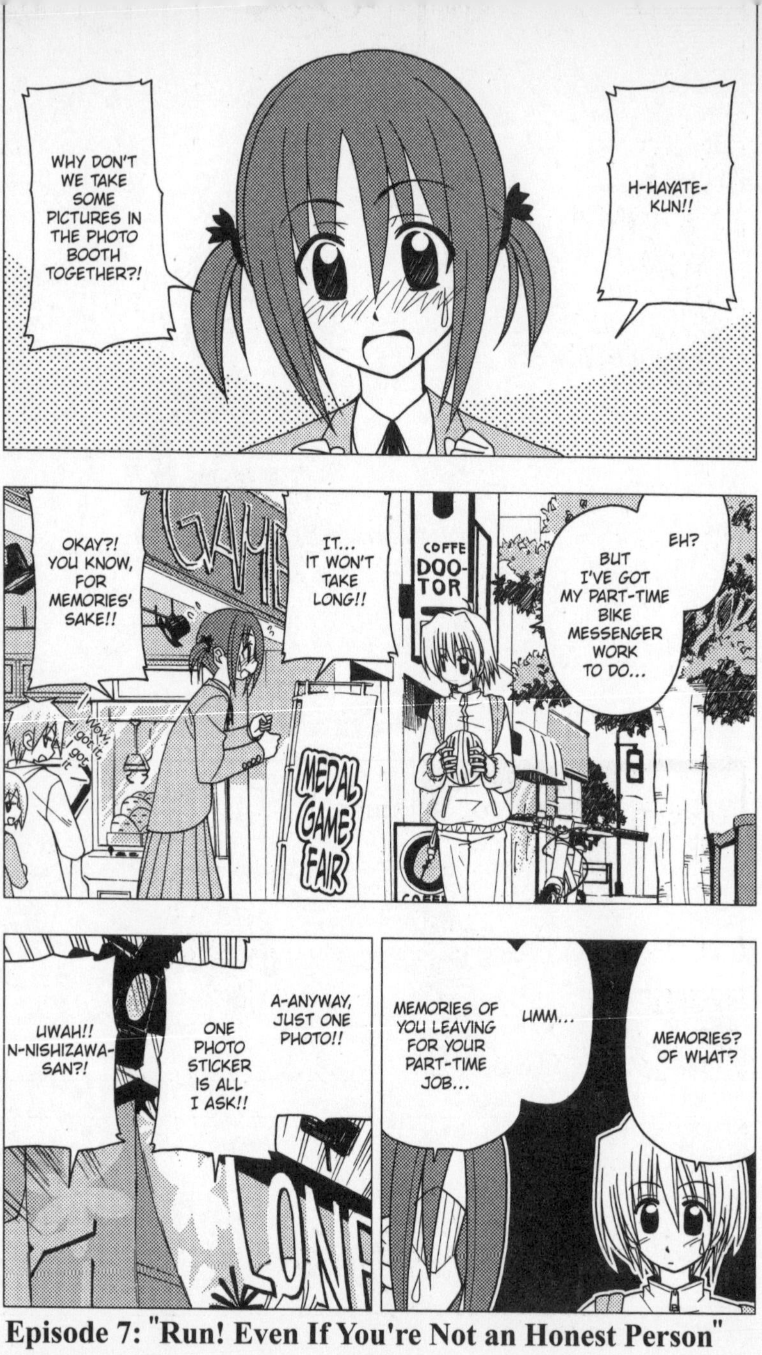
H-HAYATE-KUN!!
WHY DON'T WE TAKE SOME PICTURES IN THE PHOTO BOOTH TOGETHER?!
EH?
BUT I'VE GOT MY PART-TIME BIKE MESSENGER WORK TO DO...
COFFE DOO-TOR
IT... IT WON'T TAKE LONG!!
MEDAL GAME FAIR
OKAY?! YOU KNOW, FOR MEMORIES' SAKE!!
GAME
Wow, I got it, I got it
MEMORIES? OF WHAT?
UMM...
MEMORIES OF YOU LEAVING FOR YOUR PART-TIME JOB...
A-ANYWAY, JUST ONE PHOTO!!
ONE PHOTO STICKER IS ALL I ASK!!
UWAH!! N-NISHIZAWA-SAN?!
LONE

Episode 7: "Run! Even If You're Not an Honest Person"

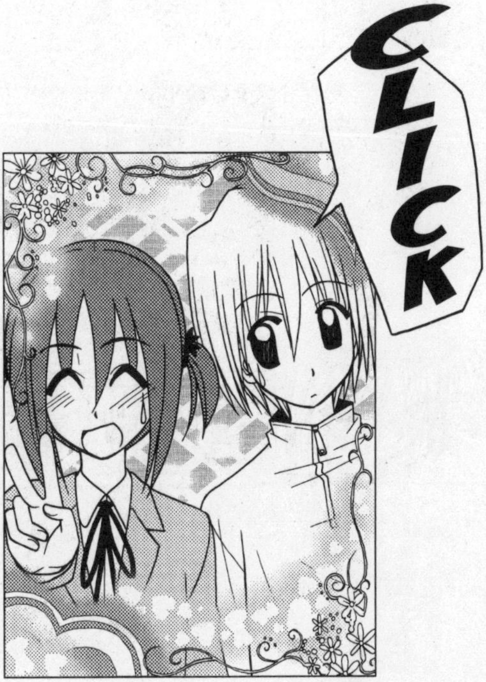
CLICK

Episode 7: "Run! Even If You're Not an Honest Person"

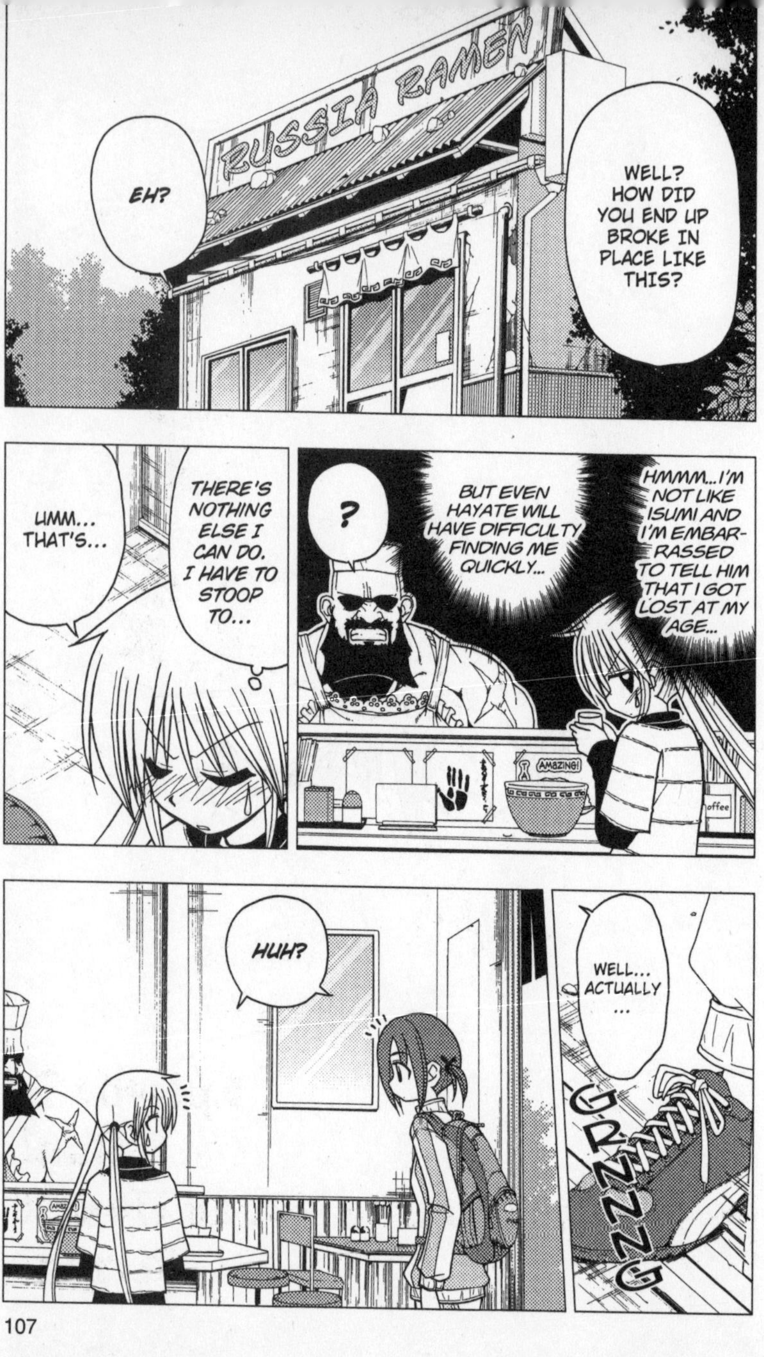
RUSSIA RAMEN
WELL? HOW DID YOU END UP BROKE IN PLACE LIKE THIS?
EH?
HMMM...I'M NOT LIKE ISUMI AND I'M EMBARRASSED TO TELL HIM THAT I GOT LOST AT MY AGE...
BUT EVEN HAYATE WILL HAVE DIFFICULTY FINDING ME QUICKLY...
?
AMAZING!
THERE'S NOTHING ELSE I CAN DO. I HAVE TO STOOP TO...
UMM... THAT'S...
WELL... ACTUALLY ...
GRNNNG
HUH?

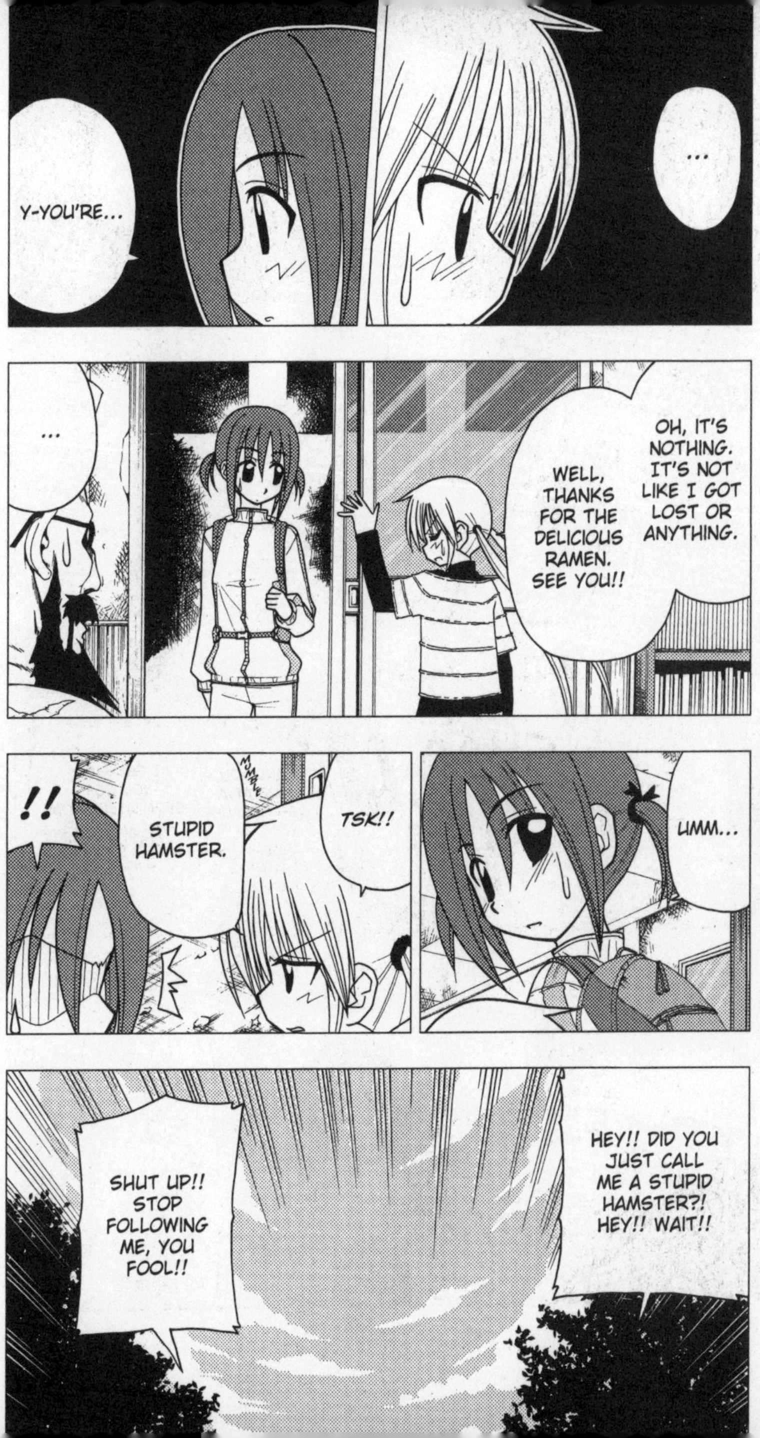
...
Y-YOU'RE...
OH, IT'S NOTHING. IT'S NOT LIKE I GOT LOST OR ANYTHING.
WELL, THANKS FOR THE DELICIOUS RAMEN. SEE YOU!!
...
UMM...
TSK!!
STUPID HAMSTER.
!!
HEY!! DID YOU JUST CALL ME A STUPID HAMSTER?! HEY!! WAIT!!
SHUT UP!! STOP FOLLOWING ME, YOU FOOL!!

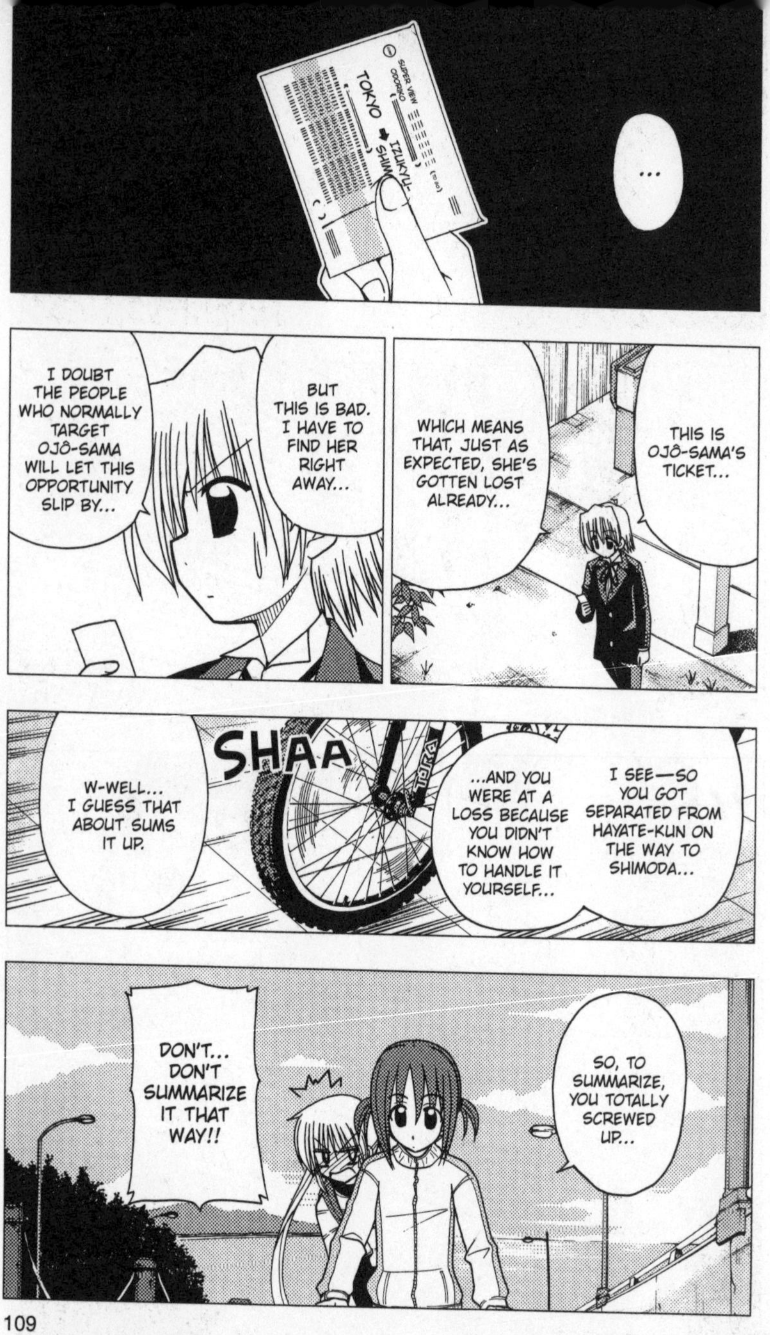
SUPER VIEW
ODORIKO
IZUKYU-
TOKYO
SHIM
...
THIS IS OJÔ-SAMA'S TICKET...
WHICH MEANS THAT, JUST AS EXPECTED, SHE'S GOTTEN LOST ALREADY...
BUT THIS IS BAD. I HAVE TO FIND HER RIGHT AWAY...
I DOUBT THE PEOPLE WHO NORMALLY TARGET OJÔ-SAMA WILL LET THIS OPPORTUNITY SLIP BY...
I SEE—SO YOU GOT SEPARATED FROM HAYATE-KUN ON THE WAY TO SHIMODA...
...AND YOU WERE AT A LOSS BECAUSE YOU DIDN'T KNOW HOW TO HANDLE IT YOURSELF...
TORA
SHAA
W-WELL... I GUESS THAT ABOUT SUMS IT UP.
SO, TO SUMMARIZE, YOU TOTALLY SCREWED UP...
DON'T... DON'T SUMMARIZE IT THAT WAY!!

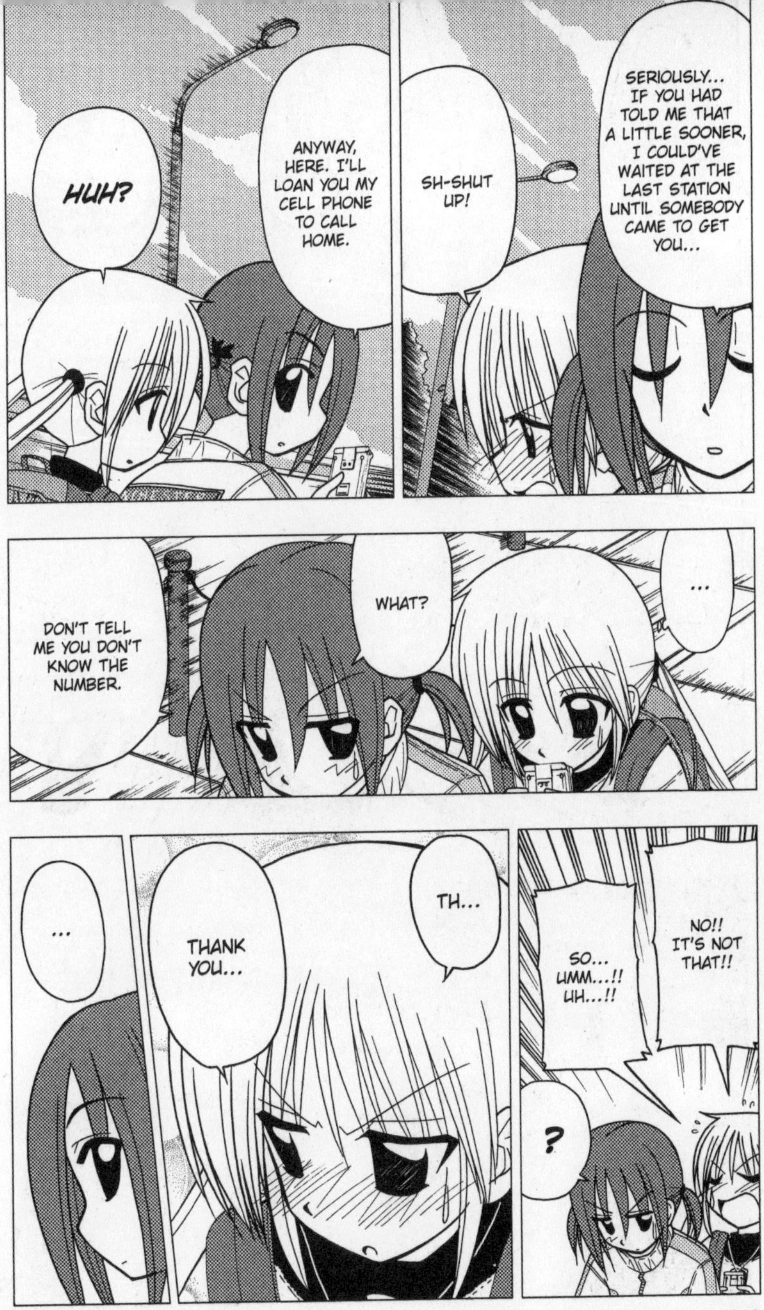
SERIOUSLY... IF YOU HAD TOLD ME THAT A LITTLE SOONER, I COULD'VE WAITED AT THE LAST STATION UNTIL SOMEBODY CAME TO GET YOU...
SH-SHUT UP!
ANYWAY, HERE. I'LL LOAN YOU MY CELL PHONE TO CALL HOME.
HUH?
...
WHAT?
DON'T TELL ME YOU DON'T KNOW THE NUMBER.
NO!! IT'S NOT THAT!!
SO... UMM...!! UH...!!
?
TH...
THANK YOU...
...

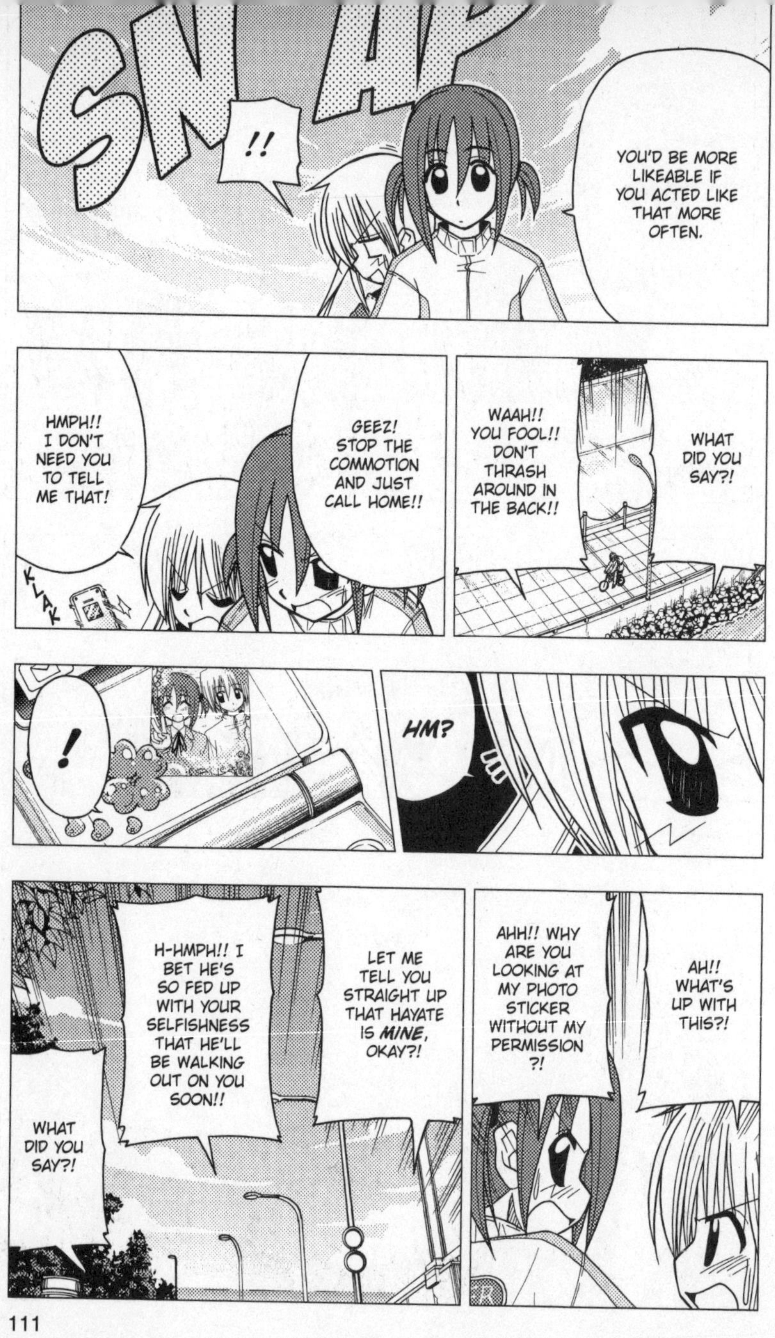
YOU'D BE MORE LIKEABLE IF YOU ACTED LIKE THAT MORE OFTEN.
SNAP
!!
WHAT DID YOU SAY?!
WAAH!! YOU FOOL!! DON'T THRASH AROUND IN THE BACK!!
GEEZ! STOP THE COMMOTION AND JUST CALL HOME!!
HMPH!! I DON'T NEED YOU TO TELL ME THAT!
KLAK
HM?
!
AH!! WHAT'S UP WITH THIS?!
AHH!! WHY ARE YOU LOOKING AT MY PHOTO STICKER WITHOUT MY PERMISSION?!
LET ME TELL YOU STRAIGHT UP THAT HAYATE IS *MINE*, OKAY?!
H-HMPH!! I BET HE'S SO FED UP WITH YOUR SELFISHNESS THAT HE'LL BE WALKING OUT ON YOU SOON!!
WHAT DID YOU SAY?!

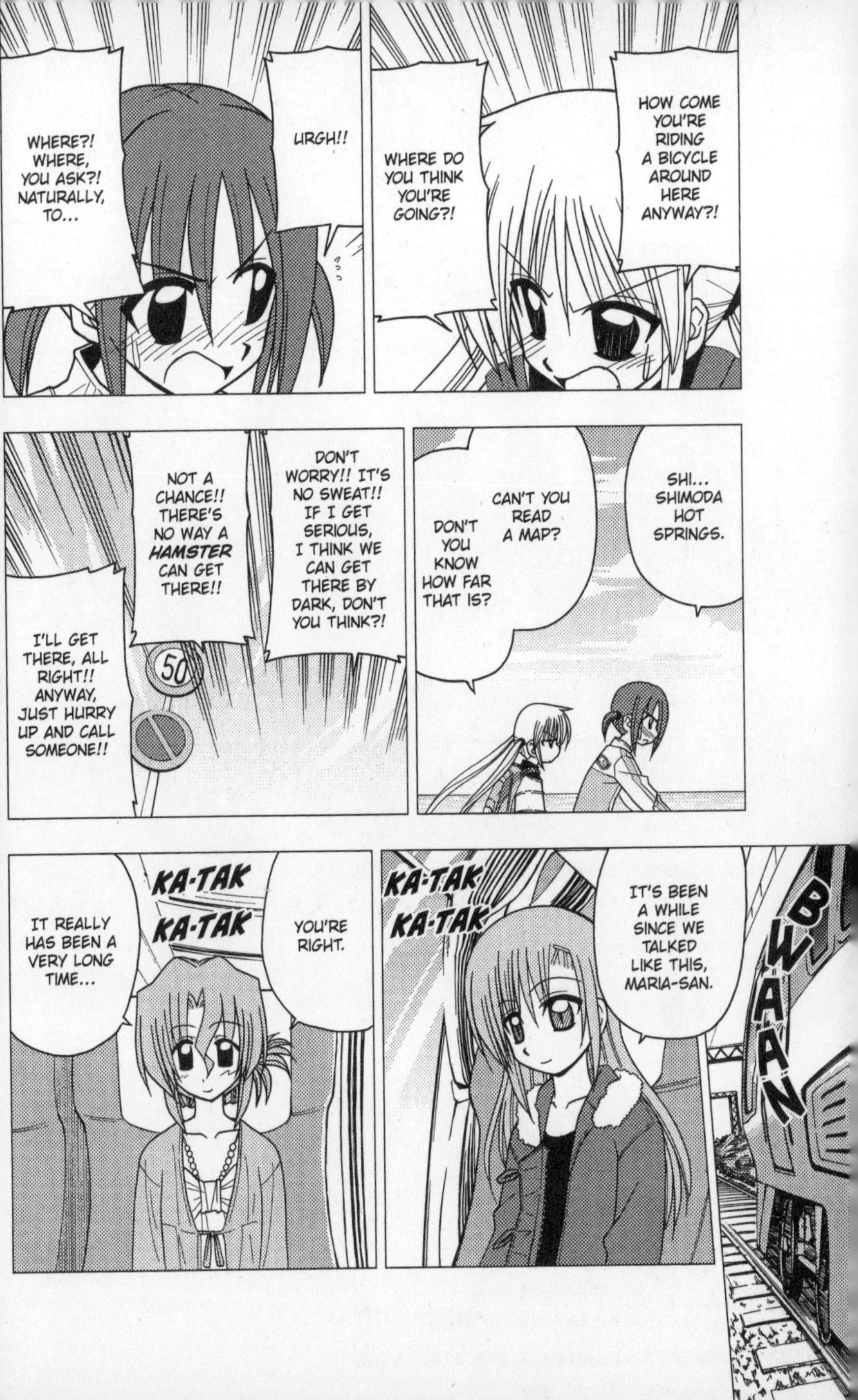
HOW COME YOU'RE RIDING A BICYCLE AROUND HERE ANYWAY?!
WHERE DO YOU THINK YOU'RE GOING?!
URGH!!
WHERE?! WHERE, YOU ASK?! NATURALLY, TO...
SHI... SHIMODA HOT SPRINGS.
CAN'T YOU READ A MAP?
DON'T YOU KNOW HOW FAR THAT IS?
DON'T WORRY!! IT'S NO SWEAT!! IF I GET SERIOUS, I THINK WE CAN GET THERE BY DARK, DON'T YOU THINK?!
NOT A CHANCE!! THERE'S NO WAY A *HAMSTER* CAN GET THERE!!
50
I'LL GET THERE, ALL RIGHT!! ANYWAY, JUST HURRY UP AND CALL SOMEONE!!
BWAAN
IT'S BEEN A WHILE SINCE WE TALKED LIKE THIS, MARIA-SAN.
KA-TAK KA-TAK
YOU'RE RIGHT.
KA-TAK KA-TAK
IT REALLY HAS BEEN A VERY LONG TIME...

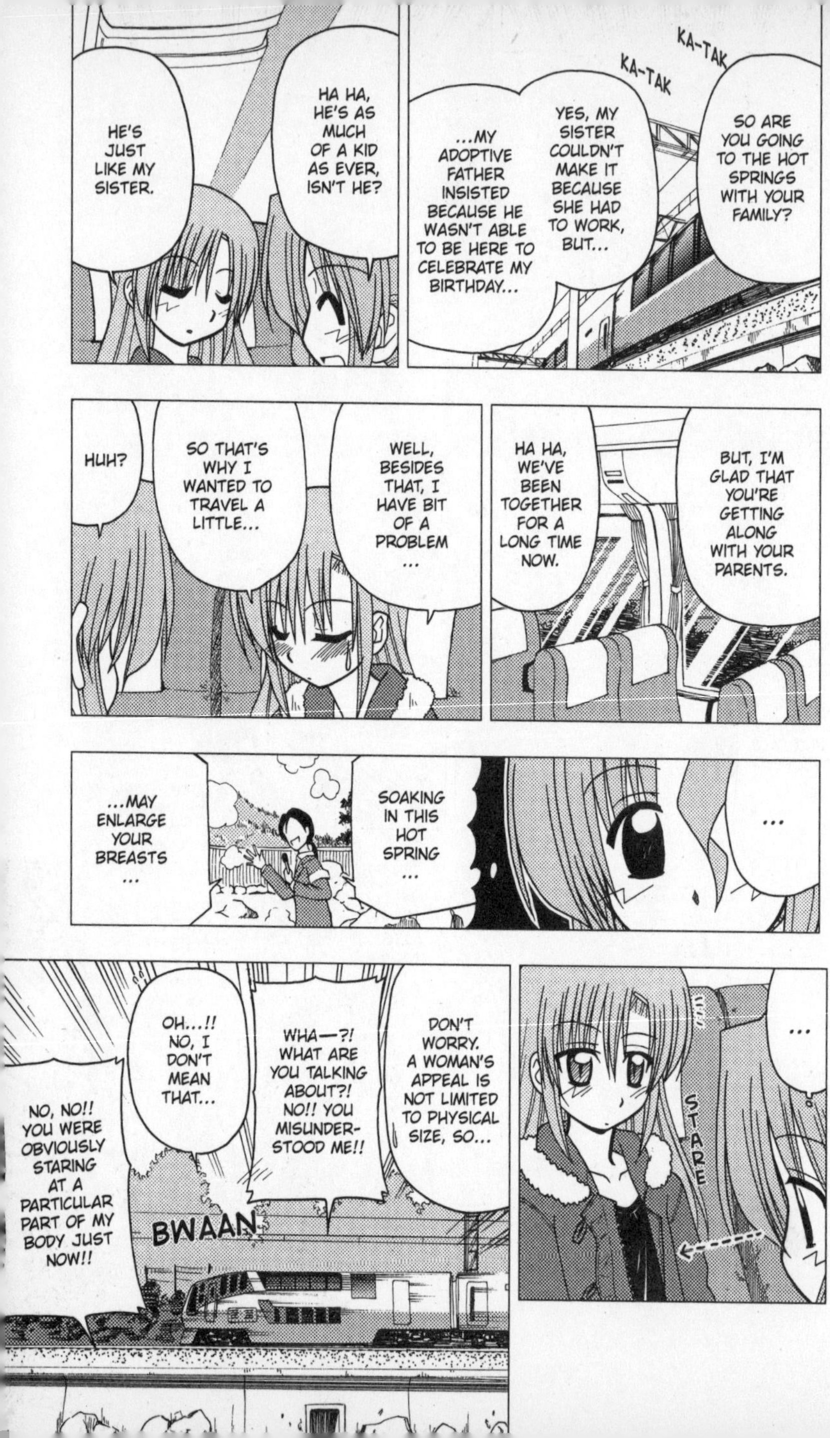
KA-TAK
KA-TAK
SO ARE YOU GOING TO THE HOT SPRINGS WITH YOUR FAMILY?
YES, MY SISTER COULDN'T MAKE IT BECAUSE SHE HAD TO WORK, BUT...
...MY ADOPTIVE FATHER INSISTED BECAUSE HE WASN'T ABLE TO BE HERE TO CELEBRATE MY BIRTHDAY...
HA HA, HE'S AS MUCH OF A KID AS EVER, ISN'T HE?
HE'S JUST LIKE MY SISTER.
BUT, I'M GLAD THAT YOU'RE GETTING ALONG WITH YOUR PARENTS.
HA HA, WE'VE BEEN TOGETHER FOR A LONG TIME NOW.
WELL, BESIDES THAT, I HAVE BIT OF A PROBLEM...
SO THAT'S WHY I WANTED TO TRAVEL A LITTLE...
HUH?
...
SOAKING IN THIS HOT SPRING...
...MAY ENLARGE YOUR BREASTS...
...
STARE
DON'T WORRY. A WOMAN'S APPEAL IS NOT LIMITED TO PHYSICAL SIZE, SO...
WHA—?! WHAT ARE YOU TALKING ABOUT?! NO!! YOU MISUNDERSTOOD ME!!
OH...!! NO, I DON'T MEAN THAT...
NO, NO!! YOU WERE OBVIOUSLY STARING AT A PARTICULAR PART OF MY BODY JUST NOW!!
BWAAN

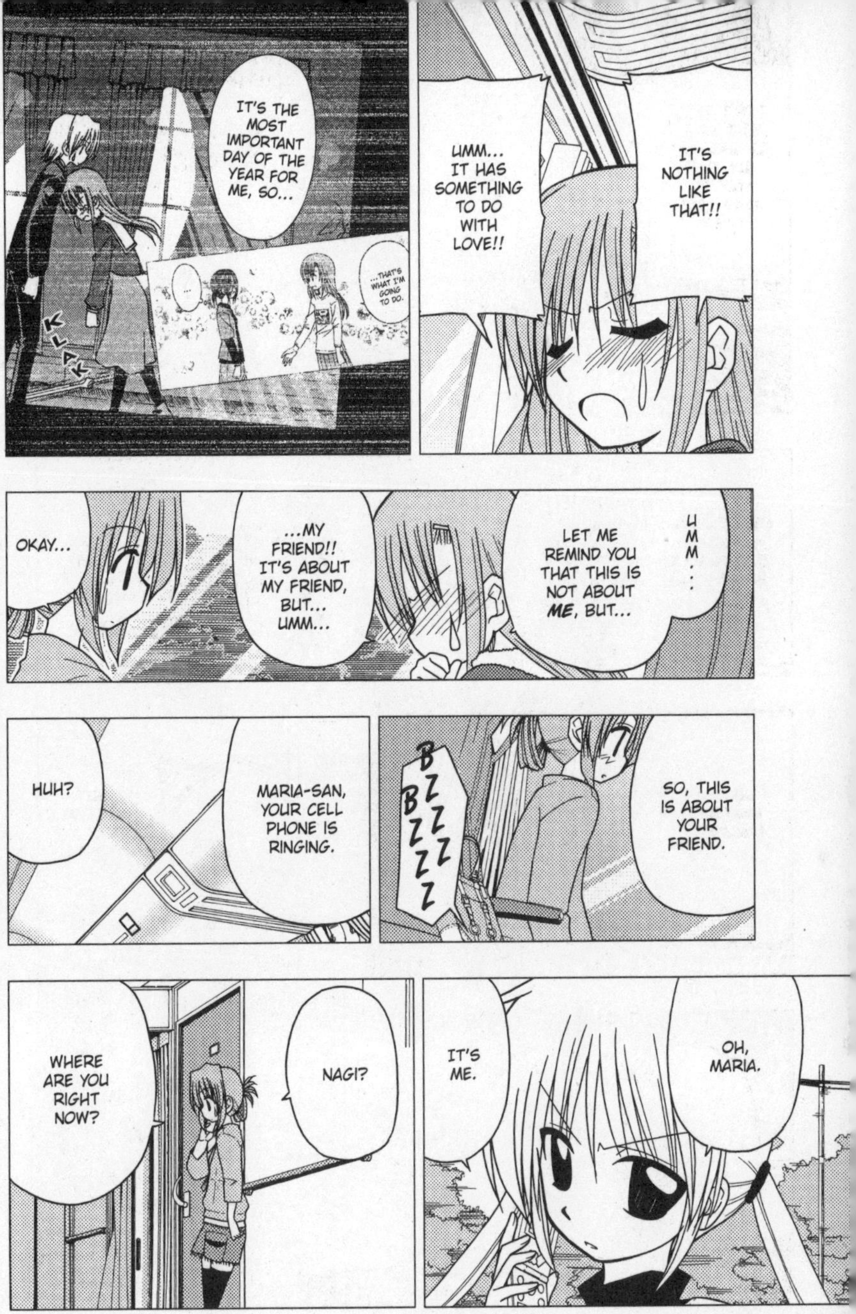
IT'S NOTHING LIKE THAT!!
UMM... IT HAS SOMETHING TO DO WITH LOVE!!
IT'S THE MOST IMPORTANT DAY OF THE YEAR FOR ME, SO...
...THAT'S WHAT I'M GOING TO DO.
...
KLAK
UMM...
LET ME REMIND YOU THAT THIS IS NOT ABOUT *ME*, BUT...
...MY FRIEND!! IT'S ABOUT MY FRIEND, BUT... UMM...
OKAY...
SO, THIS IS ABOUT YOUR FRIEND.
BZZZ BZZZZ
MARIA-SAN, YOUR CELL PHONE IS RINGING.
HUH?
OH, MARIA.
IT'S ME.
NAGI?
WHERE ARE YOU RIGHT NOW?

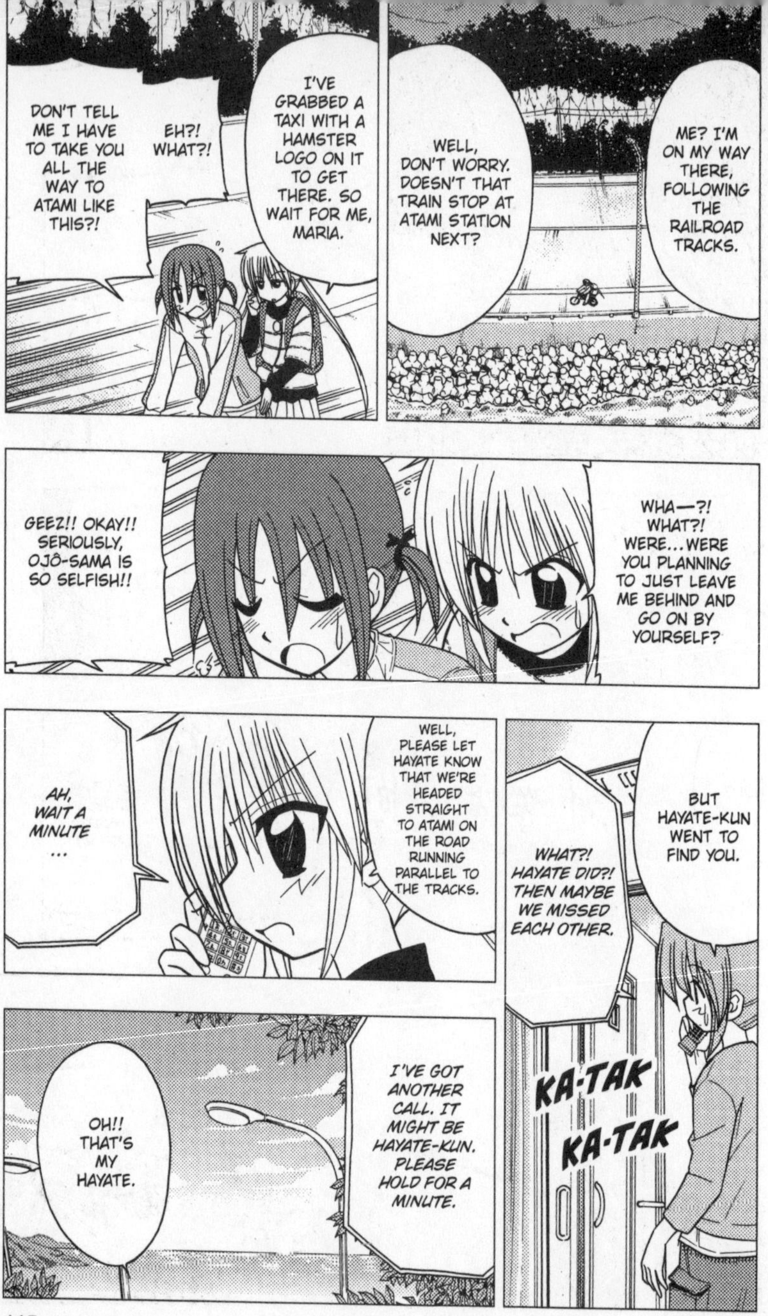
ME? I'M ON MY WAY THERE, FOLLOWING THE RAILROAD TRACKS.
WELL, DON'T WORRY. DOESN'T THAT TRAIN STOP AT ATAMI STATION NEXT?
I'VE GRABBED A TAXI WITH A HAMSTER LOGO ON IT TO GET THERE. SO WAIT FOR ME, MARIA.
EH?! WHAT?!
DON'T TELL ME I HAVE TO TAKE YOU ALL THE WAY TO ATAMI LIKE THIS?!
WHA—?! WHAT?! WERE...WERE YOU PLANNING TO JUST LEAVE ME BEHIND AND GO ON BY YOURSELF?
GEEZ!! OKAY!! SERIOUSLY, OJÔ-SAMA IS SO SELFISH!!
BUT HAYATE-KUN WENT TO FIND YOU.
WHAT?! HAYATE DID?! THEN MAYBE WE MISSED EACH OTHER.
KA-TAK
KA-TAK
WELL, PLEASE LET HAYATE KNOW THAT WE'RE HEADED STRAIGHT TO ATAMI ON THE ROAD RUNNING PARALLEL TO THE TRACKS.
AH, WAIT A MINUTE ...
I'VE GOT ANOTHER CALL. IT MIGHT BE HAYATE-KUN. PLEASE HOLD FOR A MINUTE.
OH!! THAT'S MY HAYATE.

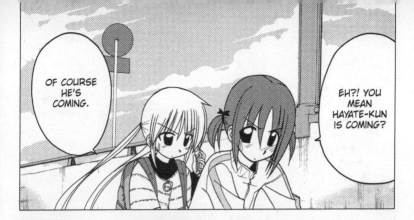

OF COURSE HE'S COMING.

EH?! YOU MEAN HAYATE-KUN IS COMING?

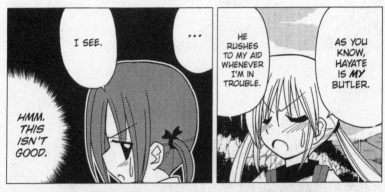

I SEE.

...

HMM. THIS ISN'T GOOD.

HE RUSHES TO MY AID WHENEVER I'M IN TROUBLE.

AS YOU KNOW, HAYATE IS *MY* BUTLER.

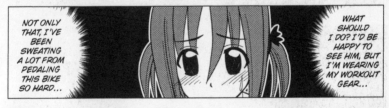

NOT ONLY THAT, I'VE BEEN SWEATING A LOT FROM PEDALING THIS BIKE SO HARD...

WHAT SHOULD I DO? I'D BE HAPPY TO SEE HIM, BUT I'M WEARING MY WORKOUT GEAR...

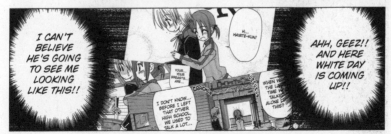

I CAN'T BELIEVE HE'S GOING TO SEE ME LOOKING LIKE THIS!!

H... HAYATE-KUN!

YOUR... YOUR BREASTS... ARE...

I DON'T KNOW... BEFORE I LEFT THAT OTHER HIGH SCHOOL, WE USED TO TALK A LOT...

CRACKLE

WHEN WAS THE LAST TIME WE TALKED ALONE LIKE THIS?

AHH, GEEZ!! AND HERE WHITE DAY IS COMING UP!!

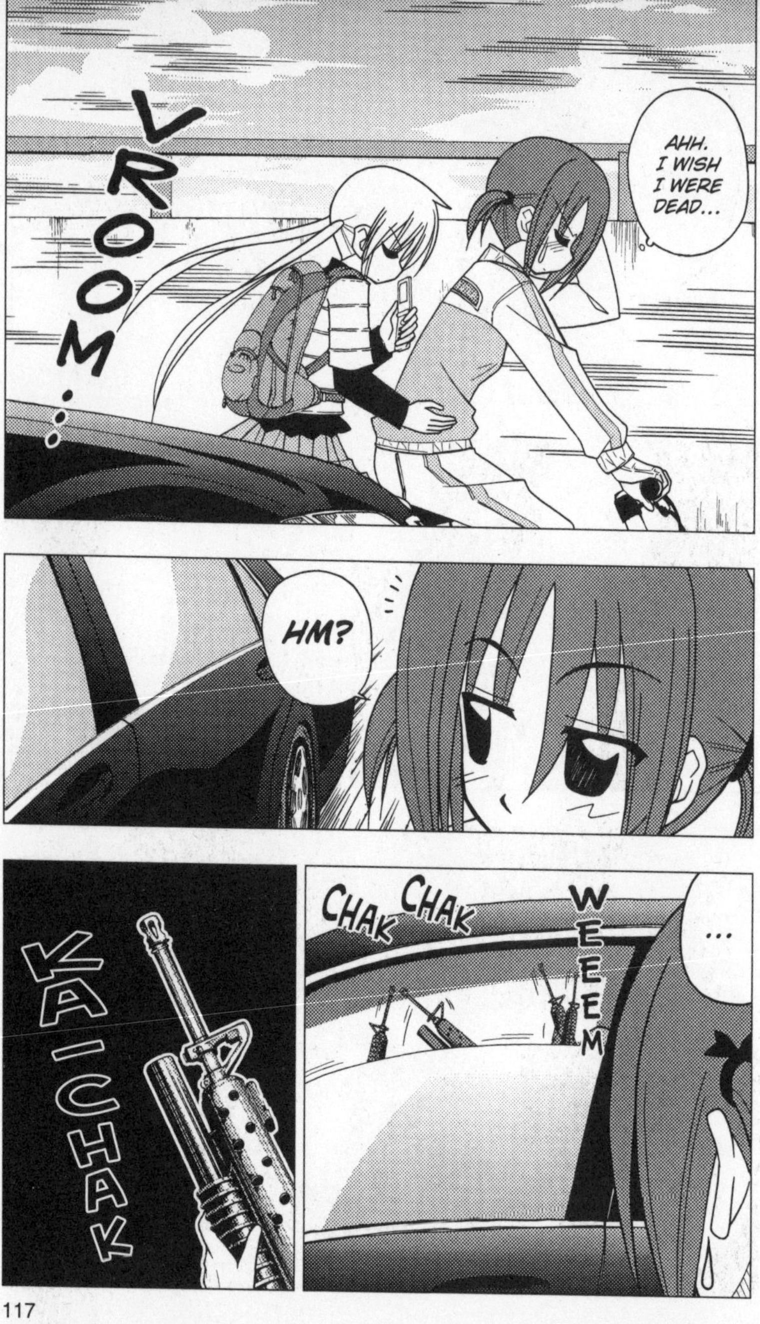
AHH. I WISH I WERE DEAD...
VROOM...
HM?
...
WEEEM
CHAK
CHAK
KAICHAK

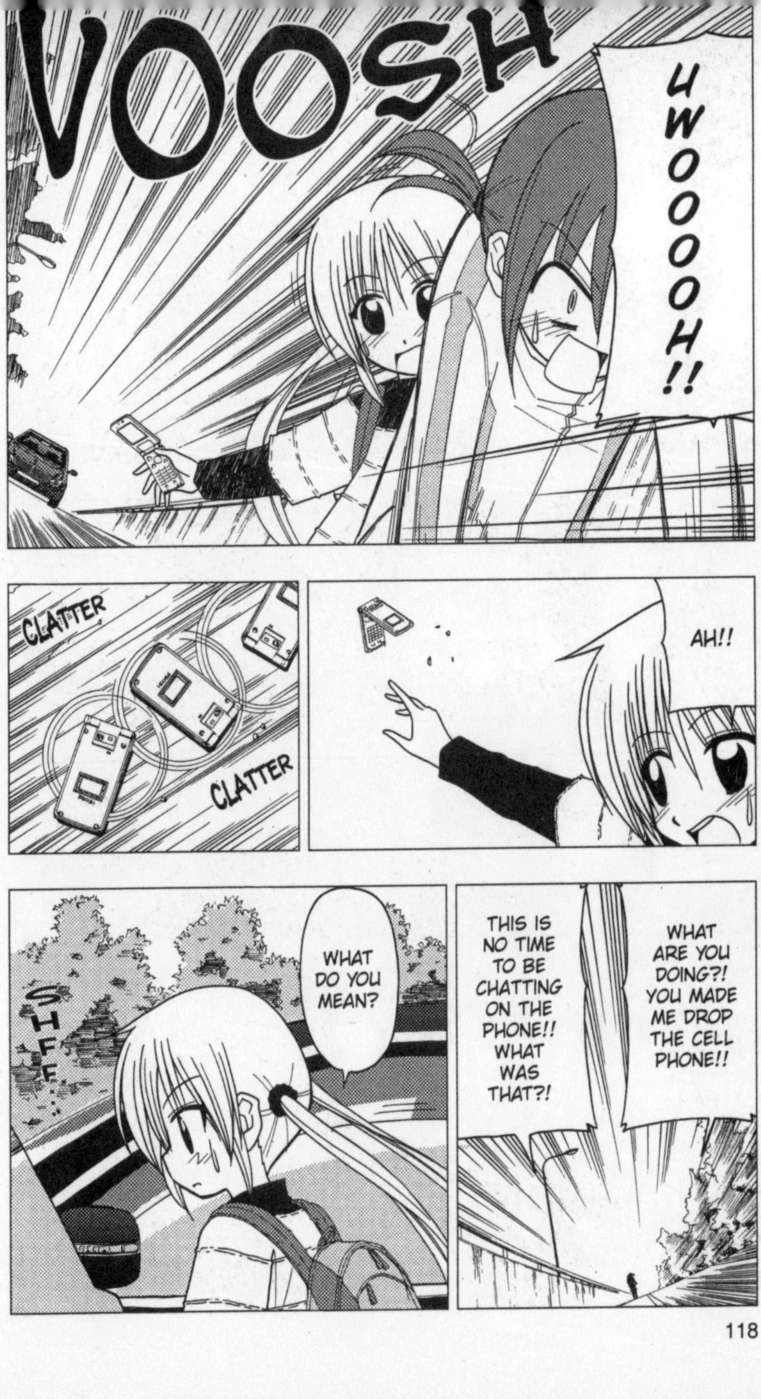
UWOOOOOH!!
VOOSH
AH!!
CLATTER
CLATTER
WHAT ARE YOU DOING?! YOU MADE ME DROP THE CELL PHONE!!
THIS IS NO TIME TO BE CHATTING ON THE PHONE!! WHAT WAS THAT?!
WHAT DO YOU MEAN?
SHFF...

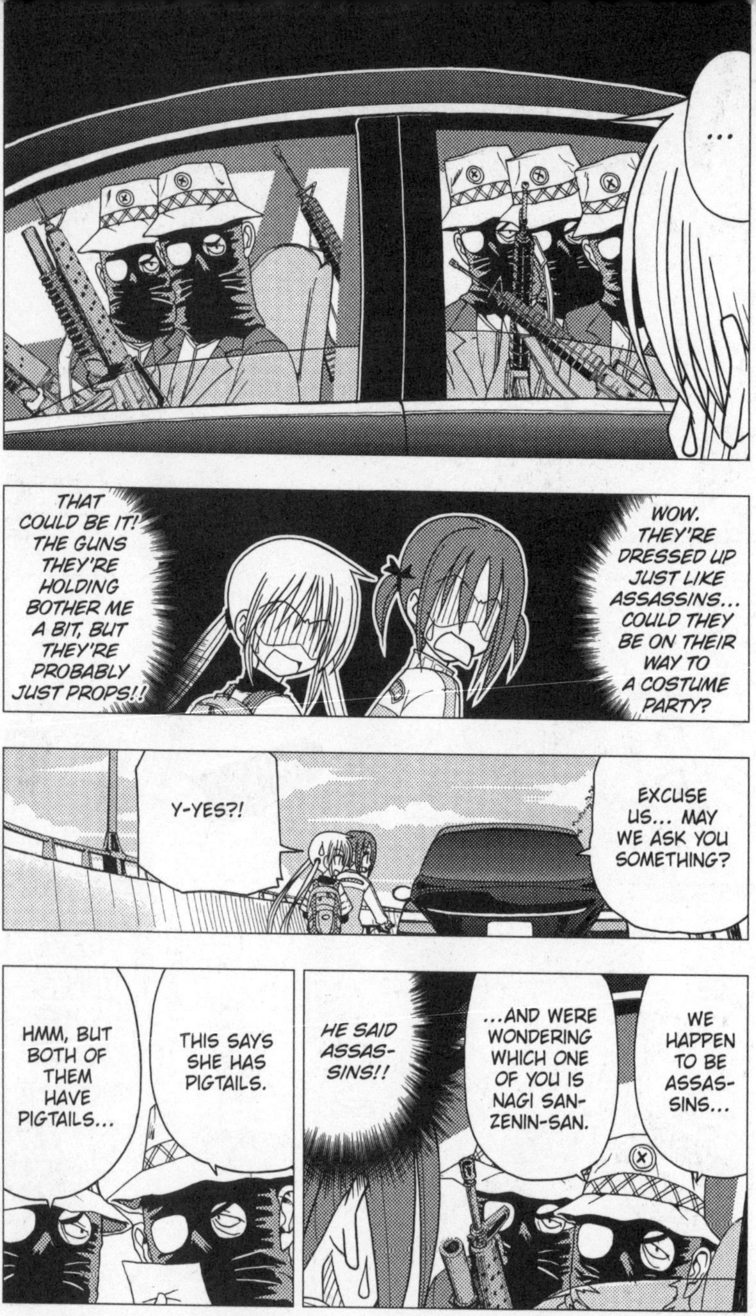
...
WOW. THEY'RE DRESSED UP JUST LIKE ASSASSINS... COULD THEY BE ON THEIR WAY TO A COSTUME PARTY?
THAT COULD BE IT! THE GUNS THEY'RE HOLDING BOTHER ME A BIT, BUT THEY'RE PROBABLY JUST PROPS!!
EXCUSE US... MAY WE ASK YOU SOMETHING?
Y-YES?!
WE HAPPEN TO BE ASSAS-SINS...
...AND WERE WONDERING WHICH ONE OF YOU IS NAGI SAN-ZENIN-SAN.
HE SAID ASSAS-SINS!!
THIS SAYS SHE HAS PIGTAILS.
HMM, BUT BOTH OF THEM HAVE PIGTAILS...

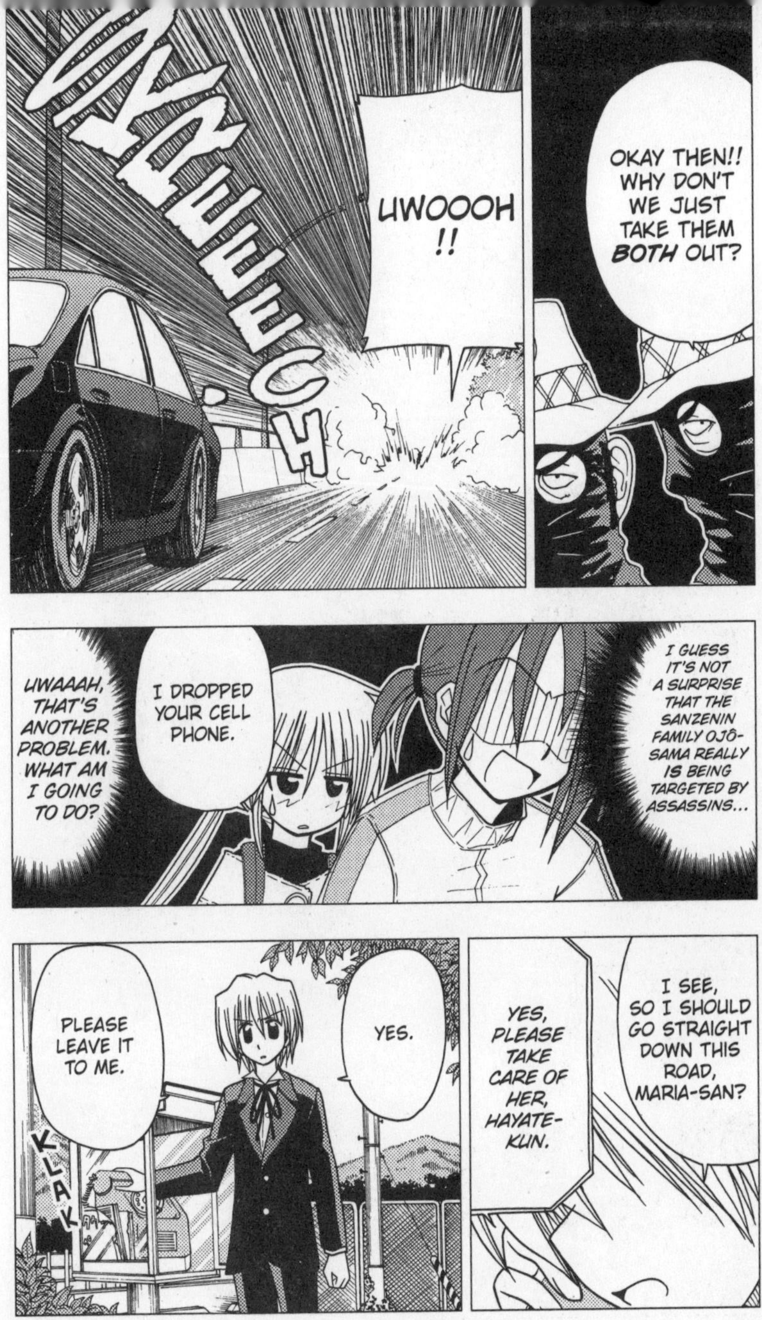
OKAY THEN!! WHY DON'T WE JUST TAKE THEM *BOTH* OUT?
UWOOOH !!
I GUESS IT'S NOT A SURPRISE THAT THE SANZENIN FAMILY OJÔ-SAMA REALLY IS BEING TARGETED BY ASSASSINS...
I DROPPED YOUR CELL PHONE.
UWAAAH, THAT'S ANOTHER PROBLEM. WHAT AM I GOING TO DO?
I SEE, SO I SHOULD GO STRAIGHT DOWN THIS ROAD, MARIA-SAN?
YES, PLEASE TAKE CARE OF HER, HAYATE-KUN.
YES.
PLEASE LEAVE IT TO ME.
KLAK

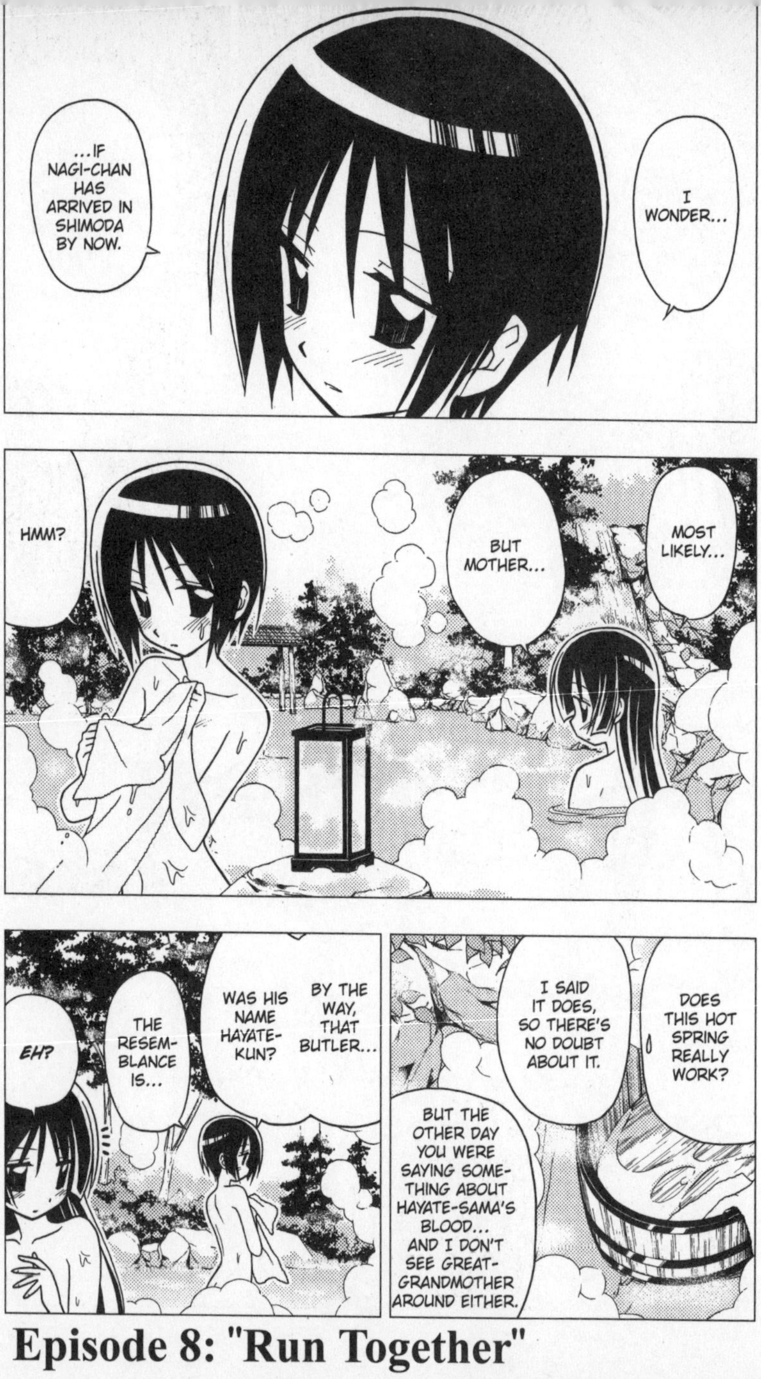
I WONDER...
...IF NAGI-CHAN HAS ARRIVED IN SHIMODA BY NOW.
MOST LIKELY...
BUT MOTHER...
HMM?
DOES THIS HOT SPRING REALLY WORK?
I SAID IT DOES, SO THERE'S NO DOUBT ABOUT IT.
BUT THE OTHER DAY YOU WERE SAYING SOME-THING ABOUT HAYATE-SAMA'S BLOOD... AND I DON'T SEE GREAT-GRANDMOTHER AROUND EITHER.
BY THE WAY, THAT BUTLER...
WAS HIS NAME HAYATE-KUN?
THE RESEM-BLANCE IS...
EH?

Episode 8: "Run Together"

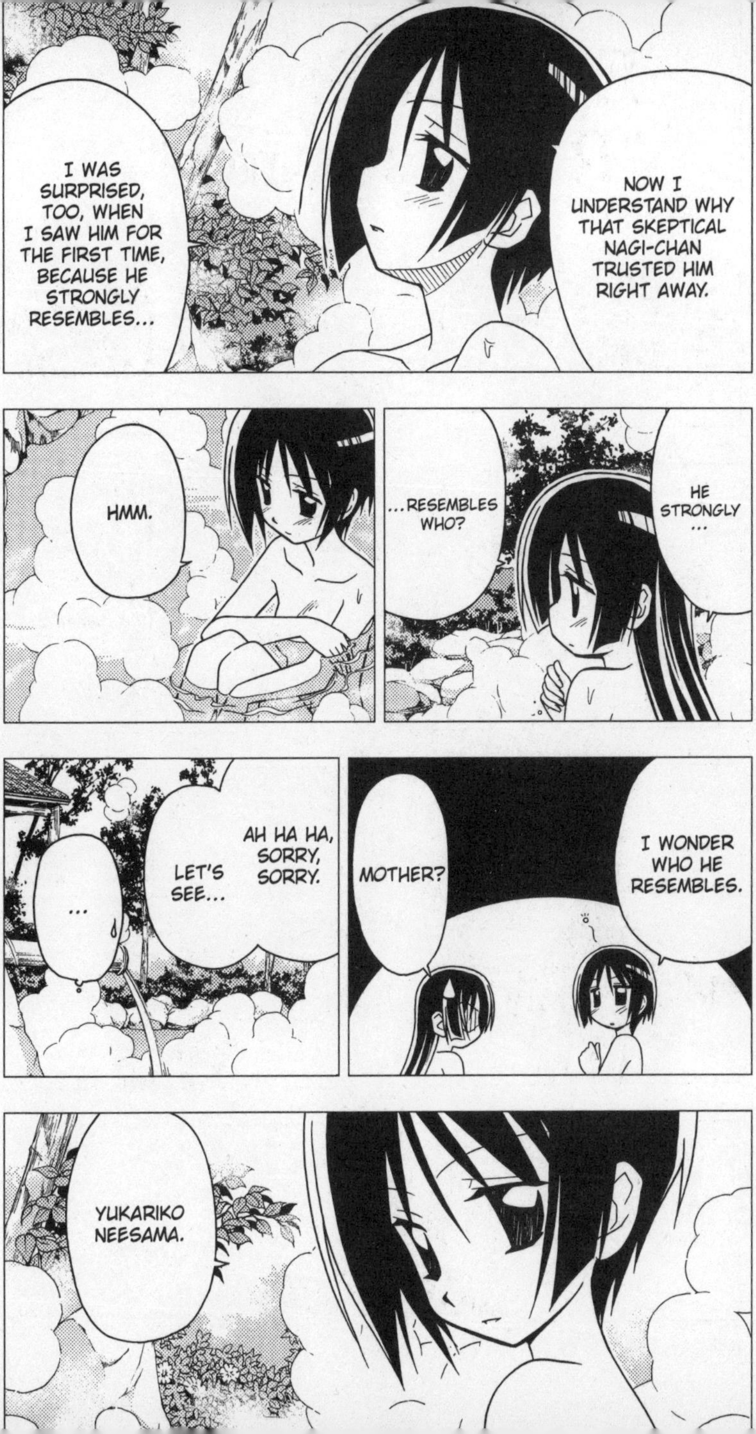
NOW I UNDERSTAND WHY THAT SKEPTICAL NAGI-CHAN TRUSTED HIM RIGHT AWAY.
I WAS SURPRISED, TOO, WHEN I SAW HIM FOR THE FIRST TIME, BECAUSE HE STRONGLY RESEMBLES...
HE STRONGLY ...
...RESEMBLES WHO?
HMM.
I WONDER WHO HE RESEMBLES.
MOTHER?
AH HA HA, SORRY, SORRY.
LET'S SEE...
...
YUKARIKO NEESAMA.

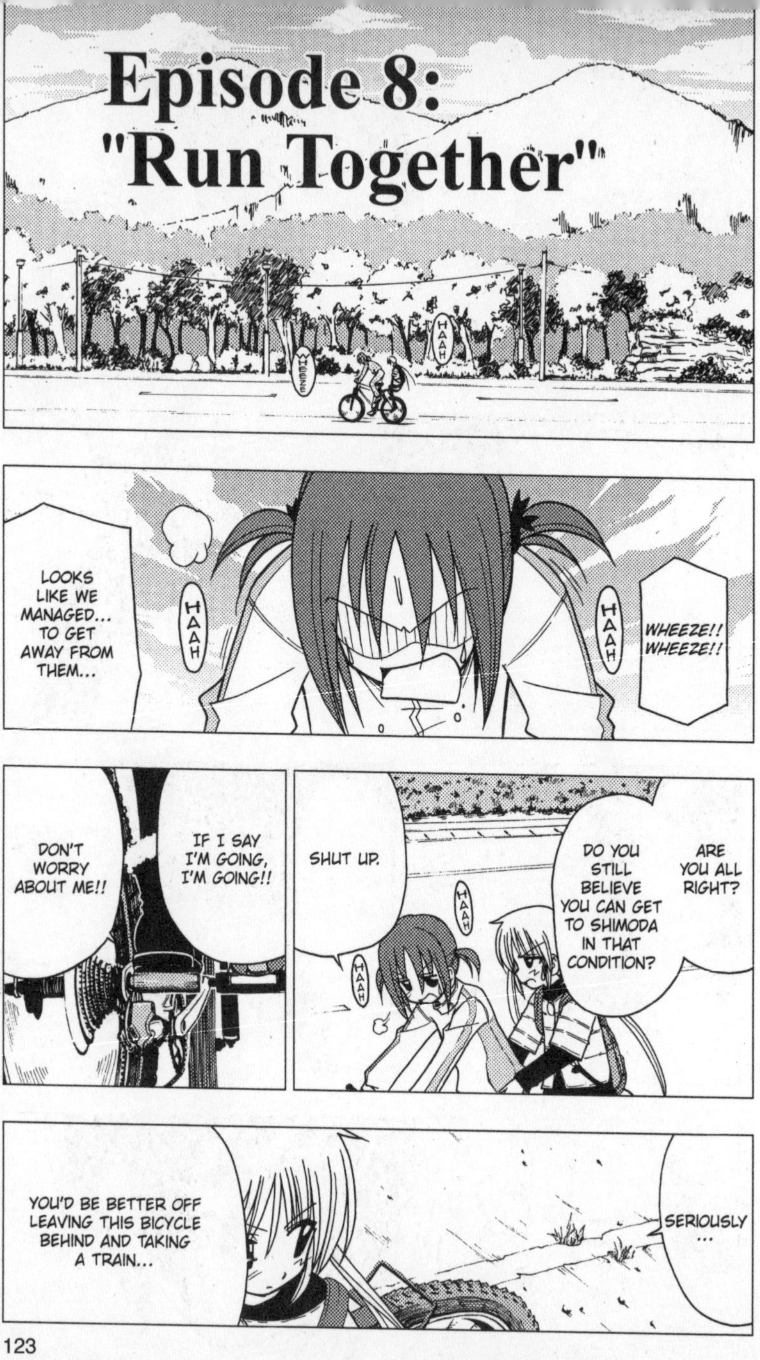
Episode 8: "Run Together"
HAAH
WHEEZE
WHEEZE!! WHEEZE!!
HAAH
HAAH
LOOKS LIKE WE MANAGED... TO GET AWAY FROM THEM...
ARE YOU ALL RIGHT?
DO YOU STILL BELIEVE YOU CAN GET TO SHIMODA IN THAT CONDITION?
HAAH
HAAH
SHUT UP.
IF I SAY I'M GOING, I'M GOING!!
DON'T WORRY ABOUT ME!!
SERIOUSLY...
YOU'D BE BETTER OFF LEAVING THIS BICYCLE BEHIND AND TAKING A TRAIN...

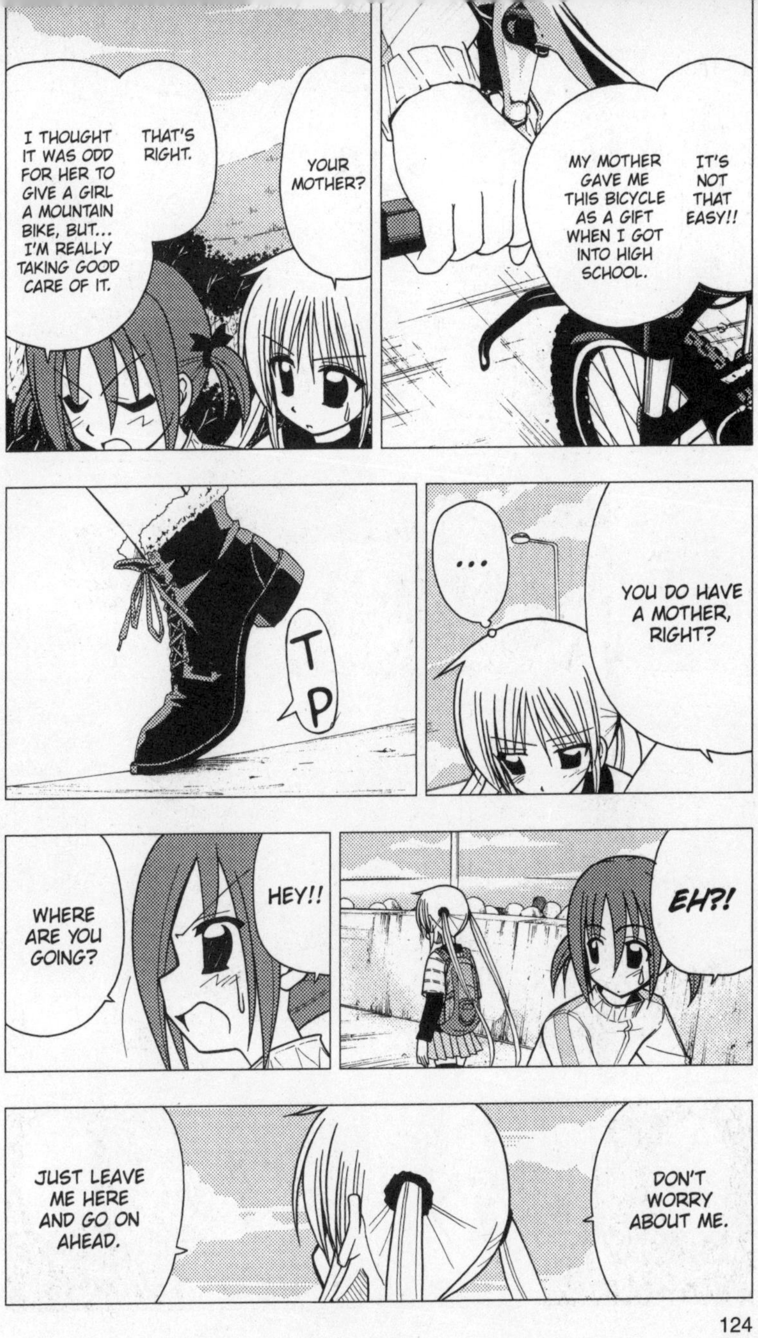
IT'S NOT THAT EASY!!
MY MOTHER GAVE ME THIS BICYCLE AS A GIFT WHEN I GOT INTO HIGH SCHOOL.
YOUR MOTHER?
THAT'S RIGHT.
I THOUGHT IT WAS ODD FOR HER TO GIVE A GIRL A MOUNTAIN BIKE, BUT... I'M REALLY TAKING GOOD CARE OF IT.
YOU DO HAVE A MOTHER, RIGHT?
...
TP
EH?!
HEY!!
WHERE ARE YOU GOING?
DON'T WORRY ABOUT ME.
JUST LEAVE ME HERE AND GO ON AHEAD.

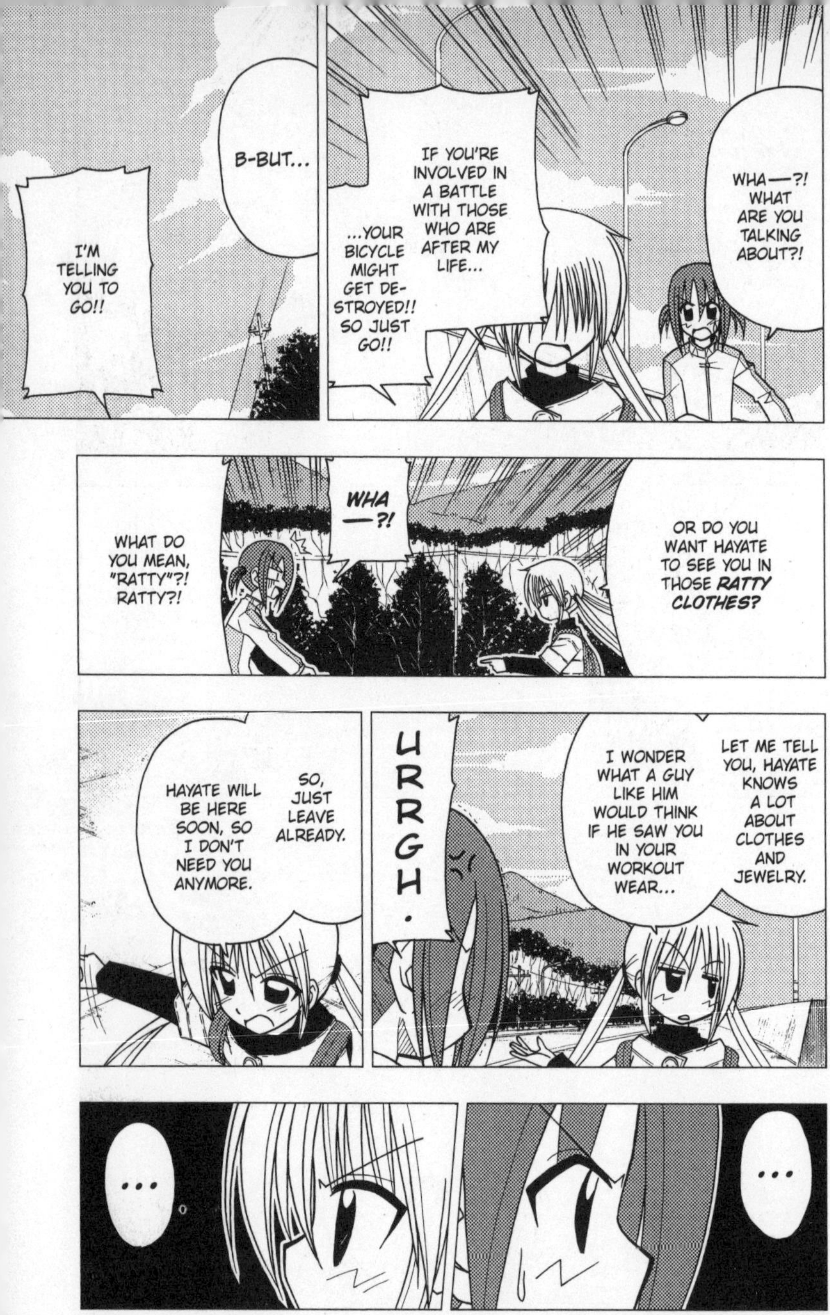
WHA—?! WHAT ARE YOU TALKING ABOUT?!
IF YOU'RE INVOLVED IN A BATTLE WITH THOSE WHO ARE AFTER MY LIFE...
...YOUR BICYCLE MIGHT GET DE-STROYED!! SO JUST GO!!
B-BUT...
I'M TELLING YOU TO GO!!
OR DO YOU WANT HAYATE TO SEE YOU IN THOSE *RATTY CLOTHES?*
WHA—?!
WHAT DO YOU MEAN, "RATTY"?! RATTY?!
LET ME TELL YOU, HAYATE KNOWS A LOT ABOUT CLOTHES AND JEWELRY.
I WONDER WHAT A GUY LIKE HIM WOULD THINK IF HE SAW YOU IN YOUR WORKOUT WEAR...
URRGH.
SO, JUST LEAVE ALREADY.
HAYATE WILL BE HERE SOON, SO I DON'T NEED YOU ANYMORE.
...
...

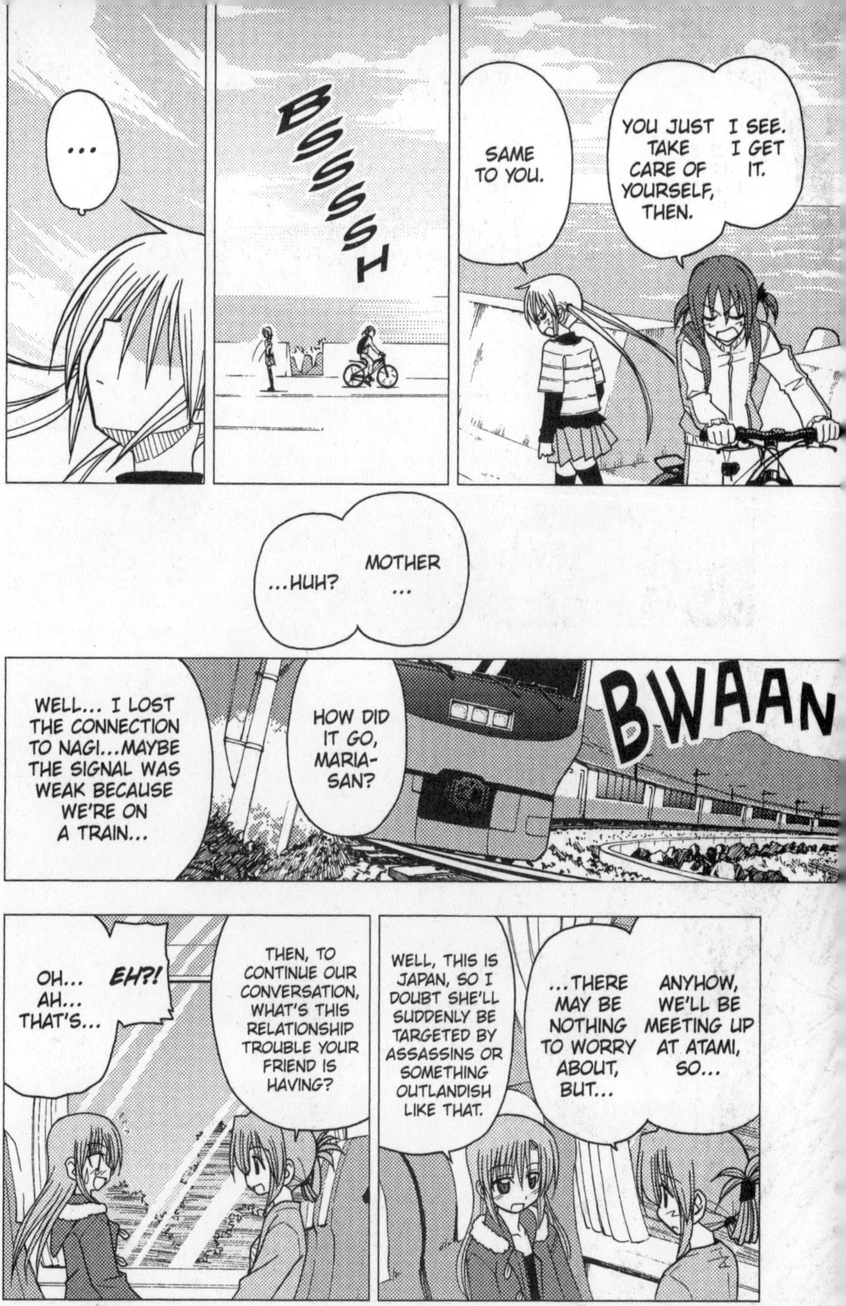
I SEE. I GET IT.
YOU JUST TAKE CARE OF YOURSELF, THEN.
SAME TO YOU.
BSSSSH
...
MOTHER ...
...HUH?
BWAAN
HOW DID IT GO, MARIA-SAN?
WELL... I LOST THE CONNECTION TO NAGI...MAYBE THE SIGNAL WAS WEAK BECAUSE WE'RE ON A TRAIN...
ANYHOW, WE'LL BE MEETING UP AT ATAMI, SO...
...THERE MAY BE NOTHING TO WORRY ABOUT, BUT...
WELL, THIS IS JAPAN, SO I DOUBT SHE'LL SUDDENLY BE TARGETED BY ASSASSINS OR SOMETHING OUTLANDISH LIKE THAT.
THEN, TO CONTINUE OUR CONVERSATION, WHAT'S THIS RELATIONSHIP TROUBLE YOUR FRIEND IS HAVING?
EH?!
OH... AH... THAT'S...

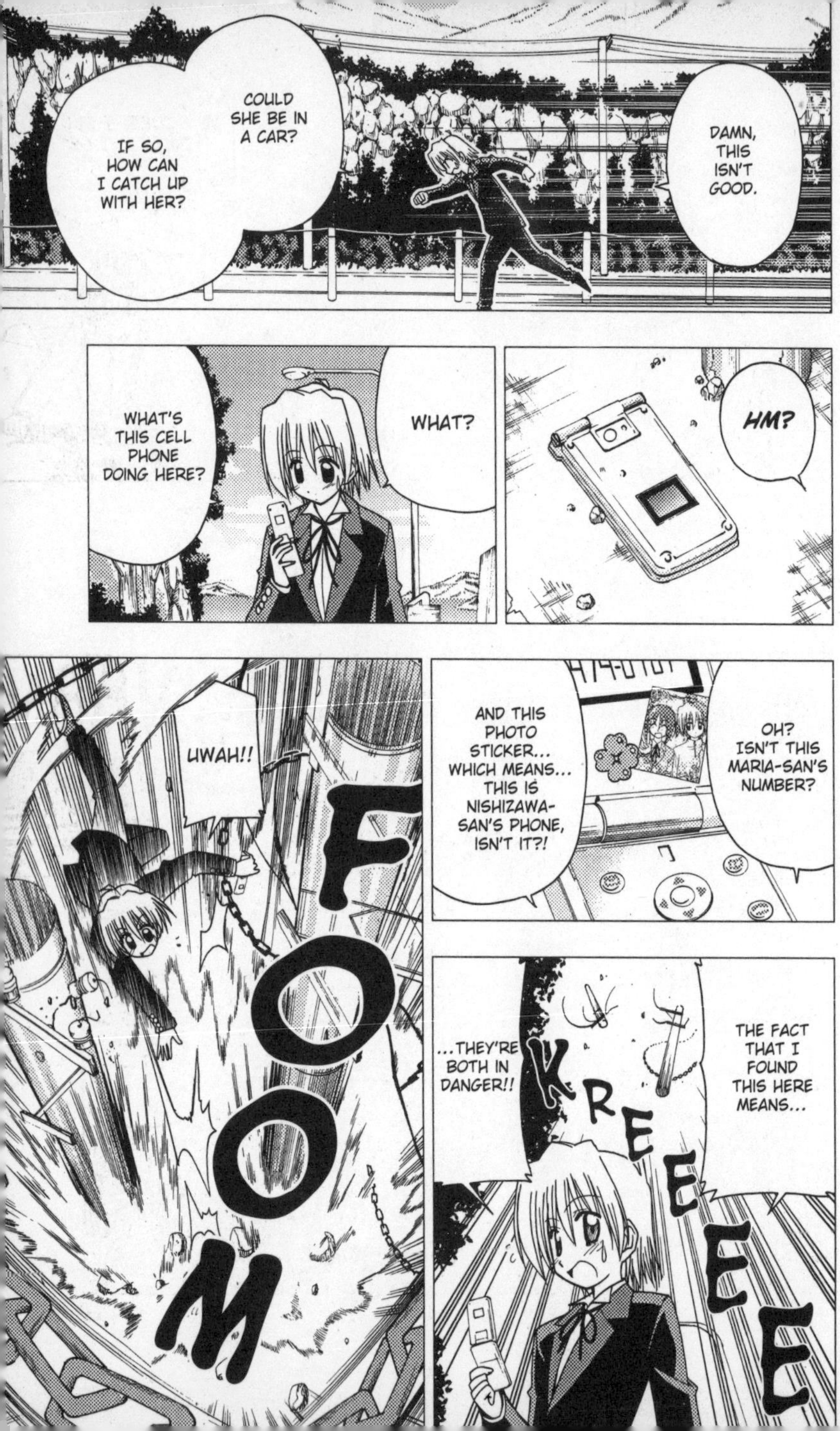
DAMN, THIS ISN'T GOOD.
COULD SHE BE IN A CAR?
IF SO, HOW CAN I CATCH UP WITH HER?
HM?
WHAT?
WHAT'S THIS CELL PHONE DOING HERE?
OH? ISN'T THIS MARIA-SAN'S NUMBER?
AND THIS PHOTO STICKER... WHICH MEANS... THIS IS NISHIZAWA-SAN'S PHONE, ISN'T IT?!
THE FACT THAT I FOUND THIS HERE MEANS...
KREEEEEE
...THEY'RE BOTH IN DANGER!!
UWAH!!
FOOOM

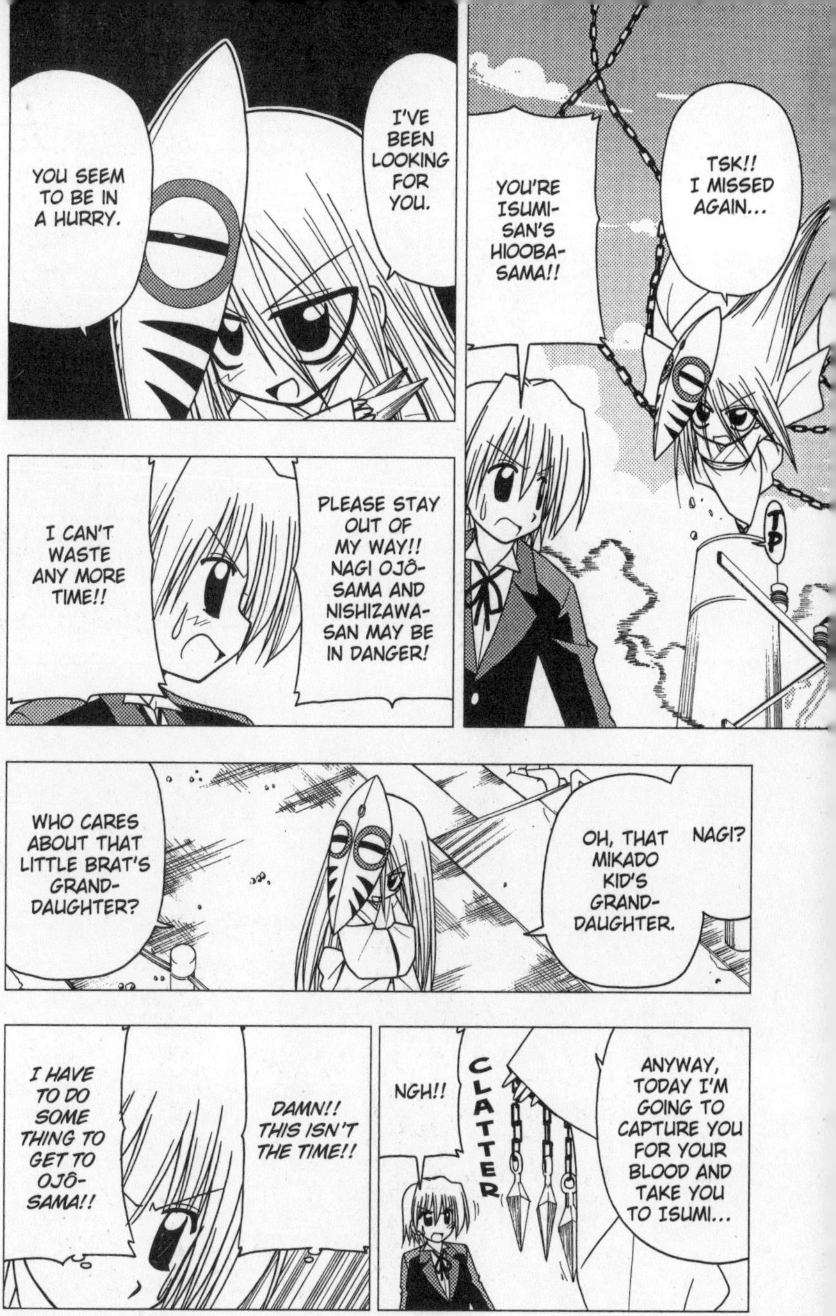
TSK!! I MISSED AGAIN...
YOU'RE ISUMI-SAN'S HIOOBA-SAMA!!
TP
I'VE BEEN LOOKING FOR YOU.
YOU SEEM TO BE IN A HURRY.
PLEASE STAY OUT OF MY WAY!! NAGI OJÔ-SAMA AND NISHIZAWA-SAN MAY BE IN DANGER!
I CAN'T WASTE ANY MORE TIME!!
NAGI?
OH, THAT MIKADO KID'S GRAND-DAUGHTER.
WHO CARES ABOUT THAT LITTLE BRAT'S GRAND-DAUGHTER?
ANYWAY, TODAY I'M GOING TO CAPTURE YOU FOR YOUR BLOOD AND TAKE YOU TO ISUMI...
CLATTER
NGH!!
DAMN!! THIS ISN'T THE TIME!!
I HAVE TO DO SOME THING TO GET TO OJÔ-SAMA!!

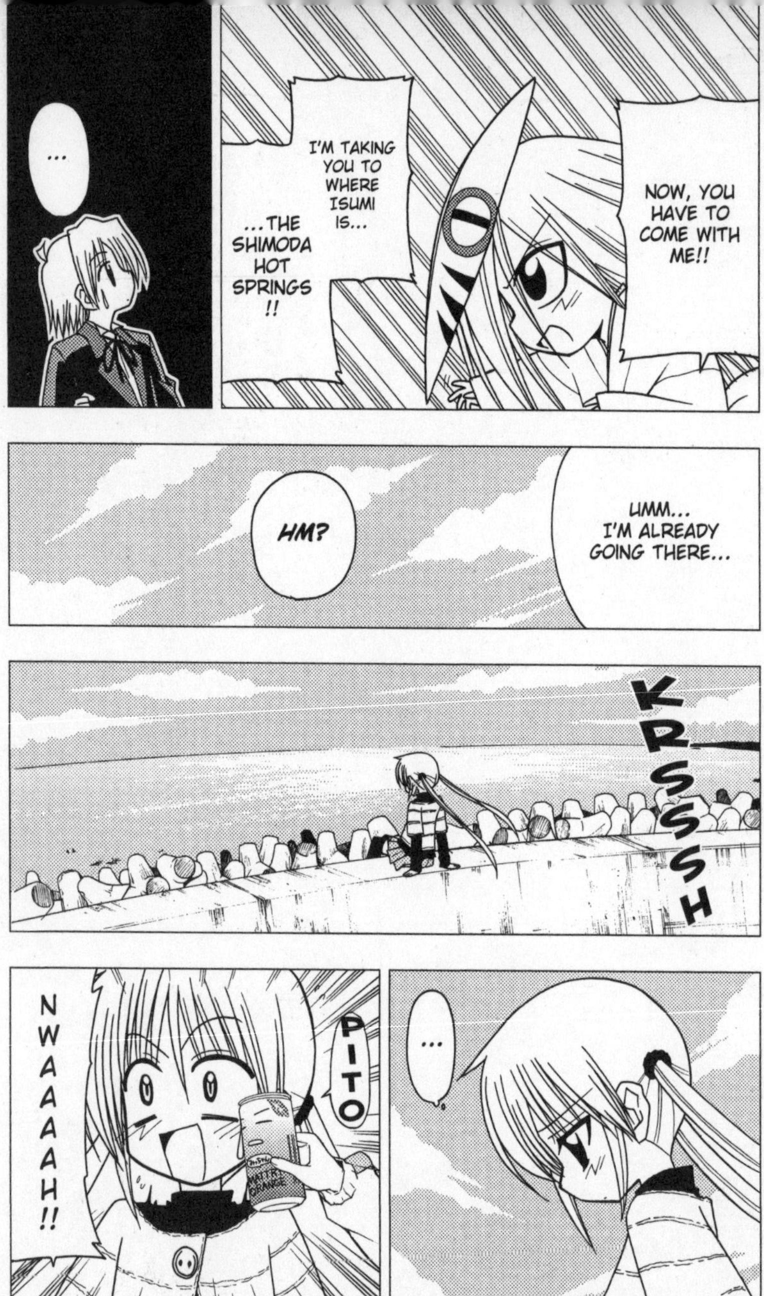
NOW, YOU HAVE TO COME WITH ME!!
I'M TAKING YOU TO WHERE ISUMI IS...
...THE SHIMODA HOT SPRINGS!!
...
UMM... I'M ALREADY GOING THERE...
HM?
KRSSSH
...
PITO
NWAAAAAAH!!

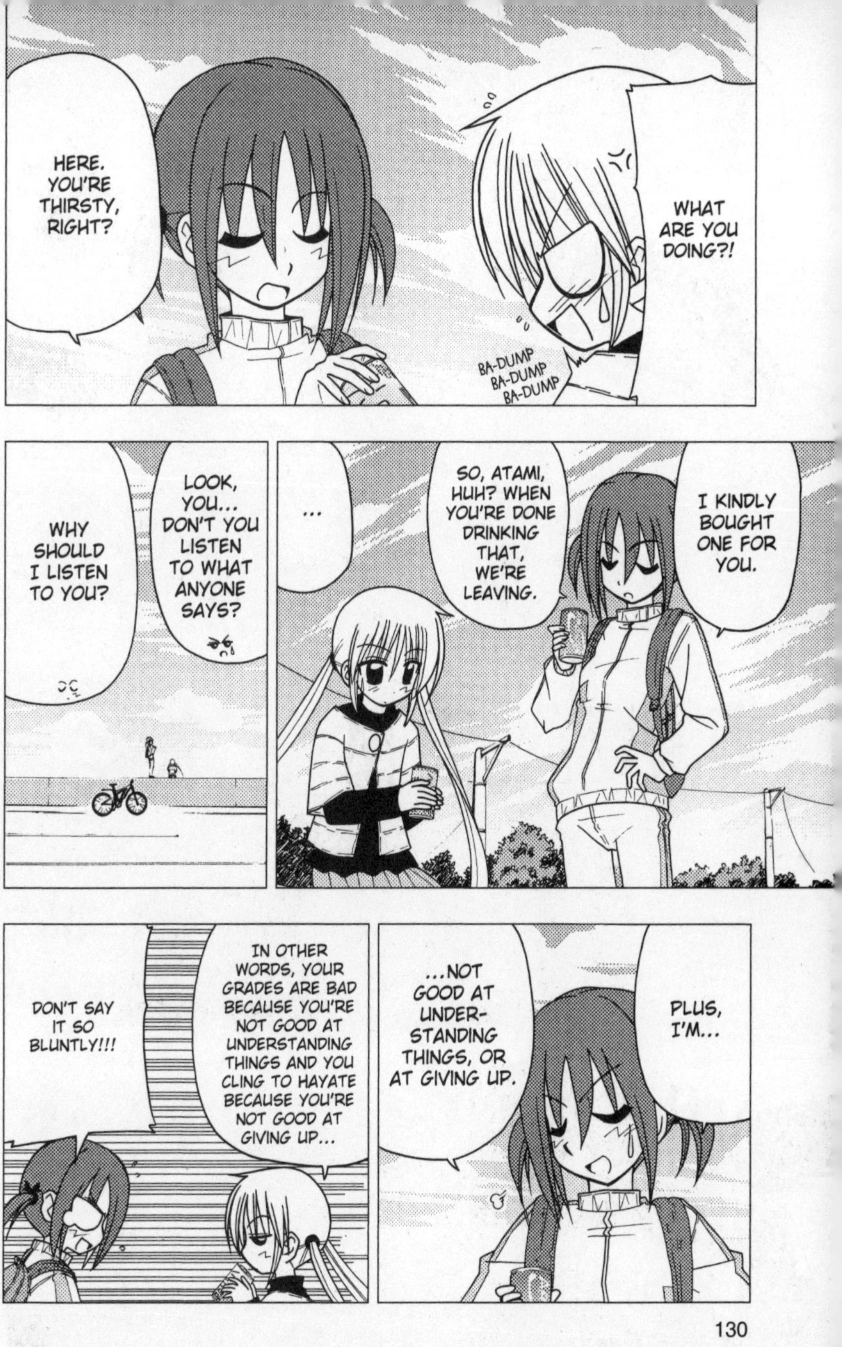
HERE. YOU'RE THIRSTY, RIGHT?
WHAT ARE YOU DOING?!
BA-DUMP BA-DUMP BA-DUMP
I KINDLY BOUGHT ONE FOR YOU.
SO, ATAMI, HUH? WHEN YOU'RE DONE DRINKING THAT, WE'RE LEAVING.
...
LOOK, YOU... DON'T YOU LISTEN TO WHAT ANYONE SAYS?
WHY SHOULD I LISTEN TO YOU?
PLUS, I'M...
...NOT GOOD AT UNDER-STANDING THINGS, OR AT GIVING UP.
IN OTHER WORDS, YOUR GRADES ARE BAD BECAUSE YOU'RE NOT GOOD AT UNDERSTANDING THINGS AND YOU CLING TO HAYATE BECAUSE YOU'RE NOT GOOD AT GIVING UP...
DON'T SAY IT SO BLUNTLY!!!

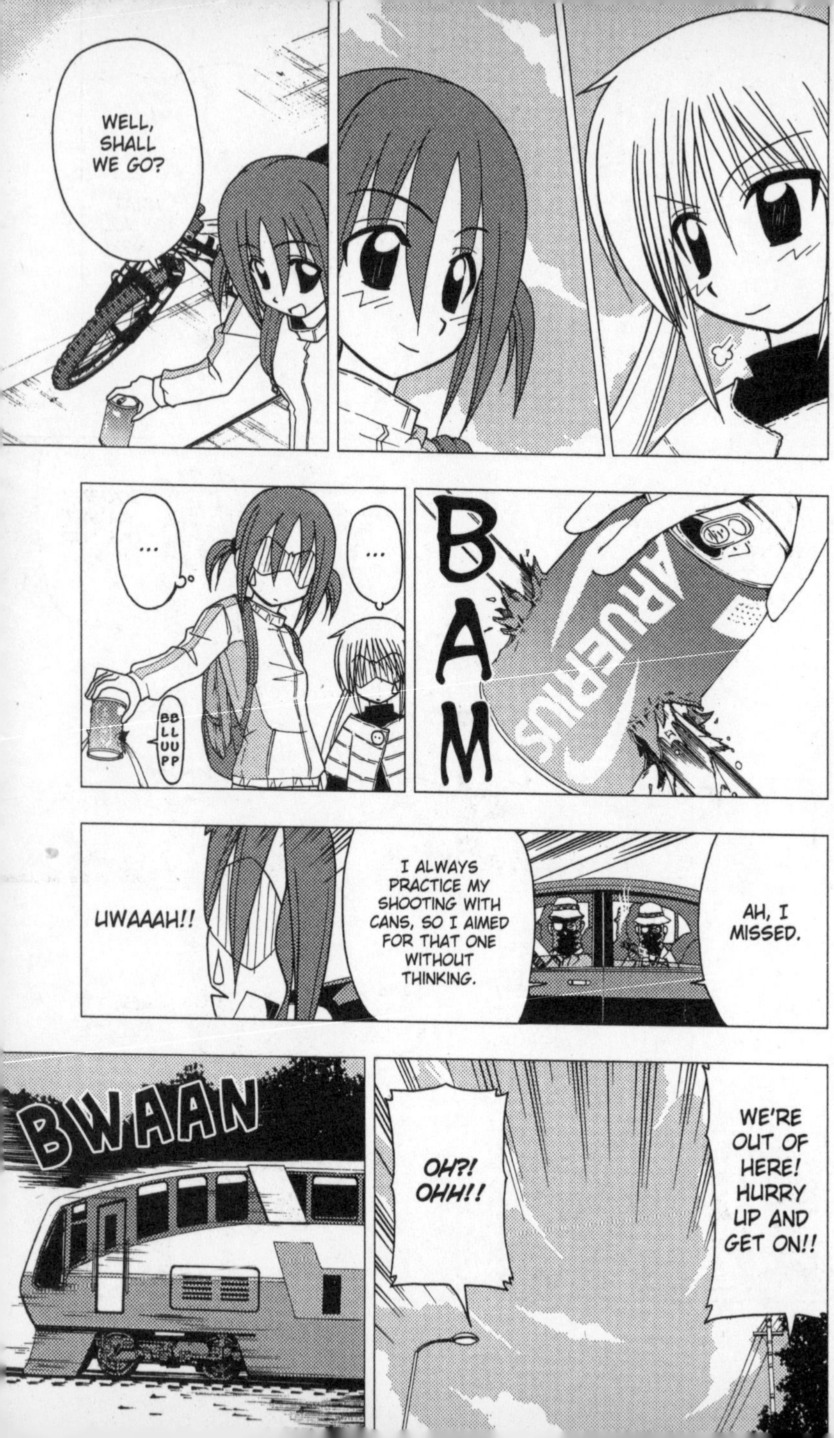
WELL, SHALL WE GO?
BAM
ARUERIUS
...
...
BBLLUUPP
AH, I MISSED.
I ALWAYS PRACTICE MY SHOOTING WITH CANS, SO I AIMED FOR THAT ONE WITHOUT THINKING.
UWAAAH!!
WE'RE OUT OF HERE! HURRY UP AND GET ON!!
OH?! OHH!!
BWAAN

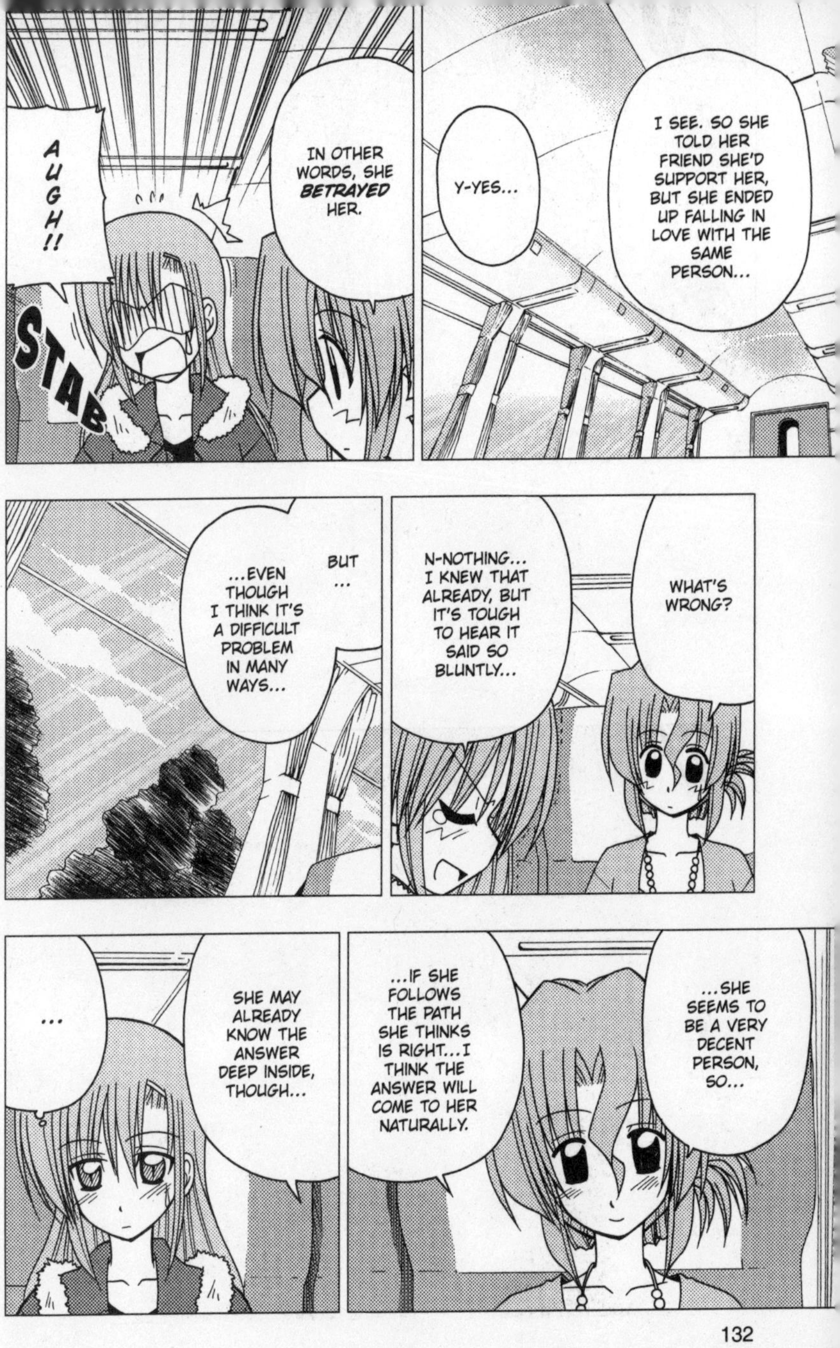
I SEE. SO SHE TOLD HER FRIEND SHE'D SUPPORT HER, BUT SHE ENDED UP FALLING IN LOVE WITH THE SAME PERSON...
Y-YES...
IN OTHER WORDS, SHE *BETRAYED* HER.
AUGH!!
STAB
WHAT'S WRONG?
N-NOTHING... I KNEW THAT ALREADY, BUT IT'S TOUGH TO HEAR IT SAID SO BLUNTLY...
BUT ...
...EVEN THOUGH I THINK IT'S A DIFFICULT PROBLEM IN MANY WAYS...
...SHE SEEMS TO BE A VERY DECENT PERSON, SO...
...IF SHE FOLLOWS THE PATH SHE THINKS IS RIGHT...I THINK THE ANSWER WILL COME TO HER NATURALLY.
SHE MAY ALREADY KNOW THE ANSWER DEEP INSIDE, THOUGH...
...

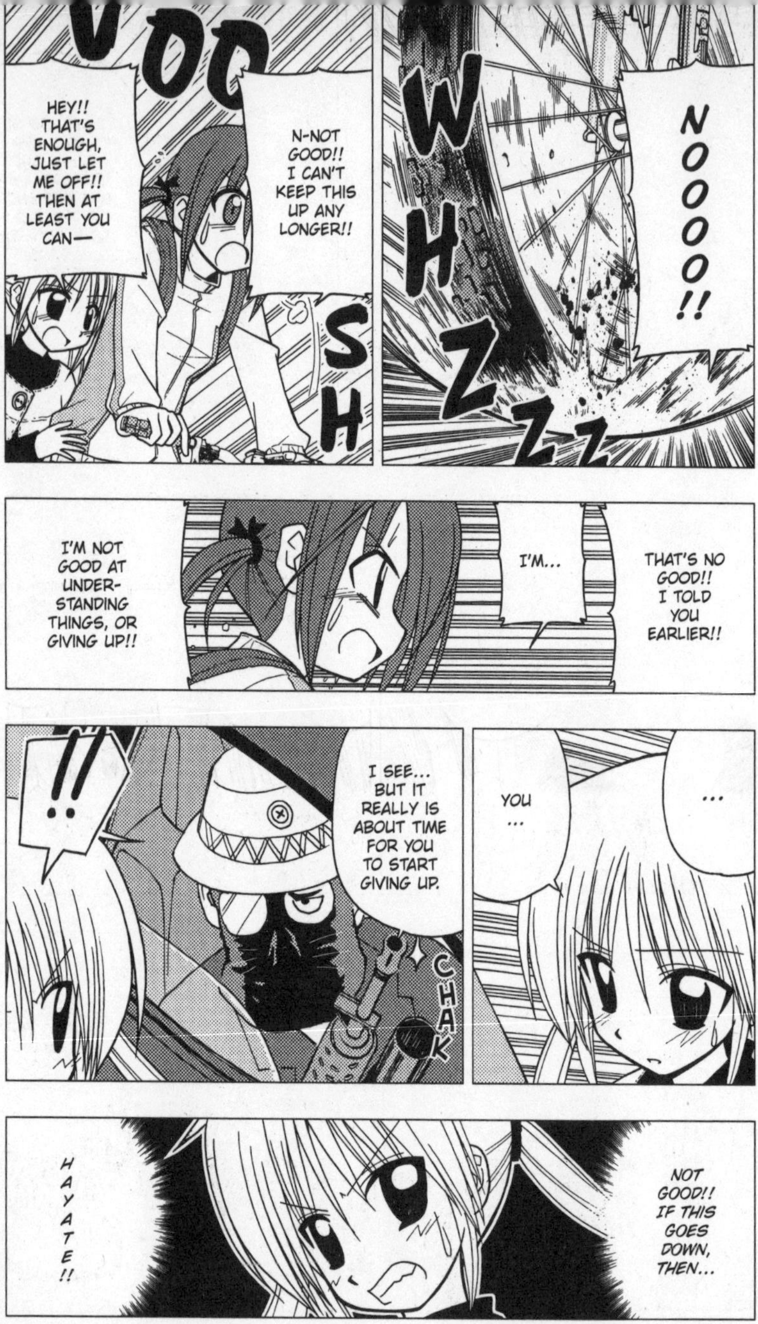
NOOOOO!!
WHZZZ
VOO
N-NOT GOOD!! I CAN'T KEEP THIS UP ANY LONGER!!
HEY!! THAT'S ENOUGH, JUST LET ME OFF!! THEN AT LEAST YOU CAN—
SH
THAT'S NO GOOD!! I TOLD YOU EARLIER!!
I'M...
I'M NOT GOOD AT UNDER-STANDING THINGS, OR GIVING UP!!
...
YOU ...
I SEE... BUT IT REALLY IS ABOUT TIME FOR YOU TO START GIVING UP.
CHAK
!!
NOT GOOD!! IF THIS GOES DOWN, THEN...
HAYATE!!

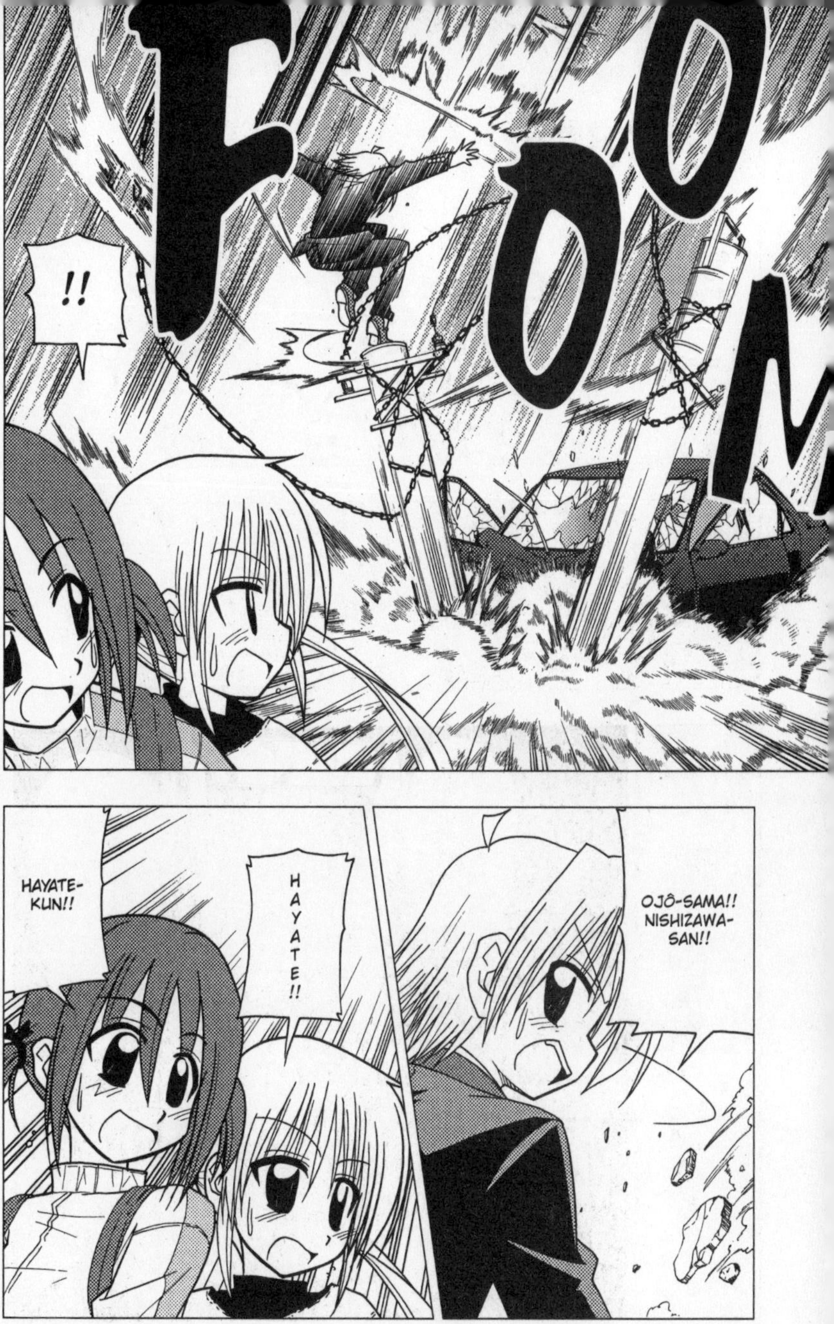
FOOM
!!
OJÔ-SAMA!! NISHIZAWA-SAN!!
HAYATE!!
HAYATE-KUN!!

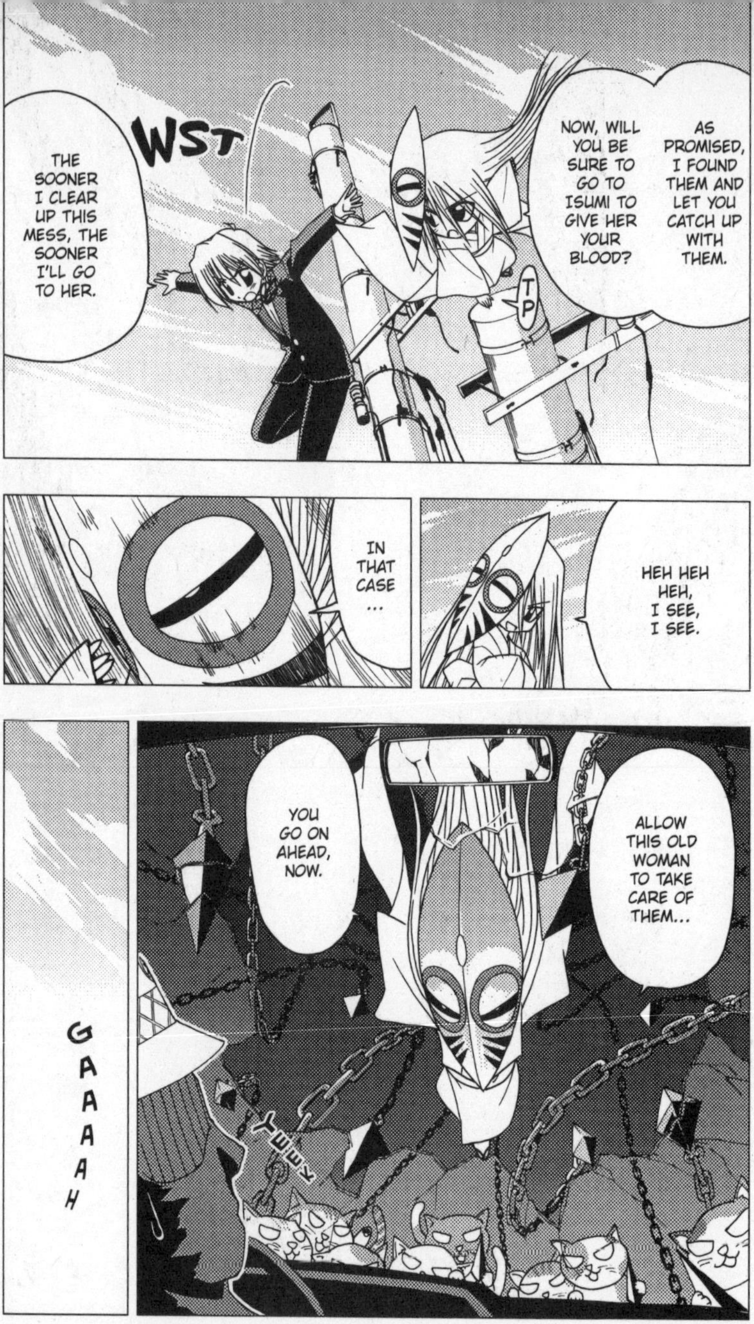
AS PROMISED, I FOUND THEM AND LET YOU CATCH UP WITH THEM.
NOW, WILL YOU BE SURE TO GO TO ISUMI TO GIVE HER YOUR BLOOD?
TP
WST
THE SOONER I CLEAR UP THIS MESS, THE SOONER I'LL GO TO HER.
HEH HEH HEH, I SEE, I SEE.
IN THAT CASE ...
ALLOW THIS OLD WOMAN TO TAKE CARE OF THEM...
YOU GO ON AHEAD, NOW.
YEEK
GAAAAAH

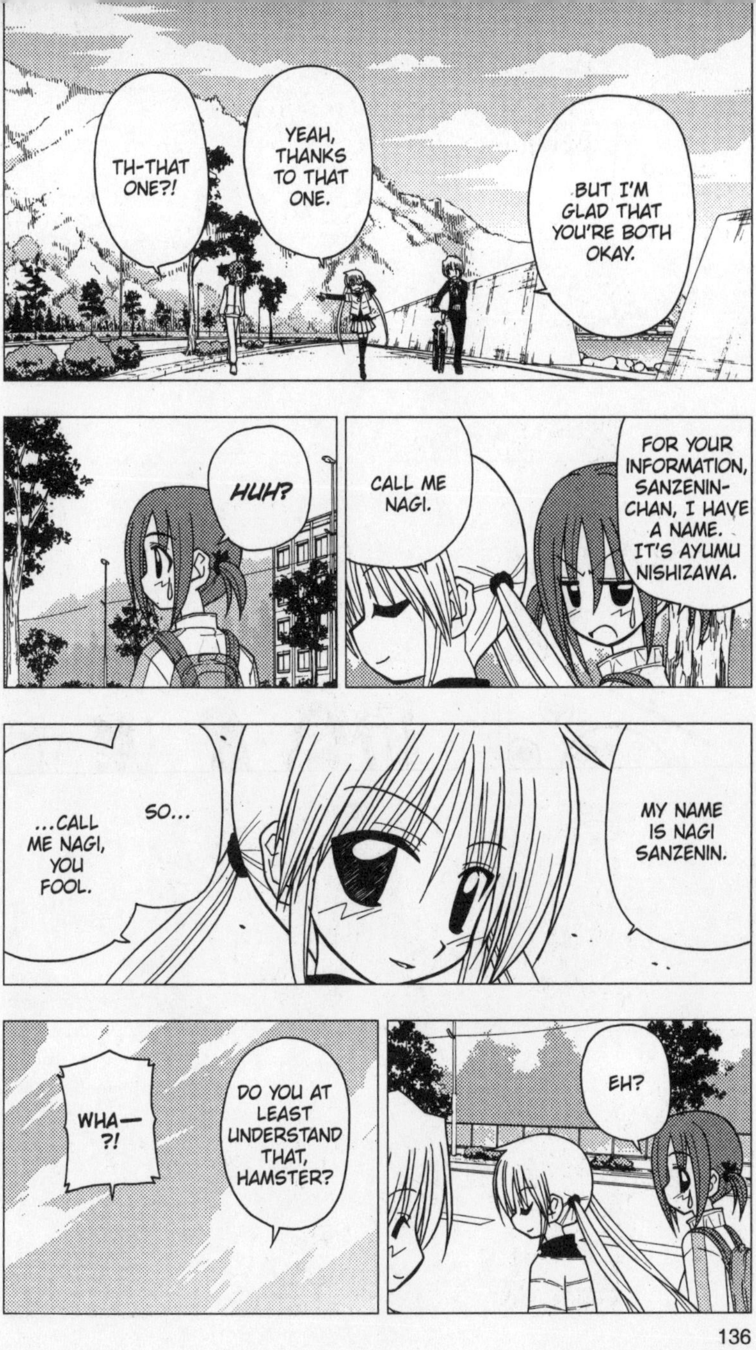
BUT I'M GLAD THAT YOU'RE BOTH OKAY.
YEAH, THANKS TO THAT ONE.
TH-THAT ONE?!
FOR YOUR INFORMATION, SANZENIN-CHAN, I HAVE A NAME. IT'S AYUMU NISHIZAWA.
CALL ME NAGI.
HUH?
MY NAME IS NAGI SANZENIN.
SO...
...CALL ME NAGI, YOU FOOL.
EH?
DO YOU AT LEAST UNDERSTAND THAT, HAMSTER?
WHA— ?!

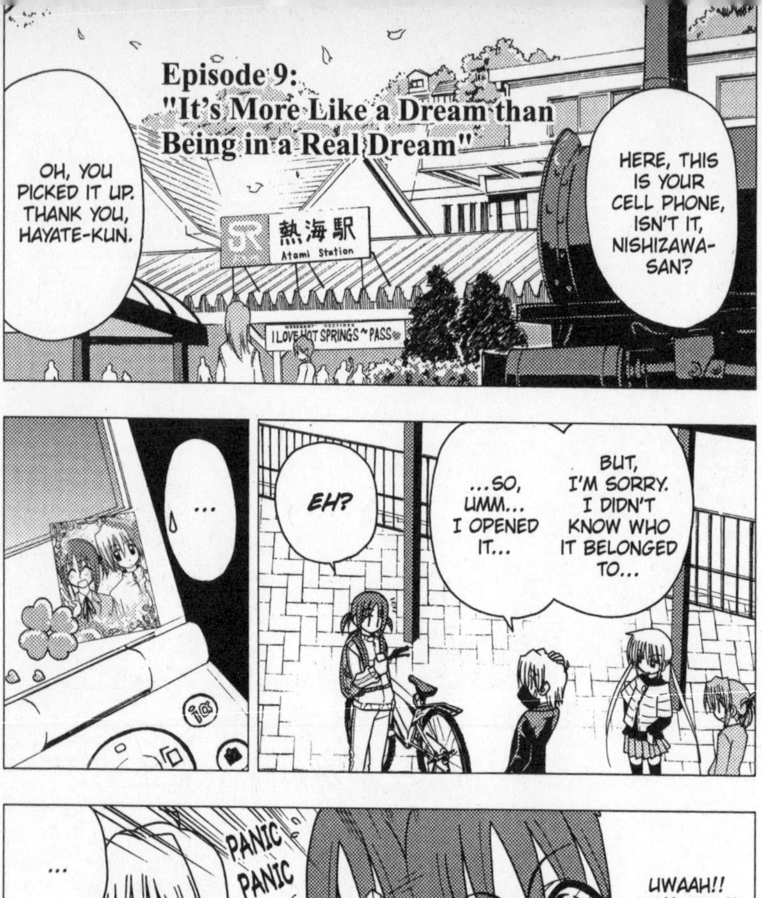
Episode 9:
"It's More Like a Dream than Being in a Real Dream"
熱海駅
Atami Station
I LOVE HOT SPRINGS ~ PASS
HERE, THIS IS YOUR CELL PHONE, ISN'T IT, NISHIZAWA-SAN?
OH, YOU PICKED IT UP. THANK YOU, HAYATE-KUN.
BUT, I'M SORRY. I DIDN'T KNOW WHO IT BELONGED TO...
...SO, UMM... I OPENED IT...
EH?
...
UWAAH!! UH!! THIS!! THIS IS...
PANIC PANIC
...
EITHER WAY, NISHIZAWA-SAN...
...THANK YOU VERY MUCH FOR TAKING CARE OF NAGI.
HUH?
NO, NO...
IT WAS NOTHING, REALLY.

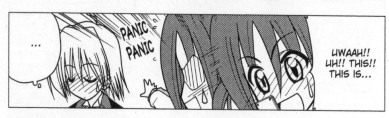

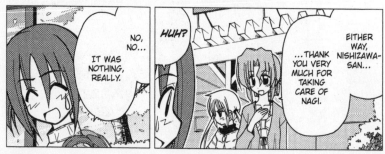

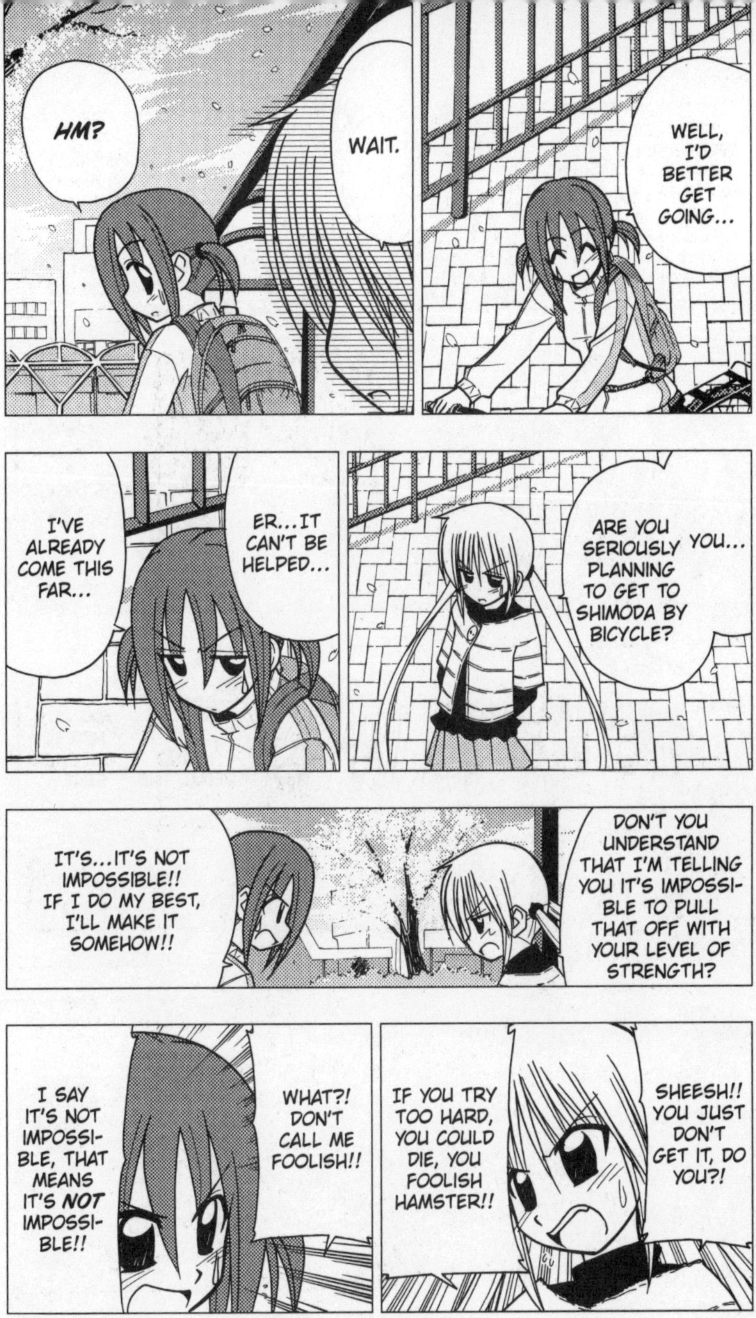
WELL, I'D BETTER GET GOING...
WAIT.
HM?
YOU...
ARE YOU SERIOUSLY PLANNING TO GET TO SHIMODA BY BICYCLE?
ER...IT CAN'T BE HELPED...
I'VE ALREADY COME THIS FAR...
DON'T YOU UNDERSTAND THAT I'M TELLING YOU IT'S IMPOSSIBLE TO PULL THAT OFF WITH YOUR LEVEL OF STRENGTH?
IT'S...IT'S NOT IMPOSSIBLE!! IF I DO MY BEST, I'LL MAKE IT SOMEHOW!!
SHEESH!! YOU JUST DON'T GET IT, DO YOU?!
IF YOU TRY TOO HARD, YOU COULD DIE, YOU FOOLISH HAMSTER!!
WHAT?! DON'T CALL ME FOOLISH!!
I SAY IT'S NOT IMPOSSIBLE, THAT MEANS IT'S *NOT* IMPOSSIBLE!!

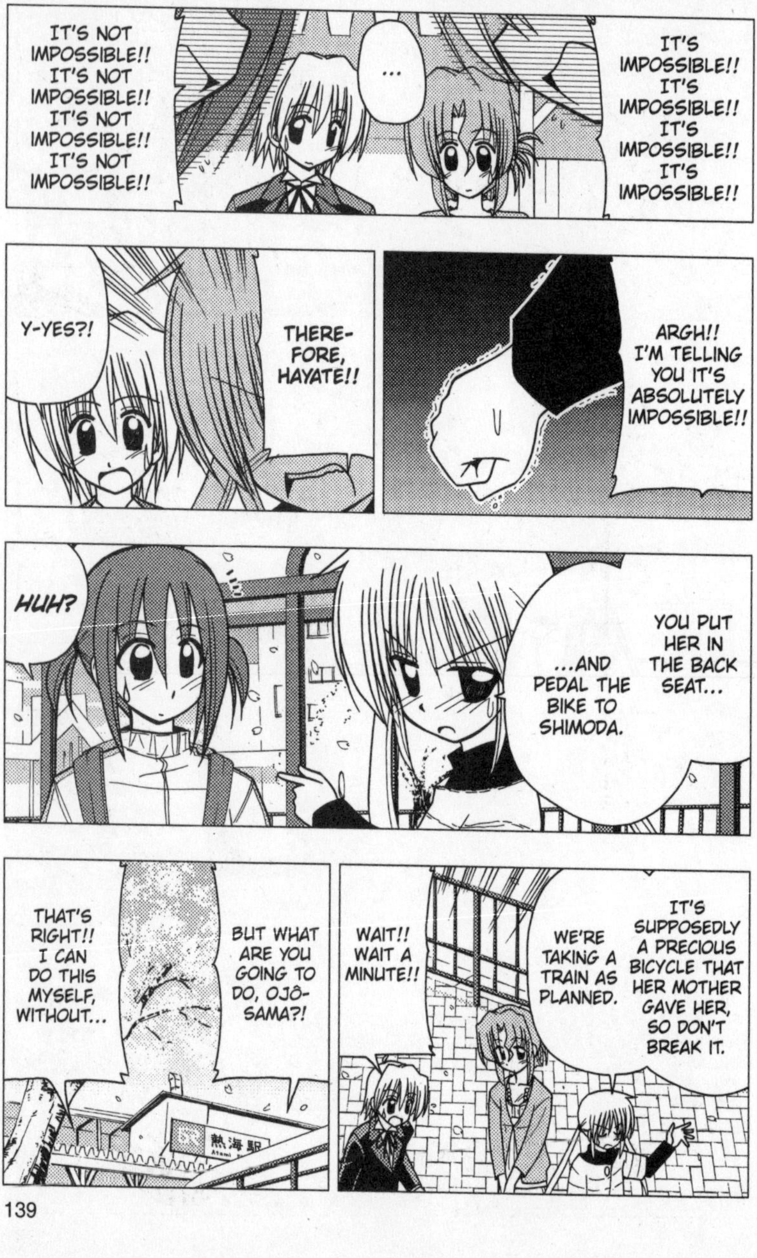
IT'S IMPOSSIBLE!! IT'S IMPOSSIBLE!! IT'S IMPOSSIBLE!! IT'S IMPOSSIBLE!!
...
IT'S NOT IMPOSSIBLE!! IT'S NOT IMPOSSIBLE!! IT'S NOT IMPOSSIBLE!! IT'S NOT IMPOSSIBLE!!
ARGH!! I'M TELLING YOU IT'S ABSOLUTELY IMPOSSIBLE!!
THERE-FORE, HAYATE!!
Y-YES?!
YOU PUT HER IN THE BACK SEAT...
...AND PEDAL THE BIKE TO SHIMODA.
HUH?
IT'S SUPPOSEDLY A PRECIOUS BICYCLE THAT HER MOTHER GAVE HER, SO DON'T BREAK IT.
WE'RE TAKING A TRAIN AS PLANNED.
WAIT!! WAIT A MINUTE!!
BUT WHAT ARE YOU GOING TO DO, OJÔ-SAMA?!
THAT'S RIGHT!! I CAN DO THIS MYSELF, WITHOUT...
熱海駅

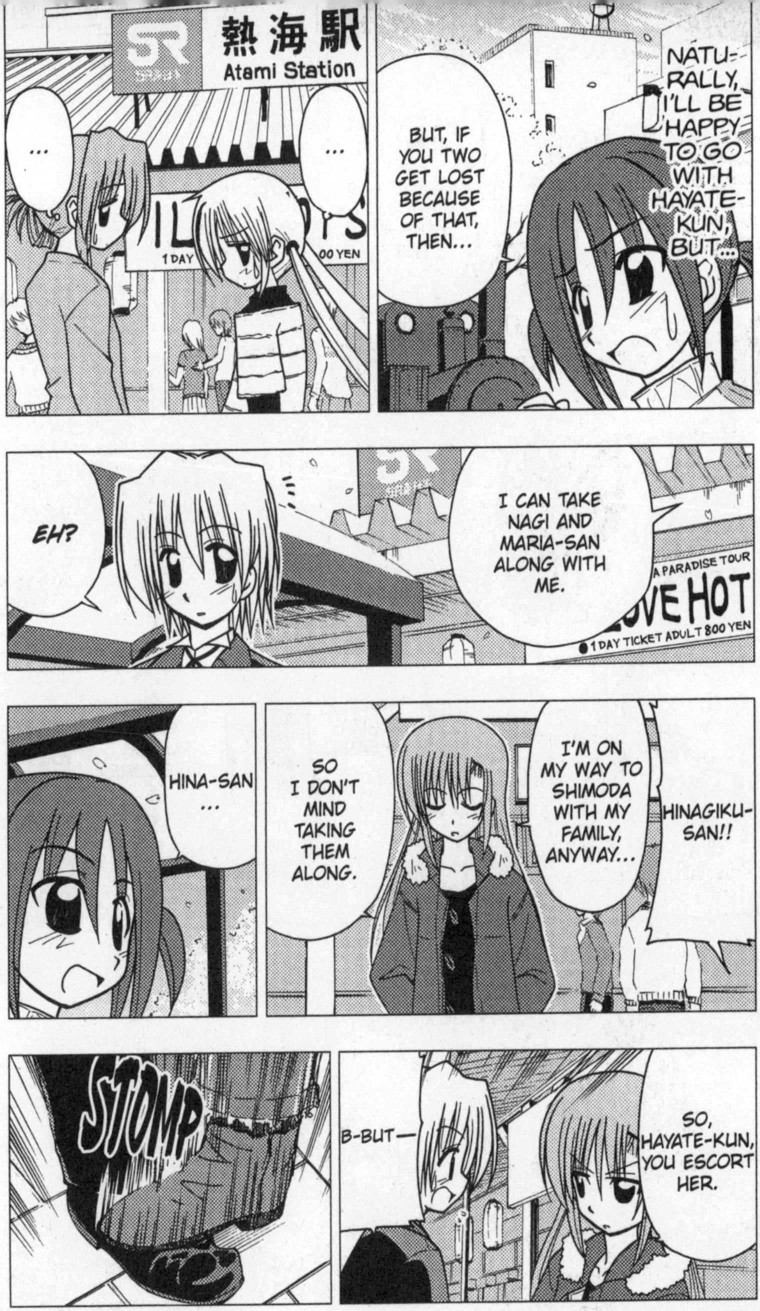
NATURALLY, I'LL BE HAPPY TO GO WITH HAYATE-KUN, BUT...
BUT, IF YOU TWO GET LOST BECAUSE OF THAT, THEN...
熱海駅
Atami Station
...
...
1 DAY
00 YEN
I CAN TAKE NAGI AND MARIA-SAN ALONG WITH ME.
A PARADISE TOUR
LOVE HOT
1 DAY TICKET ADULT 800 YEN
EH?
HINAGIKU-SAN!!
I'M ON MY WAY TO SHIMODA WITH MY FAMILY, ANYWAY...
SO I DON'T MIND TAKING THEM ALONG.
HINA-SAN ...
SO, HAYATE-KUN, YOU ESCORT HER.
B-BUT—
STOMP

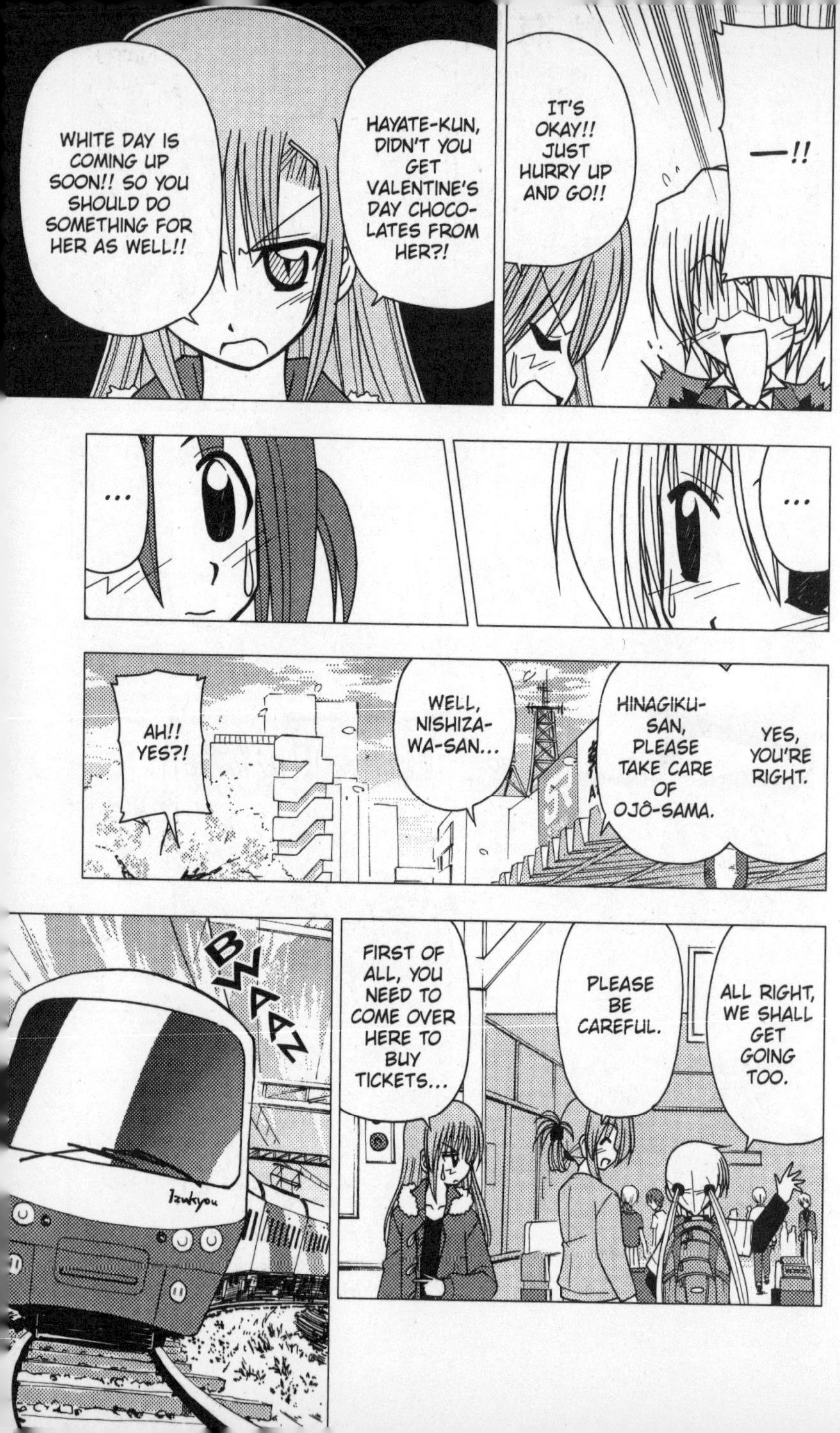
—!!
IT'S OKAY!! JUST HURRY UP AND GO!!
HAYATE-KUN, DIDN'T YOU GET VALENTINE'S DAY CHOCOLATES FROM HER?!
WHITE DAY IS COMING UP SOON!! SO YOU SHOULD DO SOMETHING FOR HER AS WELL!!
...
...
YES, YOU'RE RIGHT.
HINAGIKU-SAN, PLEASE TAKE CARE OF OJÔ-SAMA.
WELL, NISHIZAWA-SAN...
AH!! YES?!
ALL RIGHT, WE SHALL GET GOING TOO.
PLEASE BE CAREFUL.
FIRST OF ALL, YOU NEED TO COME OVER HERE TO BUY TICKETS...
BWAAN
Izukyou

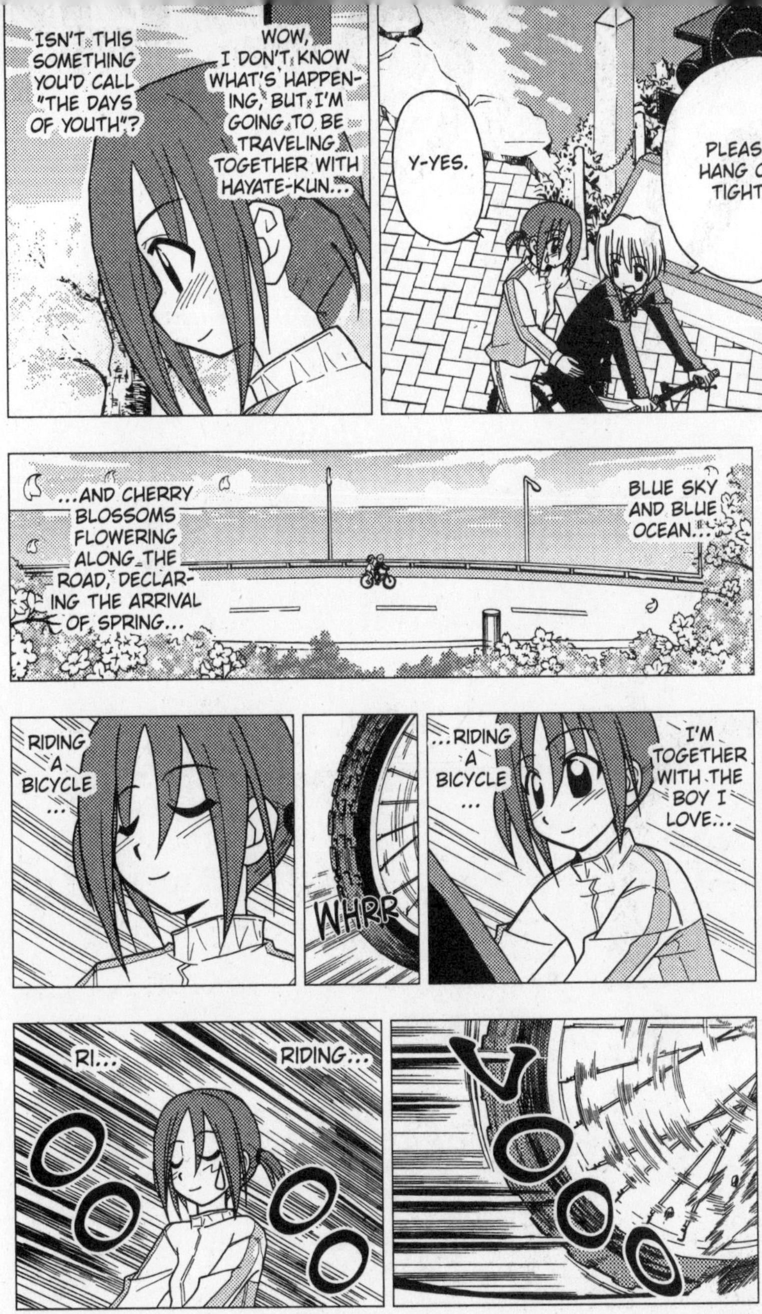
PLEASE HANG ON TIGHT.
Y-YES.
WOW, I DON'T KNOW WHAT'S HAPPENING, BUT I'M GOING TO BE TRAVELING TOGETHER WITH HAYATE-KUN...
ISN'T THIS SOMETHING YOU'D CALL "THE DAYS OF YOUTH"?
BLUE SKY AND BLUE OCEAN...
...AND CHERRY BLOSSOMS FLOWERING ALONG THE ROAD, DECLARING THE ARRIVAL OF SPRING...
I'M TOGETHER WITH THE BOY I LOVE...
...RIDING A BICYCLE ...
WHRR
RIDING A BICYCLE ...
VOOOOO
RIDING...
RI...
OOOOO

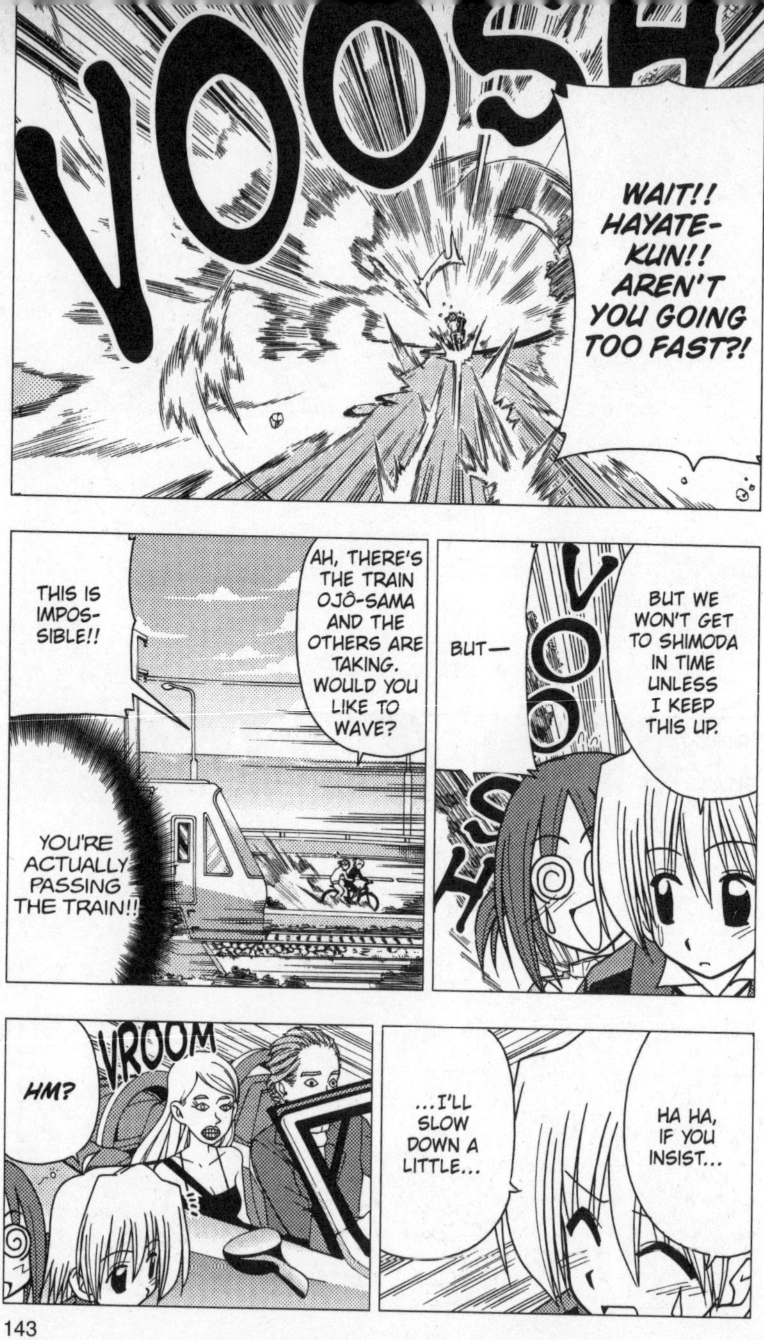
VOOSH!
WAIT!! HAYATE-KUN!! AREN'T YOU GOING TOO FAST?!
BUT WE WON'T GET TO SHIMODA IN TIME UNLESS I KEEP THIS UP.
BUT—
VOOSH
AH, THERE'S THE TRAIN OJÔ-SAMA AND THE OTHERS ARE TAKING. WOULD YOU LIKE TO WAVE?
THIS IS IMPOSSIBLE!!
YOU'RE ACTUALLY PASSING THE TRAIN!!
HA HA, IF YOU INSIST...
...I'LL SLOW DOWN A LITTLE...
VROOM
HM?

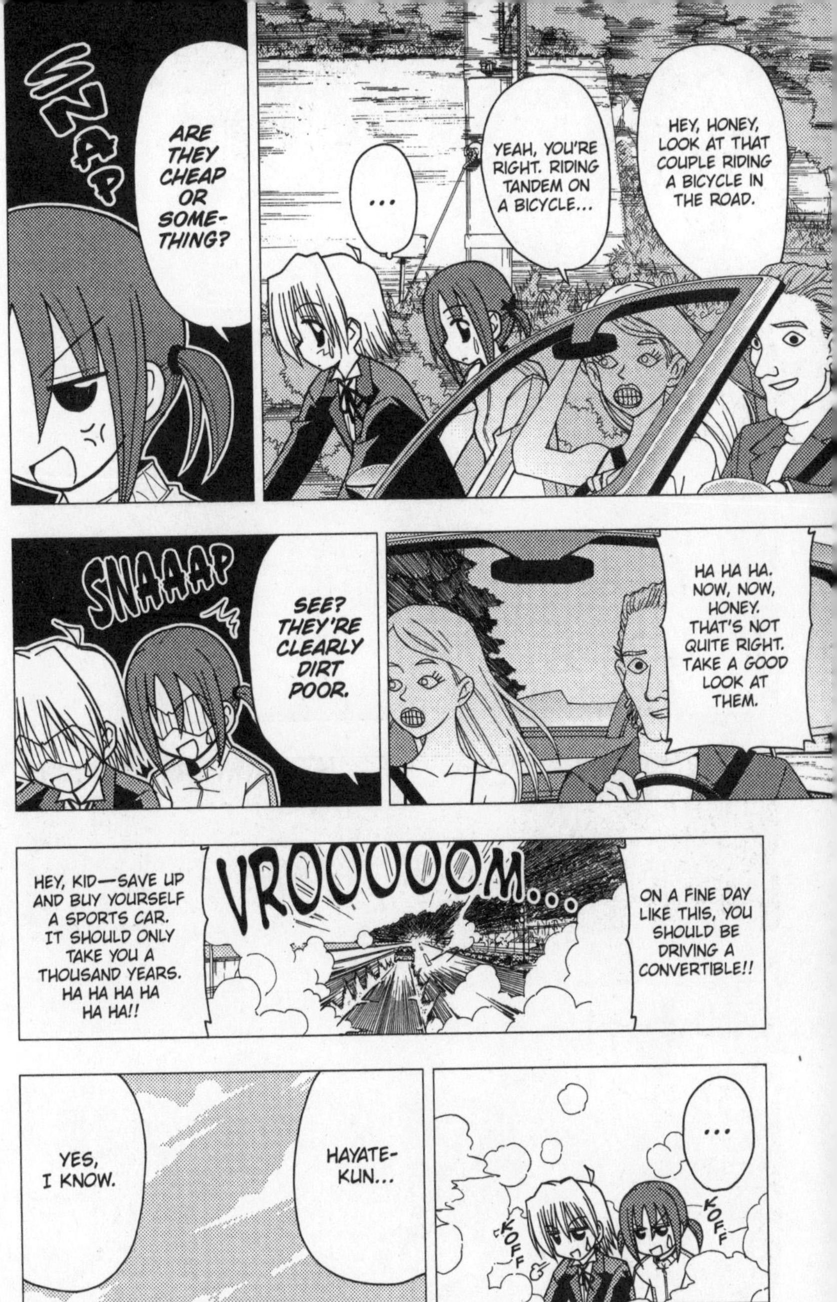
HEY, HONEY, LOOK AT THAT COUPLE RIDING A BICYCLE IN THE ROAD.
YEAH, YOU'RE RIGHT. RIDING TANDEM ON A BICYCLE...
...
ARE THEY CHEAP OR SOME-THING?
SNAP
HA HA HA. NOW, NOW, HONEY. THAT'S NOT QUITE RIGHT. TAKE A GOOD LOOK AT THEM.
SEE? THEY'RE CLEARLY DIRT POOR.
SNAAAP
ON A FINE DAY LIKE THIS, YOU SHOULD BE DRIVING A CONVERTIBLE!!
VROOOOOM...
HEY, KID—SAVE UP AND BUY YOURSELF A SPORTS CAR. IT SHOULD ONLY TAKE YOU A THOUSAND YEARS. HA HA HA HA HA HA!!
...
KOFF
KOFF
HAYATE-KUN...
YES, I KNOW.

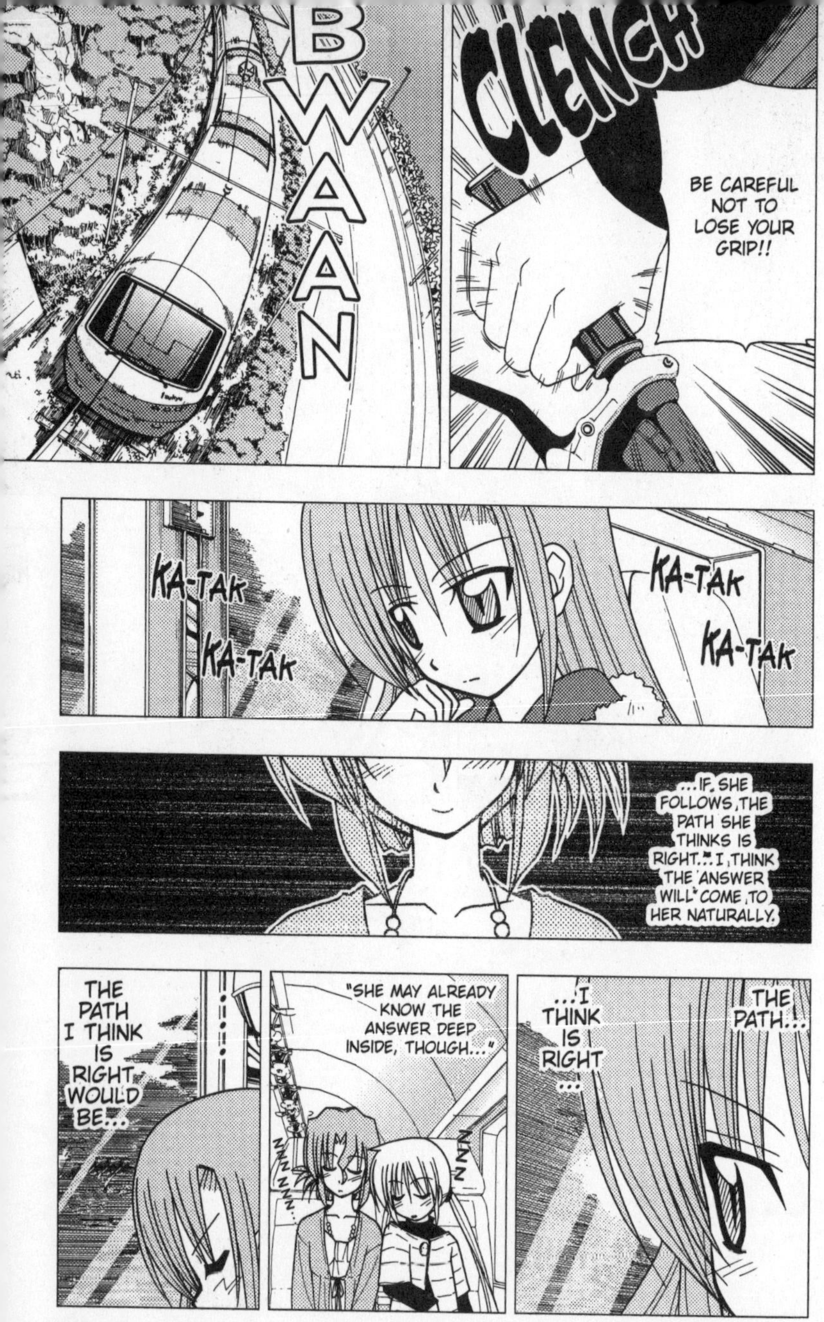
CLENCH
BE CAREFUL NOT TO LOSE YOUR GRIP!!
BWAAN
KA-TAK
KA-TAK
KA-TAK
KA-TAK
...IF SHE FOLLOWS THE PATH SHE THINKS IS RIGHT... I THINK THE ANSWER WILL COME TO HER NATURALLY.
THE PATH...
...I THINK IS RIGHT...
"SHE MAY ALREADY KNOW THE ANSWER DEEP INSIDE, THOUGH..."
ZNN
ZNN ZNN...
THE PATH I THINK IS RIGHT WOULD BE...

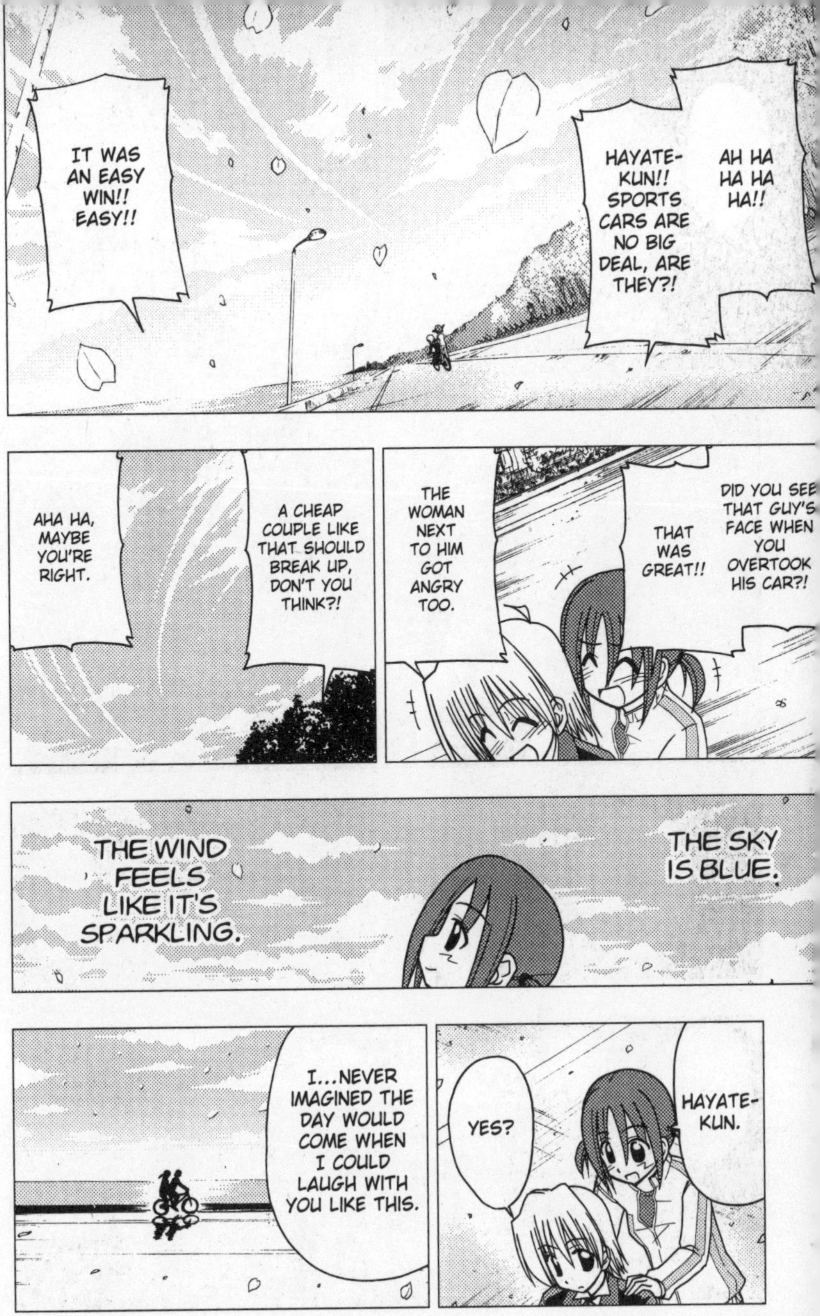
AH HA HA HA HA!!
HAYATE-KUN!! SPORTS CARS ARE NO BIG DEAL, ARE THEY?!
IT WAS AN EASY WIN!! EASY!!
DID YOU SEE THAT GUY'S FACE WHEN YOU OVERTOOK HIS CAR?!
THAT WAS GREAT!!
THE WOMAN NEXT TO HIM GOT ANGRY TOO.
A CHEAP COUPLE LIKE THAT SHOULD BREAK UP, DON'T YOU THINK?!
AHA HA, MAYBE YOU'RE RIGHT.
THE SKY IS BLUE.
THE WIND FEELS LIKE IT'S SPARKLING.
HAYATE-KUN.
YES?
I...NEVER IMAGINED THE DAY WOULD COME WHEN I COULD LAUGH WITH YOU LIKE THIS.

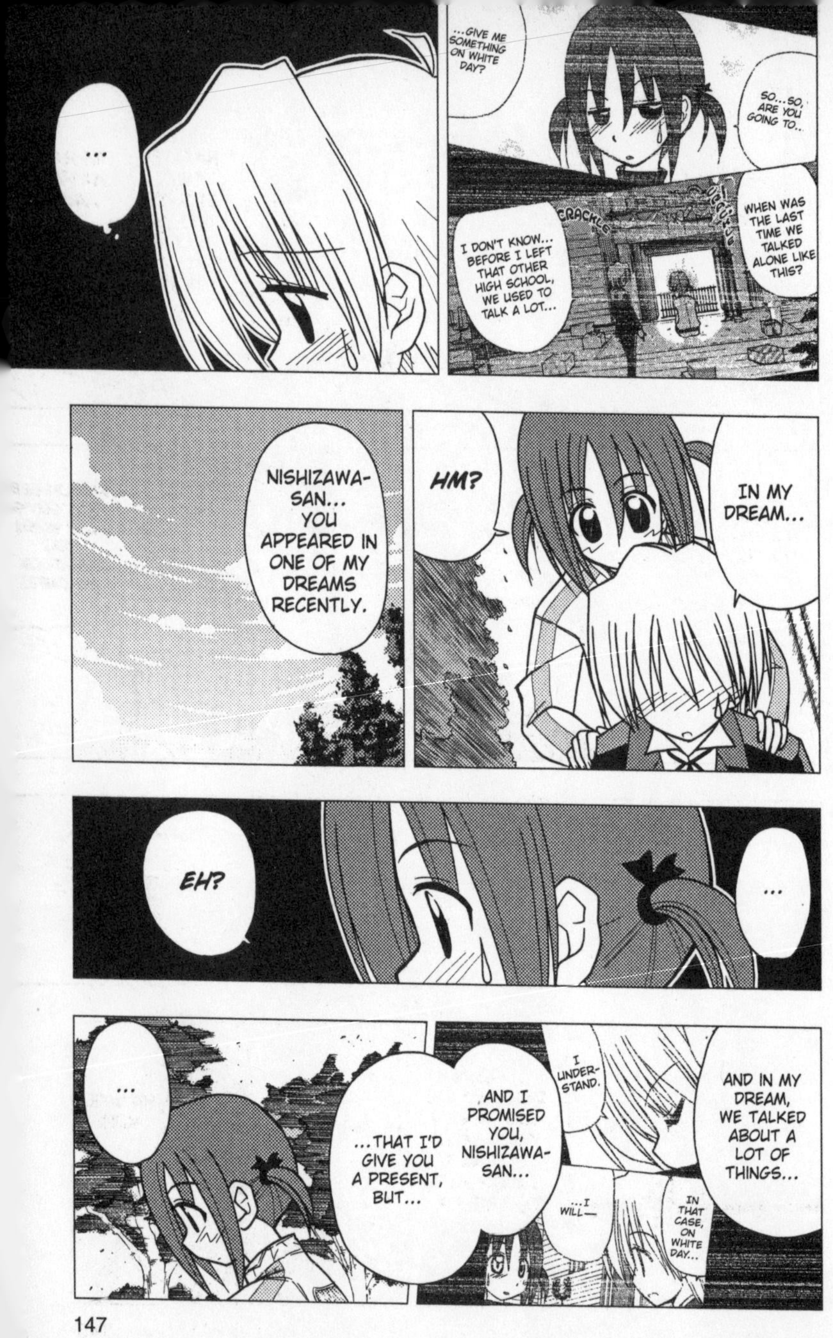
SO... SO, ARE YOU GOING TO..
...GIVE ME SOMETHING ON WHITE DAY?
WHEN WAS THE LAST TIME WE TALKED ALONE LIKE THIS?
CRACKLE
I DON'T KNOW... BEFORE I LEFT THAT OTHER HIGH SCHOOL, WE USED TO TALK A LOT...
...
IN MY DREAM...
HM?
NISHIZAWA-SAN... YOU APPEARED IN ONE OF MY DREAMS RECENTLY.
...
EH?
AND IN MY DREAM, WE TALKED ABOUT A LOT OF THINGS...
I UNDERSTAND.
IN THAT CASE, ON WHITE DAY...
...I WILL—
AND I PROMISED YOU, NISHIZAWA-SAN...
...THAT I'D GIVE YOU A PRESENT, BUT...
...

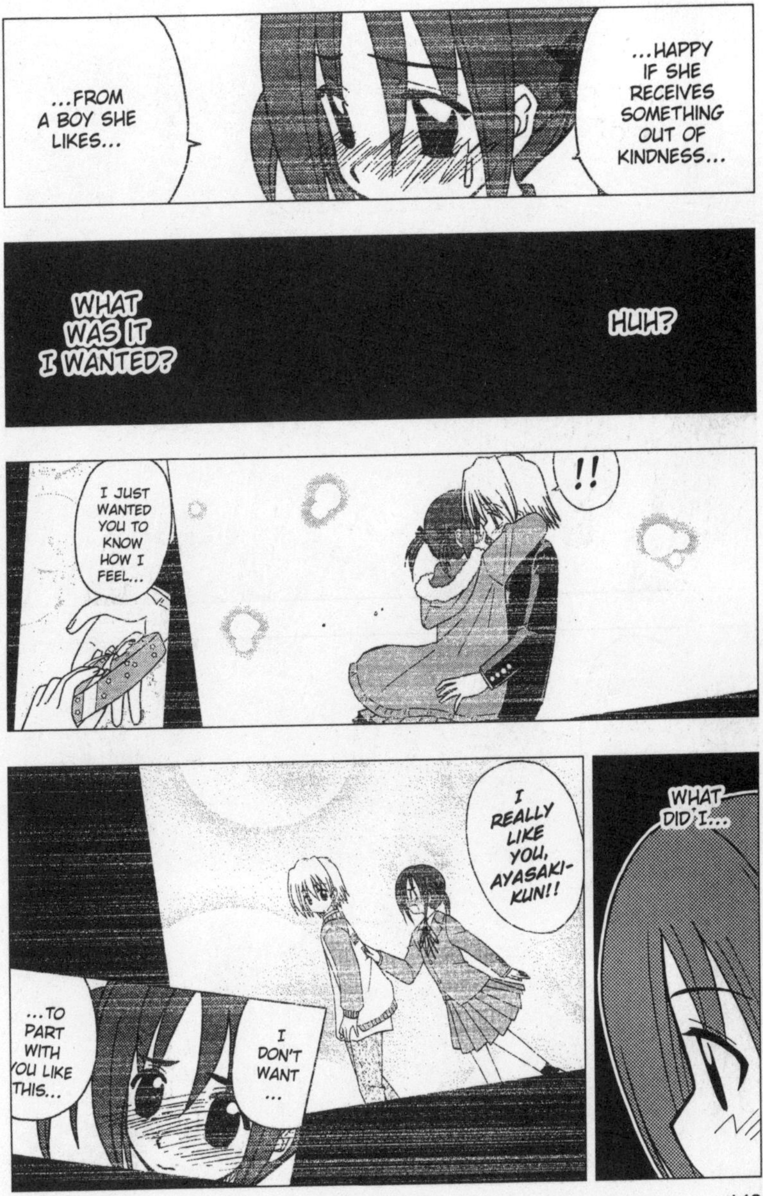
...HAPPY IF SHE RECEIVES SOMETHING OUT OF KINDNESS...
...FROM A BOY SHE LIKES...
HUH?
WHAT WAS IT I WANTED?
!!
I JUST WANTED YOU TO KNOW HOW I FEEL...
WHAT DID I...
I REALLY LIKE YOU, AYASAKI-KUN!!
I DON'T WANT...
...TO PART WITH YOU LIKE THIS...

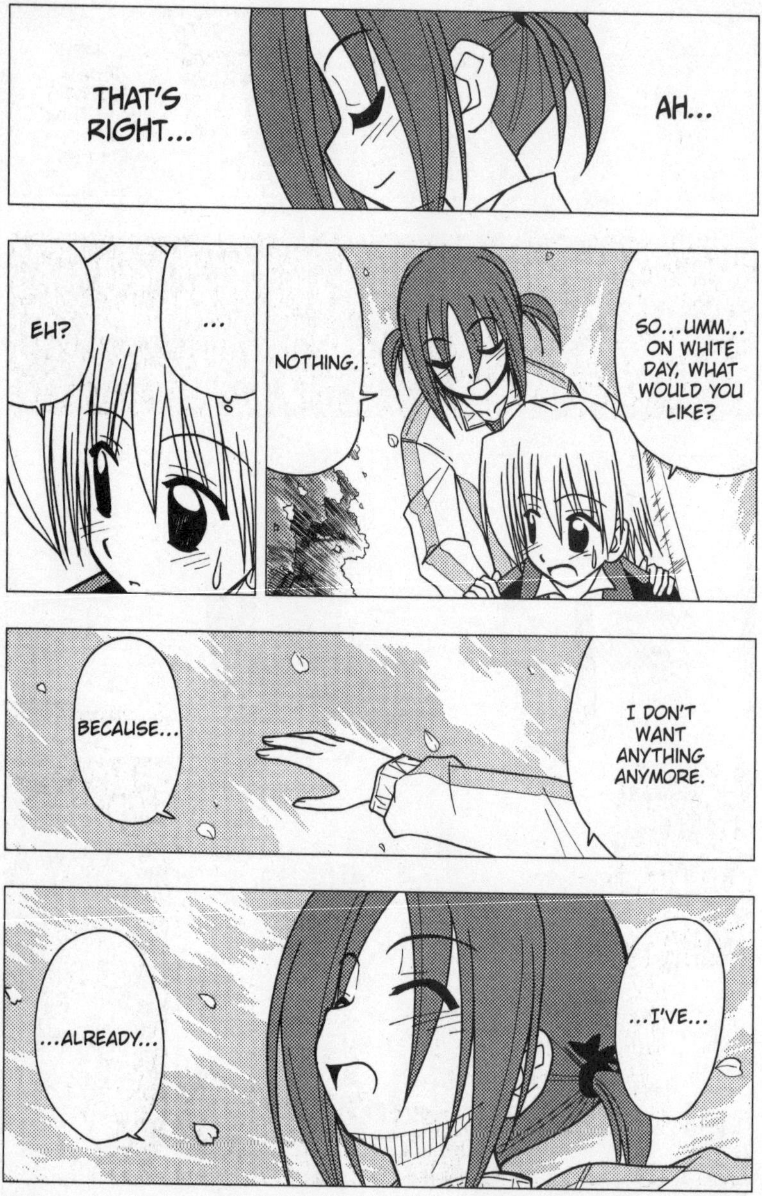
AH...
THAT'S RIGHT...
SO...UMM... ON WHITE DAY, WHAT WOULD YOU LIKE?
NOTHING.
...
EH?
I DON'T WANT ANYTHING ANYMORE.
BECAUSE...
...I'VE...
...ALREADY...

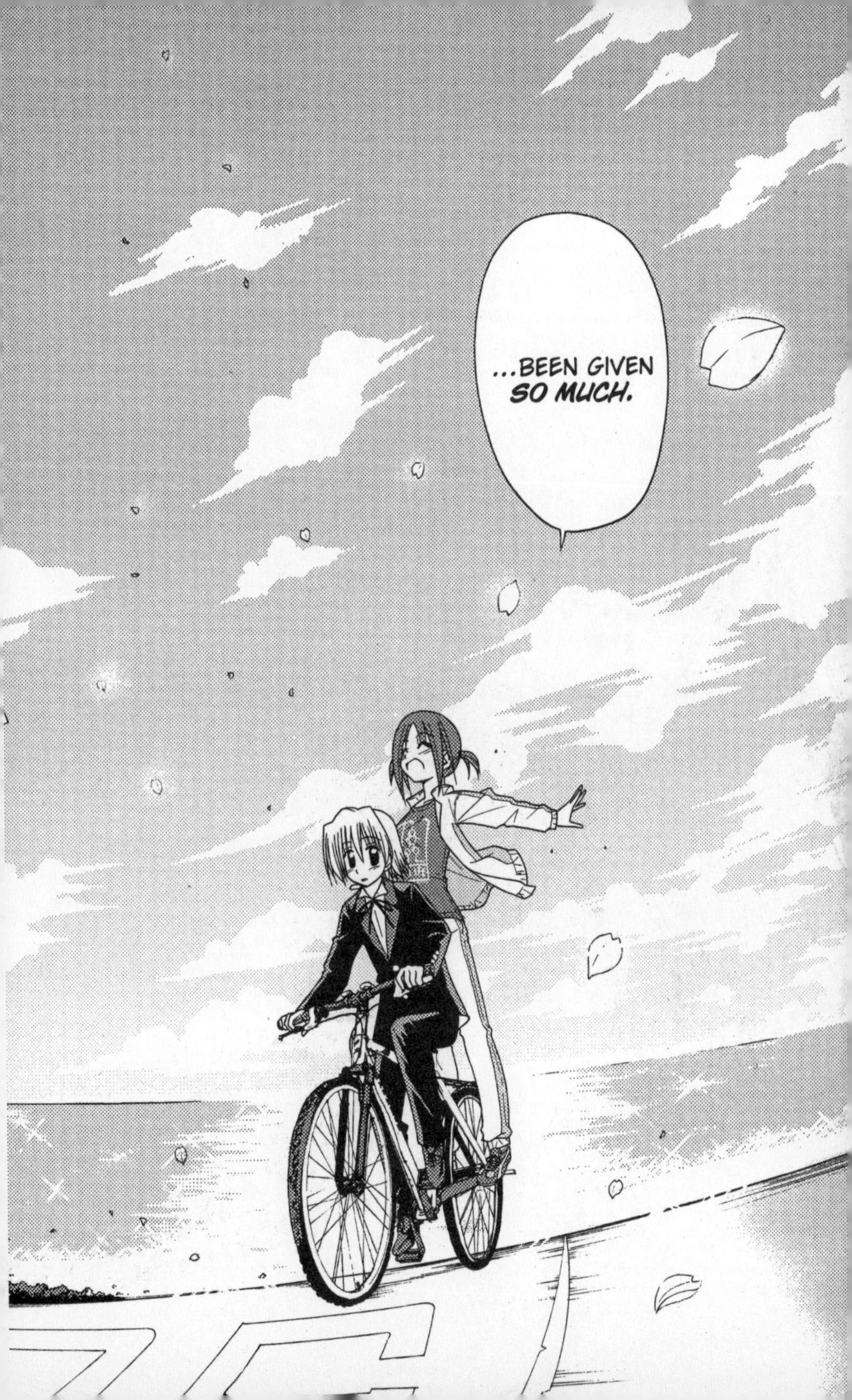
...BEEN GIVEN SO MUCH.

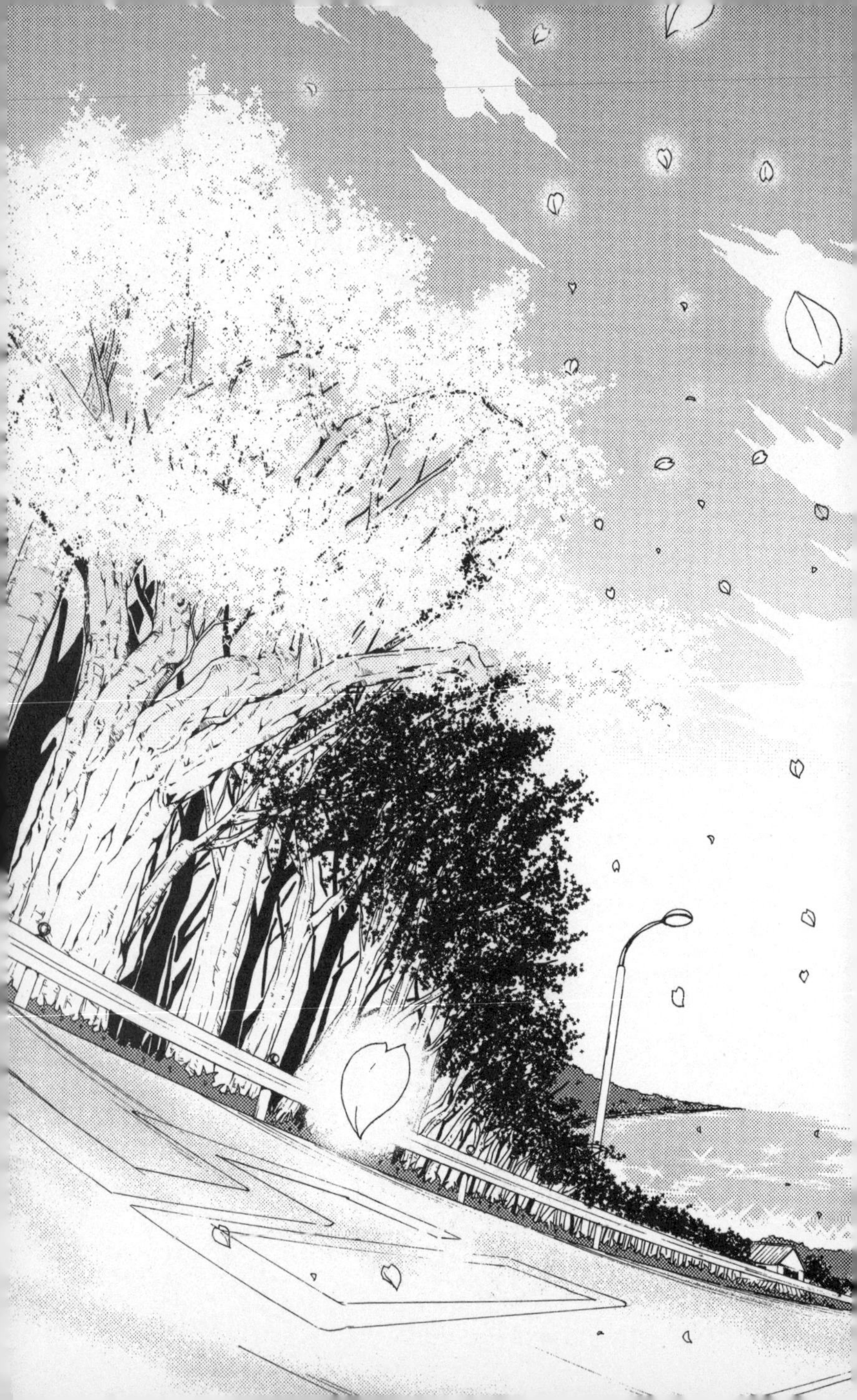

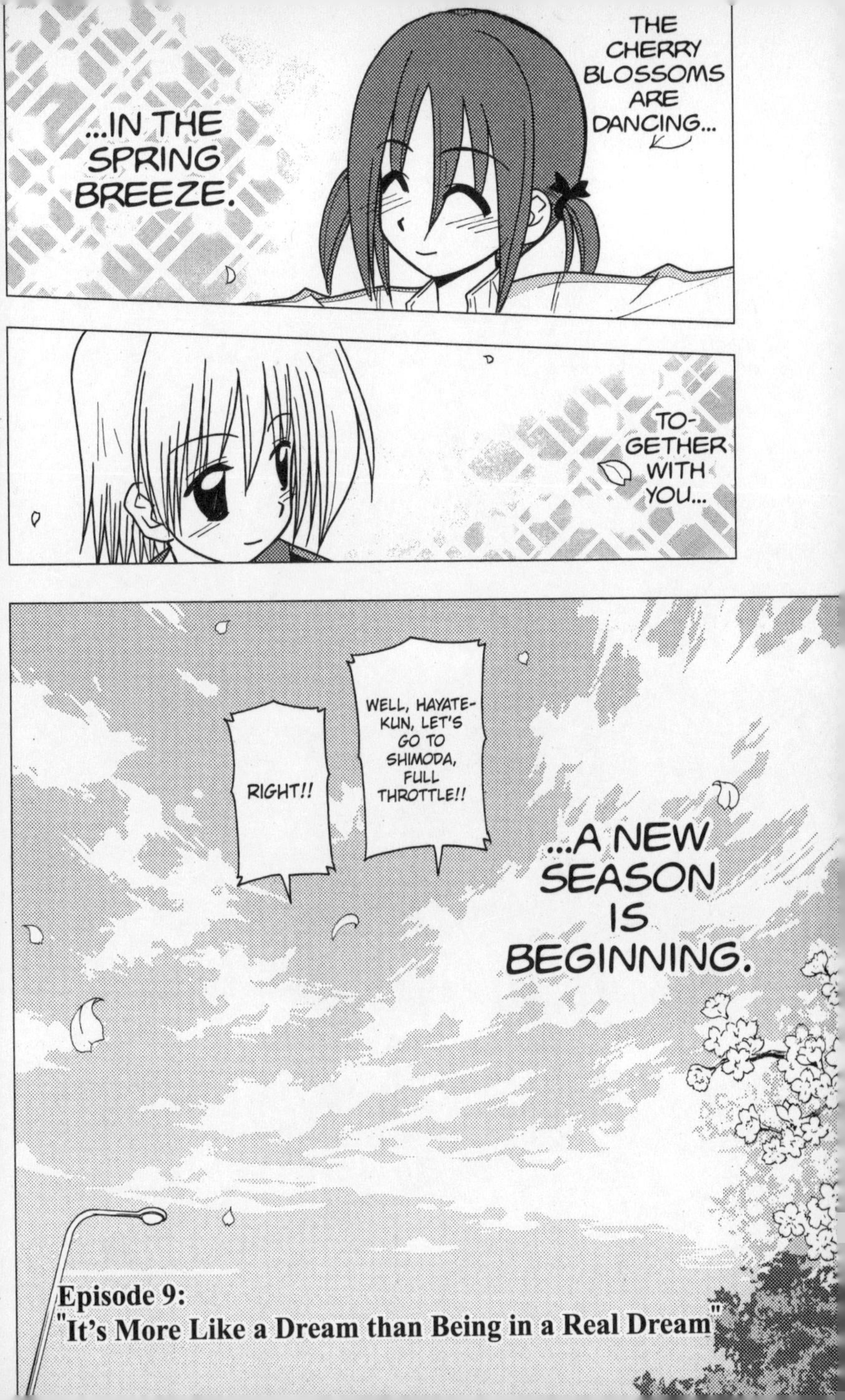
THE CHERRY BLOSSOMS ARE DANCING...
...IN THE SPRING BREEZE.
TO-GETHER WITH YOU...
WELL, HAYATE-KUN, LET'S GO TO SHIMODA, FULL THROTTLE!!
RIGHT!!
...A NEW SEASON IS BEGINNING.
Episode 9:
"It's More Like a Dream than Being in a Real Dream"

Episode 10: "Kiwa Kiwa Last Boy"

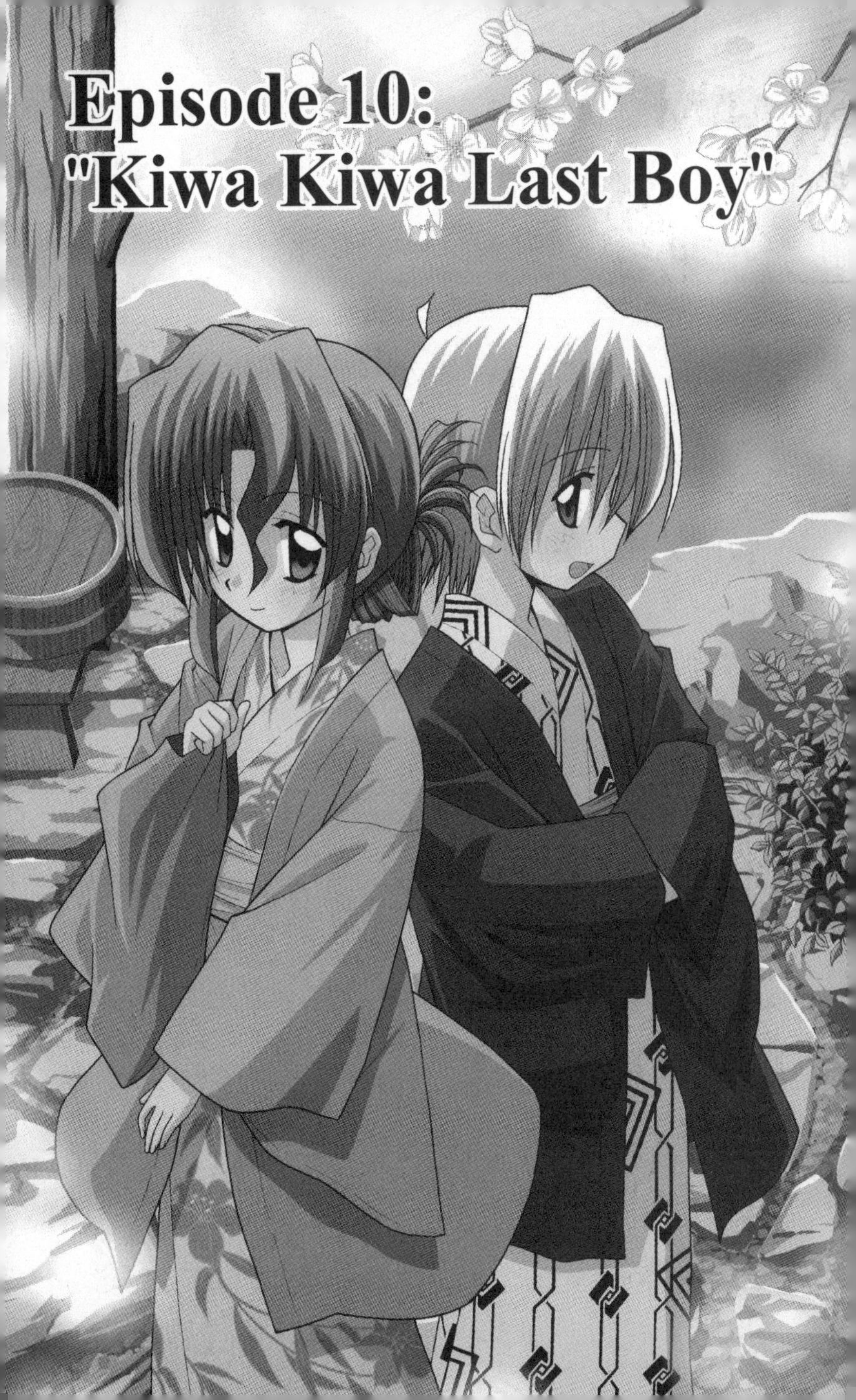

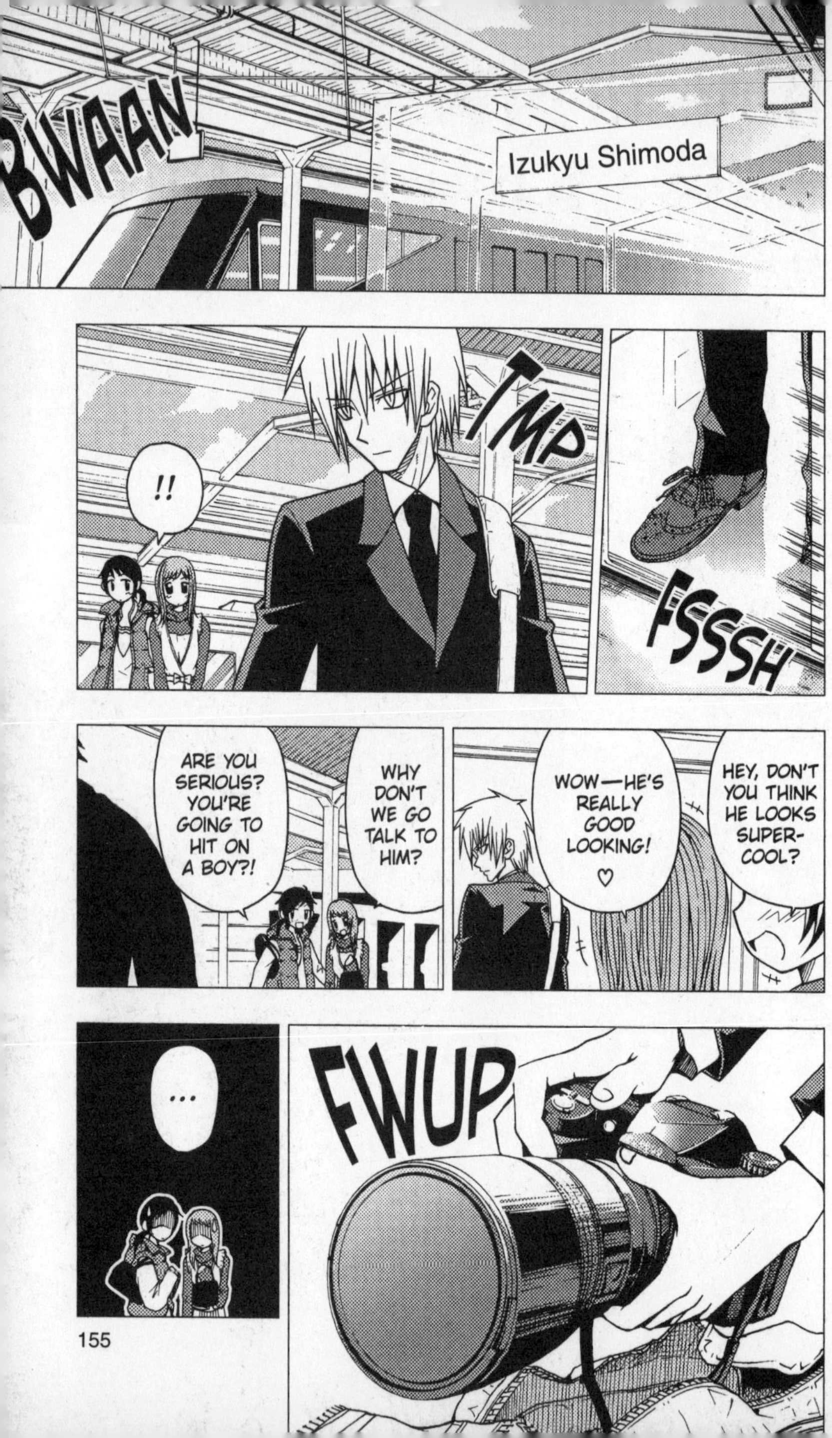
BWAAN
Izukyu Shimoda
FSSSH
TMP
!!
HEY, DON'T YOU THINK HE LOOKS SUPER-COOL?
WOW—HE'S REALLY GOOD LOOKING! ♡
WHY DON'T WE GO TALK TO HIM?
ARE YOU SERIOUS? YOU'RE GOING TO HIT ON A BOY?!
FWUP
...

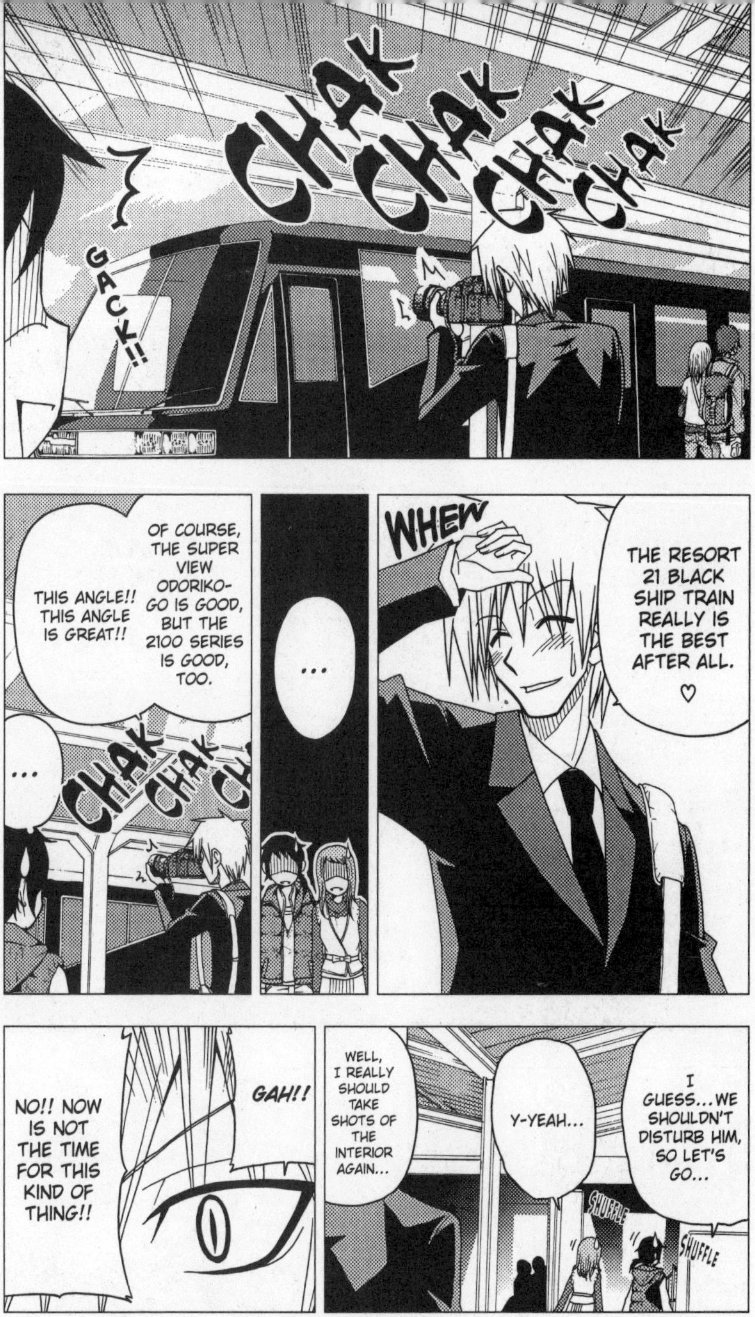
CHAK CHAK CHAK CHAK
GACK!!
WHEW
THE RESORT 21 BLACK SHIP TRAIN REALLY IS THE BEST AFTER ALL. ♡
...
OF COURSE, THE SUPER VIEW ODORIKO-GO IS GOOD, BUT THE 2100 SERIES IS GOOD, TOO.
THIS ANGLE!! THIS ANGLE IS GREAT!!
...
CHAK CHAK
I GUESS...WE SHOULDN'T DISTURB HIM, SO LET'S GO...
Y-YEAH...
SHUFFLE SHUFFLE
WELL, I REALLY SHOULD TAKE SHOTS OF THE INTERIOR AGAIN...
GAH!!
NO!! NOW IS NOT THE TIME FOR THIS KIND OF THING!!

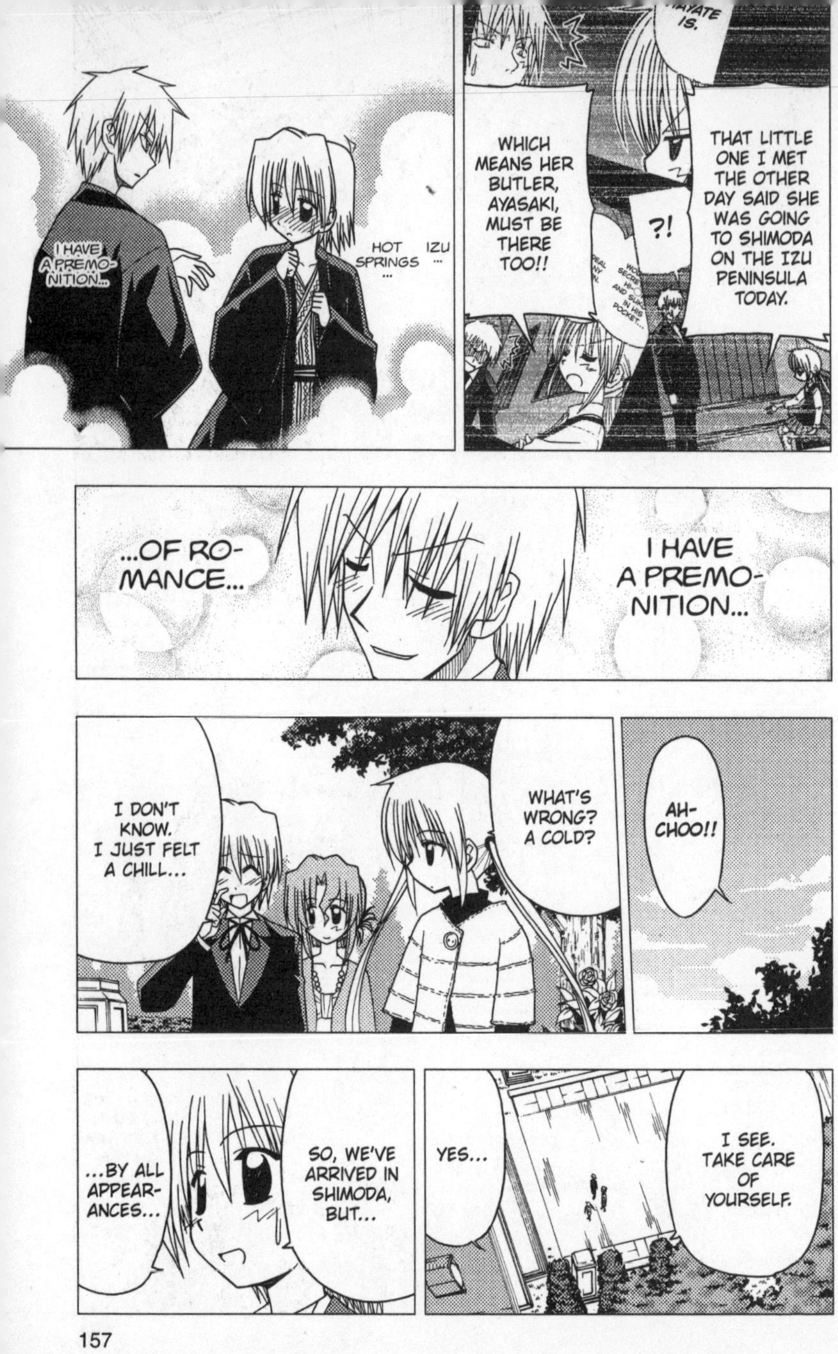
HAYATE IS.
THAT LITTLE ONE I MET THE OTHER DAY SAID SHE WAS GOING TO SHIMODA ON THE IZU PENINSULA TODAY.
?!
WHICH MEANS HER BUTLER, AYASAKI, MUST BE THERE TOO!!
IZU ...
HOT SPRINGS ...
I HAVE A PREMO-NITION...
I HAVE A PREMO-NITION...
...OF RO-MANCE...
AH-CHOO!!
WHAT'S WRONG? A COLD?
I DON'T KNOW. I JUST FELT A CHILL...
I SEE. TAKE CARE OF YOURSELF.
YES...
SO, WE'VE ARRIVED IN SHIMODA, BUT...
...BY ALL APPEAR-ANCES...

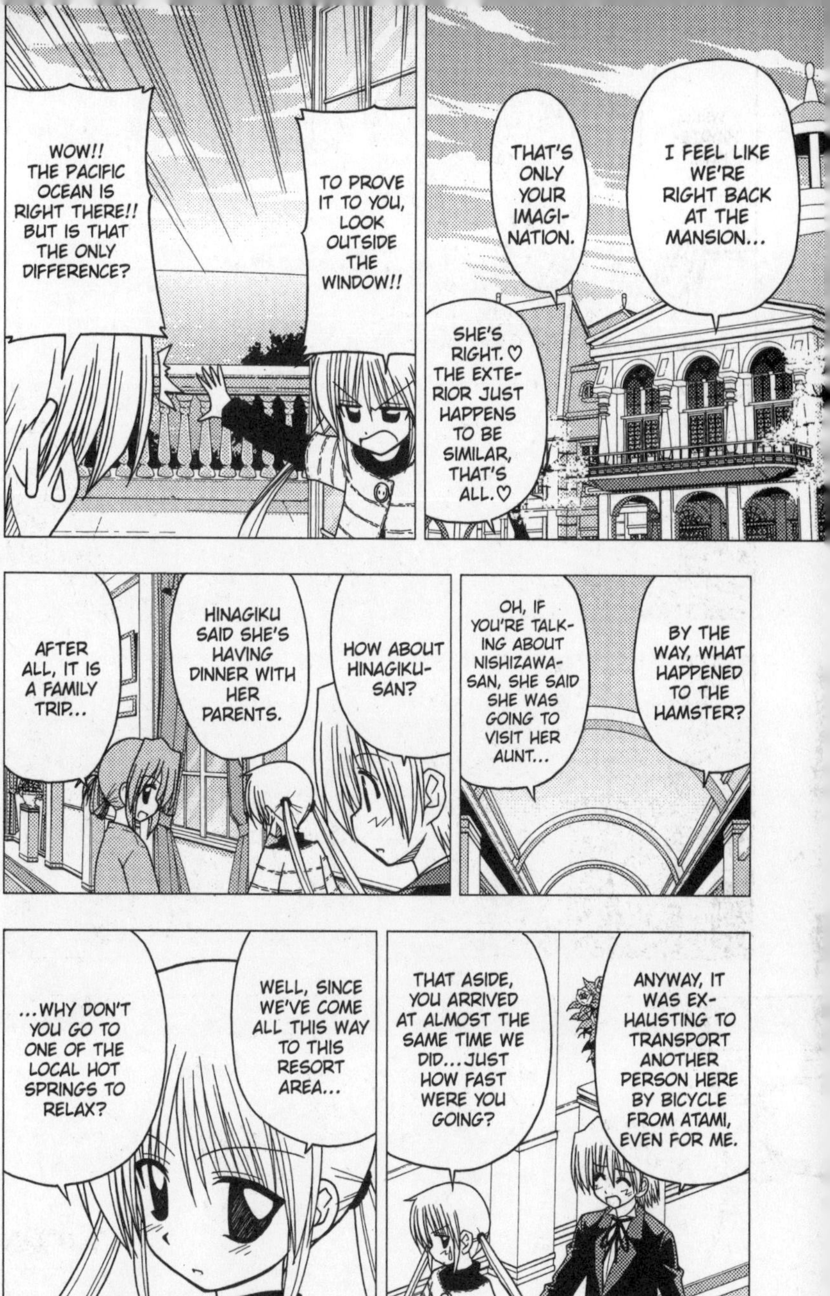
I FEEL LIKE WE'RE RIGHT BACK AT THE MANSION...
THAT'S ONLY YOUR IMAGINATION.
SHE'S RIGHT.♡ THE EXTERIOR JUST HAPPENS TO BE SIMILAR, THAT'S ALL.♡
TO PROVE IT TO YOU, LOOK OUTSIDE THE WINDOW!!
WOW!! THE PACIFIC OCEAN IS RIGHT THERE!! BUT IS THAT THE ONLY DIFFERENCE?
BY THE WAY, WHAT HAPPENED TO THE HAMSTER?
OH, IF YOU'RE TALKING ABOUT NISHIZAWA-SAN, SHE SAID SHE WAS GOING TO VISIT HER AUNT...
HOW ABOUT HINAGIKU-SAN?
HINAGIKU SAID SHE'S HAVING DINNER WITH HER PARENTS.
AFTER ALL, IT IS A FAMILY TRIP...
ANYWAY, IT WAS EXHAUSTING TO TRANSPORT ANOTHER PERSON HERE BY BICYCLE FROM ATAMI, EVEN FOR ME.
THAT ASIDE, YOU ARRIVED AT ALMOST THE SAME TIME WE DID... JUST HOW FAST WERE YOU GOING?
WELL, SINCE WE'VE COME ALL THIS WAY TO THIS RESORT AREA...
...WHY DON'T YOU GO TO ONE OF THE LOCAL HOT SPRINGS TO RELAX?

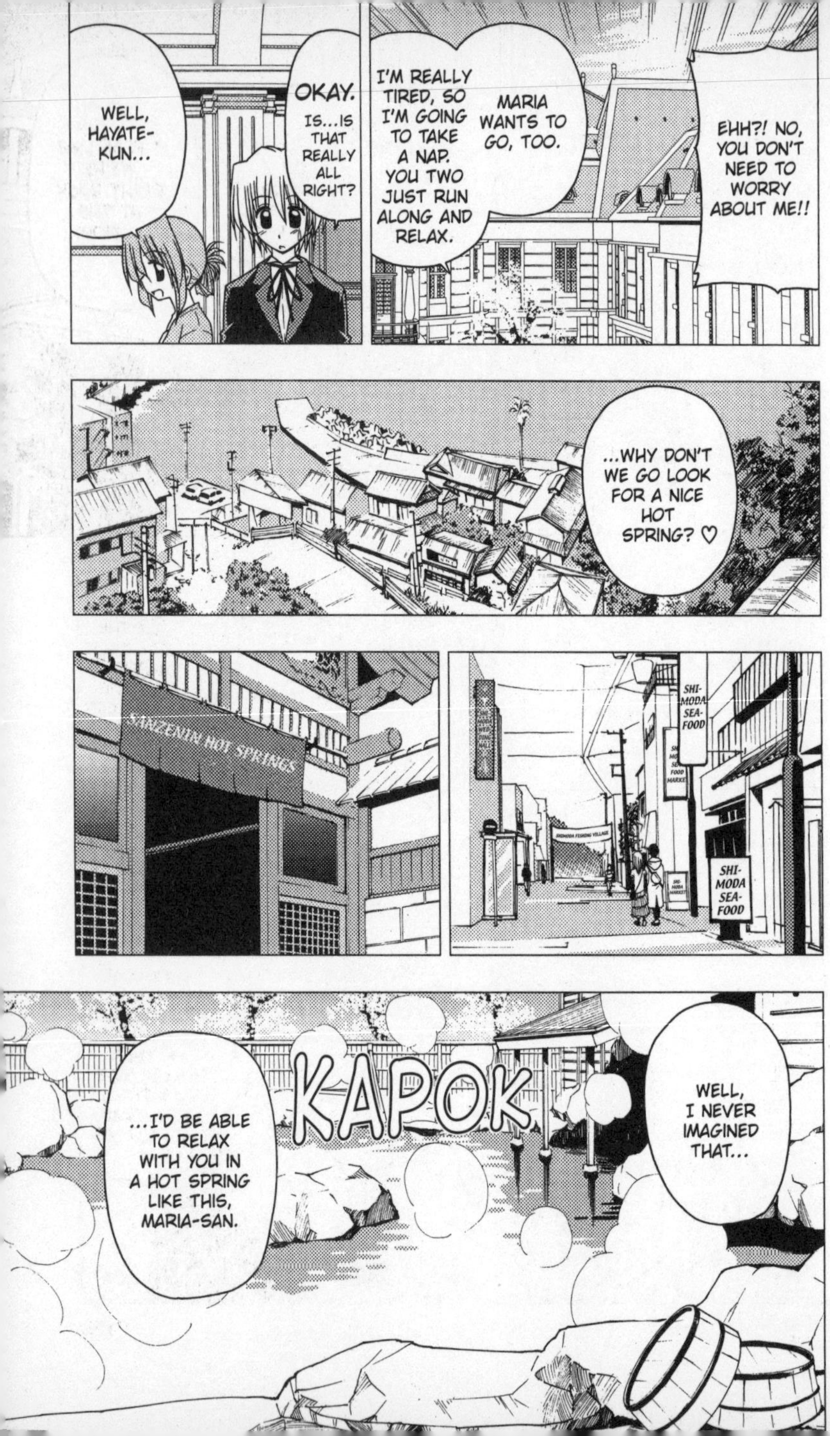
EHH?! NO, YOU DON'T NEED TO WORRY ABOUT ME!!
MARIA WANTS TO GO, TOO.
I'M REALLY TIRED, SO I'M GOING TO TAKE A NAP. YOU TWO JUST RUN ALONG AND RELAX.
OKAY.
IS...IS THAT REALLY ALL RIGHT?
WELL, HAYATE-KUN...
...WHY DON'T WE GO LOOK FOR A NICE HOT SPRING? ♡
SHI-MODA SEA-FOOD
SHI-MODA WED-DING HALL
SHIMODA FISHING VILLAGE
SHI-MODA SEA-FOOD
SANZENIN HOT SPRINGS
WELL, I NEVER IMAGINED THAT...
KAPOK
...I'D BE ABLE TO RELAX WITH YOU IN A HOT SPRING LIKE THIS, MARIA-SAN.

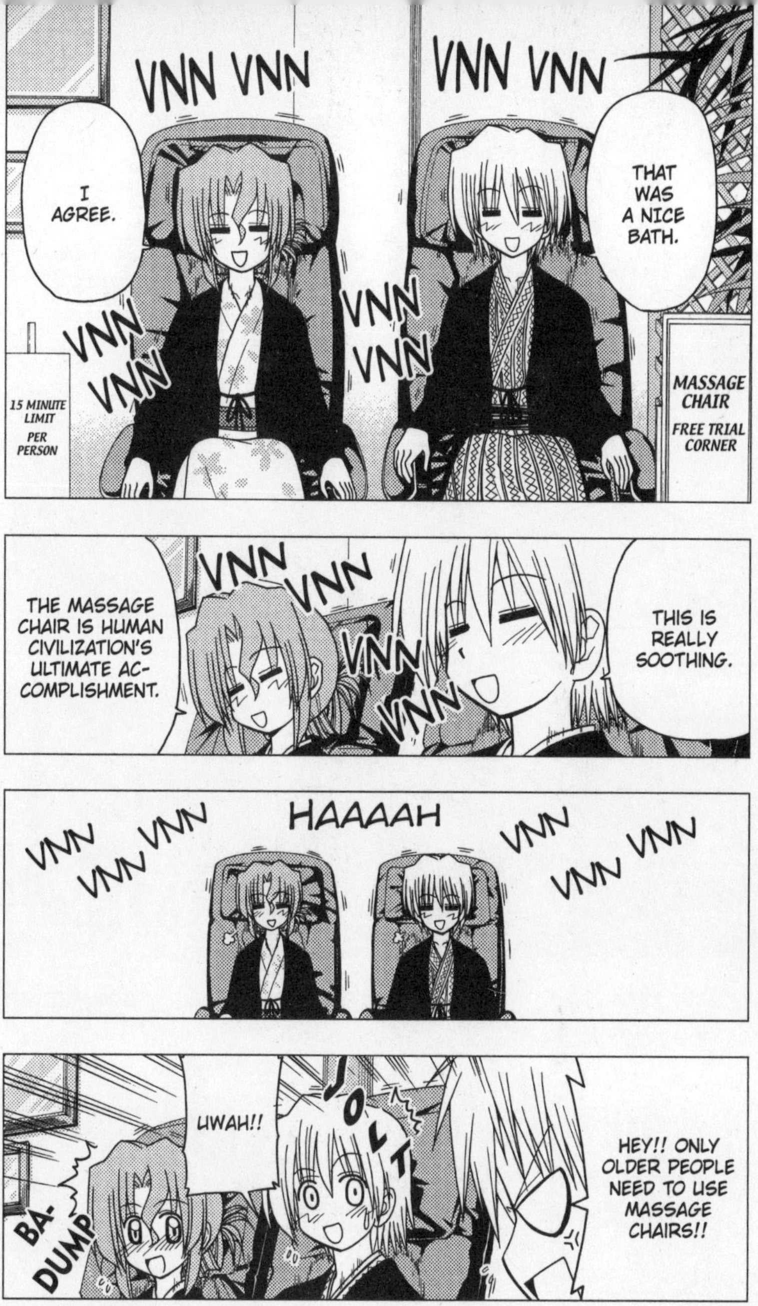
VNN VNN
THAT WAS A NICE BATH.
VNN VNN
I AGREE.
MASSAGE CHAIR
FREE TRIAL CORNER
VNN VNN
VNN VNN
15 MINUTE LIMIT PER PERSON
THIS IS REALLY SOOTHING.
VNN VNN
VNN VNN
THE MASSAGE CHAIR IS HUMAN CIVILIZATION'S ULTIMATE AC-COMPLISHMENT.
VNN VNN
VNN VNN
HAAAAH
VNN VNN
VNN VNN
HEY!! ONLY OLDER PEOPLE NEED TO USE MASSAGE CHAIRS!!
JOLT
UWAH!!
BA-DUMP

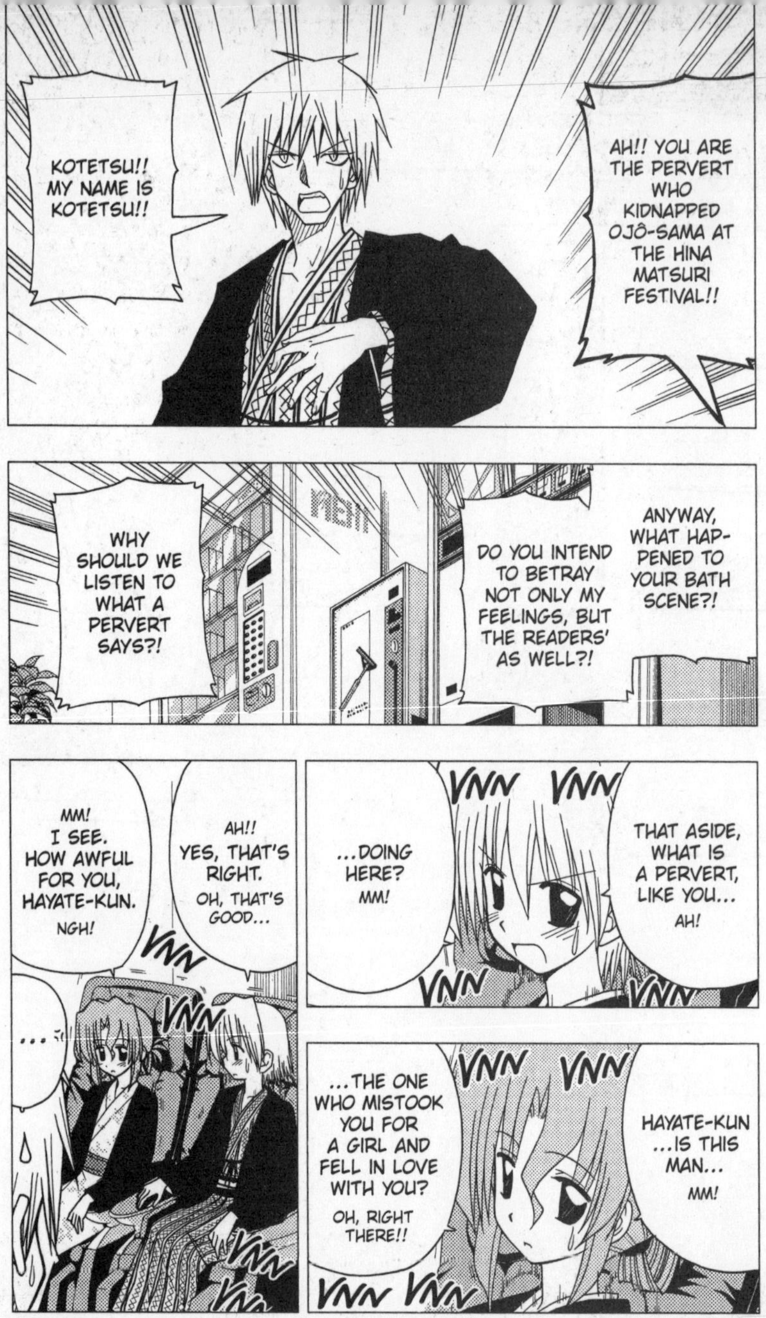
AH!! YOU ARE THE PERVERT WHO KIDNAPPED OJÔ-SAMA AT THE HINA MATSURI FESTIVAL!!
KOTETSU!! MY NAME IS KOTETSU!!
ANYWAY, WHAT HAP-PENED TO YOUR BATH SCENE?!
DO YOU INTEND TO BETRAY NOT ONLY MY FEELINGS, BUT THE READERS' AS WELL?!
WHY SHOULD WE LISTEN TO WHAT A PERVERT SAYS?!
VNN VNN
THAT ASIDE, WHAT IS A PERVERT, LIKE YOU... AH!
...DOING HERE? MM!
VNN VNN
VNN VNN
HAYATE-KUN ...IS THIS MAN... MM!
...THE ONE WHO MISTOOK YOU FOR A GIRL AND FELL IN LOVE WITH YOU? OH, RIGHT THERE!!
VNN VNN
AH!! YES, THAT'S RIGHT. OH, THAT'S GOOD...
MM! I SEE. HOW AWFUL FOR YOU, HAYATE-KUN. NGH!
VNN
VNN
VNN

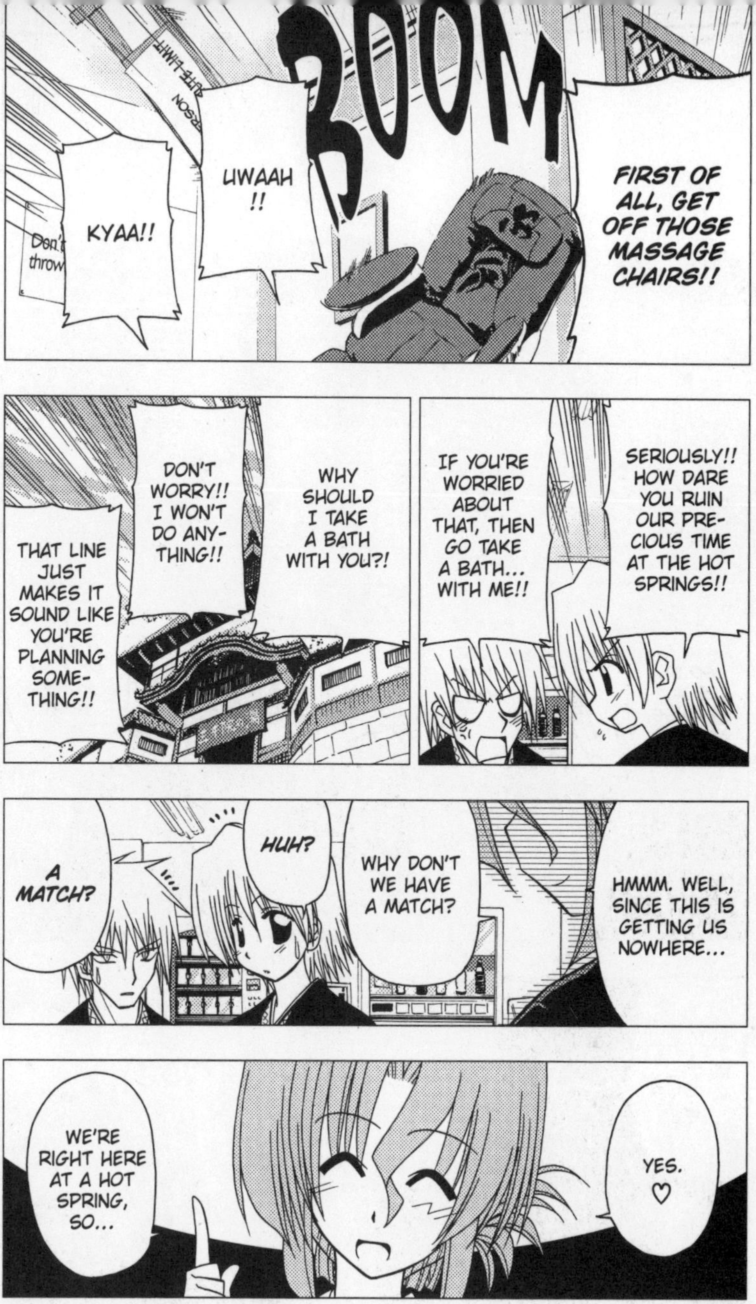
FIRST OF ALL, GET OFF THOSE MASSAGE CHAIRS!!
BOOM
UWAAH !!
KYAA!!
SERIOUSLY!! HOW DARE YOU RUIN OUR PRE-CIOUS TIME AT THE HOT SPRINGS!!
IF YOU'RE WORRIED ABOUT THAT, THEN GO TAKE A BATH... WITH ME!!
WHY SHOULD I TAKE A BATH WITH YOU?!
DON'T WORRY!! I WON'T DO ANY-THING!!
THAT LINE JUST MAKES IT SOUND LIKE YOU'RE PLANNING SOME-THING!!
HMMM. WELL, SINCE THIS IS GETTING US NOWHERE...
WHY DON'T WE HAVE A MATCH?
HUH?
A MATCH?
YES. ♡
WE'RE RIGHT HERE AT A HOT SPRING, SO...

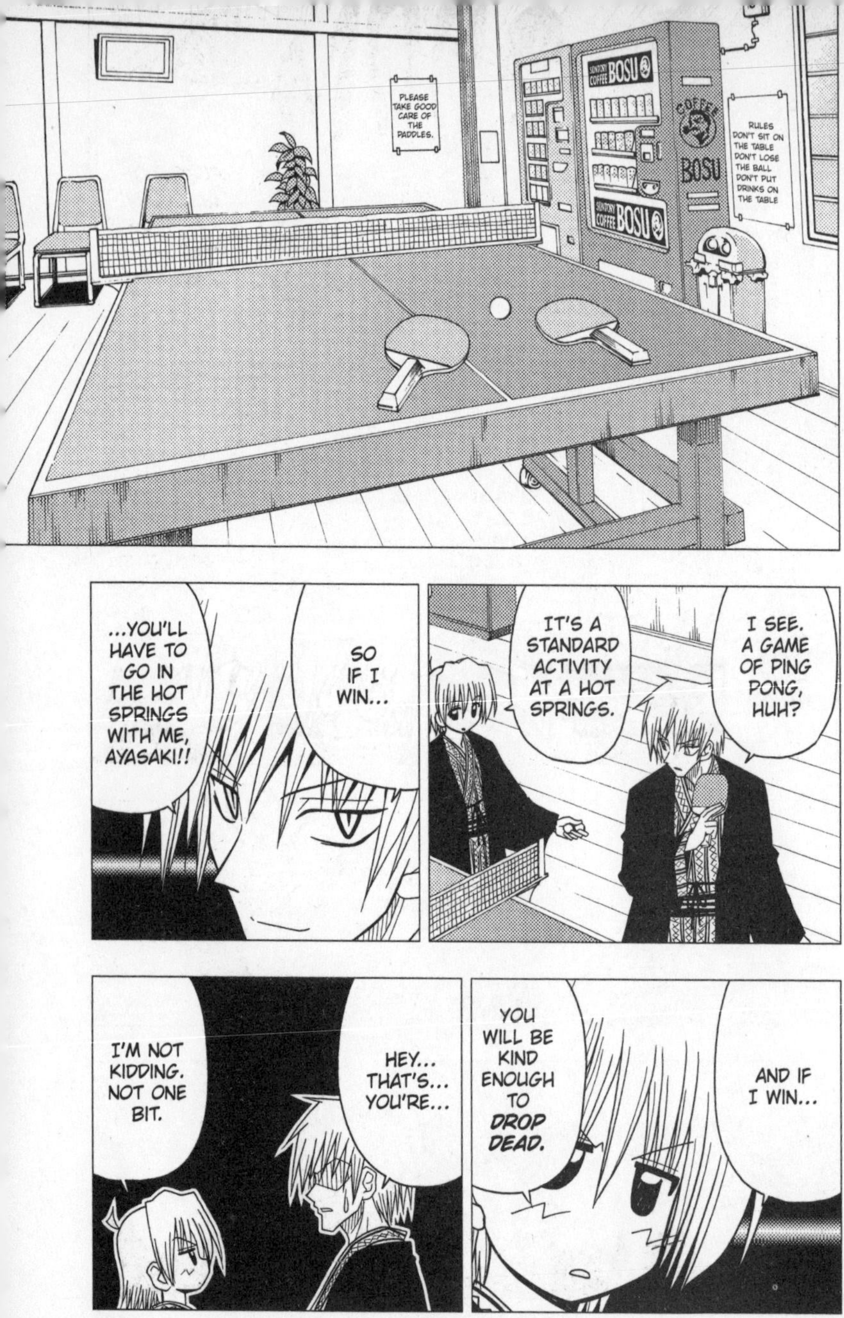
RULES
DON'T SIT ON THE TABLE
DON'T LOSE THE BALL
DON'T PUT DRINKS ON THE TABLE
COFFEE BOSU
SUNTORY COFFEE BOSU
SUNTORY COFFEE BOSU
PLEASE TAKE GOOD CARE OF THE PADDLES.
I SEE. A GAME OF PING PONG, HUH?
IT'S A STANDARD ACTIVITY AT A HOT SPRINGS.
SO IF I WIN...
...YOU'LL HAVE TO GO IN THE HOT SPRINGS WITH ME, AYASAKI!!
AND IF I WIN...
YOU WILL BE KIND ENOUGH TO *DROP DEAD.*
HEY... THAT'S... YOU'RE...
I'M NOT KIDDING. NOT ONE BIT.

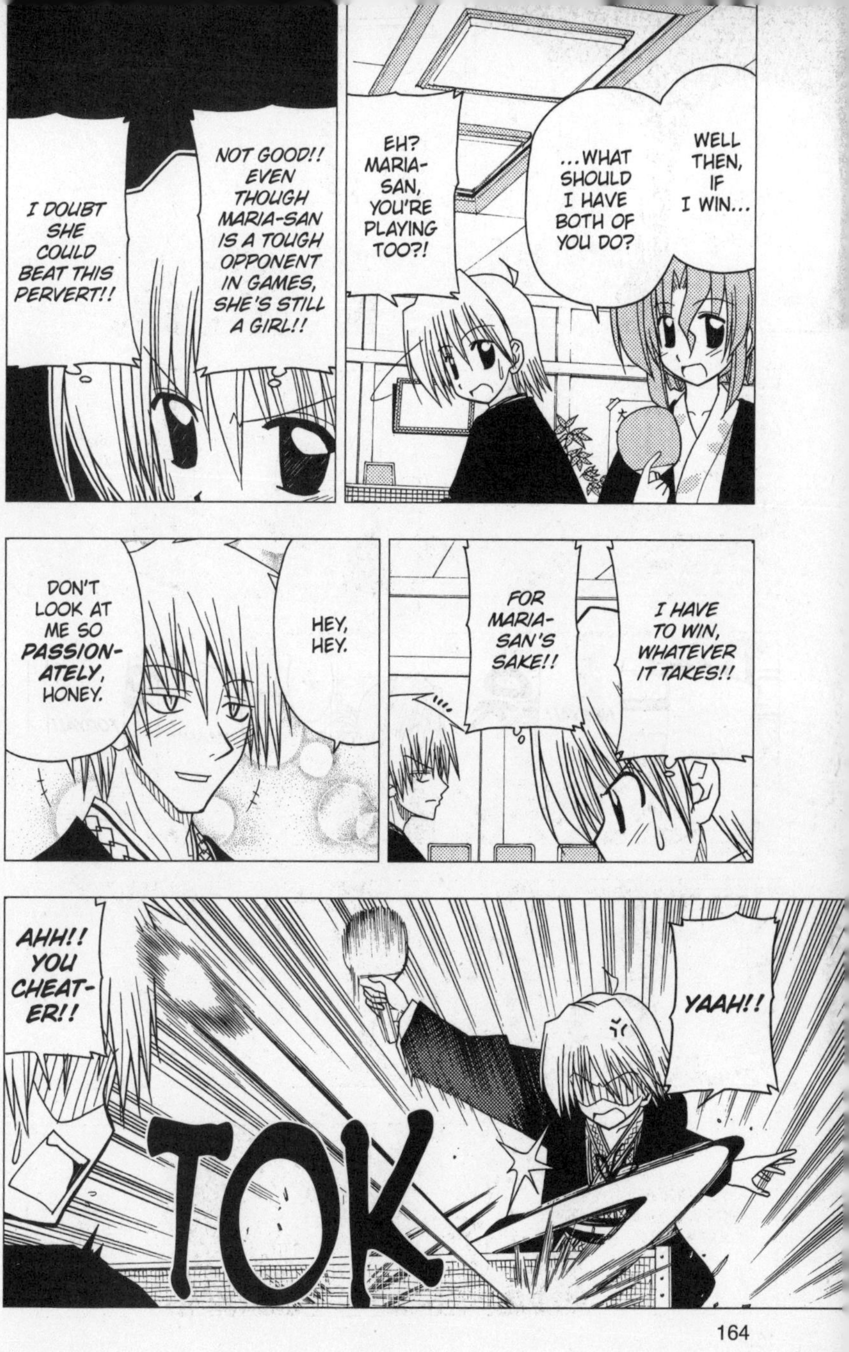
WELL THEN, IF I WIN...
...WHAT SHOULD I HAVE BOTH OF YOU DO?
EH? MARIA-SAN, YOU'RE PLAYING TOO?!
NOT GOOD!! EVEN THOUGH MARIA-SAN IS A TOUGH OPPONENT IN GAMES, SHE'S STILL A GIRL!!
I DOUBT SHE COULD BEAT THIS PERVERT!!
I HAVE TO WIN, WHATEVER IT TAKES!!
FOR MARIA-SAN'S SAKE!!
HEY, HEY.
DON'T LOOK AT ME SO PASSION-ATELY, HONEY.
YAAH!!
TOK
AHH!! YOU CHEAT-ER!!

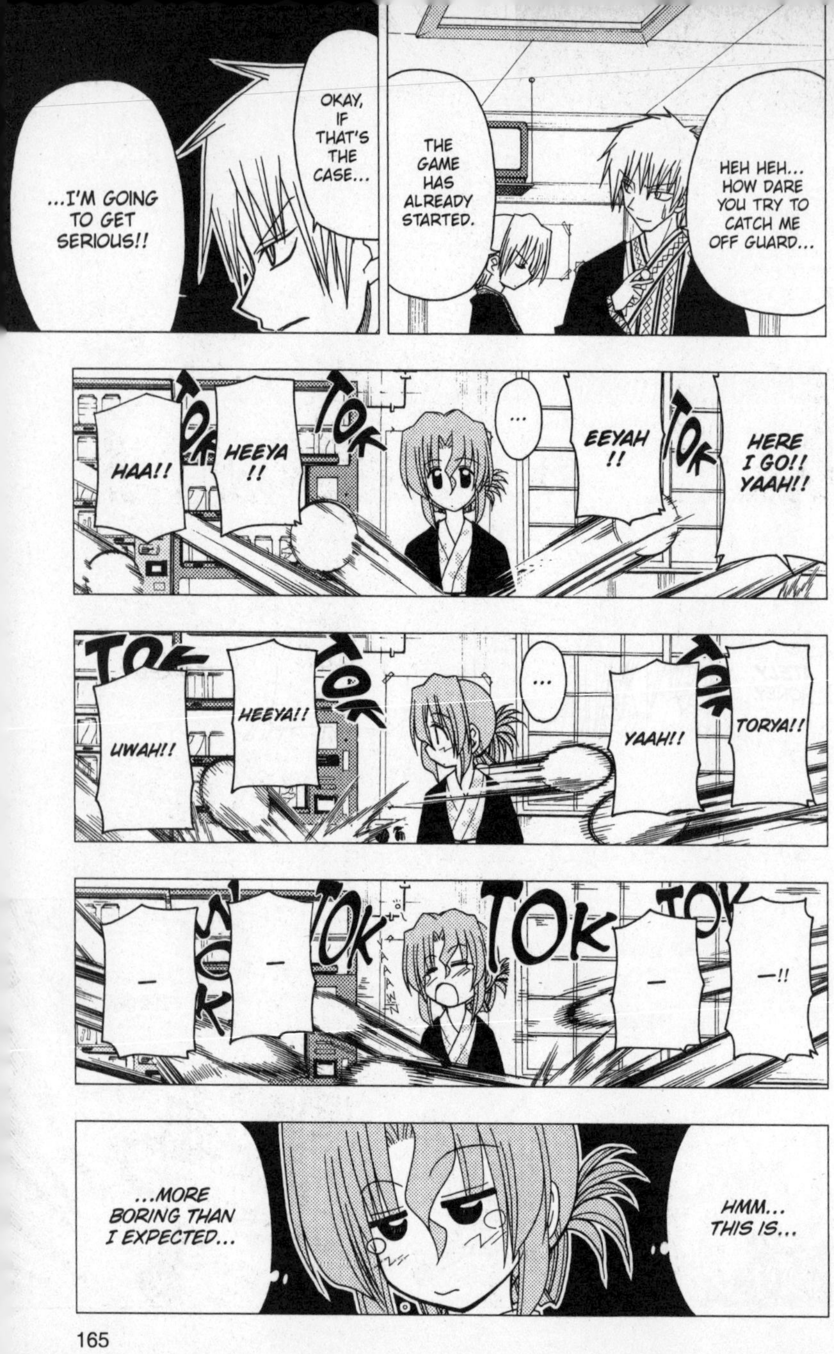
HEH HEH... HOW DARE YOU TRY TO CATCH ME OFF GUARD...
THE GAME HAS ALREADY STARTED.
OKAY, IF THAT'S THE CASE...
...I'M GOING TO GET SERIOUS!!
HERE I GO!! YAAH!!
TOK
EEYAH!!
...
TOK
HEEYA!!
TOK
HAA!!
TORYA!!
TOK
YAAH!!
...
TOK
HEEYA!!
TOK
UWAH!!
—!!
TOK
—
TOK
TOK
—
—
HMM... THIS IS...
...MORE BORING THAN I EXPECTED...

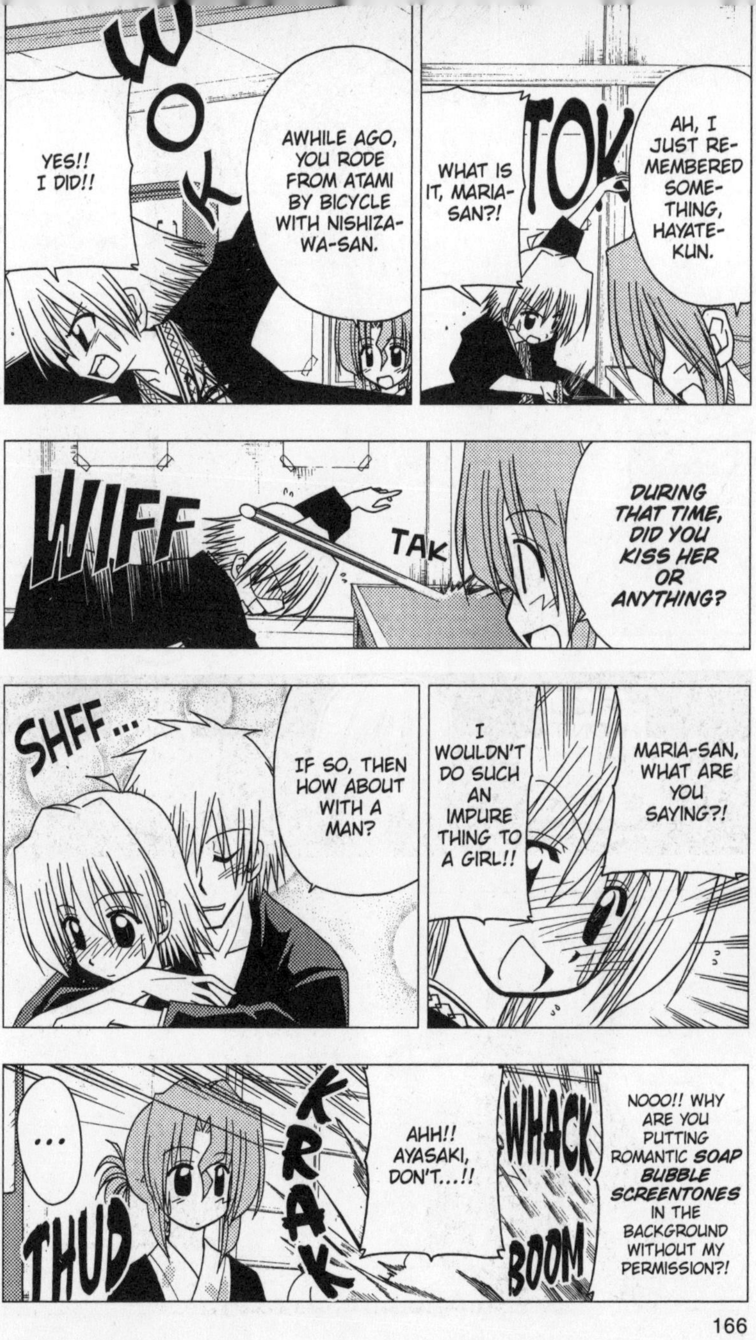
AH, I JUST RE-MEMBERED SOME-THING, HAYATE-KUN.
TOK
WHAT IS IT, MARIA-SAN?!
AWHILE AGO, YOU RODE FROM ATAMI BY BICYCLE WITH NISHIZA-WA-SAN.
WOK
YES!! I DID!!
DURING THAT TIME, DID YOU KISS HER OR ANYTHING?
TAK
WIFF
MARIA-SAN, WHAT ARE YOU SAYING?!
I WOULDN'T DO SUCH AN IMPURE THING TO A GIRL!!
IF SO, THEN HOW ABOUT WITH A MAN?
SHFF...
NOOO!! WHY ARE YOU PUTTING ROMANTIC SOAP BUBBLE SCREENTONES IN THE BACKGROUND WITHOUT MY PERMISSION?!
WHACK
BOOM
AHH!! AYASAKI, DON'T...!!
KRAK
...
THUD

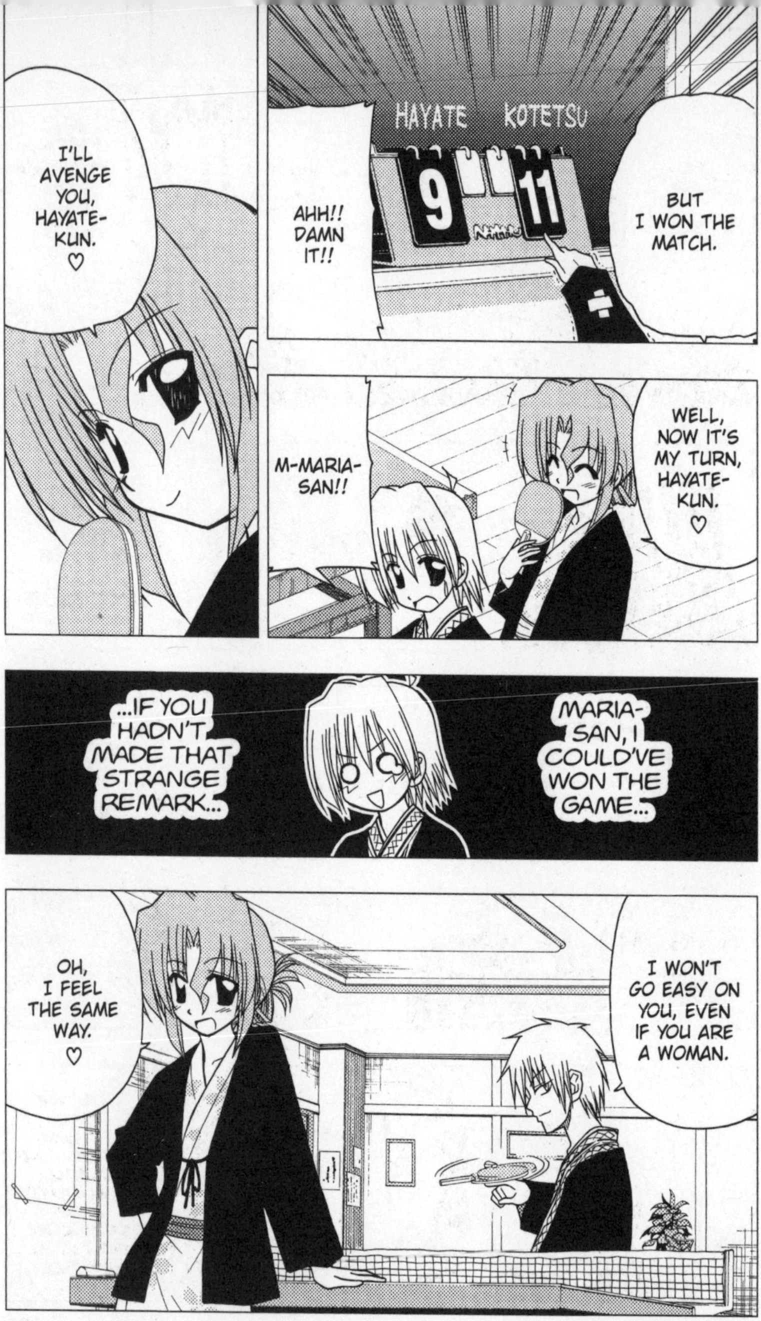
HAYATE KOTETSU
9 11
BUT I WON THE MATCH.
AHH!! DAMN IT!!
WELL, NOW IT'S MY TURN, HAYATE-KUN. ♡
M-MARIA-SAN!!
I'LL AVENGE YOU, HAYATE-KUN. ♡
MARIA-SAN, I COULD'VE WON THE GAME...
...IF YOU HADN'T MADE THAT STRANGE REMARK...
I WON'T GO EASY ON YOU, EVEN IF YOU ARE A WOMAN.
OH, I FEEL THE SAME WAY. ♡

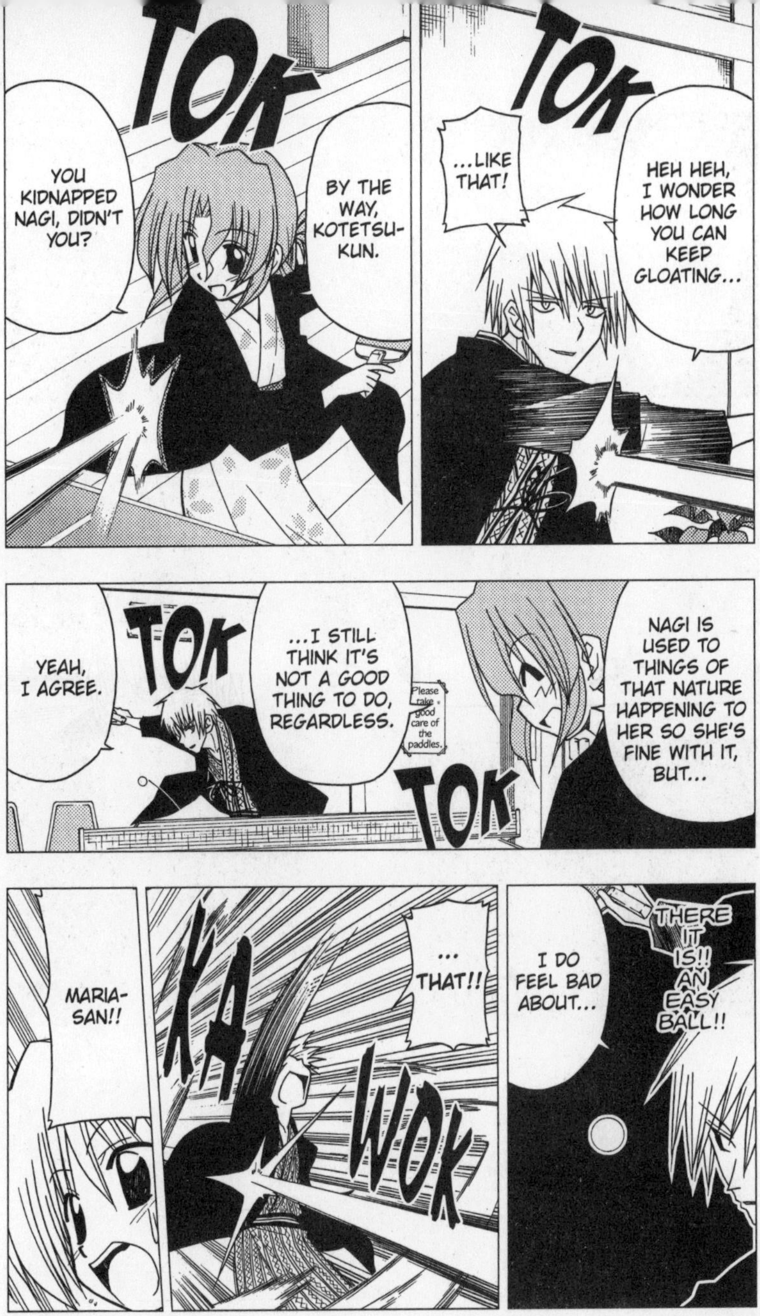
TOK
HEH HEH, I WONDER HOW LONG YOU CAN KEEP GLOATING...
...LIKE THAT!
TOK
BY THE WAY, KOTETSU-KUN.
YOU KIDNAPPED NAGI, DIDN'T YOU?
NAGI IS USED TO THINGS OF THAT NATURE HAPPENING TO HER SO SHE'S FINE WITH IT, BUT...
TOK
Please take good care of the paddles.
...I STILL THINK IT'S NOT A GOOD THING TO DO, REGARDLESS.
TOK
YEAH, I AGREE.
THERE IT IS!! AN EASY BALL!!
I DO FEEL BAD ABOUT...
...THAT!!
KA WOK
MARIA-SAN!!

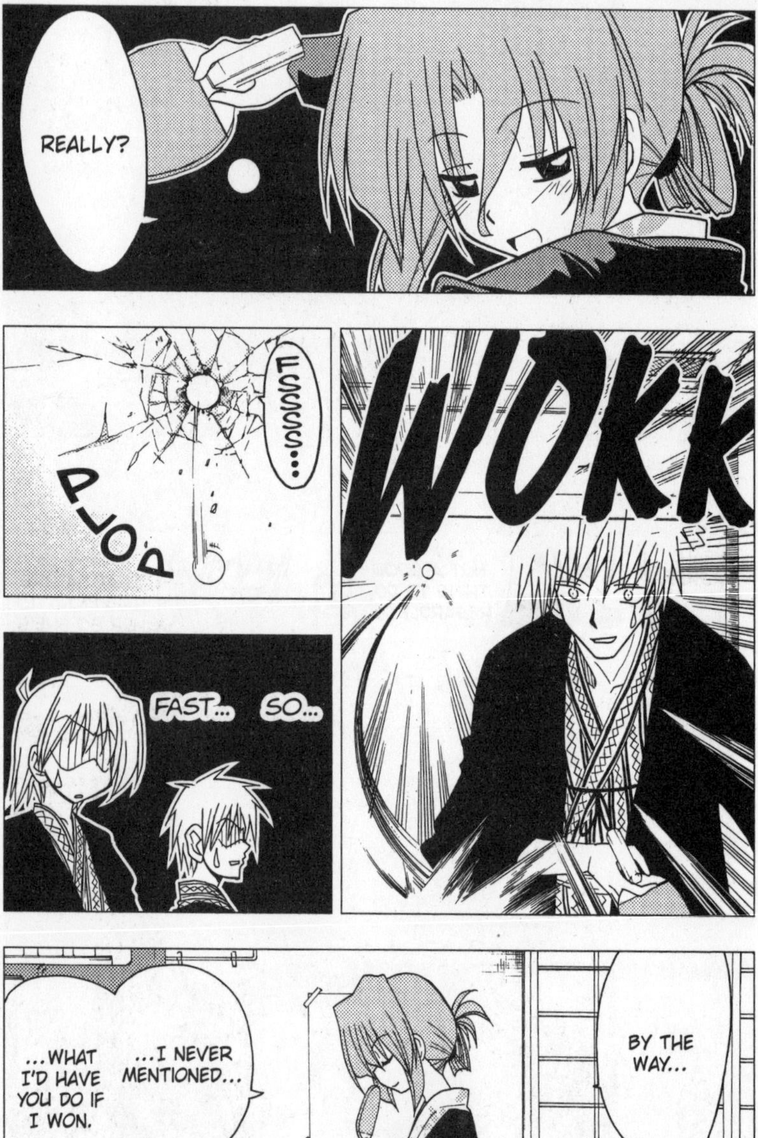
REALLY?
WOKK
FSSSS...
PLOP
FAST... SO...
BY THE WAY...
...I NEVER MENTIONED...
...WHAT I'D HAVE YOU DO IF I WON.

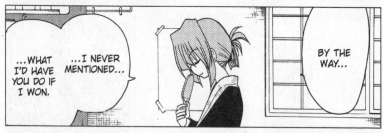

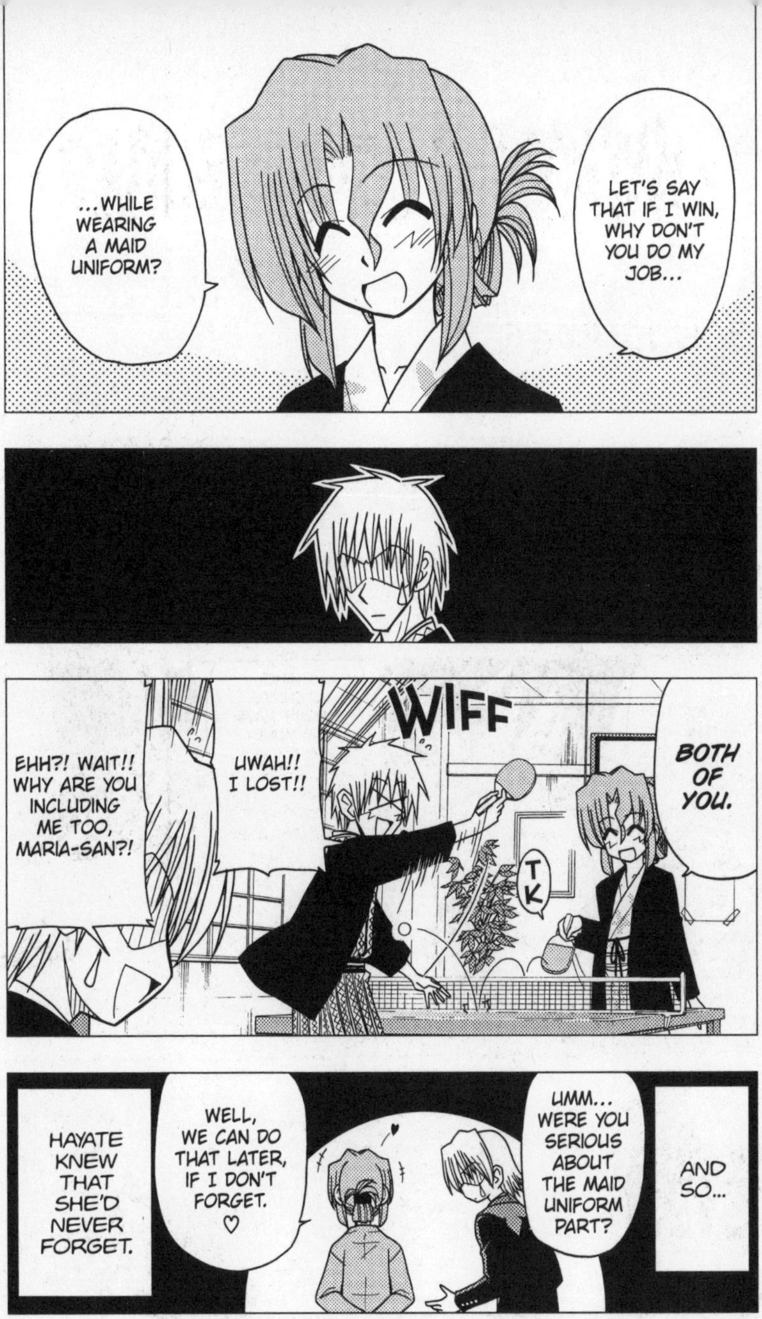
LET'S SAY THAT IF I WIN, WHY DON'T YOU DO MY JOB...
...WHILE WEARING A MAID UNIFORM?
BOTH OF YOU.
WIFF
TK
UWAH!! I LOST!!
EHH?! WAIT!! WHY ARE YOU INCLUDING ME TOO, MARIA-SAN?!
AND SO...
UMM... WERE YOU SERIOUS ABOUT THE MAID UNIFORM PART?
WELL, WE CAN DO THAT LATER, IF I DON'T FORGET. ♡
HAYATE KNEW THAT SHE'D NEVER FORGET.

- HAYATE THE COMBAT BUTLER -

BONUS PAGE

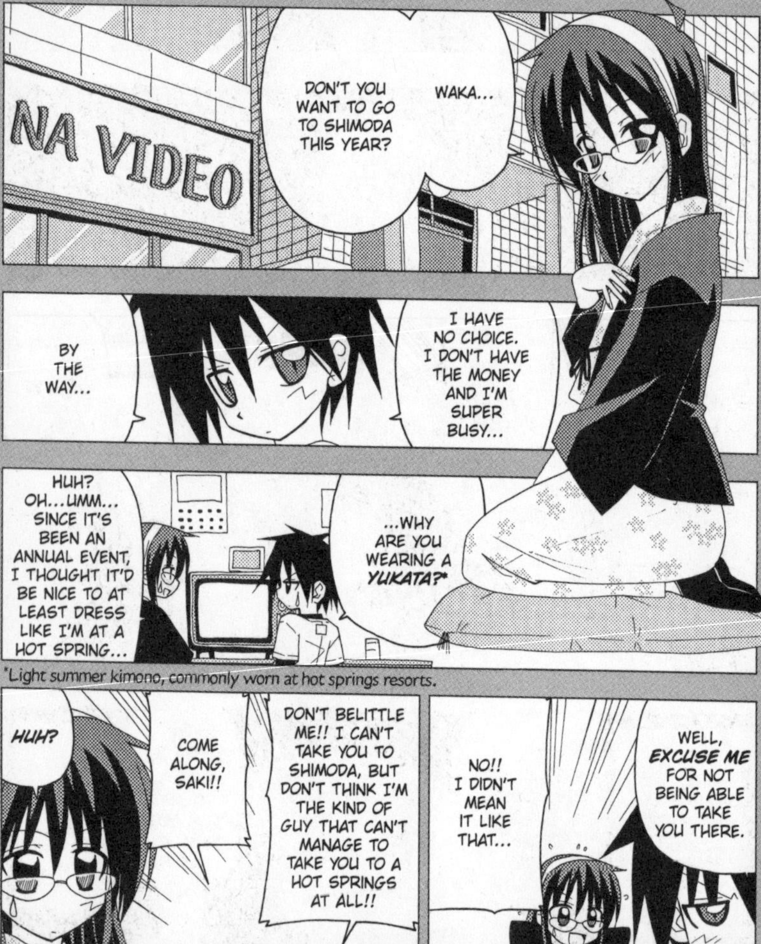

WAKA...
DON'T YOU WANT TO GO TO SHIMODA THIS YEAR?
NA VIDEO
I HAVE NO CHOICE. I DON'T HAVE THE MONEY AND I'M SUPER BUSY...
BY THE WAY...
...WHY ARE YOU WEARING A *YUKATA?**
HUH? OH...UMM... SINCE IT'S BEEN AN ANNUAL EVENT, I THOUGHT IT'D BE NICE TO AT LEAST DRESS LIKE I'M AT A HOT SPRING...
WELL, ***EXCUSE ME*** FOR NOT BEING ABLE TO TAKE YOU THERE.
NO!! I DIDN'T MEAN IT LIKE THAT...
DON'T BELITTLE ME!! I CAN'T TAKE YOU TO SHIMODA, BUT DON'T THINK I'M THE KIND OF GUY THAT CAN'T MANAGE TO TAKE YOU TO A HOT SPRINGS AT ALL!!
COME ALONG, SAKI!!
HUH?

*Light summer kimono, commonly worn at hot springs resorts.

☜ This continues on the next, next, next page.

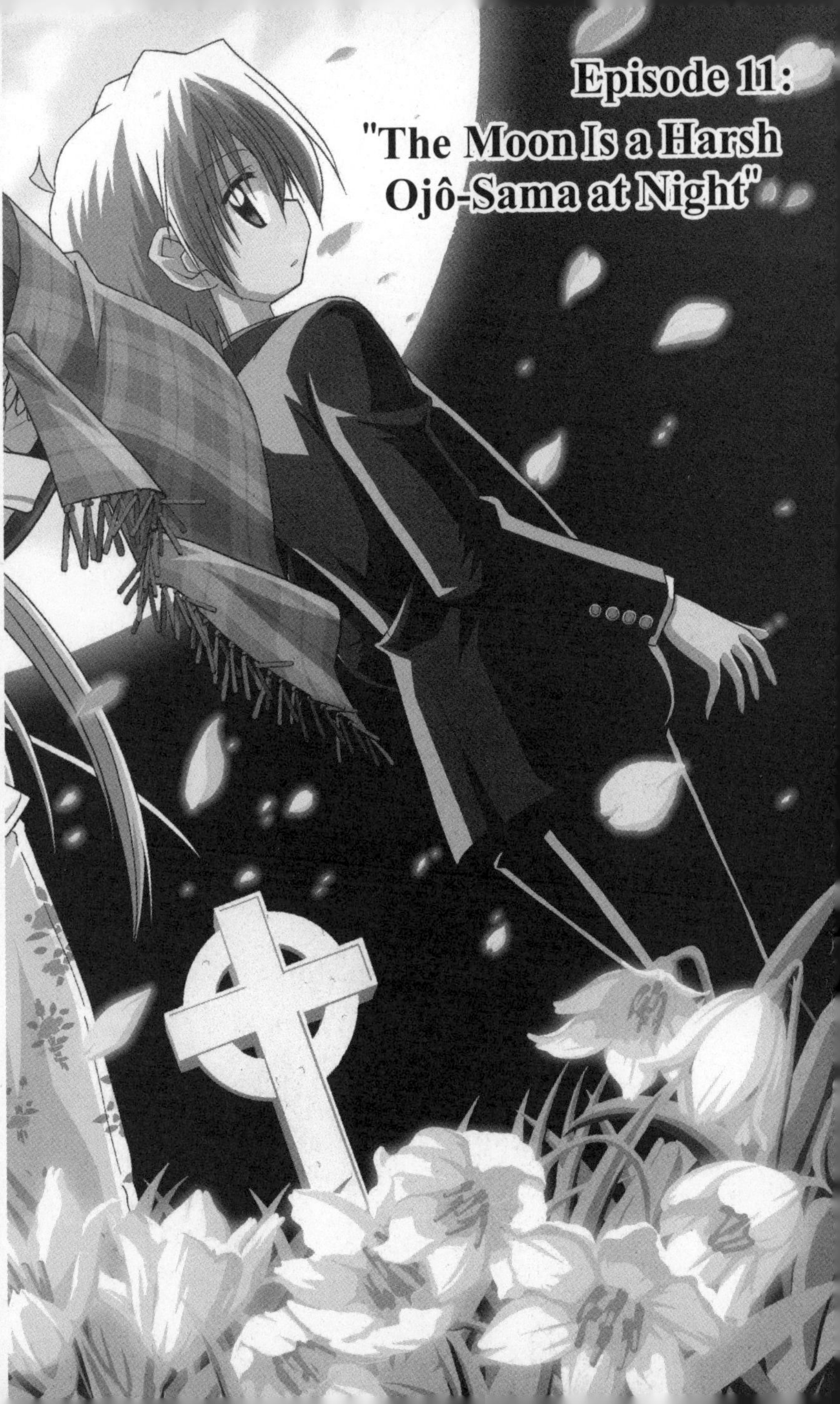
Episode 11:
"The Moon Is a Harsh
Ojô-Sama at Night"

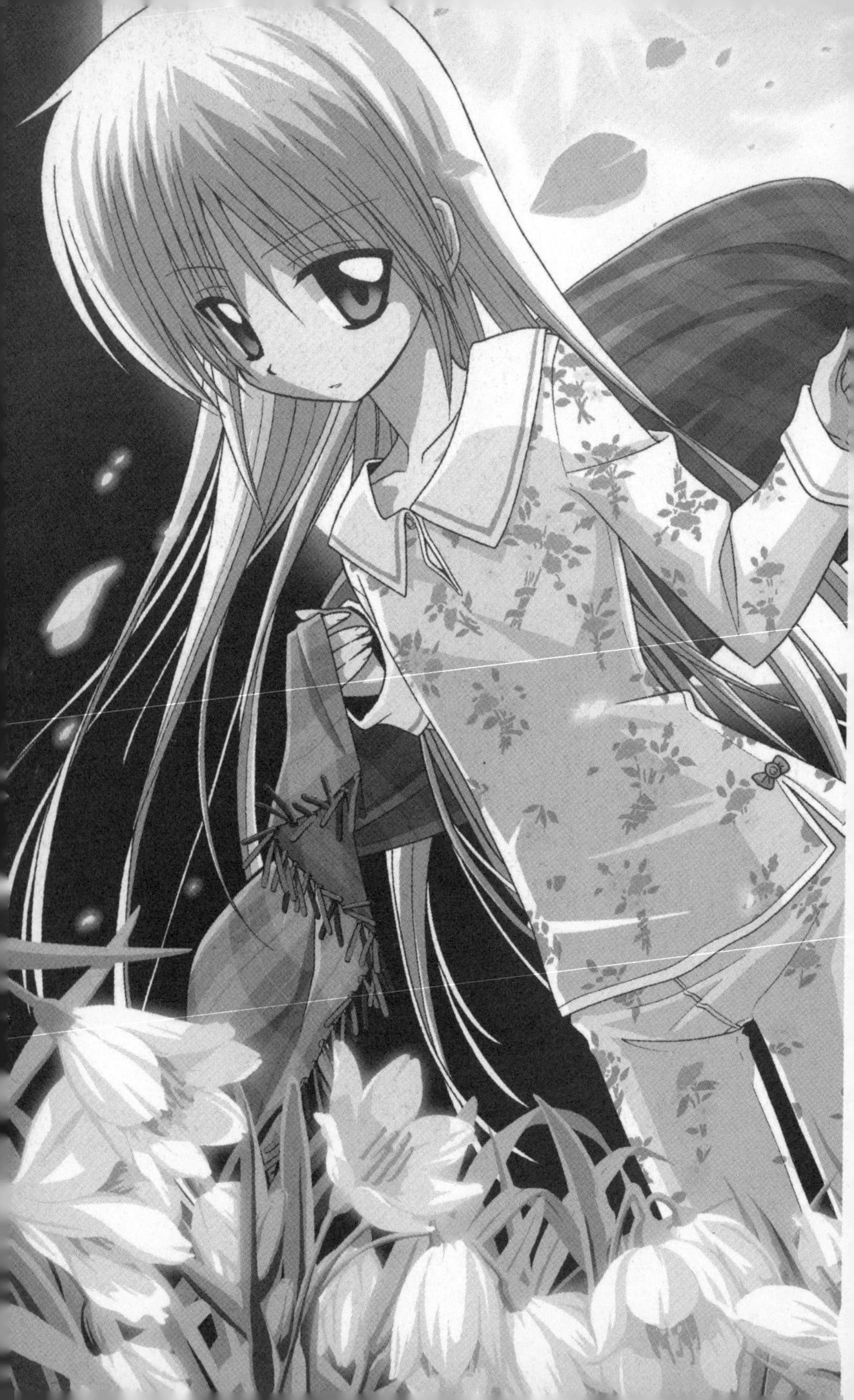

The bonus page story continues.

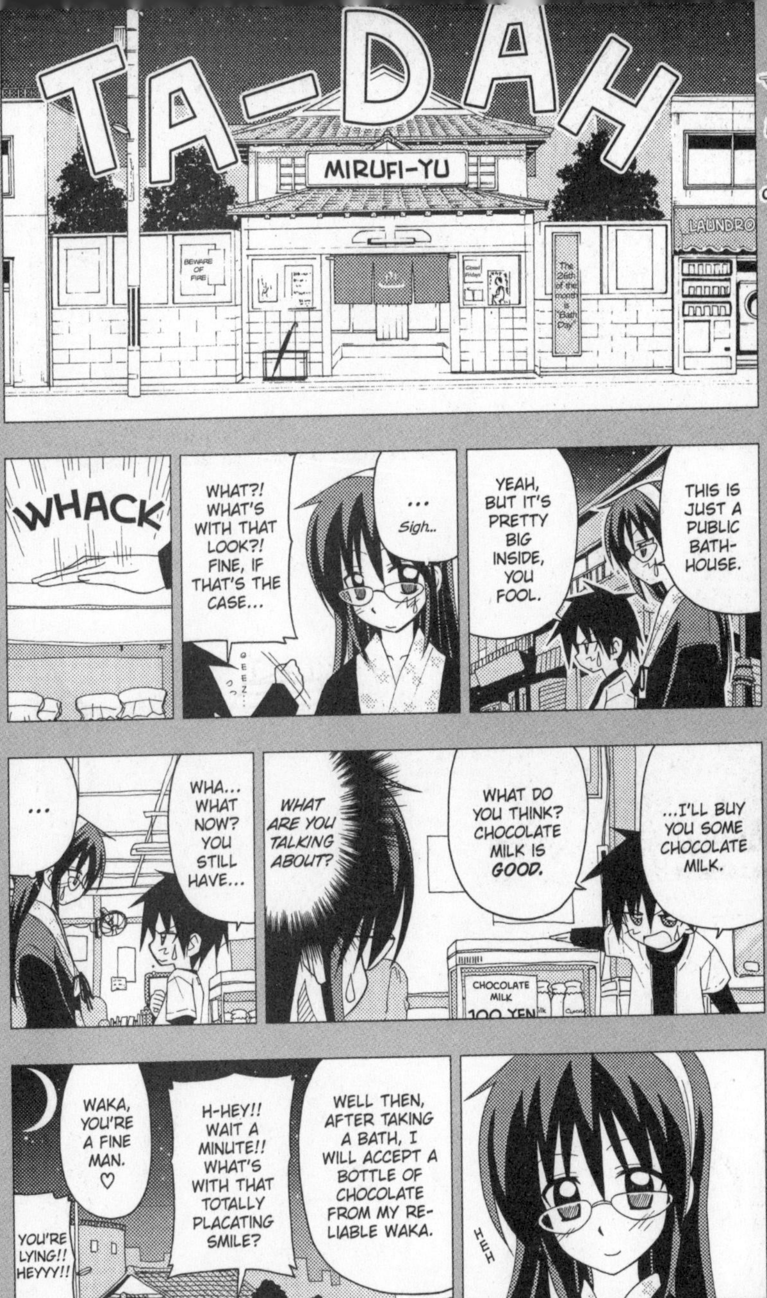
TA-DAH
MIRUFI-YU
BEWARE OF FIRE
Closed Fridays
The 26th of the month is "Bath Day"
LAUNDRO
THIS IS JUST A PUBLIC BATH-HOUSE.
YEAH, BUT IT'S PRETTY BIG INSIDE, YOU FOOL.
... Sigh..
WHAT?! WHAT'S WITH THAT LOOK?! FINE, IF THAT'S THE CASE...
GEEZ...
WHACK
...I'LL BUY YOU SOME CHOCOLATE MILK.
WHAT DO YOU THINK? CHOCOLATE MILK IS *GOOD.*
CHOCOLATE MILK 100 YEN
WHAT ARE YOU TALKING ABOUT?
WHA... WHAT NOW? YOU STILL HAVE...
...
HEH
WELL THEN, AFTER TAKING A BATH, I WILL ACCEPT A BOTTLE OF CHOCOLATE FROM MY RE-LIABLE WAKA.
H-HEY!! WAIT A MINUTE!! WHAT'S WITH THAT TOTALLY PLACATING SMILE?
WAKA, YOU'RE A FINE MAN. ♡
YOU'RE LYING!! HEYYY!!

There's no particular punch line...

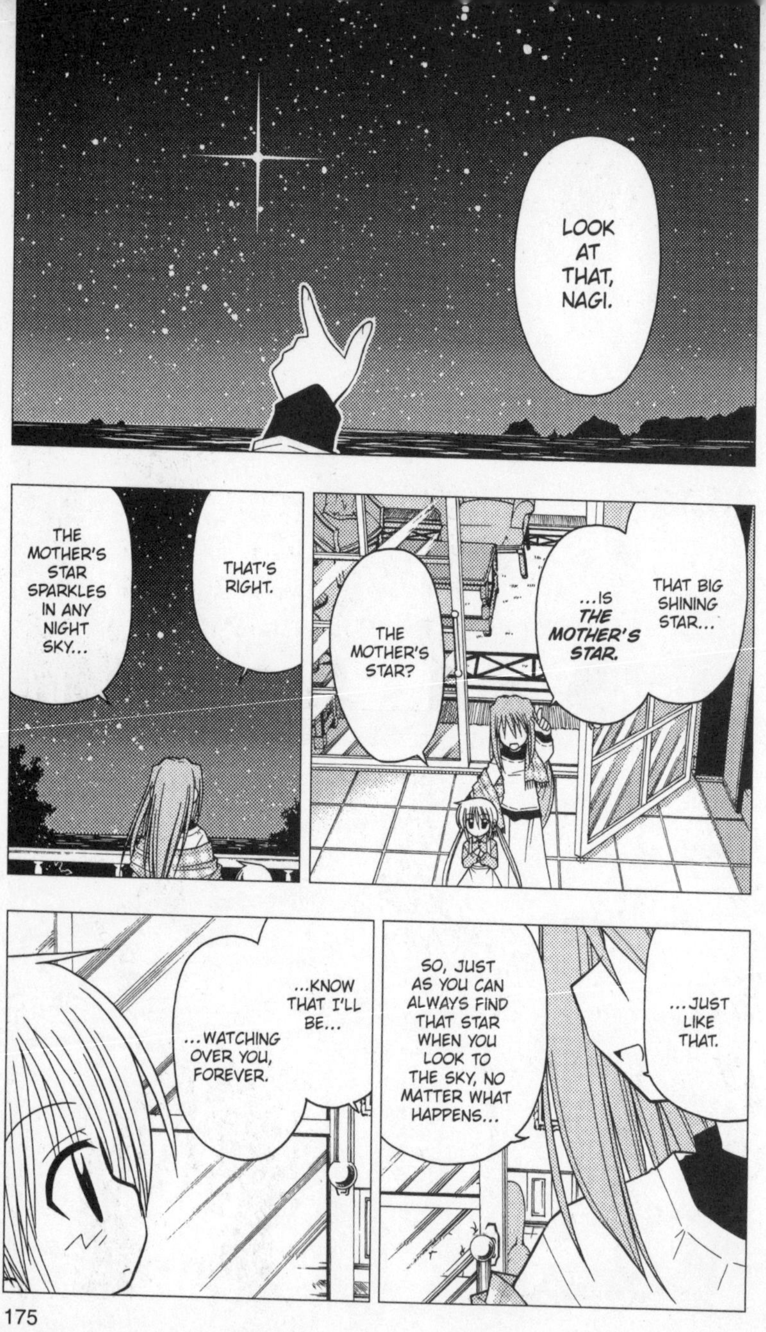
LOOK AT THAT, NAGI.
THAT BIG SHINING STAR...
...IS *THE MOTHER'S STAR.*
THE MOTHER'S STAR?
THAT'S RIGHT.
THE MOTHER'S STAR SPARKLES IN ANY NIGHT SKY...
...JUST LIKE THAT.
SO, JUST AS YOU CAN ALWAYS FIND THAT STAR WHEN YOU LOOK TO THE SKY, NO MATTER WHAT HAPPENS...
...KNOW THAT I'LL BE...
...WATCHING OVER YOU, FOREVER.

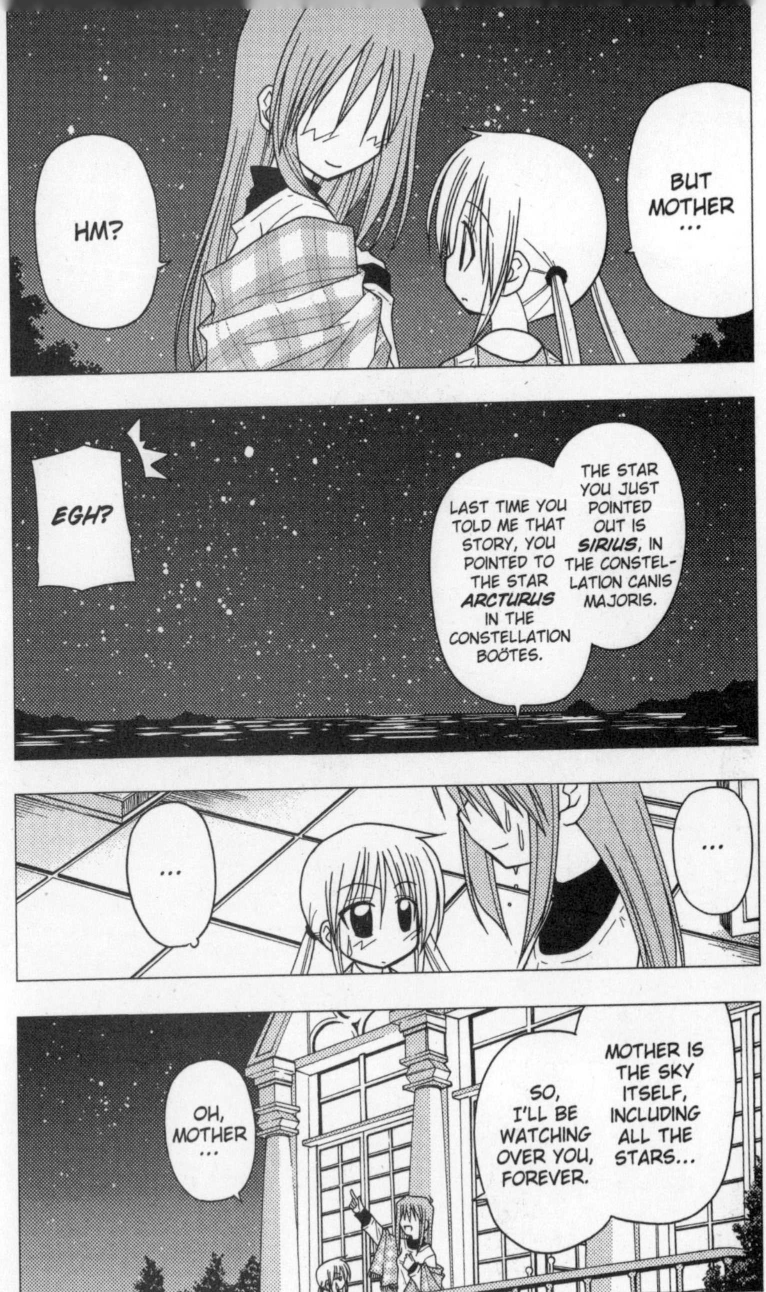
BUT MOTHER ...
HM?
LAST TIME YOU TOLD ME THAT STORY, YOU POINTED TO THE STAR ARCTURUS IN THE CONSTELLATION BOÖTES.
THE STAR YOU JUST POINTED OUT IS SIRIUS, IN THE CONSTELLATION CANIS MAJORIS.
EGH?
...
...
MOTHER IS THE SKY ITSELF, INCLUDING ALL THE STARS...
SO, I'LL BE WATCHING OVER YOU, FOREVER.
OH, MOTHER ...

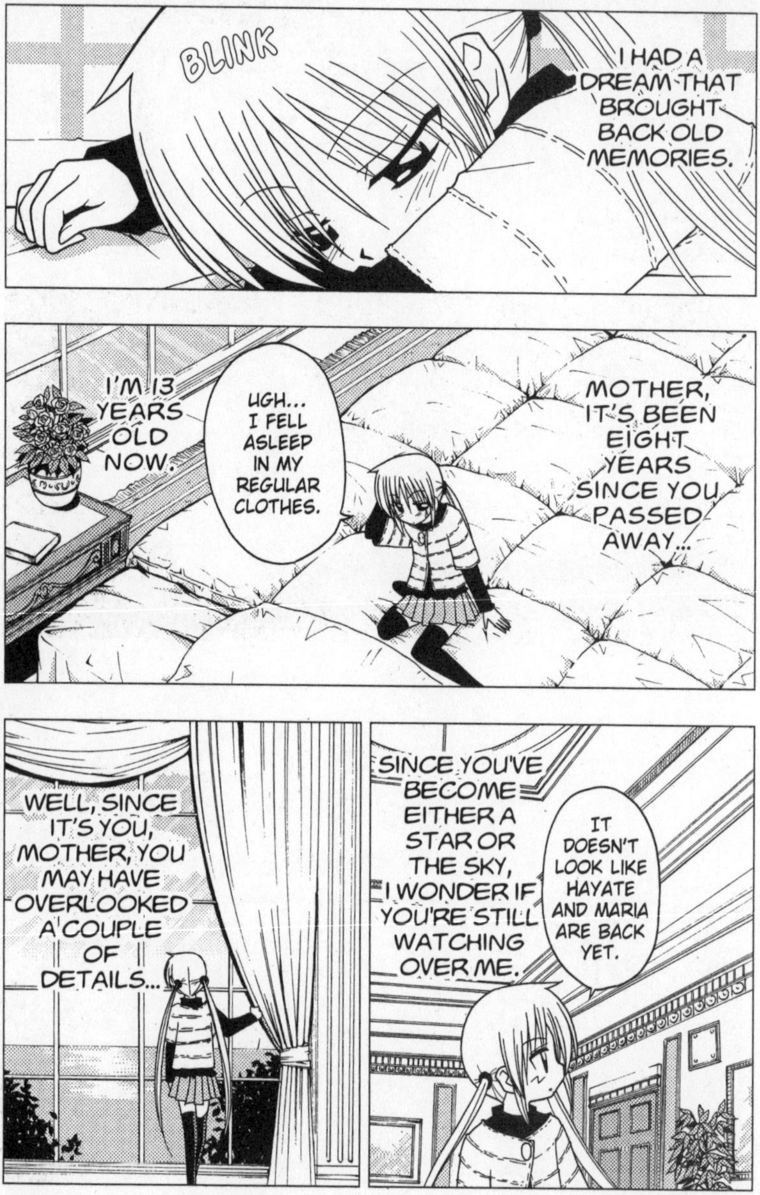
BLINK
I HAD A DREAM THAT BROUGHT BACK OLD MEMORIES.
MOTHER, IT'S BEEN EIGHT YEARS SINCE YOU PASSED AWAY...
UGH... I FELL ASLEEP IN MY REGULAR CLOTHES.
I'M 13 YEARS OLD NOW.
SINCE YOU'VE BECOME EITHER A STAR OR THE SKY, I WONDER IF YOU'RE STILL WATCHING OVER ME.
IT DOESN'T LOOK LIKE HAYATE AND MARIA ARE BACK YET.
WELL, SINCE IT'S YOU, MOTHER, YOU MAY HAVE OVERLOOKED A COUPLE OF DETAILS...

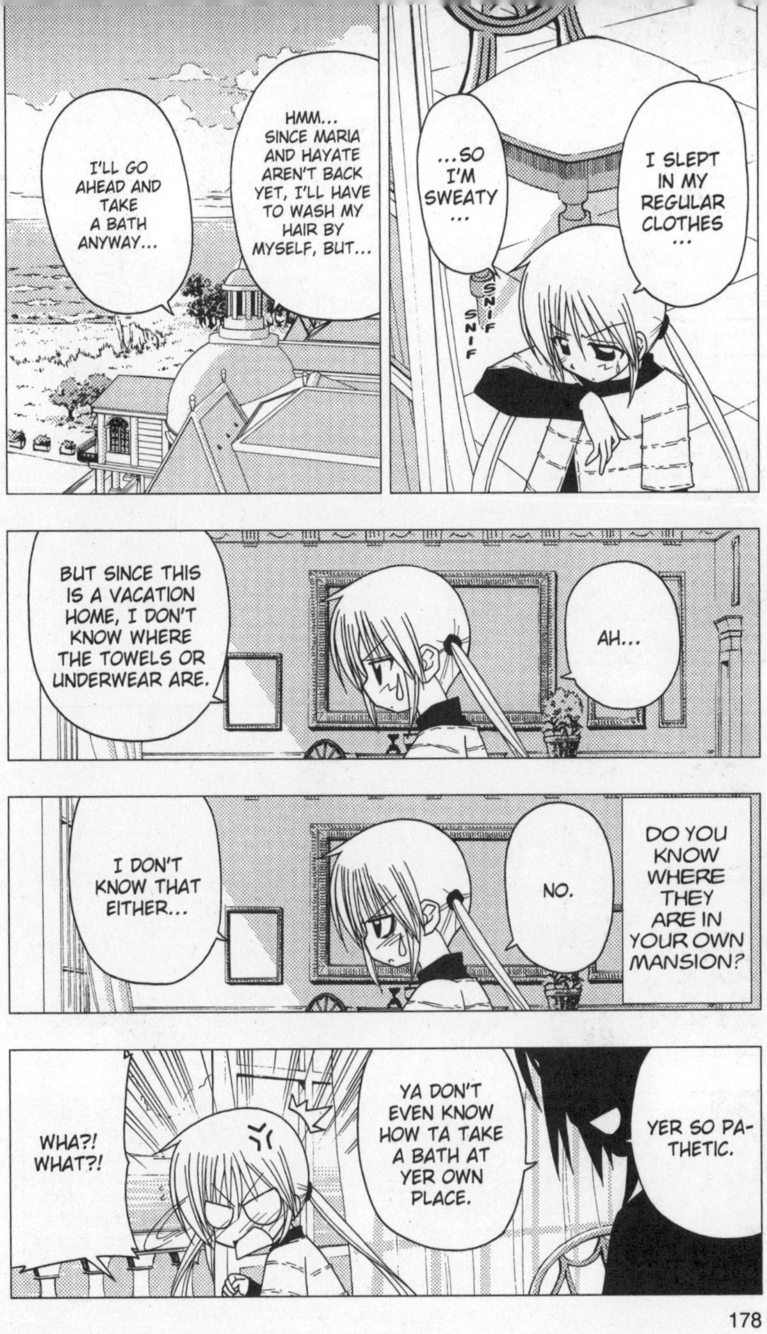
I SLEPT IN MY REGULAR CLOTHES...
...SO I'M SWEATY...
SNIF SNIF
HMM... SINCE MARIA AND HAYATE AREN'T BACK YET, I'LL HAVE TO WASH MY HAIR BY MYSELF, BUT...
I'LL GO AHEAD AND TAKE A BATH ANYWAY...
AH...
BUT SINCE THIS IS A VACATION HOME, I DON'T KNOW WHERE THE TOWELS OR UNDERWEAR ARE.
DO YOU KNOW WHERE THEY ARE IN YOUR OWN MANSION?
NO.
I DON'T KNOW THAT EITHER...
YER SO PATHETIC.
YA DON'T EVEN KNOW HOW TA TAKE A BATH AT YER OWN PLACE.
WHA?! WHAT?!

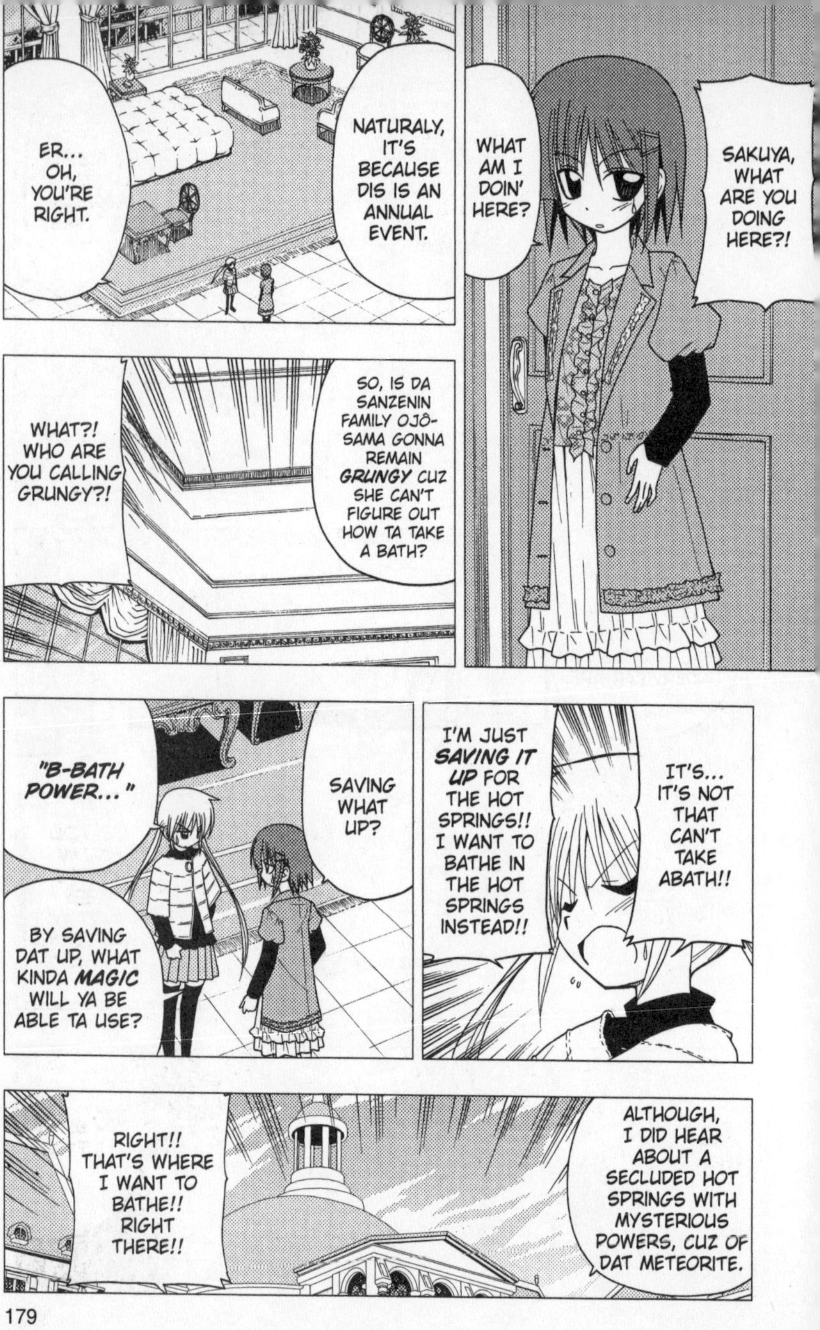
SAKUYA, WHAT ARE YOU DOING HERE?!
WHAT AM I DOIN' HERE?
NATURALY, IT'S BECAUSE DIS IS AN ANNUAL EVENT.
ER... OH, YOU'RE RIGHT.
SO, IS DA SANZENIN FAMILY OJÔ-SAMA GONNA REMAIN ***GRUNGY*** CUZ SHE CAN'T FIGURE OUT HOW TA TAKE A BATH?
WHAT?! WHO ARE YOU CALLING GRUNGY?!
IT'S... IT'S NOT THAT CAN'T TAKE ABATH!!
I'M JUST ***SAVING IT UP*** FOR THE HOT SPRINGS!! I WANT TO BATHE IN THE HOT SPRINGS INSTEAD!!
SAVING WHAT UP?
"B-BATH POWER..."
BY SAVING DAT UP, WHAT KINDA ***MAGIC*** WILL YA BE ABLE TA USE?
ALTHOUGH, I DID HEAR ABOUT A SECLUDED HOT SPRINGS WITH MYSTERIOUS POWERS, CUZ OF DAT METEORITE.
RIGHT!! THAT'S WHERE I WANT TO BATHE!! RIGHT THERE!!

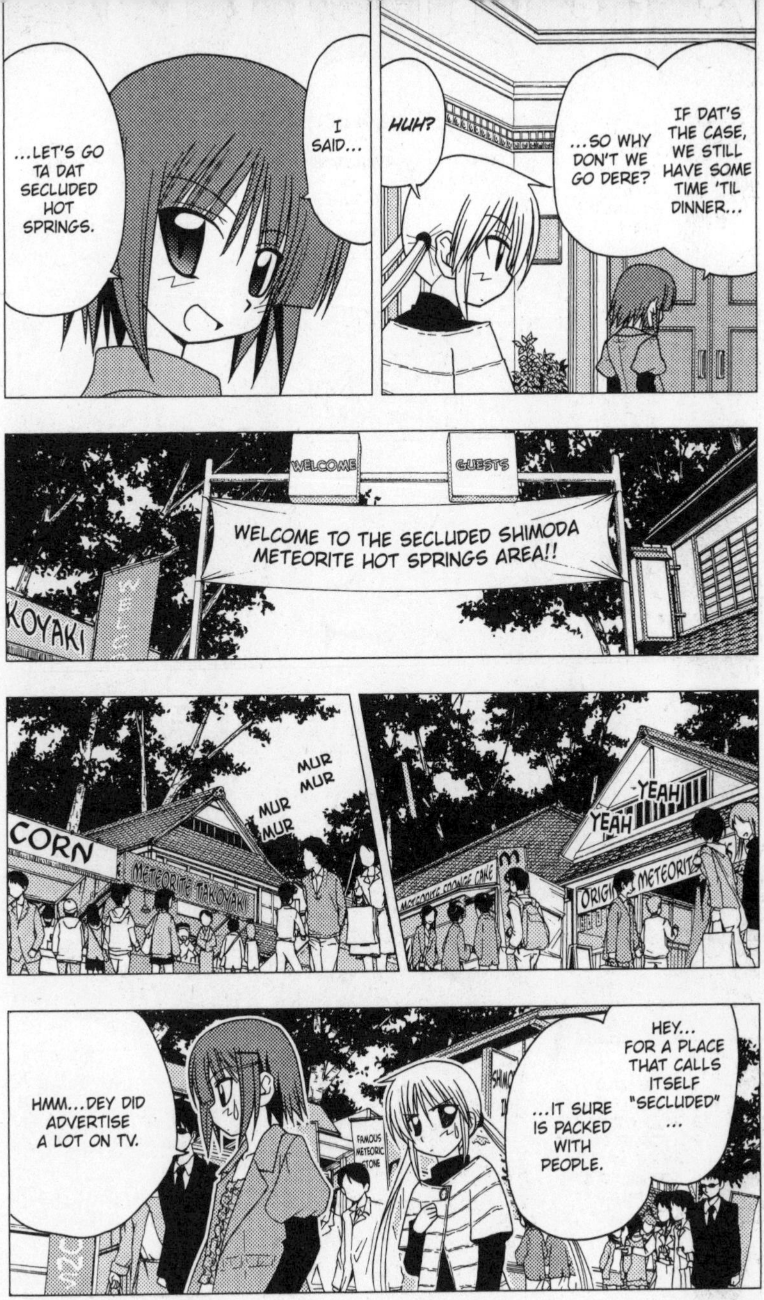
HUH?
IF DAT'S THE CASE, WE STILL HAVE SOME TIME 'TIL DINNER...
...SO WHY DON'T WE GO DERE?
I SAID...
...LET'S GO TA DAT SECLUDED HOT SPRINGS.
WELCOME
GUESTS
WELCOME TO THE SECLUDED SHIMODA METEORITE HOT SPRINGS AREA!!
KOYAKI
YEAH
YEAH
MUR MUR
MUR MUR
CORN
METEORITE TAKOYAKI
HEY... FOR A PLACE THAT CALLS ITSELF "SECLUDED"...
...IT SURE IS PACKED WITH PEOPLE.
FAMOUS METEORIC STONE
HMM...DEY DID ADVERTISE A LOT ON TV.

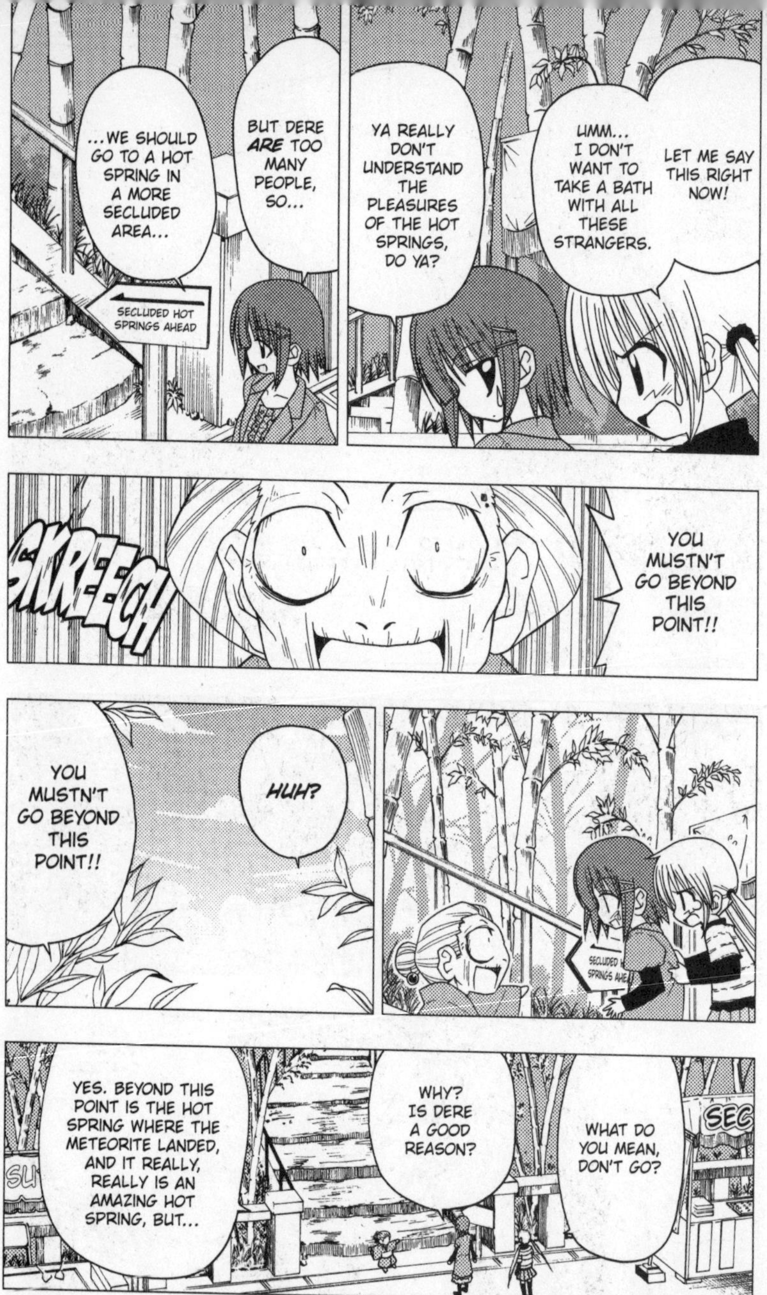
LET ME SAY THIS RIGHT NOW!
UMM... I DON'T WANT TO TAKE A BATH WITH ALL THESE STRANGERS.
YA REALLY DON'T UNDERSTAND THE PLEASURES OF THE HOT SPRINGS, DO YA?
BUT DERE *ARE* TOO MANY PEOPLE, SO...
...WE SHOULD GO TO A HOT SPRING IN A MORE SECLUDED AREA...
SECLUDED HOT SPRINGS AHEAD
YOU MUSTN'T GO BEYOND THIS POINT!!
SKREEECH
HUH?
YOU MUSTN'T GO BEYOND THIS POINT!!
WHAT DO YOU MEAN, DON'T GO?
WHY? IS DERE A GOOD REASON?
YES. BEYOND THIS POINT IS THE HOT SPRING WHERE THE METEORITE LANDED, AND IT REALLY, REALLY IS AN AMAZING HOT SPRING, BUT...

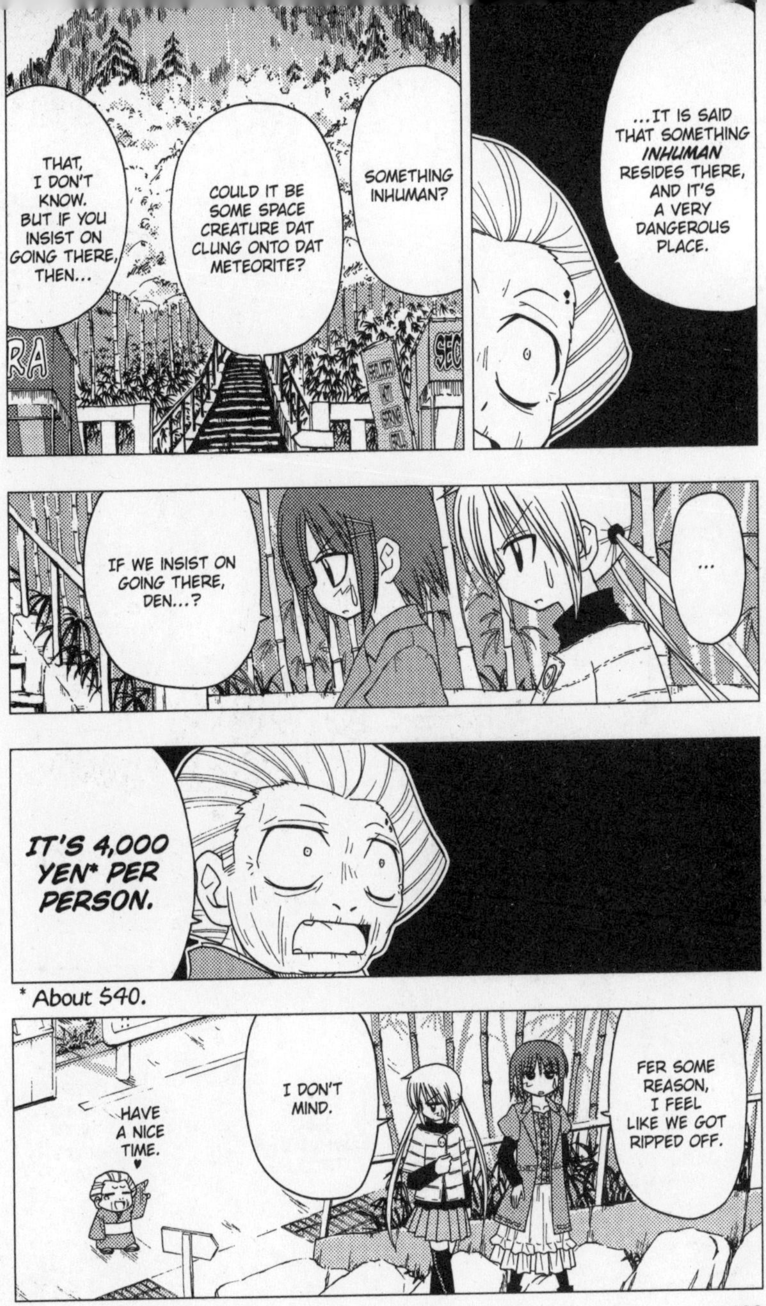
...IT IS SAID THAT SOMETHING *INHUMAN* RESIDES THERE, AND IT'S A VERY DANGEROUS PLACE.
SOMETHING INHUMAN?
COULD IT BE SOME SPACE CREATURE DAT CLUNG ONTO DAT METEORITE?
THAT, I DON'T KNOW. BUT IF YOU INSIST ON GOING THERE, THEN...
...
IF WE INSIST ON GOING THERE, DEN...?
IT'S 4,000 YEN* PER PERSON.
FER SOME REASON, I FEEL LIKE WE GOT RIPPED OFF.
I DON'T MIND.
HAVE A NICE TIME. ♥

* About $40.

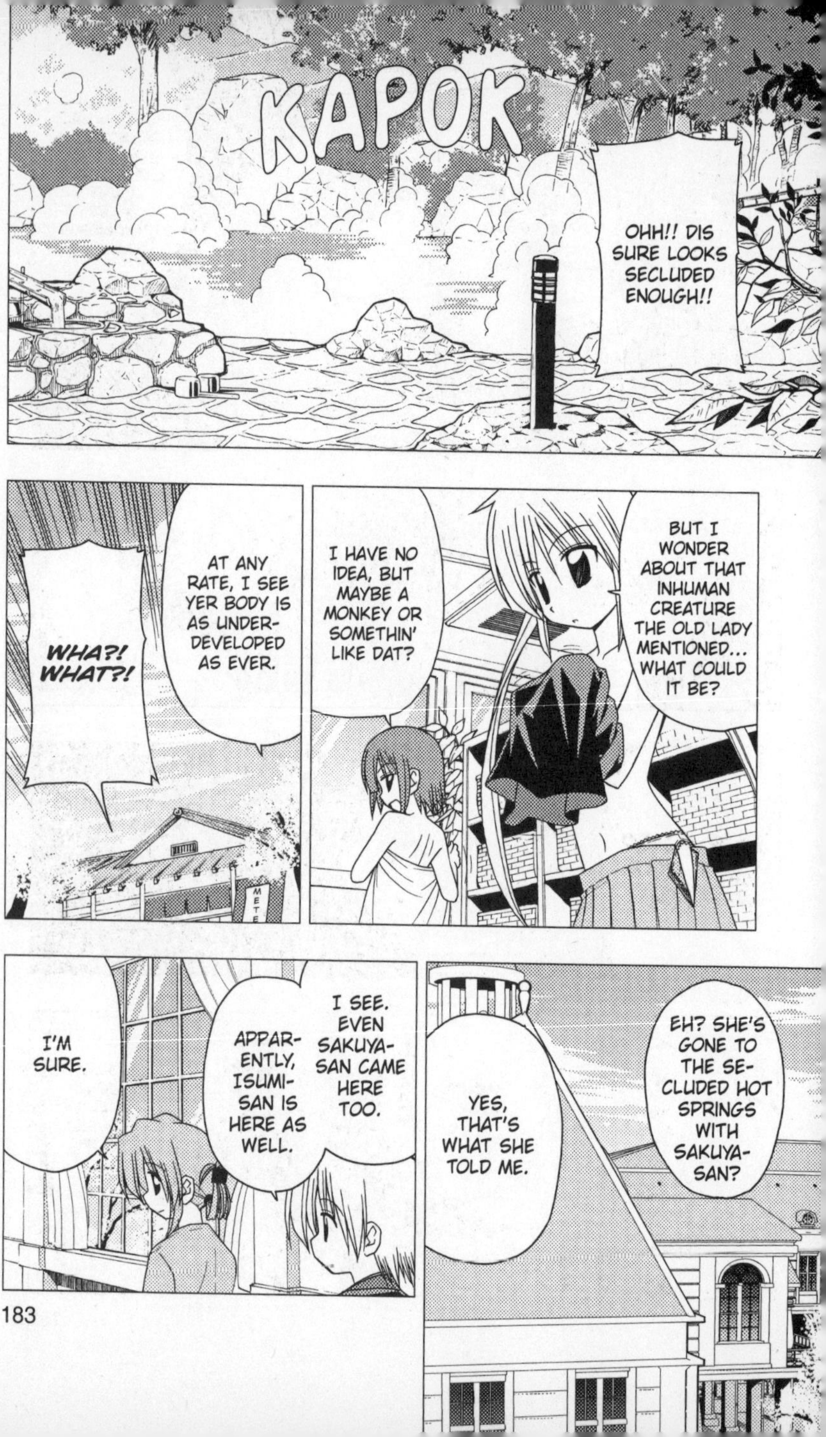
KAPOK
OHH!! DIS SURE LOOKS SECLUDED ENOUGH!!
BUT I WONDER ABOUT THAT INHUMAN CREATURE THE OLD LADY MENTIONED... WHAT COULD IT BE?
I HAVE NO IDEA, BUT MAYBE A MONKEY OR SOMETHIN' LIKE DAT?
AT ANY RATE, I SEE YER BODY IS AS UNDER-DEVELOPED AS EVER.
WHA?! WHAT?!
EH? SHE'S GONE TO THE SE-CLUDED HOT SPRINGS WITH SAKUYA-SAN?
YES, THAT'S WHAT SHE TOLD ME.
I SEE. EVEN SAKUYA-SAN CAME HERE TOO.
APPAR-ENTLY, ISUMI-SAN IS HERE AS WELL.
I'M SURE.

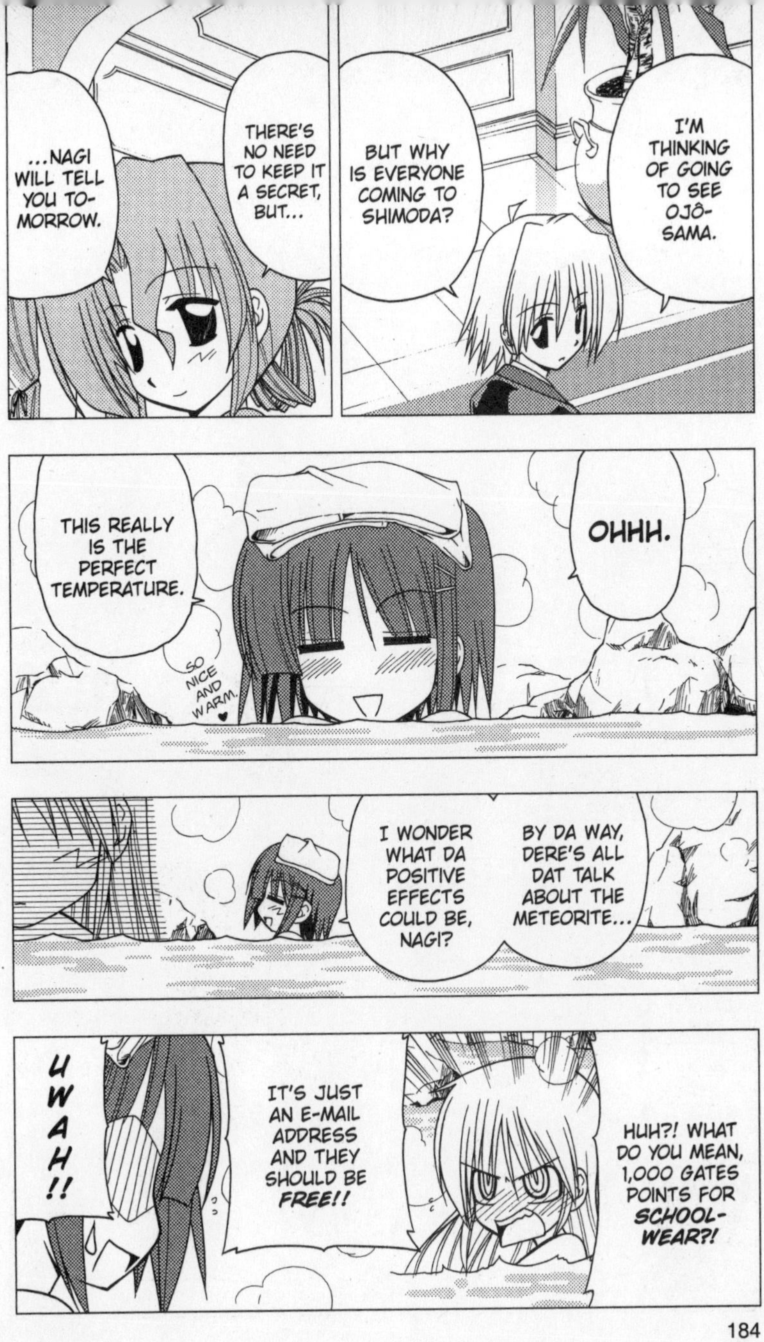
I'M THINKING OF GOING TO SEE OJÔ-SAMA.
BUT WHY IS EVERYONE COMING TO SHIMODA?
THERE'S NO NEED TO KEEP IT A SECRET, BUT...
...NAGI WILL TELL YOU TO-MORROW.
OHHH.
THIS REALLY IS THE PERFECT TEMPERATURE.
SO NICE AND WARM. ♥
BY DA WAY, DERE'S ALL DAT TALK ABOUT THE METEORITE...
I WONDER WHAT DA POSITIVE EFFECTS COULD BE, NAGI?
HUH?! WHAT DO YOU MEAN, 1,000 GATES POINTS FOR *SCHOOL-WEAR?!*
IT'S JUST AN E-MAIL ADDRESS AND THEY SHOULD BE *FREE!!*
UWAH!!

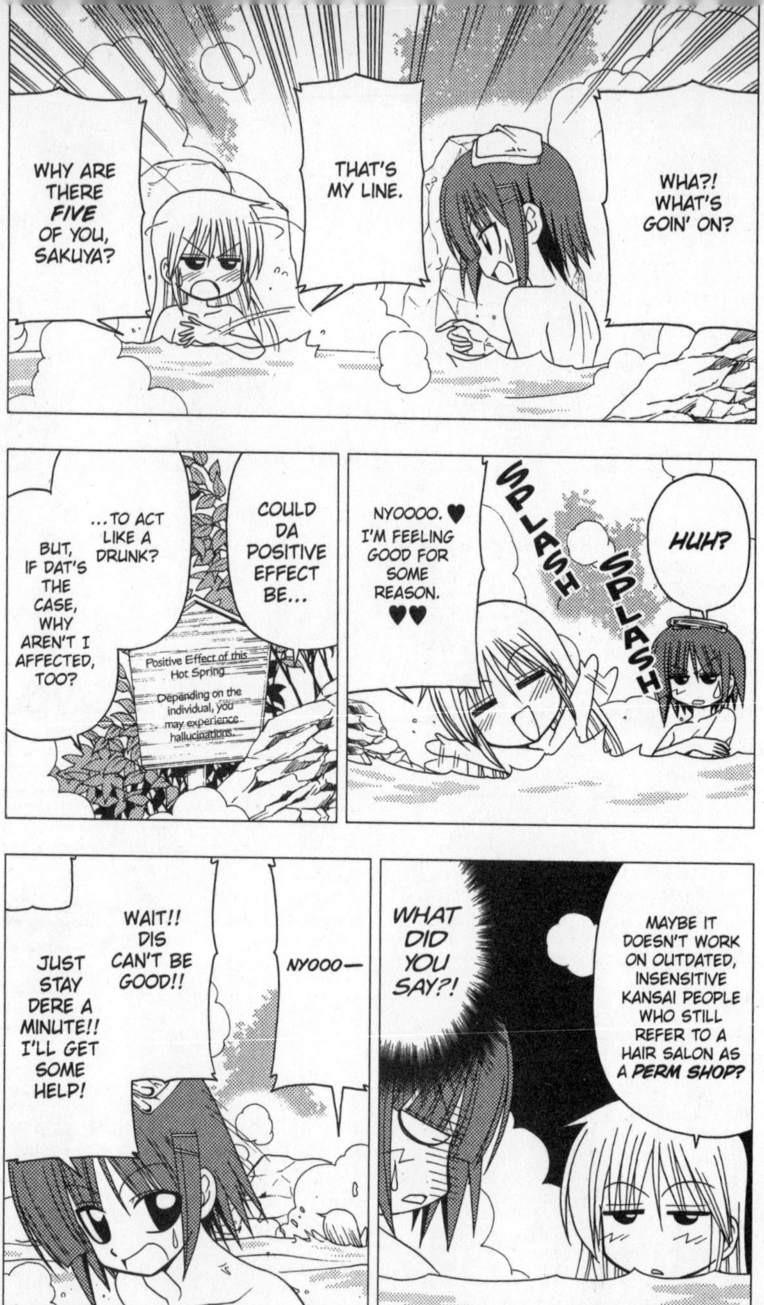
WHA?! WHAT'S GOIN' ON?
THAT'S MY LINE.
WHY ARE THERE *FIVE* OF YOU, SAKUYA?
HUH?
SPLASH
SPLASH
NYOOOO. ♥ I'M FEELING GOOD FOR SOME REASON. ♥♥
COULD DA POSITIVE EFFECT BE...
...TO ACT LIKE A DRUNK?
BUT, IF DAT'S THE CASE, WHY AREN'T I AFFECTED, TOO?
Positive Effect of this Hot Spring
Depending on the individual, you may experience hallucinations.
MAYBE IT DOESN'T WORK ON OUTDATED, INSENSITIVE KANSAI PEOPLE WHO STILL REFER TO A HAIR SALON AS A *PERM SHOP?*
WHAT DID YOU SAY?!
NYOOO—
WAIT!! DIS CAN'T BE GOOD!!
JUST STAY DERE A MINUTE!! I'LL GET SOME HELP!

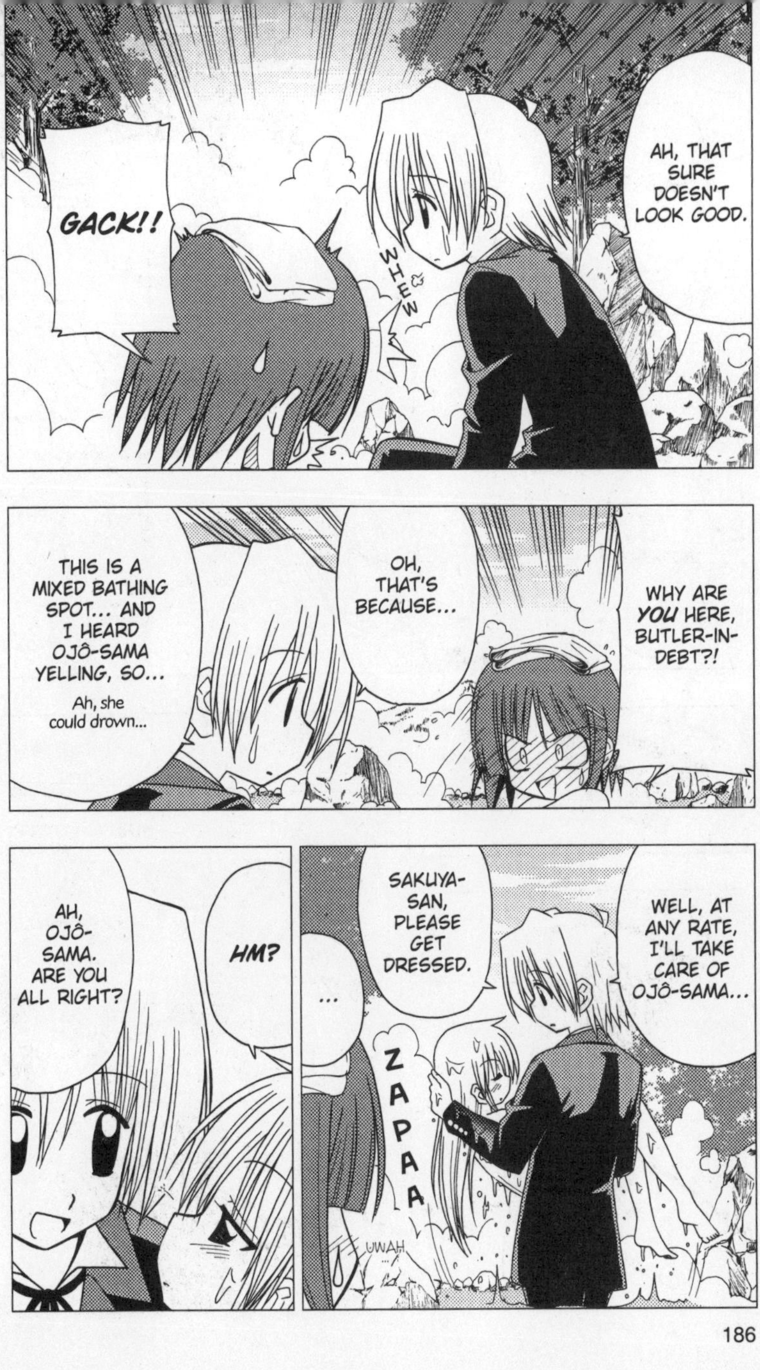
AH, THAT SURE DOESN'T LOOK GOOD.
WHEW
GACK!!
WHY ARE *YOU* HERE, BUTLER-IN-DEBT?!
OH, THAT'S BECAUSE...
THIS IS A MIXED BATHING SPOT... AND I HEARD OJÔ-SAMA YELLING, SO...
Ah, she could drown...
WELL, AT ANY RATE, I'LL TAKE CARE OF OJÔ-SAMA...
SAKUYA-SAN, PLEASE GET DRESSED.
...
ZAPAA
UWAH ...!
HM?
AH, OJÔ-SAMA. ARE YOU ALL RIGHT?

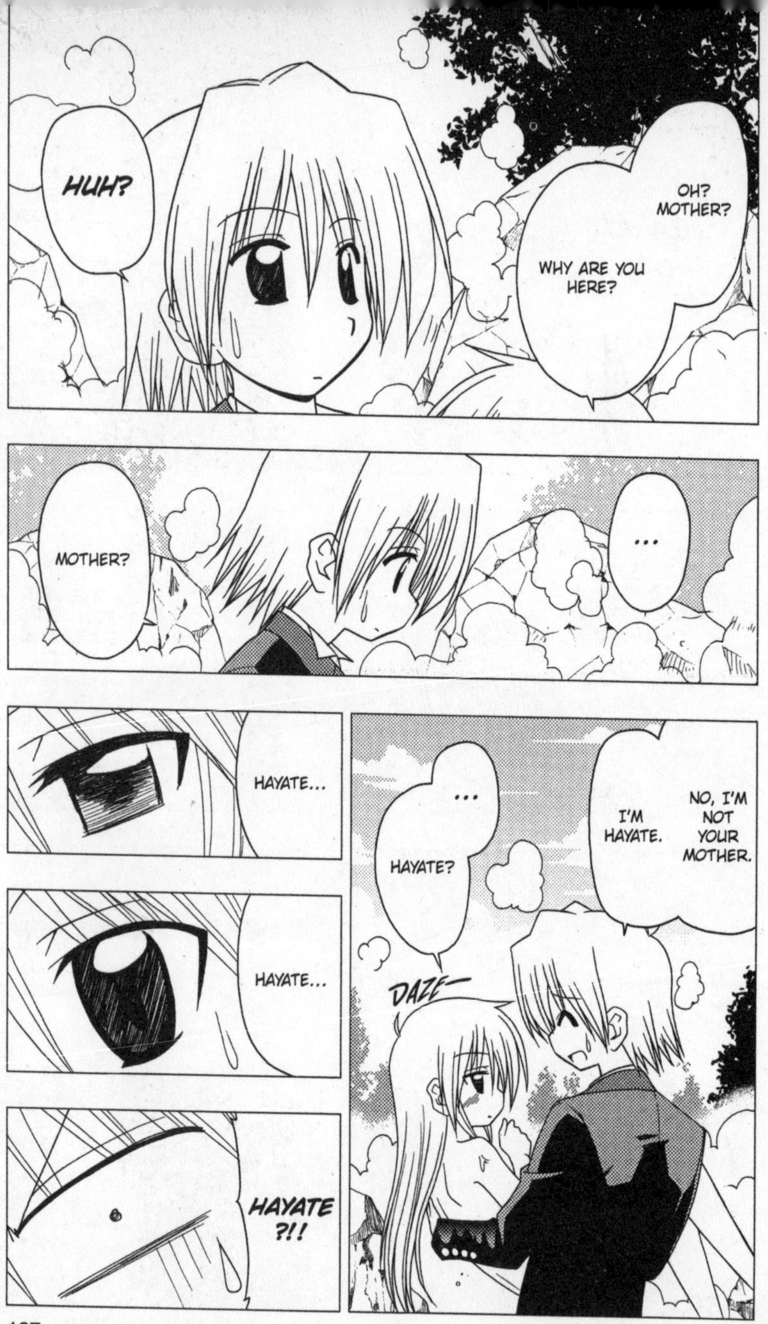

HUH?

OH? MOTHER?

WHY ARE YOU HERE?

MOTHER?

...

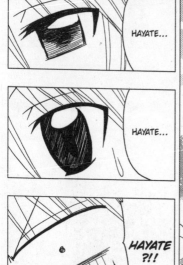

HAYATE...

HAYATE...

HAYATE ?!!

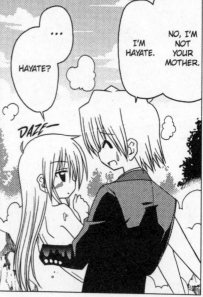

...

HAYATE?

I'M HAYATE.

NO, I'M NOT YOUR MOTHER.

DAZE—

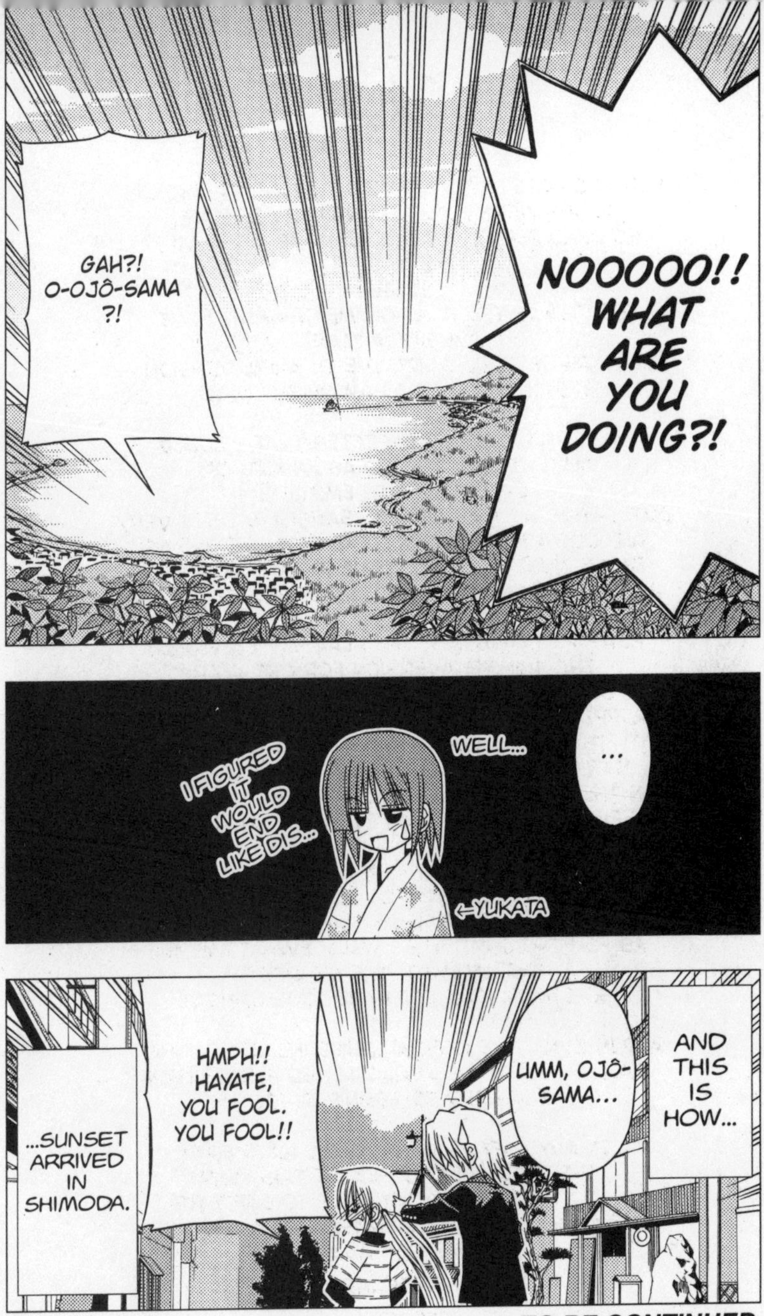
NOOOOO!! WHAT ARE YOU DOING?!
GAH?! O-OJÔ-SAMA ?!
...
WELL...
I FIGURED IT WOULD END LIKE DIS...
←YUKATA
AND THIS IS HOW...
UMM, OJÔ-SAMA...
HMPH!! HAYATE, YOU FOOL. YOU FOOL!!
...SUNSET ARRIVED IN SHIMODA.

TO BE CONTINUED

FOR THE PAGE LAYOUT IN THIS VOLUME, THE BONUS
PAGES WERE INSERTED INTO THE EPISODE,
SO BE CAREFUL.☆(BE CAREFUL ABOUT WHAT?)

THERE!
SO THIS IS THE 11TH VOLUME OF *HAYATE THE
COMBAT BUTLER!*
AND AS OF APRIL 2007, THE TV ANIME VERSION
BEGAN, AIRING AT 10 AM ON TV TOKYO.

HONESTLY, I NEVER EXPECTED THAT I COULD
MAKE IT THIS FAR, SO AS AN AUTHOR,
I'M FILLED WITH EMOTION.
BUT THIS IS NO TIME TO FEEL SATISFIED. I GET VERY
ANXIOUS ABOUT MEETING THE EXPECTATIONS OF
THOSE INVOLVED IN RECOMMENDING THIS MANGA,
AS WELL AS THE EXPECTATIONS OF YOU, THE FANS.

FOR THE TIME BEING, THE PLAN IS TO CONTINUE
THE ANIMATED VERSION FOR ONE YEAR
(FOUR 3-MONTH SEASONS)—UNLESS IT GETS
DROPPED DUE TO LOW RATINGS—SO PLEASE STICK
WITH IT AND SEE WHAT HAPPENS IN THE LONG RUN.
NATURALLY, I'LL CONTINUE TO WORK HARDER
ON THE MANGA AS WELL, SO PLEASE CONTINUE TO
SUPPORT ME MORE THAN EVER IN THAT REGARD.

IN MAY, A NOVELIZED VERSION OF *HAYATE THE
COMBAT BUTLER* WILL BE COMING OUT.
I WAS IN CHARGE OF ILLUSTRATING IT.
AS FOR THE CONTENTS...WELL, EVEN I AM ONLY
FAMILIAR WITH THE SYNOPSIS,
SO I'M LOOKING FORWARD TO READING IT.

AND IN JUNE, THE OFFICIAL GUIDE INCLUDING "THAT"
SHOULD FINALLY BE AVAILABLE, SO PLEASE LOOK
FORWARD TO SEEING IT, TOO.

IN ANY CASE, I THINK YOU'LL HAVE MANY
OPPORTUNITIES TO SEE US THIS YEAR,
SO I HOPE YOU'LL CONTINUE TO SUPPORT
ME AS ALWAYS. ALSO, PLEASE CHECK THE WEB
SUNDAY SITE AS WELL.☆
HTTP://WEBSUNDAY.NET

SEE YOU!

Smiling Onmyôji

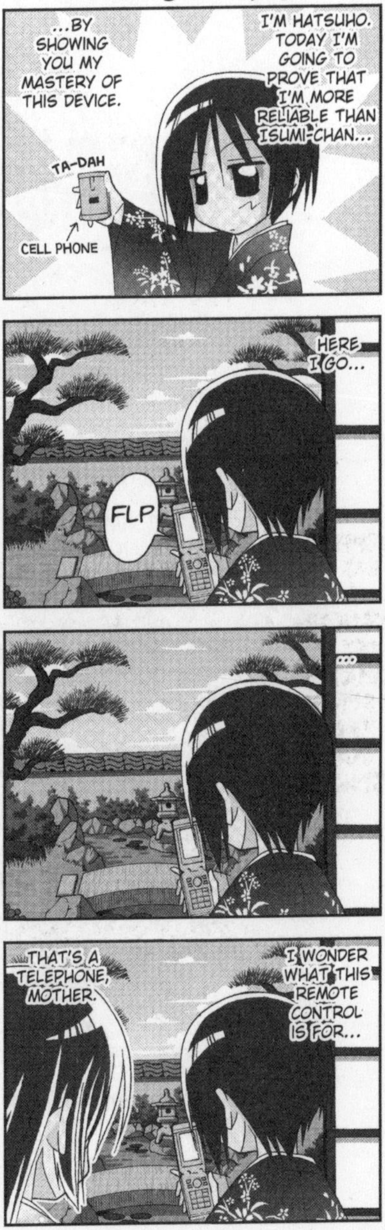
I'M HATSUHO. TODAY I'M GOING TO PROVE THAT I'M MORE RELIABLE THAN ISUMI-CHAN...
...BY SHOWING YOU MY MASTERY OF THIS DEVICE.
TA-DAH
CELL PHONE
HERE I GO...
FLP
...
I WONDER WHAT THIS REMOTE CONTROL IS FOR...
THAT'S A TELEPHONE, MOTHER.

Douman Seiman

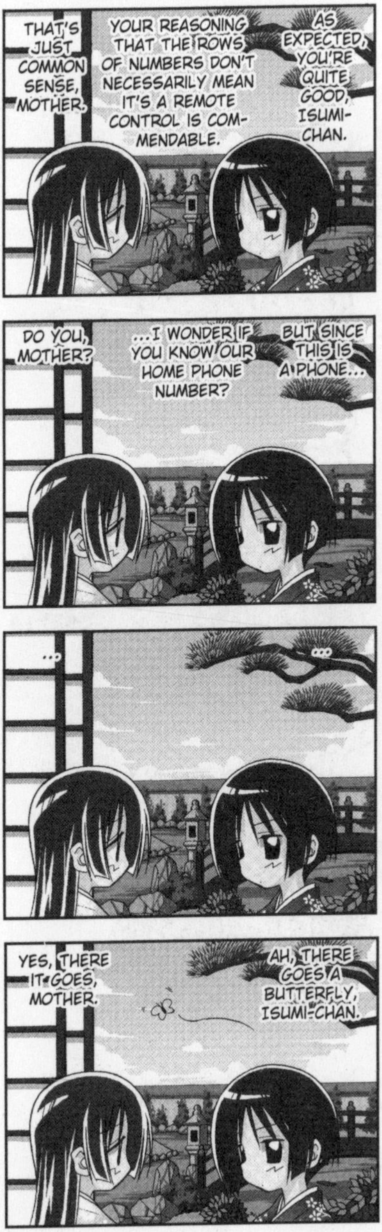
AS EXPECTED, YOU'RE QUITE GOOD, ISUMI-CHAN.
YOUR REASONING THAT THE ROWS OF NUMBERS DON'T NECESSARILY MEAN IT'S A REMOTE CONTROL IS COMMENDABLE.
THAT'S JUST COMMON SENSE, MOTHER.
BUT SINCE THIS IS A PHONE...
...I WONDER IF YOU KNOW OUR HOME PHONE NUMBER?
DO YOU, MOTHER?
...
...
AH, THERE GOES A BUTTERFLY, ISUMI-CHAN.
YES, THERE IT GOES, MOTHER.

HAYATE THE COMBAT BUTLER
VOL. 11

STORY AND ART BY
KENJIRO HATA

English Adaptation/Mark Giambruno
Translation/Yuki Yoshioka & Cindy H. Yamauchi
Touch-up Art & Lettering/HudsonYards
Design/Yukiko Whitley
Editor/Shaenon K. Garrity

Editor in Chief, Books/Alvin Lu
Editor in Chief, Magazines/Marc Weidenbaum
VP, Publishing Licensing/Rika Inouye
VP, Sales & Product Marketing/Gonzalo Ferreyra
VP, Creative/Linda Espinosa
Publisher/Hyoe Narita

Printed in Canada

Published by VIZ Media, LLC
P.O. Box 77010
San Francisco, CA 94107

10 9 8 7 6 5 4 3 2 1
First printing, May 2009

store.viz.com

www.viz.com

PARENTAL ADVISORY
HAYATE THE COMBAT BUTLER is rated T+ for Older Teen and is recommended for ages 16 and up. This volume contains strong language, realistic and fantasy violence, and crude humor.
T+ FOR OLDER TEEN
ratings.viz.com

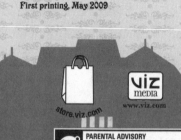

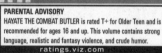

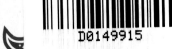

ayate the combat butler 11

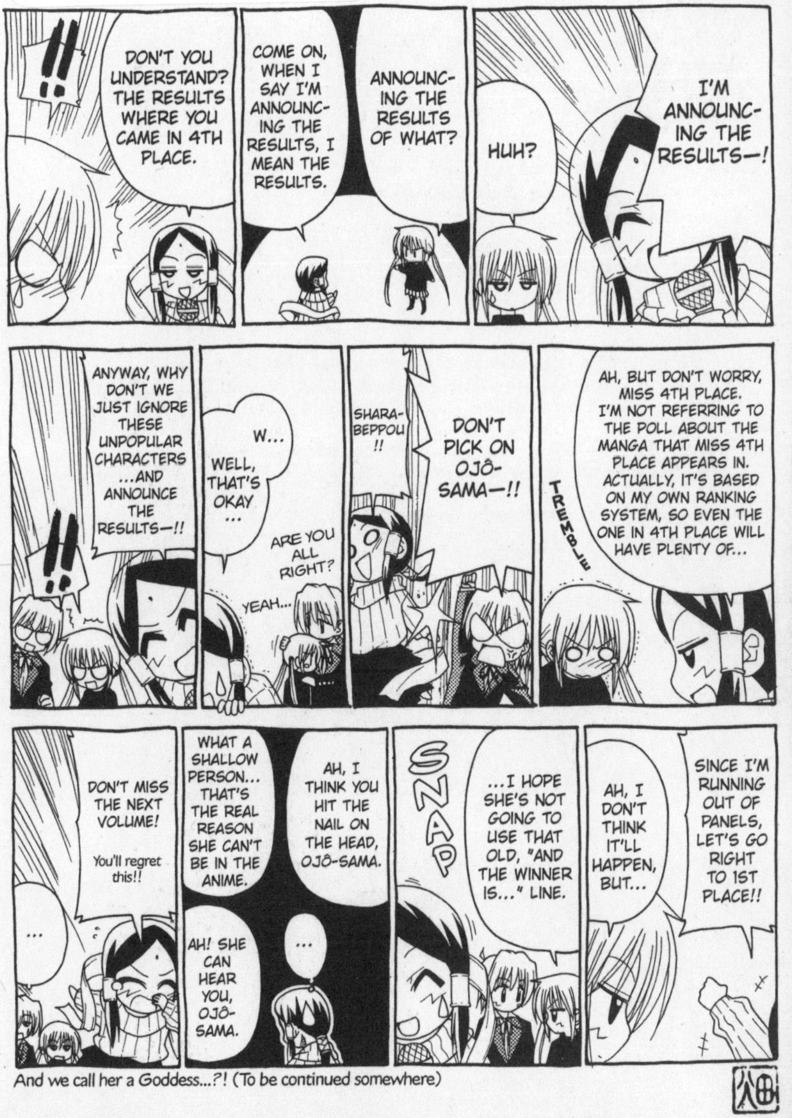
I'M ANNOUNCING THE RESULTS—!
HUH?
ANNOUNCING THE RESULTS OF WHAT?
COME ON, WHEN I SAY I'M ANNOUNCING THE RESULTS, I MEAN THE RESULTS.
DON'T YOU UNDERSTAND? THE RESULTS WHERE YOU CAME IN 4TH PLACE.
!!
AH, BUT DON'T WORRY, MISS 4TH PLACE. I'M NOT REFERRING TO THE POLL ABOUT THE MANGA THAT MISS 4TH PLACE APPEARS IN. ACTUALLY, IT'S BASED ON MY OWN RANKING SYSTEM, SO EVEN THE ONE IN 4TH PLACE WILL HAVE PLENTY OF...
TREMBLE
DON'T PICK ON OJÔ-SAMA—!!
SHARA-BEPPOU!!
W...
WELL, THAT'S OKAY...
ARE YOU ALL RIGHT?
YEAH...
ANYWAY, WHY DON'T WE JUST IGNORE THESE UNPOPULAR CHARACTERS ...AND ANNOUNCE THE RESULTS—!!
!!
SINCE I'M RUNNING OUT OF PANELS, LET'S GO RIGHT TO 1ST PLACE!!
AH, I DON'T THINK IT'LL HAPPEN, BUT...
...I HOPE SHE'S NOT GOING TO USE THAT OLD, "AND THE WINNER IS..." LINE.
SNAP
AH, I THINK YOU HIT THE NAIL ON THE HEAD, OJÔ-SAMA.
WHAT A SHALLOW PERSON... THAT'S THE REAL REASON SHE CAN'T BE IN THE ANIME.
...
AH! SHE CAN HEAR YOU, OJÔ-SAMA.
DON'T MISS THE NEXT VOLUME!
You'll regret this!!
...

And we call her a Goddess...?! (To be continued somewhere)